THE HIDDEN POWER OF SYSTEMS THINKING

The Hidden Power of Systems Thinking: Governance in a Climate Emergency is a persuasive, lively book that shows how systems thinking can be harnessed to effect profound, complex change.

In the age of the Anthropocene, the need for new ways of thinking and acting has become urgent. But patterns of obstacles are apparent in any action, be they corporate interests, lobbyists, or outdated political and government systems. Ison and Straw show how and why failure in governance is at the heart of the collective incapacity to tackle the climate and biodiversity emergencies. They go beyond analysis of the problem and demonstrate how incorporating systems thinking into governance at every level would enable us to break free of historical shackles. They propose 26 principles for systemic governance.

This book will be inspiring reading for students applying their systemic methods, specialists in change management or public administration, activists for 'whole system change' and decision makers wanting to effect challenging transformations. It is for anyone with the ambition to create a sustainable and fair world.

Ray Ison is Professor of Systems at the UK Open University (OU). As part of ASTiP (Applied Systems Thinking in Practice Group) he is responsible with colleagues for managing a post-graduate program in Systems Thinking in Practice. He has held a number of leadership posts within the international Systems and Cybernetics community including Presidencies of the IFSR (International Federation for Systems Research) and ISSS (International Society for the Systems Sciences). His research field is systems praxeology, institutional innovation and systemic governance.

Ed Straw is Visiting Fellow at the OU's ASTiP group. He has seen government from every angle: as a citizen and consumer, adviser to several government ministers, Chair of Demos and Relate and as a specialist on government task forces. He was a consultant on both the Conservative and Labour government's public sector reforms, and a 'moderniser' for the UK Labour party. As a partner at PricewaterhouseCoopers (PwC) and Coopers & Lybrand, he was a global and UK board director.

SYSTEMS THINKING

Series Editors
Gerald Midgley University of Hull, UK

Systems Thinking theory and practice is gaining ground in the worlds of social policy and management.

The Routledge Systems Thinking series is designed to make this complex subject as easy for busy practitioners and researchers to understand as possible. It provides a range of reference books, textbooks and research books on a array of themes in systems thinking, from theoretical introductions to the systems thinking approach and its history, through practical guides to the implementation of systems thinking in the world, through to in depth case studies that are significant for their profound impact.

This series is an essential reference point for anyone looking for innovative ways to effect systemic change, or engaging with complex problems.

Managing Creativity
A Systems Thinking Journey
José-Rodrigo Córdoba-Pachón

Systems Thinking in a Turbulent World
A Search for New Perspectives
Anthony Hodgson

The Hidden Power of Systems Thinking
Governance in a Climate Emergency
Ray Ison and Ed Straw

For more information about this series, please visit: https://www.routledge.com/Systems-Thinking/book-series/STHINK

THE HIDDEN POWER OF SYSTEMS THINKING

Governance in a Climate Emergency

Ray Ison and Ed Straw

Routledge
Taylor & Francis Group

LONDON AND NEW YORK

First published 2020
by Routledge
2 Park Square, Milton Park, Abingdon, Oxon OX14 4RN

and by Routledge
52 Vanderbilt Avenue, New York, NY 10017

Routledge is an imprint of the Taylor & Francis Group, an informa business

British Library Cataloguing-in-Publication Data
A catalogue record for this book is available from the British Library

Library of Congress Cataloging-in-Publication Data
A catalog record has been requested for this book

ISBN: 978-1-138-49398-8 (hbk)
ISBN: 978-1-138-49399-5 (pbk)
ISBN: 978-1-351-02690-1 (ebk)

Typeset in Bembo
by Deanta Global Publishing Services, Chennai, India

DEDICATION

Ray Ison

To *Nicky Ison* who strives every day to put into effect the changes we write about and for *Philip Wallis*, who, in a life tragically cut short, sought the transformations at the heart of this book.

p 218 Evaluation is a system preserving
* activity but are not cybernetic— circular
causal chains that move from action to sensing to
comparison to the desired purpose, + back to action

p224 PAPAI S does not work (Trump)
problem analysis Policy Approval Implementation Solution
Feedback should be embedded in implementation

p225 Systemic experimentation is not the norm
p226 Policy as a distinct end is dead. But purpose
is alive + awaits our embrace.
Lasting beneficial change becomes circular,
cybernetic, experimental, and deliberative, all within
the values of inquiry + not personal power.
Instead think of it as an infinite game of a process
of ongoing open deliberation.
Humans/societies are diverse experiments linked
to each other
p227 Crafting experiments 1) have own humility
• cybernetic feedback, deliberation open decision-making
+ be systemic.

p228 8 experimentation tests
p229 Asking for change will not work
construct the system to require change.
p229 Allocate authority to the second chamber
create design authorities — design standards.
p230 We need multiple perspectives, second-order
cybernetic feedback, knowing-in-action, emerging
standards. "A Resultive" design
Use EDD (Engage Deliberate Decide)
Not DAD (Decide Announce Defend)
p235 Principles for systemic governing are collective
emergent, cybernetic. Ask "what would
make good change happen?"
p240 Approach each decision in a spirit of inquiry
and learning
p255 We have the capacity to consolidate and
accelerate this shift — face up to what has to be
done + do it, with vigor + determination. Let
no obstacle get in the way. If you have power, use it.
p255 where to apply it? Where is my sphere of
influence?
p257 systems practices you can use
every day.

CONTENTS

ILLUSTRATIONS

Figures

Table

Boxes

PREFACE

It is not necessary to change. Survival is not mandatory.[1]

This book is an invitation to think differently. Because the world is in a fix. 'If we always do what we've always done, we'll always get what we've always got'.[2] To *do* differently, we have first to *think* differently. Now, before it is too late.

The 'fix' or quandary the world is in is this:

- The risk to our planetary home gets worse by the day, and yet we continue to pollute, deplete and destabilise it. Our understanding and awareness of what we are doing expands and matures, and yet our practical response is still not much more than partial recycling and drawing on some renewable sources of energy. Climate change has become climate chaos, and yet it is still acceptable to emit greenhouse gases *en masse*. Why?
- Inequality in power and wealth is widespread, ruling elites abound, and yet we are apparently powerless to change this. Are we trapped?
- Mass consumerism is today's god – seemingly here forever, and yet discontent is common. Is there more to life than the next shopping trip?
- Individual freedom arising from wealth and technology has never been higher, and yet lived democracy is in retreat. The terms of our participation are set by the corporate state, and yet we have no control over those terms. Does neoliberal economics rule?
- Short-termism is the norm in the decisions of big companies, governments, political parties and the news media, and yet most leaders know that the world needs decisions for the long term. Is there a way out?

Problems with governance

All over the world, people are trying to use elections and political parties to acquire a fair share of the national cake, exercise some degree of power, stabilise their societies, extinguish corruption, enforce justice and the rule of law, preserve the planet for human habitation, protect indigenous homelands and/or to prevent the errors of governments. In practice, what is achieved are two steps forwards and two similar or different steps backwards. Good things do happen, but the fundamentals remain the same. Sometimes things get worse. In 'democratic' states the addiction to party politics has become a means of maintaining the underlying status quo. This is palliative, not curative; necessary – along with protest – but far from sufficient.

The operators of these 'systems' – politicians, administrators, officials – can be as much victims as their servants. From the inside, independence of mind, job security and wide experience are required to see what is really going on. Very few insiders have all three of these advantages. They can be trapped, too, by their ambition, and by cashmere terms and conditions that are too good to leave. We are all human, obliged to pursue jobs and careers within organisations as they are. This is not a book about 'good' and 'bad' people, but about the *settings* in which people work that may produce good and bad outcomes.

Despite their manifest failings, we cling to decrepit institutions – the rules and norms we invent for ourselves. We boost our political participation in the hope that somehow a different party will deliver us. New leaders may emerge and, with great intentions and hope, set up new parties. Extremes arise as the middle ground continues to demonstrate its meta-impotence. Independence movements spring up as yet another way out. Some scholars are predicting the end of democracy, some the rise of fascism. Others argue the merits of one-party states.

Our experience and studies lead to a quite different conclusion, and one that does not entail the continuing diminution of the quality of our lives. We have operated in this world of government and politics, and sought to use it for the ends we consider important. After years of trying – and serial disappointments – we realised that we were looking in the wrong place. The process of political parties-elections-governments is no match for climate change, nor for the other 'fixes'.

What is to be done

What it takes is for us all to *think* differently – to see our problems in a fresh light, to step back from the daily news noise, and to gain a deep understanding of **why** what happens, happens. To do this asks us to become aware of why we hold the views we do – especially if those views are termed 'beliefs'. We have to shun gut reactions and simplistic 'cures'; to ignore appeals to our base emotions; to not accept how things are run; to consider, without preconceptions, how the world works. To think ... and then to think about our thinking.

As we think differently, public discourse will move away from being framed by a naïve acceptance that existing 'operating systems' are 'givens', to understanding how these systems have to be recast for today's situation. Locally, the innovations now occurring in the way decisions are made and put into practice will become widespread. This combination of thinking, talking and acting will then provide the platform to change the institutions, including constitutions and laws that determine, in large part, the relationship between humans and their environment, with each other and with other species. New ways of living and enacting governance are required. In the course of this book, we hope that the means to resolve the puzzling predicament we are in will become clear.

Taking actions that make a difference may seem like a tall order. From where many of us sit today, it is. But a swift glance backwards says it is not. Big change is the norm. Look at the prevailing economic systems of 40 years ago. They did not converge relentlessly on a single means of producing and allocating goods and services but were diversified: from multiple forms of regulated market capitalism to mutuals, to worker and customer cooperatives, to substantive public sector provision, to state communism. Look back to the pre-internet, authority-curated Information Age. Look back to our limited knowledge and practice of parenting. Look back at the steady rise of democracies as an assortment of dictatorships, monarchies, apartheid nations, and one party states have fallen to the people. Consider, too, that the form of democracy common today has only been in existence for about a century. Observe the spread of feminism, the expanding appreciation of diversity, and the shift of religion from the centre to the sidelines of societies as attitudes have been transformed. These all represent huge changes in 'systems' and cultures.

The nature of change

Climate change, however, does not listen to the morning's news program, read the newspapers or hear the latest announcements by a government. It does not instruct hurricanes and tornadoes to stand down, floods to recede, the sun to turn down the heat, or wildfires to be extinguished in response to a policy announcement, a president's tweet or a denier's assertion. The planet will do what the planet will do. Hopes, beliefs and adversarial arguments are extraneous to it.

Change may happen – or just emerge. Purposeful change is also possible. The existence of constitutions in new-world or post-apartheid countries is testimony to what concerned citizens can do. Change may be first-order – doing what is already done but better. Arguments about efficiency fall into this category. Purposeful second-order change is also possible – change that changes whole systems. Second-order change concerns itself with effectiveness in relation to purpose. But no change is purely deterministic – there are always surprise and emergence. This book concerns itself with how we can collectively shift to, and sustain, second-order change, including governing for emergence, within an unfolding Anthropocene.

The Anthropocene is the geological age of such great human impact on the natural world causing the climate crisis, mass species extinction and other deleterious effects (see Box 1.1 for a detailed explanation).

If an innocent child is brought up in an authoritarian and punitive way, that child will grow up to be dysfunctional. The solution is not to wish this consequence away, to ignore this systemic inevitability of family life or to attempt to control her/his behaviour sometime in the future, but to change the upbringing. The parents have the power to behave badly, just as we have the power – for now – to behave harmfully towards the planet. But let's think. We cannot exist without the planet. We are part of it. It is part of us. The planet will only respond if we act, stop its physical abuse, and care for it.

We are not alone in this quest. People all around the world are already acting. The Organisation for Economic Cooperation and Development (OECD), representing the 36 largest national economies, is working hard to introduce systems thinking to decision making in governments. Many others are heading in the same direction. Constitutions are being adapted to give agency to the biosphere, through rights for water and for rivers. The rule of law is being applied by some judiciaries to ensure companies are responsible for the effects of their operations on the planet. The prevailing 'acceptable' behaviour of the ultra-wealthy in avoiding taxes is being challenged, for example, by Rutger Bregman at the 2019 World Economic Forum in Davos.[3] Perhaps most significantly, people locally – frustrated by the failure of their governments to act for them – are collectively organising systemically to improve their lives. These and other innovations are reported in the following chapters.

Why we have written this book

An academic met a practitioner at SCiO – the lightly named forum for 'Systems and Cybernetics in Organisations' specialists. Mutual interest in systems of governing was instant, as was a personal frustration borne of observing continuing waste in every direction whilst knowing it to be unnecessary. A collaboration began: Ed joined Ray's group at the Open University, and informal research gathered pace. We were searching for material on our current predicament to add to our own research – from examples of the causes of good and bad government and the economic and political malaise, to the social and psychological origins of our inadequate actions, some hidden deep in our minds. The bones of a book were assembled. The idea at its core was to convey Applied Systems Thinking in Practice (STiP) to the general reader along with the analysis to show that there is a way out of here. This is a hard ask – we can only hope to have succeeded.

Who are we?

Ray was brought up in a farming community where 'systemic sensibility' is a way of life. Of necessity and at times of survival, farmers have a deep connection with their environment – or the biosphere – and the effects of climate, land use, resource use, animal behaviour, reliance on neighbours, far-off markets and supply chains. Farming is always prey to the economic system and world food commodity prices, as well as to politics and its remote decision making. These lead to the unintended consequences experienced in the field, whether from the subsidy regime or desk-bound agricultural research and development. Fifty years of educating people in systems thinking at the UK Open University (OU) has made clear that everyone is born with systemic sensibility. This is then developed or lost. If lost, it can be reacquired.

Ed has spent a career lifetime in and around national and local government, in political parties, international and national business, media companies, large and small charities, and a global partnership. All the while, he was observing the successes and failures of each and their causes in practice. We think this combination of our experiences and education is a powerful platform from which to explore today's world.

Other than the personal challenge, our other motivation is of real concern for the future. On a very personal level, we fear for our children and grandchildren. Once you weigh up the science of climate change and the state of the biosphere versus the capacity of the human world to act on the scale and with the speed needed, it is difficult not to get scared. Our overriding motivation is to help prevent what appears to be becoming increasingly likely. We do fear for anyone alive in the rest of the twenty-first century.

What is the book for?

Our purpose is to stimulate, to provide a fresh way of looking at the world, and to propose ways to get us out of the fix. This is not a book of persuasion, to be accepted or rejected. But it asks: Where are you? At the end of the day, it is your choice. Everybody has a two-way relationship with the planet. This book is an invitation to join in the quest to craft different futures. Along the way you can explore whether you retain your systemic sensibilities. If the answer is no, then we offer pathways of recovery and for moving beyond sensibility to build systems literacy and capability in systems thinking in practice. An analogy for the systems journey can be found in all practice situations. Take music or football. Some people are born with, or soon develop, a musical or football *sensibility*. This can be strengthened or lost. If you want to take your practice further, then sensibility alone is not enough. The next step is to invest in developing music or football *literacy* – the capacity to read and perhaps write music or to read a game and know all the moves. To be effective in your practice, there is yet another step – to work to develop the capability to put sensibility and literacy into *practice*, to effect 'good' performances, often with others.

We have to raise our sights. In a nutshell, this is what systems thinking is. Think of it as using a wide-angle lens, becoming adept at bringing different aspects into focus, extracting our minds from the apparent givens determining what and how things are done and observing them from outside, looking over, under, behind, and forward. We encourage you to talk to others to bring multiple perspectives to your situations of interest.

Organisation of the book

Our contention is that *Systems Thinking in Practice* (STiP) provides the means to understand and fundamentally alter the systems governing our lives, and that this will rescue and protect the planet for us and for all natural life. This may appear to be a big claim. We suggest revisiting that claim once you have digested the book. Bear in mind, too, that the means to care for the planet are exactly the same means required to right the present imbalances in power, wealth, and well-being, and to give us fresh meaning in life.

To fully appreciate the 'red threads' of systems-thinking understanding will involve some work on the part of the reader. This means being open to new concepts as well as being prepared to look afresh at some familiar concepts and language. To help in this task, we have created a glossary of terms (Appendix 2). Gaining some familiarity with them now is likely to enrich your reading. Please do not read the list as a set of definitions but as explanations of concepts that can be put to use. Because of the linear (or systematic) structure of a book, there must be an element of hope – that if you read on, what is at first unclear will begin to make sense.

Following an introduction, the book is organised into three parts. Chapter 1 – Introduction – describes the human problematique (the complex of issues associated with a topic, considered collectively – see the Glossary for further explanation). The scene is set, the Anthropocene described, and forecasts of our demise set in the context of uncertainty. Do we want to take such an enormous risk due to insufficient action? The underlying causes are identified in the form of the economic, political, governmental, technological, and social systems. The chapter charts some of the many obstacles in our minds to transforming those systems. All are human inventions. All are capable of change.

Part 1 applies systems thinking to why governance and governments are failing. Chapter 2 introduces a generalised 'diamond' model of contemporary governance. It explores why the model is inadequate for the modern world, the pervasive nature of institutions, and the model's elements of the state, the law, the private sector and the media, and civil society. Each element has significant deficiencies. Such is the current volume and depth of critique from inside and outside government, few would cling on to the notion that our systems of governing are working. Despite mostly good intentions, they are not producing results. Political and technological lock-in to institutions, policies, interests, lobby groups and the like is a common governance failing. The advantage of choosing to see governance in systemic terms is that what might otherwise seem impossibly complicated can be understood and acted upon to change.

Chapter 3 explores the emergent dysfunctionalities arising from the relationships between the elements of the diamond model. Business and government in the prevailing economic system are examined, as the once occasional but now ubiquitous practice of preferential lobbying demonstrates how and why the existing systems are causing planetary, democratic and social destruction.

Chapter 4 asks: What is missing from the model of governance? Three new elements are introduced – the biosphere, technosphere and social purpose – creating a new model, new relationships and a very different systemic dynamic in three dimensions.

Part 2 answers the question What is systems thinking in practice? Chapter 5 describes day-to-day examples of effecting systemic change in a health service and in flood defence as accessible entry points. Using systems thinking in practice is not rocket science and can be used in everyday situations. Using 'I' statements and active listening – simple theory-informed practices – to make feedback work better in human communication is a case in point.

Chapter 6 sets out the panoply of the journey from 'systemic sensibility' to 'systems literacy'. It offers preparation for developing your own STiP, as there is no single way to do it. The differences between first-order and second-order change are assessed, as are the implications of pursuing systematic or systemic change. Through what lens – or framing – do you see a situation of concern (for which the word problem is often used)? What traditions of understanding may be behind your thinking? Where is the boundary around the situation drawn and who drew it and why? Treat this chapter as a 'starter pack' or a 'refresher'. Don't feel under any obligation to digest it all, but if you are tempted to pursue this in more depth, do look at the resources that are free to access on the OU's OpenLearn platform[4] or in many informative publications.[5]

Part 3 contains our proposals for applying STiP to governing. It is one thing to point to the systemic failure of our governing systems – as many have. But when seeking the next step, most commentators advocate first-order change only – changes within the current system to make it more effective. We advocate second-order change – the invention of a new system of governing.

Chapter 7 explores the constraints and possibilities for transforming the three-dimensional model – a device to facilitate discourse, conversation and negotiation about what could be. As the old can be a debilitating encumbrance on the new, there is a need to know how to liberate thinking and practice from shackles that foster only first-order change. Means to give agency to the biosphere, take responsibility for the technosphere and reclaim social purpose from an ineffective state are set out. We offer four metaphors taken from sailing and music that reveal understandings 'missing in action' in current governance systems.

Chapter 8 describes the new practices and institutions for systemic governing. The chapter's ambition is to explore innovations that can change the relationship between practice and institutions. These include principles for systemic learning, the essential place of social learning and the purposeful pursuit of social purpose, systemic action research, and institutionalising STiP in organisations.

Chapter 9 analyses the role and primacy of a constitution, how it stops the wrong things from happening and makes the right things happen. The relationship between a constitution, the ethos of the people in power and national culture determines outcomes. Seeking a solution in these 'enactors' behaving better is dismissed. Today's constitutions are out of their depth. Innovations to incorporate the biosphere in constitutions are occurring. The means for change is described. It is only by changing the rules by which governments operate that the biosphere can be protected and the major inequalities rebalanced.

Chapter 10 examines how to create beneficial change, starting from the appreciation that most of government is a political experiment. The systematic norm of Problem-Analysis-Policy-Approval-Implementation-Solution (PAPAIS) does not work. Results, decisions, and actions currently treated as separate entities must become part of the whole of making beneficial change: from the 'end-state' fallacy to experimentation as the norm, and from the 'tiny top' to distributed change. The fourth separation of powers is invoked. Its purpose is to concentrate governments' attention on outcomes or results through the vital role of cybernetic feedback – through the new institution of the 'Resulture', the crafting of experiments through ten tests, vetting decision making, design authorities and failure investigation, abandonment and enforcement powers, along with the depoliticisation of social purpose functions in society.

Chapter 11, drawing on the whole book, sets out the principles to govern and live in the Anthropocene and to restore or establish balance and justice in the distribution of wealth, power, and well-being. These principles range from 'The World Can't Run On Lies' to 'Giving Agency to the Biosphere'. Many of the new principles set out here have arisen from innovations around the world.

Chapter 12 explores the question: What next? Do you, the reader, as an individual have the will, which will then combine with the wills of others to create a collective, unstoppable force for second-order change? A short response is offered of how the 'will to change' might be garnered through acts that are collective, individual, and at work. Responses will create the drama of our lives now and into the future.

Appendix 1 explores how we have come to write what is here. It offers vignettes of what is entailed in thinking differently by reflecting on our own life journeys.

Although written by two people, the book contains three voices. 'We' dominates in the many places we converge. Sometimes Ed's voice takes over, sometimes Ray's. We hope this provides a change of rhythm, and is not disruptive to the reader. It allows us to be responsible for what we say.

The examples used to illustrate are written from our experiences and research. These are extensive, but may require some interpretation or adaptation to fit your national circumstances. Application of the concepts of STiP should bridge this gap.

We are very aware that much of the thinking in this book has been undertaken and applied by many around the world in all sorts of places. Our purpose is to cohere these, integrate them with our original work, and foster the reinvention of systems of governance. And soon!

Notes

1 W. Edwards Deming, 1900–1993, American engineer, mathematical physicist, professor and quality specialist, credited with a significant role in the post-war rise of Japan to become the world's second largest economy.
2 Henry Ford's maxim, slightly adapted.
3 https://www.theguardian.com/business/2019/feb/01/rutger-bregman-world-economic-forum-davos-speech-tax-billionaires-capitalism (Accessed February 23 2019).
4 https://www.open.edu/openlearn/science-maths-technology/engineering-technology/systems-thinking-free-courses (Accessed November 21 2018).
5 See, for example, Armson, R. 2011. *Growing Wings on the Way. Systems Thinking for Messy Situations*. Axminster: Triarchy Press, or Ison, R.L. 2017. *Systems Practice: How to Act in a Climate-Change World*. London: Springer and Milton Keynes: The Open University.

ACKNOWLEDGEMENTS

Any book makes demands on those around its authors. This book is no exception. We acknowledge the support of our partners Cathy Humphreys and Lindsey Colbourne and Ed's son and daughter Edison and Odette. We are particularly grateful to Monica Shelley for her help in making the book more readable through consistency in expression, argument and formatting, to Freya Hudson for her detailed editing, and to Simon Kneebone for his unstinting capacity to turn an idea into fine drawings.

Our roles at the Open University (OU) have created a platform from which to create this book; we are very grateful to our OU colleagues in the ASTiP Group and the School of Engineering & Innovation (E&I). Academic colleagues past and present are all acknowledged for the insights and solidarity they have offered. We also acknowledge the support of Professor Simon Lee and the Open University Strategic Research Area for Citizenship & Governance. The support of the secretarial and administrative staff of E&I, Angela, Angie, Donna, Mahruk, Olivia and Sharon is acknowledged.

The heuristics presented in Chapters 2 and 4 were first developed by Ray in a conversation with Yongping Wei and John Colvin in Lanzhou, Gansu, China. As always, their insights and collaboration facilitated emergence in understanding.

Support and insight, through comments and conversations, were provided by Tim Albin, Simon Caulkin, Ken Coghill, Julian Corner, Mark Draper, Linda John, Bruce Lagay, Pete Miles, Michael Mulvey, Tom Parker, Barbara Schmidt-Abbey, Benjamin Taylor and Yonging Wei, as well as through a multitude of ad hoc discussions with friends and colleagues.

We also thank the staff at Routledge, particularly Alexandra Atkinson and Professor Gerald Midgley, the editor-in-chief of this book series, and Professor Lee Godden and Dr Frederick Steier for their reviews of the book.

We are grateful for permissions to reproduce text and figures which are acknowledged in the Notes sections throughout the book. In particular we acknowledge (i) The Financial Times for permission to reproduce material from Caulkin, Simon (2012) On management: A big problem (Chapter 2); (ii) The publishers of Foreign Policy for permission to reproduce Figure 2.5 from Khanna, P. and Francis, D. 2016; (iii) The World Economic Forum for permission to reproduce Figure 3.1 from Burrow, S. 17 January 2018; (iv) John Wiley and Sons for permission to reproduce figures originally published in Systems Research & Behavioral Science, especially Lane, D.C (2016) in Box 8.1 (Chapter 8); (v) Tim Hollo for permission to cite from his work in Chapter 8; (vi) Julian Corner, CEO of Lankelly Chase for permission to use material in Chapter 8; (vii) The Australian Prevention Partnership Centre and The Tasmanian Department of Health for permission to reproduce Figure 12.1 and (viii) The Open University for figures and material drawn from within the STiP program.

ABBREVIATIONS

AGM	Annual General Meeting
APSC	Australian Public Service Commission
ASNL	At School and Not Learning
ASTiP	Applied Systems Thinking in Practice
BBC	British Broadcasting Corporation
CBI	Confederation of British Industry
CCC	Climate Change Committee
CEO	Chief Executive Officer
CFC	Chlorofluorocarbons
CLC	Community Legal Centres
CMA	Catchment Management Authority
CoP	Community of Practice
CPS	Crown Prosecution Service
CSH	Critical Systems Heuristics
DAD	Decide-Announce-Defend
DEA	Digital Economies Act
EA	Environment Agency
ECHR	European Court of Human Rights
EDD	Engage-Deliberate-Decide
EO	Executive Officer
EPA	Environmental Protection Agency
EPR	Extended Producer Responsibility
ESD	Ecologically Sustainable Development
ETS	EU Emissions Trading System
EU	European Union
EUSG	European School of Governance
FT	Financial Times

GCSE	General Certificate of Secondary Education
GDP	Gross Domestic Product
GHG	Greenhouse Gas
GM	Genetically Modified
GP	General Practitioner
HAS	Human Activity System
HFC	Hydrofluorocarbons
ICJ	International Court of Justice
IEC	International Electrotechnical Commission
IHI	Institute for Health Improvement
IPCC	Intergovernmental Panel on Climate Change
ISO	International Organization for Standardization
LC	Lankelly Chase
M&E	Monitoring & Evaluation
MDB	(Australian) Murray Darling Basin
MIA	Metaphor Impact Assessment
MP	Member of Parliament
MSc	Master's of Science
NGO	Non-Governmental Organisation
NIC	National Infrastructure Committee
NLE	Neoliberal Economic
NPC	New Philanthropy Capital
OECD	Organisation for Economic Co-operation and Development
OPSI	Observatory of Public Sector Innovation
OU	Open University
PAPAIS	Problem-Analysis-Policy-Approval-Implementation-Solution
PDSA	Plan-Do-Study-Act
PL	Preferential Lobbying
PM	Prime Minister
PR	Public Relations
QE	Quantitative Easing
R&D	Research & Development
SA	South Africa
SAR	Systemic Action Research
SDG	Sustainable Development Goals
SM	Systems Modelling
SLCP	Short-Lived Climate Pollutant
SSM	Soft Systems Methodology
STiP	Systems Thinking in Practice
STP	Systems Thinking Practitioner
VM	Values Modes
UK	United Kingdom
UN	United Nations
UNFCCC	United Nations Framework Convention on Climate Change

US(A)	United States (of America)
USSR	Union of Soviet Socialist Republics
WEF	World Economic Forum
WFD	Water Framework Directive
WHO	World Health Organisation

Reinventing governments

p146 good design for better fit
p147 scenarioing as praxis
p147 Re framing about purposeful action p 163
p148 sequence
  1) frame choices (D)
  2) Bring in multiple perspectives
  3) Formulate systems of interest & boundaries (C)
  4) Design for purpose (E)

p150 CAS is a framing, an invented term
  for praxis, not a term to classify
phenomena — knowing, not fixed, objective
or reified knowledge

p153 Governing metaphor - a helms person
steering a viable course in response to feedback
from the world - currents + winds in an unfolding
context steering/ sailing/ navigating

p153 governance/ governing is a duality
  enacted as a form of praxis (theory-informed
practical action) as departure sailing p154

p155 another example is
  an institution/ organisation — Berlin
          governance   phil harmonic
  the orchestrated performance is governing
            jazz   performance

p156 a trajectory self-correcting metaphor
  institutions + shoes technology = shoes
  governance , governing & walking.
  comfort = co-evolution , impacting the path

p158 Human activity system HAS — a human
  activity system for transformation.

p164 new governance model is for reconfiguring
  power relations, practices & relational dynamics
  freed from structure-determinations, & ready
  to reallocate resources

p170 systemic design = human centered
  design to multi stakeholder systems.

p176 5 factor that enable or constrain action.
p178   social learning & negotiation of priorities
in relation to the phenomena it seeks to
address and be celised, improvised, co-designed
performances of to meet higher purposes.

Business-as-usual? Or governance reform with systems thinking in practice?

The great intersection of the 21st century: a pathway to choose, or create, as we journey into an uncertain, unknowable future?

1

INTRODUCTION

Crafting a viable future?

1.1 Our human-created 'problematique'

Contemporary lived experience is of a deteriorating human–environment relationship. Expressions of this relational breakdown are far from new. Explorer and scholar Alexander von Humboldt[1] was aware from at least 1799 of the 'destruction of forests and of humankind's long term changes to the environment', including 'ruthless irrigation and the great mass of steam and gases produced in industrial centres'. The so-called 'greenhouse effect' in which temperatures inside the Earth's atmosphere rise because of the properties of gases such as carbon dioxide and methane, had been postulated in 1824 and demonstrated from experimental observations by John Tyndall in 1859. Numerous scholars and insightful thinkers have been open to the predicament of humankind, but few have framed their concerns in terms that begin with thinking about our own thinking and thus what we humans do when we do what we do.[2,3]

Human existential angst came into its own following the development of the atomic bomb, captured in phrases like 'mutually assured destruction'. So far, the global governance response to this possibility has worked. But it requires constant vigilance. The hole in the ozone shield was the first time modern societies realised that environmental deterioration was potentially dangerous. Widespread death from skin cancer awaited. For the first time too, many acknowledged that collective human behaviour had caused this dire situation and could cure it.[4] 'Ozone hole deniers' did not feature.[5]

Despite this warning, the human world charged ahead, treating the planet as an infinite resource and an infinite dumping ground. In the meantime, and in the background, scientists were studying how and why the climate behaved as it did in order to improve weather forecasting for global food production, shipping, water provision, and holiday making. They also noticed worrying trends. The mean global temperature had risen. Today it is just over 1°C above the pre-industrial period and it rises by 0.17°C each decade. This might not seem like a lot, but it is. If the world continued on this trend, our world – our habitat – would degenerate severely.

These signals of alarm have surfaced in different ways in public consciousness. Those preferring to do nothing sought to deny these long-term trends. Having lost this argument, they then sought to deny that they were human-induced. This argument has been lost too. As the science developed, so the thesis expanded. Humankind was not just igniting the climate but stomping all over the biosphere – the part of the earth's crust, waters and atmosphere that support life of all forms. Thus was born the term the 'Anthropocene' (see Box 1.1).

BOX 1.1 THE ANTHROPOCENE

The Anthropocene is a term formulated in 2000 by earth scientists Paul Crutzen and Eugene Stoermer to designate a new geological era in which human influences are so great that they are affecting 'whole Earth dynamics' through a range of biophysical and social processes.

The International Working Group on the Anthropocene[6] notes that human impacts on the Earth include:

- Erosion and sediment transport associated with a variety of anthropogenic processes, including colonisation, agriculture, urbanisation and global warming.
- Changes in the chemical composition of the atmosphere, oceans and soils, with significant anthropogenic perturbations of the cycles of elements such as carbon, nitrogen, phosphorus and various metals.
- Environmental conditions generated by these perturbations [including] global warming, ocean acidification and spreading oceanic 'dead zones'.
- Degradation of the biosphere both on land and in the sea, as a result of habitat loss, predation, species invasions and the physical and chemical changes noted above.[7]

Homo sapiens has now become a major agent in shaping the circumstances of its own existence.[8] Acceptance of the explanations that make the case for the Anthropocene – including human-induced climate change – also means accepting that we are in a period new in human history.[9] This is the issue of our time, perhaps of all times, and thus the greatest challenge to all human endeavour.

The human threat goes well beyond the climate to its air, water, land, fellow animals, flora, fauna and other resources. Imagine a bird spray-painting its nest and chicks. That's effectively what we have done. Now we have to work out how to stop doing it and clean it off.

Many people, governments, companies and civil society organisations recognise this. China is looking more likely than most to do something significant. We shall see.[10] But, as yet, the world is in the 'Phoney War'[11] stage. There is much posturing and small actions painted into major achievements, but the fact is things continue to get worse.

So much so that the risk of 'Hothouse Earth' is drawing closer.[12] This term is used to describe a scenario in which human activity causes a higher global temperature than at any time during the past 1.2 million years, due to a breakdown in the feedback loops that regulate the planet's temperature. Systemic feedback processes operate at all levels, from the planetary to the interpersonal. Losing safeguards that come from feedback processes would mean the planet has passed a tipping point beyond which its own natural processes trigger uncontrollable warming, no matter how much we subsequently reduce our greenhouse gas emissions.

The breakdown of these feedback loops include permafrost thaw; the loss of methane hydrates from the ocean floor; weaker land and ocean carbon sinks; the loss of Arctic summer sea ice; the reduction of Antarctic sea ice and polar ice sheets; the dieback of Amazon and Northern conifer forests; and increased bacterial respiration in the oceans. Forests, oceans and permafrost currently do us a great service by storing carbon. As rising temperatures cause these carbon sinks to weaken, some will start to emit more gases into the atmosphere.[13]

The result would be sea levels as much as 60m higher – imagine any coastal city under those conditions. Much of the world would be uninhabitable, and food production would be a fraction of current output, such that the 'carrying capacity' of a Hothouse Earth would drop to 1 billion people. Whether you or we would be amongst the lucky or unlucky survivors is, of course, unknown.

Professor Schellnhuber[14] said some of these changes could be reversible, but others would be irreversible

> on time frames that matter to contemporary societies. What we do not know yet is whether the climate system can be safely parked near 2°C above pre-industrial levels, as the Paris Agreement envisages. Or if it will, once pushed so far, slip down the slope towards a hothouse planet.

The IPCC Report of October 2018 gave humanity 12 years to act to avoid climate-induced catastrophe and set the maximum safe rise in mean temperature as 1.5°C.[15]

In making the arguments of this book, it is important not to be lulled into the false sense of security that comes with official conversations about climate change (and other areas of public discourse). Many of these conversations are couched in terms of rises in global mean temperatures of 1.5, 2 or 3°C. This language can be misleading because for a shift of this magnitude to occur, it means that there is to be unparalleled variation and surprise. If you understand how a normal distribution works, then Figure 1.1 explains what will happen.

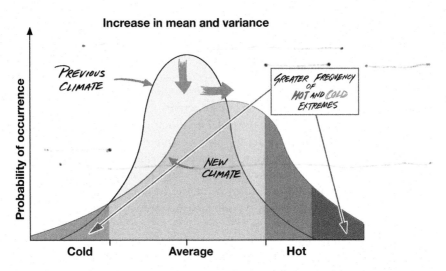

FIGURE 1.1 How climate change will operate through shifts in the 'shape' of the normal distribution of temperatures.[16]

The normal distribution for temperature is moving to the right and the tails of the distribution (i.e. variation in both hot and cold temperatures) will increase, though not perhaps as much for the cold. The other language trap is that mean temperatures rarely ever occur. Under climate change, it will be extreme temperatures and their duration that will have the most impact. These effects have already been seen in the buckling of steel railway lines in Melbourne in 2009, an extreme heatwave period, when more people died from high temperature or heat island effects (the failure of night-time temperatures to be low enough to relieve heat stress) than the major bushfire that claimed 177 lives. There have been many other examples since, including higher impact rainfall events associated with the increases in energy due to the warming of oceans and currents.

Climate change will demand more flood and storm defences and means to help populations cope with increased heat stress, especially the elderly and sick. It will also demand significant investment in re-engineering specifications used for roads, buildings, railways and sewage treatment and for managing our rivers and water supplies. The systemic effects will be huge. For example, in 2014 the Thames barrage was subjected to floods and tidal surges that almost exceeded its design capabilities. If it were to fail, London would experience major flooding. The Thames has been subjected regularly to sewage contamination in recent years because freeboards on sewage ponds, designed for less intense rainfall, have frequently overtopped due to more high-intensity rainfall. Climate change will affect all aspects of our lives, yet our news and public narratives are inadequate and our governance systems ill-prepared.

BOX 1.2 TOWARDS COLLAPSE ... OR NOT?

Jared Diamond has outlined how and why past human civilisations have collapsed.[17] Climate change was implicated in the demise of North African societies. In this same area, the price of bread, and thus food production, is said by several sources to have triggered the Arab Spring.[18] In his analyses of societal collapse, Joseph Tainter points to systemic factors set off by increasing institutional complexity and a declining capacity to act in response to environmental change in its broadest sense.[19] In the face of climate change and the systemic breakdown in the main natural cycles on which contemporary human society depends (i.e. water, carbon, nitrogen, phosphorus, and oxygen), we sit at the most profound fulcrum, or tipping point, in human history. The key question is whether we will collectively be able to make the innovations that pull us out of our current trajectory and move us towards one that offers a safer, more viable future in our ongoing co-evolution with the biosphere.

Have you ever experienced a gas leak at home? When do you call a fitter? At the first sniff? Hope it goes away by itself? Wait, because it does not smell much? Or only once there's an explosion? The world has a major gas leak. The consequence of an explosion is so great that calling the fitter today is, surely, the only safe option. This demands an expansion in the practice of the precautionary principle, the essence of which 'is captured in a number of aphorisms such as "an ounce of prevention is worth a pound of cure", "better safe than sorry", and "look before you leap".'[20]

Another common aphorism is the ancient medical principle of 'first, do no harm'. This needs to be applied to institutions and institutional decision-making processes rather than just individuals.[21] In other words, the precautionary principle has to be enacted and feature prominently in our institutions. The gas analogy raises one other important point. If we know something is taking us in the wrong direction, we do not need to wait for scientific certainty to act. Experience tells us what happens when gas explodes. Experience is already telling us about the impact of human-induced climate change.

Yes, but no one knows what *will* happen. No one knows either that the rolling apocalypse will *not* happen or that we will escape with a near miss. The issue before us is one of risk. Given that the worst case is so appalling, do we want to risk that happening by taking what transpires to be inadequate action? You may hope or believe that the planet's future is safe for us. But the planet takes no account of, or interest in, our beliefs – nor of politics. The choice is hard-edged: really take hold of human impact on the planet, or not.

If we stand back, we are collectively showing a remarkable lack of appreciation of just how lucky we are to find ourselves on this planet at this time. The physical conditions necessary to coincide for us to live in a place of such extraordinary beauty and natural diversity, so rich in resources, so benign in climate, with animal and floral companions of such wonder, are rare if not unique in the entire universe. Certainly, we know of none other. Why put all that at risk? For what?

1.2 Systems out of control

At this point, you may well be fired up to grasp the nettle, but then look around at all the obstacles and your motivation wanes.

- The world has become dominated by one 'monotheistic' economic system, seemingly unstoppable in its single-minded pursuit of profit, largely for top management, big shareholders, and financiers. In its design, this huge engine owes no responsibility to the biosphere.[22] The biosphere – along with its other 'stakeholders' of staff, consumers and communities – receives bits and pieces of protection through after-the-event regulation of the detrimental acts of companies and state enterprises. But the duty to, and for, the planet – and for us – is not part of a company's inbuilt remit, written into its business model or constitution, the means by which a social license to operate is issued. The biosphere is an afterthought for business, not a forethought. In a planet at so much risk, this is patently absurd.
- Equally, in most national constitutions, governments have no inbuilt requirements to protect and preserve the planet. Again, such as they are, they are 'bolt-ons'. The systems of governing under which governments operate are hopelessly out of date. Some work better than others – for cultural as much as constitutional reasons – but none are adequate for the *systemic reformation* we need to execute.[23] China, for example, has a quite extraordinary capacity to put its five-year plans into practice but is as likely to do the wrong thing as the right one.[24] It is experimenting with local democracy but remains highly centralised – a killer for the innovation and citizen-initiated participation needed to respond to planetary destruction.
- Democratic systems are based on competing political parties locked into antiquated and linear decision and action processes – often dominated by the preferential lobbying of large companies (Chapter 3) and others leading to state capture.[25] These systems don't work more often than they do, and are wholly unfit for the reformation needed. A political class has emerged that is separate from the people they are meant to represent. This class now includes the news media and think tanks, once sources of independent thought. Powerful leaders take every opportunity to subvert constitutional controls, often outdated, in order to do what they want and to stay in office in perpetuity, usually alongside financial corruption. Ancient religions, bent on retaining power and privilege, still control some governments, seeking to impose a set of behavioural rules as a means to gain personal power and without reference to the sanctity of our planetary home. Christianity, at least until recently, went further and declared man's dominion over all of nature. It's here for our use – and abuse.

Economic, political, governmental and technological systems have escaped our control – and have transcended our capacity to act responsibly in our relationship with the biosphere. Ironically, delusions about control and how it operates also abound. The rise of the *technosphere*, the realm of human activity that has created the technologically modified environment in which we all exist, has exacerbated this relational collapse (see Chapter 4).

The problem is that few people see these 'systems' for what they are: just one of many ways of running things. Few people, too, see how powerful 'systems' themselves are, lured by the cult of leadership and the addiction of daily politicking to perceiving that answers to our problems lie in a new leader or change in government. Such changes sometimes make a small positive difference for a limited period. Very few are ever able to transcend the words of W. Edwards Deming:[26] 'a bad system will beat a good person, every time'. It is new, strong systems of governing we need, well before strong leaders. Today's 'systems' are running beyond capacity, no matter how hard they are driven. Their engines are too small, their instrumentation lacking, and their on-board controls too flaky for the tasks required of them in the Anthropocene.

There is a crucial point here. These same 'systems' that are responsible for damaging the biosphere are also damaging us – in terms of wealth, power, well-being, products, and fear of government. The system changes necessary to restore democracy and to provide high standards of public services are the same as those needed to stabilise and maintain our relationship with the biosphere. People and nature are on the same side – only the elites are on the other. An orangutan, a spider and a poppy share our interests.

Few people, too, see where these 'systems' come from, or how to change them. The answer is, for as long as nation-states persist, that they are all articulated in a nation's constitution (whether written or enacted through tradition). It is here we must go for their reconstruction or reconstituting. No extant constitution has been designed for today's circumstances of the Anthropocene, nor for much else of modern government's role, whether in spending 40% of a nation's GDP or combating the might of global corporations (Chapter 2). Parliaments/assemblies/congresses and governments make company and other laws, international trade deals, and other treaties, which together produce (or allow) the economic system. Hence, it is termed the political economy.

Constitutions are also an act of collective self-control (Chapter 9). In various small and large ways, they impose on us rules for living together that, for the greater good, limit our individual behaviour. Constitutions are a form of institution: they are the product of human design and sense of purpose. But, like any rules-based system, the rules must achieve their desired purpose (i.e. they have to be enacted effectively). We must also have means of judging our collective acting through rigorous feedback processes (Chapter 10). If the rules are not working, then the commitment, resources, and practical skills to reconstitute the constitution are required. In this historical moment, collective discipline and capability are essential to change our own behaviours, such that we have all made a decision to alter our lifestyles to preserve an ongoing viable relationship with the planet. I will if you will.[27]

1.3 Why not act?

Let's start to think about our thinking by considering the immediate obstacles in our minds to personal change:

1. But nothing will change. This is the note of resignation often heard in relation to the many failures of government. We know a government service or decision is fundamentally flawed, we know there are better answers, but we know it will continue. Such forecast inertia is realistic. Governments lumber. If the people employed in them – and we all need a job – are content with the status quo, and the forces of renewal are insufficient to overcome their inertia, then little will change. History says it all.

As more and more power has shifted from individuals to large organisations – governments, companies, public sector agencies – and accountability of these organisations has become absent or marginal, people's capacity to enact their citizenship, in contrast to their consumerism, has become diminished.[28] This widespread sense of powerlessness encourages passivity. In this context, the likelihood of individuals rising up to take collective action is remote. Governments and the economic system have trained us to be passive. Only *the actions of powerful others can create change* becomes the spirit of the age or Zeitgeist.[29]

This sense that we cannot do anything is echoed in a survey of 1,000 people across Britain on what they valued in life.[30] It looked at compassionate values like 'helpfulness', 'equality' and 'protection of nature', and selfish values like 'wealth', 'public image' and 'success'. In the survey, 74% of respondents placed greater importance on compassionate than selfish values. But 77% believed that their fellow citizens held selfish values to be more important and compassionate values to be less important than is actually the case. 'People who hold this inaccurate view about other people's values feel significantly less positive about getting involved, they feel greater social alienation, less responsible for their communities, and less likely to fit with wider society'.[31]

In the context of climate action, this perception becomes 'They are not doing it, so there's no point in me doing it'. This 'reciprocity' inhibitor/motivator is found in other research. In Australia: 'Whether or not a householder invests in an expensive energy efficiency measure has a great deal to do with whether their friends and associates have invested in that measure' (and far less with its price). In Wales:

> The process of behavioural change is fundamentally a social one: humans are influenced by the behaviour of others around them, often to a greater extent than is at first apparent. Change can only take place in the context of a cultural shift where other people are also trying to change.[32]

2. Another source of inaction is the perception that to act as part of the biosphere will require a diminution in lifestyles, freedoms and consumption. It is seen as an unpleasant, austere, backward-looking prospect. Contentment is derived relatively. We may be starting from a rice paddy or an inner-city loft, but if life this year is easier or less hard than last year, then contentment results. The thought of going backwards is disturbing.[33]

More specific motivations play loudly alongside this directional impulse. People may say 'I like driving fast cars, flying to exotic places, eating oodles of meat, and have no wish to stop.' Keep on partying: an (environmental) recession is around the corner. Consumer values are implicit in the way we ask questions, produce data, and compose policies and practices. This is understandable as all part of a massive consumer-induced disconnect between what people do and their ability to reflect about what they do. A twenty-first-century version of good-old alienation between people and place.[34]

At this point, it helps to note that we are already going backwards. The question is which backwards do you want? To the relative who said: 'I don't want a wind turbine near my garden,' Ed replied, 'Would you rather have a turbine, a desert or a refugee camp?'

3. A rather different rationale for personal inaction is 'human ingenuity will sort it out'. Such ingenuity is not held by the non-actor. Someone else will do it. This is a high-risk strategy. Human ingenuity has sorted many things out and created many problems, not least our current state. But for those libertarian believers, it is a place to find some comfort, with some evidence.

Some entrepreneurs score high on ingenuity, leadership and vision. Some appear ethically and environmentally motivated. But few in business have the combination of wealth, education and intellect to pull off *enough* ingenious solutions. Exploitation of the planet comes in too many forms to be alleviated by the rise of 'saviour capitalists' and the 'trickle-down economics' that has produced greater inequality and the rise of migration. As Bruno Latour notes, migration exacerbated by climate change comes from without and within a nation. One group seeks a new country, whilst migrants from the inside 'remain … in place [and] experience the drama of seeing themselves left behind in their own countries'.[35]

There are insidious forms of inaction and action. Action can become institutionalised and cultural in unhelpful ways. Some societies and scientific or economic communities extol the virtues of 'progressive development'. Its aim is the exploitation of the natural world with new technologies that will make things better. Enthusiastic entrepreneurs have the power to distort innovation and investment that, if open to critical or systemic scrutiny, may not be pursued. At this time, do we really need driverless cars or missions to Mars?[36]

4. Let's move somewhere else. This has been a strategy of the last few centuries. Persecuted for religious, ethnic, social and economic reasons, groups have sought to flee, emigrate, and seek opportunity elsewhere. Decisions to move take courage, desperation, aspiration – the full gamut of human motivations. The migrations to the New World, the Americas, and Australasia are perhaps the most studied and vivid recent examples.[37] Expanding to new territories and tribal defence of extant territories are characteristics of most apes. Today we readily engage in discourses about planetary journeys and wars, suggesting that a human yearning to conquer new territory dominates our capacity to be responsible for local place and culture.

5. The ultimate rationale for inaction is simply the belief that this is how species behave. If, by eliminating predators and other controls, one species becomes dominant, its population will expand beyond the capacity of its environs to sustain it. The population collapses and equilibrium is restored. In other words, mass extermination is going to happen; it is both inevitable and a law of nature, so let it happen. Depending on your view of humanity, this might appear either callous or realistic.

These are some of the vocalised rationalisations for inaction, which may be stimulating your own thinking. Scholars have sought deeper explanations of what underlies these positions and thus how our thinking could be altered. Here is a selection.

1.4 What underlies our propensity to inaction?

1. The pace of change *Homo sapiens* is used to is extremely slow. Examining huge shifts in lifestyles in the past shows that people did not stop being hunter/gatherers and start being farmers all of a sudden. 'The change proceeded in stages, each of which involved just a small alteration in daily life', Yuval Noah Harari concludes.[38] That is the pace of change we are accustomed to.

The early stages of climate change and environmental degradation are already being felt in weather chaos, pollution and rubbish. But these are merely the early stages. To put these forces into retreat must, it may be thought, take effort, cooperation, resources, and human ingenuity of such a scale as to be beyond us. These are not small alterations. These are giant leaps. We give up before we start.

2. Your viewpoint determines the future, specifically how we view 'nature' as a risk. 'We all have to predict what risks are around us, in anything from the risk of crossing the road to the risk of climate change', concludes Mark Maslim.[39] Bringing together two theories of the myths of nature and of the myths of *human* nature, he segments people into four types. There are those perceiving nature as benign: throw anything at it and it will continue. Then there is the perception of nature as ephemeral: fragile and unforgiving, it breaks and in so doing will break you. Or it might be nature as perverse/intolerant: within limits nature can be relied on – overstep those limits and it becomes nasty. Finally, nature is capricious, or unpredictable: it may or may not be benign or ephemeral, it is beyond human control, nothing can be done. Do you relate to any of these types?

These perceptions of the behaviour of nature then fashion people's responses. 'Ephemeral' and 'perverse/intolerant' observers will act, the 'benign' and 'capricious' will not. But 'remember that individuals can be extremely fluid in their beliefs, particularly when it comes to risk and uncertainty. People will, thus, shift in their opinion depending on the evidence put forward'.[40] There is hope.

3. People are not static in their response to enforced change. We react to change, usually adversely at first, even if it is likely to be beneficial. From family upheaval to redundancy to mass immigration, people take a long time to adapt, following the classic and well-observed change curve of shock, denial, depression, anger, resignation, acceptance and understanding.

Where on this curve are we now for climate change? Certainly the shock is over. Much denial of its very existence followed, now all but ceased except in some powerful business and political redoubts. Depression and some anger are around in activists. But most people are far from acceptance and understanding. What will help the shift? Is change a property of the individual as old-fashioned cognitivists and behavioural theorists posit as well as modern-day nudgers?[41] Or is change a social process that arises out of relational dynamics as understood in social theories of learning?[42]

4. The language we speak and how it expresses the future may influence our attitude to risk and thus our propensity to act now for climate change. At first sight, this might seem a case of spurious correlation rather than cause. But in those languages like Finnish, in effect without future tenses, the individual has no linguistic separation from the future. Life is a continuum. The present is not separate from the future. Me now is also me tomorrow. What I do now is hard-wired to what happens to me then. I know I am growing old and so save money sufficiently today. Accumulating a pension for that time in my unsegmented life when I need it goes without saying. Note, 'when I need it', not 'when I *will* need it'. Don't panic.

Future tenses imply a different state: when this happens in a future separate from me today, then, yes, that. But that (a pension) is not an issue for today that requires present attention. It is in the future. English has several ways of expressing the future and is a cavalier culture in comparison with Finnish. This has its upside in creativity, humour, irreverence, but not, alas, in pension planning.

Can the same linguistic relationship to the future be seen in responses to climate? George Lakoff explains it in terms of direct and systemic causation:[43] 'Direct causation is very simple: you pick up a glass of water, you drink it, and then the glass doesn't have water in it anymore. It happens here; it happens now'. It's simple to understand and to express. 'Every language in the whole world can express direct causation in its grammar'. But the language we use cannot cope with the concept of systemic causation.

It is disturbing to ponder that history may conclude that the adoption of English as the world language was a prime reason the planet collapsed for human habitation. Time will tell.

5. Cultures shape values, and those values shape history; by the same token, our values will shape our future. The seeds of our destruction are found in the myths and metaphors that have made a culture, concludes Jeremy Lent in his epic *The Patterning Instinct*.[44] Articulated first by the philosophers of Ancient Greece, this Western pattern of meaning can be traced back to Abrahamic thought (the Old Testament), the emergence of scientism and demarcated, disciplinary silos, the commodification of the Earth as 'natural resources' and the invention of institutions and practices that exploit the resources of the Earth or diminish the quality of the relationship we humans have with the biophysical world.

Far from breaking with previous patterns of thought, Rene Descartes's famous belief that he consisted of 'a substance whose whole essence or nature is to think and whose being requires no place and depends on no material thing',[45] was an extension of Platonic and Christian cosmologies, with a crucial difference: he substituted mind for soul.

If our identity is established only in the mind, then, as the Christians insisted, our body and the rest of nature, being incapable of reason, has no intrinsic value. Descartes was explicit about this: he insisted that there is no difference 'between the machines made by craftsmen and the various bodies that nature alone composes'. The mind or soul was sacred, while the natural world possessed neither innate worth nor meaning. It existed to be remorselessly dissected and exploited.

> This worldview underpinned the scientific revolution, which brought us the astonishing marvels and benefits that have transformed our lives. But it also embedded in our minds some catastrophic root-metaphors that help to explain our current relationship to the living world. Among them are the notions of human detachment from nature, our dominion over nature, nature as a machine.[46]

These are values we see in action all around us. At the same time, the search for meaning, other than through its displacement into consumerism, is all around us too – religious fundamentalism, spirituality, low-impact living, conspiracy seeking, authenticity in leaders, fresh political parties. In their construction, governance systems for the Anthropocene cannot avoid meaning, rejecting these ancient myths and reconnecting, profoundly, with the natural world.[47]

6. The values held by each of us can and do change. By the term 'values' is meant that nest of beliefs and motivations – largely subconscious – that underpin our attitudes to everything we encounter. But people are not all the same. 'Values Modes' (VM) divides people and their motivations into 12 psychographic groups. It helps to answer the question of why people do the things and make the choices that they do and to understand the dynamics of change over time – our attitudes are not static. *What Makes People Tick*[48] describes how to communicate with each segment. This might be in social marketing, politics or campaigning for a cause.

Far from confirming that all is lost and that humanity is dooming itself to a hot watery grave, VM analysis indicates that the reverse is the case. Given a clear and specific plan, developed with targeted public deliberation, precisely communicated, and articulated by a committed and collective leadership, enough people would be ready to support and make the changes. Once in motion, most of the rest would follow – the snowball effect. A study by the Centre for Comparative and International Studies in Zurich found unexpectedly in the world's largest democracies of India and the US 'robust public support for unilateral climate policy ... [and] support declines with increasing costs, and increases with growing co-benefits and problem solving effectiveness'.[49]

7. The internet may render history as a predictor of future human behaviour less relevant. As a source of intelligence and knowledge, separate and free from the traditional controlled sources, the age of authority-curated knowledge is over. The downside of this free-for-all has been well reported – notably by the old media and the other sources it is challenging. But it is the malign end of social media and 'totalitarian corporate' AI-based intrusive marketing that is the problem, not Wikipedia, The Conversation, established science on YouTube, art history lessons, TED Talks and educational games like Minecraft. We have become a global village. Learning is advancing at a rapid pace. Our hope is that this advance will have sufficient force to put ideology and prejudice into retreat. It is the internet's power for relating and learning, not least about those blocking myths, that we seek to harness.

1.5 Observations on action and inaction

What may we conclude from theories and observations on action and inaction? Humans do change, have changed and will change. But humans need the right conditions to change beneficially. Extant 'systems' in which we now live are what's stopping us.

In turning to the concept *system*, we appreciate:

(i) The ability to bestow meanings – to 'name' things, acts, and ideas – is a source of power.
(ii) Meanings are not imprinted into things by nature, they are developed and imposed by humans.
(iii) Control of communication allows the managers of ideology to lay down the categories through which our world is perceived.
(iv) We can resist – we have agency.

There is 'an economic and political side to the formation of an idea-system, and idea-systems, once produced, become weapons in the clash of social interests'.[50]

The statement 'it is *the system* that is the problem' conveys a level of insight and recognition, but may not get us far beyond shrugs of disillusioned agreement. At other times when 'the system is the problem', what is actually at issue is the lack of a functional and effective system that achieves the purpose set for it. A collage of dysfunctional relationships is what we receive. When pressed, what is really meant when failings of 'the system' are invoked? Journalists and politicians increasingly label the source of problems as 'systemic' rather than attributing responsibility. The term can be a free pass to an acceptance of impotence or as a veil over incompetence. It is systemic, aka nothing to be done. No one is to blame and everyone is at fault. But people know that only by looking at the whole encompassing the individual will the faults be found and cured. This emerging public awareness of the real source of failings is evidence of recovering systemic sensibility: some people are thinking differently.

However, to get beyond the shrugs takes understanding of just what is going on in these systems – in a systemic way. The word 'system' comes from the Greek verb *synhistanai*, meaning 'to stand together'. A system is a perceived whole whose elements are 'interconnected'. Someone who pays particular attention to interconnections is said to be systemic. The whole may be made up of institutions, government bodies, ministers, staff, and assets, all in a complex network of relationships functioning to varying effect. Out of the end of all this, someone actually does something for or to someone. Systemic thinking and practice are about understanding what this whole is there for, how it works and embarking on its reform. This understanding has been developed into a set of concepts that are applied and adjusted or changed whilst being used to improve a situation. The technical terms draw on circular, recursive, multi-relational understandings and actions (see the Glossary in Appendix 2).

Two adjectives are derived from the noun 'system' – *systemic*, as above, and *systematic*. Think of an assembly line where a car is *systematically* put together – onto the chassis is attached the engine, gearbox and drivetrain, the axles to the drive train, the brakes and wheels to the axle and so on. In stable situations, this can work in government – issuing driving licenses for example – linear, mechanistic, causal, targets, standardisation, bureaucracy – one step follows another. The difficulty is that governments rarely work with stable situations where the end state – a car or a driving license – is predictable. Managing an economy, limiting violent crime or achieving the most good and the least bad through welfare regimes, for example, are not amenable to systematic solutions. The almost automatic use of systematic means of implementation underlies much of why governments fail. Whenever unintended consequences arise, you can be sure a government has used a systematic process for a systemic situation – biofuels is one example we will consider later. The consequences of the Anthropocene are especially uncertain, which will require both systemic and systematic responses, but in the right place. To appreciate the difference, look upon *systematic* as applicable to solids and *systemic* to fluids. When governments try to 'pick up' a fluid as if it were a solid, it slips through their fingers. As in chemistry, much of what is happening inside the fluid is unseen. This theme is developed throughout the book.

Just as seeds in a forest need light to germinate, light that comes from the death of surrounding trees, we will need to create light for new governing systems to emerge. As we look forwards to craft the new, opening up spaces for innovation and change, we should not recoil from felling the institutional timbers of our current world that took hold in a time before the Anthropocene. Fortunately, many systems thinkers before us – and the new wave of 'system changers', especially from civil society where most change will in our view originate – lay down paths of change.

Eric Wolf[51] asked in 1982 , for example,

> what difference would it make to our understanding if we looked at the world as a whole, a totality, a system, instead of a sum of self-contained societies and cultures; if we took seriously the admonition to think of human aggregates as 'inextricably involved with other aggregates, near and far, in weblike, netlike connections'.

Roy Scranton provides further insight when he says

> we can continue acting as if tomorrow will be just like yesterday, growing less and less prepared for each new disaster as it comes, and more and more desperately invested in a life we can't sustain. Or we can learn to see each day as the death of what came before, freeing ourselves to deal with whatever problems the present offers without attachment or fear.[52]

Indy Johar sums up the increasing recognition by many that

> our governance model is broken. We live in a 'systemocracy' – a world of massive inter-dependency yet we are holding on to 19th century versions of governance. This creates the illusion of sovereignty & supremacy – acting as a denial of the complexity we must confront. We need a new governance model which acknowledges our global interdependence at all scales & focuses on the quality, diversity and integrity of feedback in all its natures, whilst recognising the future is real-time and negotiatory. For us to move forward structurally, we need massive reform of our model of governance – reinventing it for the 21st century.[53]

But this dual recognition of governance failure and of systems thinking as being essential to our futures is not happening fast enough. Systems can be dissolved, or deemed not to exist, or re-invented, or re-designed, but the praxis (practical action that is theory-informed or aware) for doing this requires a combination of systemic sensibility, systems literacy and systems thinking in practice capability.[54] This is what we seek to explain in the pages that follow.

This book says we can act. We have choice. The 'systems' we experience as determining much of the way we live, work and organise are not set in stone, the immutable consequence of 'natural' laws. The systems we have are the systems we have. They can be changed, they have to be changed, so let's change them.

The next part of the book examines why governance and governments are failing.

Notes

1 As Wulf (2015) outlines in her intellectual biography of Humboldt (p. 213): Wulf, Andrea. 2015. *The Invention of Nature. The Adventures of Alexander von Humboldt. The Lost Hero of Science.* London: John Murray.
2 Ison, R.L. 2017. *How to Act in Situations of Uncertainty and Complexity in a Climate Change World.* London: Springer and Milton Keynes: The Open University.
3 The question 'What do we do when we do what we do?' is a second-order question that in its answering invites reflexivity (i.e. reflection on reflection).
4 *The Guardian* reported the resumption of deliberations by a 'little-noticed treaty [with] nothing to do with the Paris accord, the United Nations Framework Convention on Climate Change (UNFCCC) … that have dragged on since 1992, on energy sector emissions, which have resumed their rise. The Kigali amendment, which was agreed on 15 October 2016 and comes into force on 1 January 2019, will drastically reduce hydrofluorocarbons (HFCs). These heat-trapping gases are the byproduct of industrial processes such as refrigeration and can be eliminated from those processes by re-engineering. The amendment comes under the Montreal Protocol, the world's most successful international environmental treaty, which aims to stop the depletion of the ozone layer. HFCs are prime examples of short-lived climate pollutants (SLCPs), a range of chemicals that are spewed into the atmosphere by human activities and contribute to global warming.' https://www.theguardian.com/environment/2018/oct/08/kigali-amendment-little-noticed-treaty-could-help-delay-climate-catastrop he?CMP=Share_iOSApp_Other (Accessed 11 October 2018).
5 One could speculate that effective responses to CFCs, which were causing the ozone 'hole', happened before private-sector companies, aided by some governments, learnt from Big Tobacco, Big Coal, and Big Oil how to delay and obfuscate collective global action for the environment.
6 http://quaternary.stratigraphy.org/working-groups/anthropocene/ (Accessed 31 August 2018).
7 Ibid (Accessed 6 June 2016).
8 Regardless of whether one accepts the framing offered by the neologism 'Anthropocene' (others have suggested 'econocene', or 'capitalocene') it is clear that the phenomena to which it refers are real and call for transformations in our individual and collective understandings and practices.
9 Ison, R.L. and M.A. Shelley. 2016. Governing in the Anthropocene: contributions from systems thinking in practice? *Systems Research and Behavioral Science* 33 (5): 589–594.
10 China's 13th Five-Year Plan for Ecological & Environmental Protection (2016–2020) 'supports the "wars" against air, water and soil pollution. The plan has three core missions – to raise the quality of the environment, to strengthen holistic management solutions and to speed up the amendment of environmental issues'. http://chinawat errisk.org/notices/chinas-13th-five-year-plan-2016-2020/ (Accessed 21 September 2018).
11 A mock war. The Phoney War was that period at the start of World War II after the invasion of Poland during which, despite having declared war and the terms of the Anglo-Polish and Franco-Polish military alliances that obliged the United Kingdom and France to assist Poland, no Western power committed to launching a significant land offensive.
12 Steffen, Will, Johan Rockström, Katherine Richardson, Timothy M. Lenton, Carl Folke, Diana Liverman, Colin P. Summerhayes et al. 2018. Trajectories of the Earth

system in the Anthropocene. *Proceedings of the National Academy of Sciences* 115 (33): 8252–8259.

13 Ibid.

14 https://www.theguardian.com/environment/2018/aug/17/world-waking-up-to -reality-climate-change-hothouse-earth-author (Accessed 1 September 2018).

15 UN Intergovernmental Panel on Climate Change (IPCC). https://www.theguard ian.com/environment/2018/oct/08/global-warming-must-not-exceed-15c-war ns-landmark-un-report (Accessed 11 October 2018).

16 Adapted from IPCC (International Panel on Climate Change) Report, 2001.

17 Diamond, Jared. 2005. *Collapse: How Societies Choose to Fail or Succeed.* Harmondsworth: Penguin.

18 Perez, I. Climate change and rising food prices heightened Arab Spring. *Scientific American.* 4 March 2013.

19 Tainter, J. 1988. *The Collapse of Complex Societies.* Cambridge: Cambridge University Press.

20 https://en.wikipedia.org/wiki/Precautionary_principle (Accessed 21 September 2018).

21 Ibid.

22 A full explication of how and why we use the term 'biosphere' is given in Chapter 4.

23 We use the term 'systemic reformation' purposefully; the period of the Reformation in Europe combined challenges to ways of thinking about the world and the place of humans in it as well as being a period of great institutional reform. We face an even greater challenge and have less time to effect the transformations needed.

24 China Water Risk 2016. *China's 13th Five-Year Plan for Ecological & Environmental Protection (2016–2020).* http://chinawaterrisk.org/notices/chinas-13th-five-year-plan -2016-2020/ (Accessed 21 September 2018).

25 'State capture is a type of systemic political corruption in which private interests significantly influence a state's decision-making processes to their own advantage'. https ://en.wikipedia.org/wiki/State_capture (Accessed 21 September 2018).

26 W. Edwards Deming, 1900–1993.

27 Changing our relationship with the planet demands also that we change our relationships with each other – after all, many humans have done little to contribute to the Anthropocene – and we must also change our relationships with other species, what some might call conserving biodiversity.

28 In making these distinctions between citizen and consumer (values, or ways of being) we draw on the following book: Sagoff, Mark. 1988. *The Economy of the Earth.* Cambridge: Cambridge University Press.

29 Extinction Rebellion and Schools Climate Strikes are, as we write, challenging this notion hard.

30 Common Cause Foundation. 2016. *Perceptions Matter: The Common Cause UK Values Survey.*

31 Ibid.

32 Futerra. 2004. *The Rules of the Game: Evidence Base for the Climate Change Communications Strategy.*

33 A variation is parents wanting their children to have more opportunities than themselves (e.g. not to be farmers).

34 Mulvey, Michael (personal communication, September 2018).

35 Latour, Bruno. 2018. *Down to Earth: Politics in the New Climatic Regimes.* Cambridge: Polity.

36 There is a view that history says exploration is full of surprise, and may uncover something of much relevance; but exploration where? Our history to date shows a predisposition to avoid responsibility for human cohabitation with the biosphere.

37 Wolf, Eric. 1982. *Europe and the People without History.* Berkeley: University of California Press.

38 Harari, Yuval Noah. 2011. *Sapiens: A Brief History of Humankind.* New York: Vintage Books.

39 Maslim, Mark. 2004. *Global Warming: A Very Short Introduction*. Oxford: Oxford University Press.
40 Ibid.
41 In some circles these simplistic approaches to effecting behaviour change have come up for major challenges, especially in terms of their long term effectiveness as well as their theoretical and methodological validity. Nudge is 'a concept in behavioral science, political theory and economics which proposes positive reinforcement and indirect suggestions as ways to influence the behavior and decision making of groups or individuals.' Nudging is said to contrast with other ways to achieve compliance, such as education, legislation or enforcement but these are not the only approaches to effecting social change. https://en.wikipedia.org/wiki/Nudge_theory (Accessed 21 September 2018).
42 Wenger's social theory of learning starts with four premises: (i) We are social beings. Far from being trivially true, this fact is a central aspect of learning; (ii) Knowledge is a matter of competence with respect to valued enterprises – such as singing in tune, discovering scientific facts, fixing machines, writing poetry, being convivial, growing up as a boy or a girl, and so forth; (iii) Knowing is a matter of participating in the pursuit of such enterprises, that is, of active engagement in the world; (iv) Meaning – our ability to experience the world and our engagement with it as meaningful – is ultimately what learning is to produce. http://pagi.wikidot.com/wenger-social-theory-learning (Accessed 21 September 2018).
43 Winchester, F. 2016. *George Lakoff: How We Talk about Climate Change, Politics & Morals*. https://citizensclimatelobby.org/americas-linguistics-how-we-talk-about-climate-change-politics-morals/ (Accessed 13 July 2018).
44 Lent, Jeremy. 2017. *The Patterning Instinct: A Cultural History of Man's Search for Meaning*. Amherst: Prometheus Books.
45 Descartes' Arguments for Dualism. https://web.ics.purdue.edu/~curd/110WK13.html (Accessed 16 April 2019).
46 Monbiot, George. 2018. Stepping Back from the Brink. https://www.monbiot.com/2018/01/31/stepping-back-from-the-brink/ (Accessed 12 February 2019).
47 Michael Mulvey (personal communication, September 2018) makes the point that 'the word "religion" has its roots in the Latin verb "religo" meaning "to bind back together". Thus it is that humankind now needs a new way of binding itself back together, a new religion in the sense of "set of shared beliefs" that unifies rather than divides.' He asks: 'Could not the focus of such a shared belief system be "stewardship of Planet Earth for future generations or some such?"'
48 Rose, Chris. 2011. *What Makes People Tick*. Leicester: Matador.
49 Bernauer, T. and R. Gampfer. 2015. How robust is public support for unilateral climate policy? *Environmental Science & Policy* 54: 316–330.
50 Wolf, Eric. 1982. op cit.
51 Ibid.
52 Scranton, Roy. 2015. *Learning to Die in the Anthropocene: Reflections on the End of a Civilization*. San Francisco: City Lights Publishers.
53 Johar, Indy. June 2018. Medium. https://provocations.darkmatterlabs.org/the-great-restructuring-begins-dfba15d22019 (Accessed 21 September 2018).
54 In making this claim, our position is that all systems are socially constructed, even 'ecosystems' because it is we humans who invented the term 'ecosystem' and thus we can choose how to use the concept. In taking this stance we are not denying the materiality of the world and what might loosely be described as the 'laws of physics', or even 'of nature'.

PART 1

The failure of governance and governments

The edifice we have built no longer has viable foundations – we need to reform.

2

WHY GOVERNANCE
SYSTEMS ARE FAILING

2.1 Government and governance critiques

Across countries and domains there is a growing critique of contemporary governance.[1] We are far from alone in recognizing widespread systemic failure. We have worked or lived in many of these countries and have written about, researched, and attempted to transform, governance and governing in several of them. Symptoms of governance deficit vary across policy domains and scale from local to global, occurring within nations, organisations, and multilateral projects and programs.[2]

In *The Fourth Revolution*, Micklethwait and Wooldridge claim that,

> for 500 years, the West's ability to reinvent the state has enabled it to lead the world. Today, the West is weighed down by dysfunctional governments, bloated budgets and self-indulgent publics; it risks losing its edge to more autocratic Asian states.[3]

Their reform proposals range from 'government is best when it is close to the people to whom it is accountable' to the judicious and controlled use of technocrats for setting government pensions and controlling gerrymandering, and to laws that expire automatically after ten years unless explicitly renewed.[4]

In the UK, Stein Ringen argued that 'a strong government (Tony Blair's) was defeated by a weak system of governance', that 'the next government ... has proved itself equally unable' and that 'both these governments came up against concentrations of economic power that have become politically unmanageable'.[5] He examined New Labour's achievements during 1997–2007 in terms of their social-policy objectives, finding that they had achieved 'absolutely nothing' in their flagship policies of child poverty, education, social justice, and health. He highlighted problems that emerge when governments adopt command-and-control approaches that fail to mobilise citizens or stakeholders in policy development and implementation. His sobering conclusion was that no UK government, of any political persuasion, could get done what it is elected to do. 'What citizens need from their governments, then, is both the pull of good governance and the push of robust institutions'. His study revealed the depth of the malaise that arises when a country is trapped in a system shaped by historical structures and practices. His findings point to deep-seated issues in the 'system of governance' and the need for revitalisation and innovation, including strengthening modes of local or horizontal governance.[6]

In an account of Australian Federal politics from 2007–2014, Paul Kelly concludes that the 'process of debate, competition and elections leading to national progress has broken down. The business of politics is decoupled from the interests of Australia and its citizens. This decoupling constitutes the Australian crisis'.[7] He goes on to situate this state of affairs within a more general framing of the dilemma of Western democracies: 'the inability of political decision makers to address the problems of their nations'.

Laura Tingle explains the Australian situation in terms of neoliberal experiments that reduce the state, especially the civil service, creating 'a growing loss of institutional memory about how things have come about, and, more importantly perhaps, why they did. Without memory, there is no context or continuity for the making of new decisions'. For Tingle, the reasons for governance failure are largely institutional. She cites five primary causes:

1. The rise of an unstable executive at the expense of the parliament (both lacking capacity to build institutional memory).
2. The decline in the influence of the public sector.
3. The relative rise of the national security establishment (which maintains its influence and memory).
4. The transformation of the media into a channel for present-tense information, rather than a reliable repository of the historic record.
5. Increasing loss of civil rights.[8]

The Chinese government is concerned that its rising water shortage of 40 billion tonnes a year is so severe it will destabilize the whole society. So weak are the state-led responses that Philip Ball concludes that only political reform can save the environment.[9] It is estimated that every year water pollution produces 190 million casualties and about 60,000 fatalities in China. Despite a new law in 2015, China fails to acknowledge citizens' basic right to an environment fit for life. The environment is not yet 'afforded the highest level of priority on a par with laws directed at promoting economic growth and controlling population'.

Some countries have relatively new constitutions that, despite sophisticated design by today's standards, skirt the brink of systemic failure. In South Africa, 'state capture' has become rife.[10] State capture is 'a type of systemic political corruption in which private interests significantly influence a state's decision-making processes to their own advantage'. The term was first used by the World Bank (c 2000) to describe the situation in central Asian countries making the transition from Soviet communism. Small corrupt groups used their influence over government officials to appropriate government decision making in order to strengthen their own economic positions; these groups would later become known as oligarchs.[11]

Political and technological lock-in to past policies, interests, lobby groups, and the like is a common governance failure. A classic case is Eskom, a state-owned electricity utility, originally established in 1923. It is a monopoly that has suffered from poor management, South Africa-style crony capitalism, and corruption. For political rather than commercial reasons, it has become locked into the coal industry, overemployment, and underinvestment such that its debt is enough to undermine the state. In 2017, Goldman Sachs declared:

> Eskom [is] the 'biggest risk to South Africa's economy.' The company had R413 billion in debt and plans to raise an additional R340 billion (US$26 billion) – representing eight percent of South Africa's GDP. R218.2 billion of the company's debt consist of government guarantees. Exacerbating the company's financial situation was a recorded R3 billion worth of irregular expenditures in 2017.[12]

It is difficult to see how the country will extricate itself from the trap the ANC (African National Congress), with big mine owners, has created. But it is not an issue confined to the global South. Consider the complicity of the German car industry and the switch by Germany from nuclear back to polluting coal.

Lock-in can be sustained in professional fields. Because the future we will experience is not predictable from the past, many practices will have to change substantially. Mark Shapiro refers to this as *The End of Stationarity*. Stationarity is the idea that the future can be predicted and controlled by having a good set of understandings of the past from which powerful models can be built to predict, and thus control, the future.[13] Stationarity-based practice is common in many branches of science and engineering, but it will not work in a climate-change world characterised by new extremes and constant surprise (i.e. events new to human experience).

Despite West Churchman and Rittel and Webber formulating the idea of wicked problems in the late 1960s[14] and the conclusions reached by the Australian Public Service Commission in 2007 that public policy was consistently failing in situations that were 'wicked', it has taken some time for the public sectors of the world to begin to act appropriately.[15]

These critiques are all valuable and relevant. Our challenge is to locate each within a holistic model of a governance system.

2.2 The failing governance 'diamond'

Historically, the basis of governance in many nations has been the *trias politica*. Known as the 'separation of powers', its aim was 'to prevent the concentration of power and provide for checks and balances between the legislature, the executive and the judiciary'.[16] A rich cast of characters was involved in its development, ranging from Aristotle and the Roman Republic to the Plymouth Colony in North America, Baron de Montesquieu, and the evolution of the English 'constitution'. In the US, the functional elements of the separation of powers are the Legislative (Congress), the Executive (President) and the Judicial (Supreme Court).[17] Other variations exist in most countries, except in one-party states and autocracies.

The separation of powers is no longer an adequate descriptor of contemporary governance. As a model, it is restricted to the state, but other elements play a significant role in the destiny of human life within the Anthropocene. Our premise is that the current governance system operating in most nations can be understood as a 'diamond' comprising state, judiciary/law – as in the *trias politica* – plus the private sector (with which the media is currently aligned) and civil society that today plays significant roles in and beyond most nations (see Figure 2.1). This model fits with how we experience ourselves being governed – though the strength and role of each element differs within and between nations.

But if this is how things are, then this model is irredeemably flawed. This is because of inadequacies within each element, breakdowns in the systemic dynamics between elements, and because necessary elements are missing. Neither is this diamond 'forever'. Once appreciated, we can act to change it. Unlike natural diamonds, it is not a product of nature, immune to breakdown or reconfiguration. We have agency: governance can be reinvented, reconfigured, or abandoned.

The power of thinking systemically is to create ways of appreciating the complexity in a situation and of designing actions that facilitate change. That is why Figures 2.1 and (later) 4.1 are called heuristic devices. They are models not of what is but devices to enable thinking and talking about what is, or

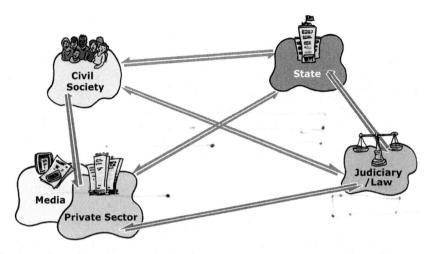

FIGURE 2.1 A generic model of the existing 'two-dimensional' governance 'diamond', no longer adequate to human circumstances.[18]

more importantly, what could be.[19] At the moment thinking systemically is not easy for most people, including many politicians. The advantage of choosing to see governance in systemic terms is that what might otherwise seem impossibly complicated can be understood and acted upon to change. Systems thinking in practice reveals patterns, elements, relations, and different forms of connectivity. Boundary judgments (what is the system-of-interest as determined by whom), feedback processes and emergent properties can be explored and reconfigured.

Using Figure 2.1 heuristically requires a particular kind of reading. It sits in two dimensions, can be understood as a set of four interrelated 'elements', or subsystems, with a fifth, the media located near or in the private sector. Effective governance/governing may or may not emerge from the interactions of these 'elements' depending on whether the components and their interactions are functional (i.e. there is good *connectivity* in the system).[20] Emergent properties arise from the dynamics within and between each element, giving rise to what we understand and experience as the state, civil society, the law, the private sector and the media.[21] But none of these 'elements' can be said to exist in and of themselves. They arise in relation to each other, generating emergent properties such as fairness, trust, security, equity, well-being, ethics and justice. Other systems thinking concepts describe the relational dynamics: interdependencies, influences, and feedback dynamics – both positive and negative (see Glossary).

What makes up the elements in Figure 2.1 are institutions and what people do (i.e. the practices, or praxes, that are explored in Chapter 6). Before moving on, a slight digression is needed to explain what institutions are, how they operate, and how they differ from organisations.

2.2.1 Institutions are pervasive

In some ways, the structural and practice elements of each of the subsystems in Figure 2.1 are easy to name. They can be mapped and depicted, though this is rarely done. Each is made up of much more than what appears at first glance. For example, states vary in their practices, rituals, codes of conduct and the like, which are all linked to informal and formal institutions. Institutions are what institutional economists call norms, or rules of the game, that we humans invent. Anyone who watched the Netflix series *The Crown*, might remember the conflict over whether the 1952 coronation of the British Queen would be televised or not.[22] Both formal and informal rules were being contested.

We humans have developed societies that have a great propensity to invent and use institutions that affect our lives in all manner of ways. Examples are when our parents expect us to have a family dinner, giving and receiving presents, losing face (in Chinese culture), driving on one side of the road, ways of voting, financial regulations – the list goes on. Our whole system of governance is enabled and constrained by a hugely complex array of institutions. Figure 2.2a is a diagram you can't possibly understand. It depicts, using a systems diagram format, all the different institutions and organisations affecting the functioning of one state agency.

Figure 2.2b is an expanded systems map. It was generated by a senior team who built up a collective picture of all the institutions and organisations that affected them doing their jobs – and thus the functioning of the Catchment Management Authority (CMA). They were also responsible for the grouping and naming of what they saw as like elements – in systems terms this is called making boundary judgments – as well as decisions as to what is inside or outside a particular subsystem or system. One of the main distinctions they drew was between organisational entities (e.g. ministries, industry associations) and institutions such as acts, strategies, policies and task forces.

Because the words 'institution' and 'organisation' are often used interchangeably and mean different things in different cultures, it is worth reviewing their etymology (the origin and historical development of a word) so as to make our use clearer (see Box 2.1). In STiP it is also important to distinguish between organisation and structure – a source of considerable confusion.

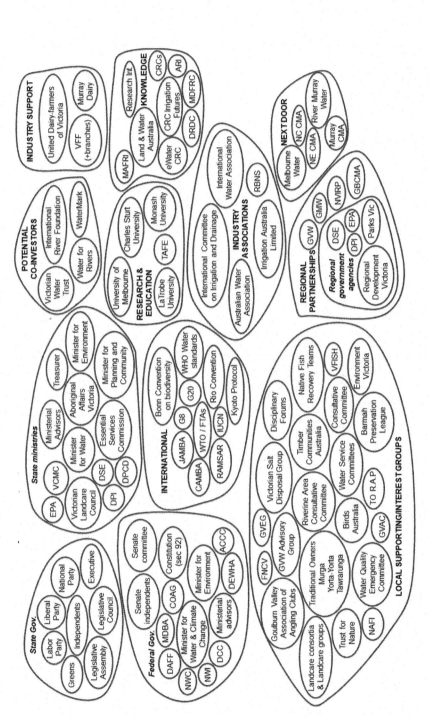

FIGURE 2.2A A systems map of the institutions and organisations that affect the governing of the Goulburn–Broken River Catchment by a Catchment Management Authority, within the State of Victoria, Australia.[23]

FIGURE 2.2B Continued.

BOX 2.1 THE DIFFERENCES BETWEEN INSTITUTION, ORGANISATION AND STRUCTURE

Institution, from the Latin *institutum*, is 'an ordinance; a purpose; a custom; precedents; principal components', literally 'thing set up'. The verb 'to institute', or 'to institutionalise' is from *institutus*: 'to establish in office, appoint; to set up, put in place; arrange; found, establish; appoint, designate; govern, administer; teach, instruct'. The words 'institution' and 'organisation' began to be conflated from about 1828 in France when an organisation or society devoted to some specific work was created, viz. the Institut National des Sciences et des Arts. This conflation has caused difficulties ever since.[24]

The etymology of 'organisation' is less obvious. Many accounts say organisations are the product of acts of organising. This implies human agency and design. The term is, however, common in biology, thus reflecting what might be described as evolutionary 'organising' through drift and 'natural selection'. We will say that organisations (the noun) are products of the action or process of organizing, ordering, or putting into systemic form; also, the arrangement and coordination of parts into a systemic whole. Organisations thus contain processes, elements (often institutions) and structures. Figure 2.1 depicts key elements understood as creating the organisation of the current governance system.

Structures are not the same as organisation, as one can change without affecting the other; for example, the cells in our body parts (structure) change all the time, but while we live their organisation (the relations between the parts) is conserved. The structures of the different elements in Figure 2.1 can be changed but the overall organisation will remain the same.

Organisations can pursue a purpose which might be understood as an emergent property of both relationships between elements (i.e. patterns of organisation) and elements, including institutions and structures. It is thus feasible, in theory at least, to agree some discernible purpose for organisations like a Ministry, a finance department, a company, a mutual or the Roman Catholic Church. Many organisations, of course, lose track of their purpose or pursue purposes that may no longer be viable or useful to a society.

The concepts in Box 2.1 are critical to understanding how to go about changing governance systems. Change is misdirected, or impossible to achieve, if there is confusion about what one is dealing with – institutions, organisations or structures. We have encountered many failed attempts at organisational change due to people only tinkering with structures. An effective organisation can sometimes be destroyed by simplistic changes in structures.

Figure 2.2 could not have been generated if not done collaboratively by the senior team[25] – no individual had a picture of the full institutional/organisational complexity. The group were astounded when they realised that no one knew everything; thus, no one person could be said to be in total control. This demonstrates one of the key STiP precepts: multiple perspectives are needed to engage successfully with complex and uncertain situations. The senior team also realised how long it took to appreciate and work within this complexity – and how much understanding was lost through staff turnover or frequent reallocation of roles, now common in public sectors. This is a major constraint to innovation and effective governance.[26]

The specific detail of Figure 2.2 is not germane to the arguments of this book. What is relevant is to realise that institutional complexity is pervasive and profound, yet poorly understood. Insightful systemic understanding of the institutional ecology of situations and organisations is in short supply. Understanding of institutions and the capability in how to act in relation to existing as well as possible future institutions, are also underdeveloped. This has two dimensions: (1) failure in the systemic design of institutions and/or social technologies, and (2) limited appreciation of the effects institutions have on the enactment, the practices, of governing (see Chapters 7 and 8).

In our experience, ministers, bureaucrats and policy makers have no hesitation in generating new institutions without knowing how they will or will not function within an extant institutional/organisational ecosystem. There is also a frequent failure to kill off institutions that are no longer valid or impinge on the efficacy of new institutions.

2.2.2 Institutions as ideology

A particular perversion has slipped into each of the elements of Figure 2.1. This concerns the extent to which something is an institution or an ideology. The classic example is 'the market'. Rationalist or neoclassical economics underpins *the ideology* of the market, and these in turn have underpinned neoliberalism and austerity. When one uses such a concept, ideally the user would articulate how they understood what a market is, how it comes into existence, and what practices it fosters or constrains. A distinction can thus be made between those who refer to THE market, and those who refer to 'market mechanisms'.

Markets always depend on historical institutions. Wherever one 'sees' or experiences a market, then it always has institutional entailments linked to context, culture, etc. The 'market' for US-style democracy did not exist in Iraq because conducive historical institutions did not exist and were not built. By contrast, Vietnam's growth as an economy was partly achieved under a closed economic model, as they knew they had to grow their institutions first. The use of market mechanisms has failed a lot: examples are the privatisation of water and electricity utilities and higher education in various countries. On the other hand, it may be that creating market mechanisms for water trade, as in the Australian Murray Darling Basin (MDB), will aid more effective water management and river health. Then again, the outcome of this experiment will depend on the governance system in which these mechanisms sit. This is the principal reason Swiss railways work well in comparison to UK railways.

The chapter now focuses on the different elements, or subsystems in Figure 2.1. The functioning of each of these elements is explored, starting with the state. Examples of systemic failings emerging in the relations – or lack of relations – between the elements are dealt with in Chapter 3.

2.3 The state

Trust in governments is in decline across the world. In a compelling set of statistics, the OECD reported[27] that from 2007 to 2014 on average, confidence in national governments declined from 45.2% to 41.8%. The steepest decline was 30%, while the highest increase was 25%. The 2016 average is similar at 42%.[28] The Swiss, at 75% had the highest confidence – perhaps no surprise, given the weight their constitution gives to decentralization and direct democracy. Australia (45%) and the UK (42%) were in the middle of the pack, the US in the lower half (35%) and Spain, Greece and Slovenia (21–18%) at the bottom.

Pia Riggirozzi[29] reports on the OECD's Latin American Economic Outlook 2018, finding that

> 75% have little or no confidence in their national governments. A survey published by Intal/Latinbarometro, found that people believe that the most reliable institution in Latin America is the church (65% confidence); followed by the armed forces (42%) and police (35%). Political parties are viewed as the most disreputable institutions – with just 15% confidence. The widespread shift to the right in Latin American politics, and in Western societies too, is not simply a partisan change – it is also evidence that democratic principles are themselves collapsing. Reconnecting the bond between citizens, public institutions and government is now critical if meaningful democracy is to serve as a means of making society fairer.

When OECD surveys reveal low trust in government, it is the state that is the problem. But there are different forms of state and thus differences in their functioning. Data for China is not in the OECD analysis. What is trust in an authoritarian state dominated by Han Chinese sensibilities and prepared to imprison and/or re-educate a million of its minority Muslim population, the Uighur?[30]

Trust is an interesting measure.[31] It is not a commodity one can seek and point to, or trade or sell. It is best considered as an emergent property of social processes and, in the case of governance, the experiences of citizens. Trust may be lost by declining quality in the relational dynamics between state and non-state actors, by forces operating more widely than the boundary of a nation state, by mismatches between what citizens expect and what they experience or receive, and myriad other factors.

The OECD data point to answers to the questions: what is good governance? And how can we say it is failing? These data suggest the need for answers in context, taking history and difference and thus expectations into account. This is why data are reported as 'trust', 'satisfaction', 'performance' rather than a set of targets or narrowly defined metrics such as the classical economic indicators like GDP, Gini coefficients, and other measures that report state-variables rather than process and rate-variables and emergent properties.

2.3.1 Organs of the state

In most nations, there is an executive branch made up of a President or Prime Minister or Chancellor with an associated office made up of 'staffers' and civil servants. Ministerial staffers may outnumber and have more power than civil servants, or vice versa. The executive sits outside the elected assembly or parliament. Many countries have a head of state – royalty, or in republics a President – who sits outside the executive (e.g. as in Germany, Austria). The state may have a written constitution or, as with the UK, an unwritten or uncodified constitution, which it may act on or ignore at will, occasionally restrained by judicial process. In some countries the constitution designates its parliament as supreme. In others, people (citizens) are supreme.

Another significant element of the state is the civil service, or public service, or state bureaucracy – a cadre of staff who are charged with a wide range of functions that contribute to governing. The state may own lots of assets, such as large land holdings, military equipment, hospitals and the like. Quangos, agencies, and parastatal organisations also sit within the state – some firmly embraced, some loosely held. Most nations have a central state-owned bank, or in the case of the US, a Federal Reserve. The central bank may act at arms-length (i.e. relatively independently from the government of the day) as in Germany and the Netherlands, or be under central control – Norway and India.[32] To fully understand the current set of organs in any state requires an appreciation of history.

2.3.2 Why states are failing

By understanding how the different elements in Figure 2.1 have come into being, how they have evolved and been configured over time, and how they constrain or enhance the praxis of governing, the mistakes and inadequacies of the past can be recognised and eliminated. Most governance reform would benefit from a state-led, 'green-field-site approach', but there is a danger that even this strategy can fall into the trap where stakeholders use the same thinking and practices and institutions that created the current mess because of 'non-reflexive reinvention'.[33] There are many reasons why states are failing. Here is a sample.

Exploring the history of bureaucracy is revealing. The German sociologist Max Weber (1864–1920) argued that bureaucracy constitutes the 'most efficient and rational way in which one can organize human activity and that systematic processes and organized hierarchies are necessary to maintain order, maximize efficiency, and eliminate favoritism'.[34] Note the focus Weber placed on systematic process and hierarchy. For Weber, standardisation was the main means to achieve efficiency and eliminate favouritism (i.e. there was an inbuilt rejection of local or contextual variation or difference). Weberian understandings pervade bureaucracies, whether in the state or in other organisations. They do what they do, as that's what they do. Imposing further bureaucracy is a practice that feels like control and improvement. Organisations needing to reduce costs often use bureaucracy to do this, but thereby only increase them. Those in charge of bureaucracies generally perceive themselves at the centre, and the centre does, of course, think it knows best.

Today one has to be sceptical of the Weberian agenda and beware of being 'flattened' by the 'roll-out' of a centralised project, programme, or policy. Take that phrase 'rolling-out government policy' and ask 'What does the metaphor of: policy as capable of being rolled out to somewhere or over something reveal and conceal?' It promotes a model of governance as centre-to-periphery, implies a stabilized, pre-formed policy that is relevant across contexts, and has at its core some dubious theoretical assumptions about human behaviour change and communication. If metaphor theory seems a step too far, then when contemplating policy or practice development, ask the question, 'Is what we are talking about systematic or systemic or both?'[35] 'Rolling-out policy' is a systematic metaphor, as it doesn't usually build in feedback and it may preclude those with interests in an issue from building their stakeholding by negotiating (1) what is at issue, and (2) what purpose a governance intervention serves. Appreciating the differences between a systemic and a systematic metaphor opens up space for reflexive inquiry and the proposing of new metaphors (see Chapter 7).

Consultation of interested parties about a proposed policy has also been bureaucratised. Consultation rarely achieves its espoused purpose (see Chapter 8). As a participant in community consultations around the implementation of Ecologically Sustainable Development (ESD), Ray experienced the constraining power of government-imposed framings. ESD, despite its origins and underlying theoretical base, was framed as a triple-bottom line phenomenon: social, economic, and environmental.[36] In practice, just as the UN's Sustainable Development Goals have framings based on continued economic growth and market capitalism, the ESD designers privileged the economic, even though it is but one of a range of means of being social. At the time, this unleashed a discourse about trade-offs, but what was never traded off was the economic. In fact quite the reverse, it was always favoured over the other two.

In the Sydney consultations, participants in the meeting proposed, and had carried by a vote of those present, a reframing of ESD based on citizen, not consumer, values (following distinctions made by Mark Sagoff in his book, *The Economy of the Earth*).[37] This outcome did little to shift the government-led consultation-juggernaut, which stayed within its economic-focused framings. Naïve consultation and ethically dubious attempts at stakeholder engagement alienate.

They leave those who have committed feeling exploited, ignored and ultimately alienated: a systemic set of phenomena that has emerged in many places in the last 40 years.

The vital role of health and safety-at-work regulation has been bureaucratised too, with centre-to-periphery rules made and rolled out in response to specific accidents or other damage to humans. Inevitably, many rules miss their purpose, tying up work and home in complexity and time-wasting, and giving good regulation a bad name. Exploitation of dumb regulation by tradespeople and business has become a source of profit, not safety. The end result of these types of regulation is to transfer wealth from citizens to the private sector, without any economic or safety output. 'Good regulation' is being failed by Weberian bureaucracy.

Based on his UK study,[38] Ringen called for the reinvention of local governance in ways that break out of the traps bequeathed by Weberian thinking and institutions that attempt to standardise and deliver through command and control measures and public policy prescriptions. What Ringen saw as a trajectory towards systemic failure has come to pass. The political theatre that has played out in the UK and Europe after the 2016 Brexit vote is testimony to his claims. The praxis of governance is inadequate in the face of what needs to be governed because double work *has* to be done but is *not being* done – new institutions have to be developed, old ones abandoned, and then ways of enacting the new institutions have to be learnt – all whilst there are contestations between the Executive, the Parliaments (Westminster, Scotland, Wales and Northern Ireland), the law, the private sector, and civil society in a nation divided over the issue. To undertake this mammoth task, 3,000 new civil servants were recruited (as of early 2018) with another 5,000 to come following significant cuts from austerity policies,[39] and thereby the massive loss of memory for governing.[40]

Another failing is the rational policy project cycle with prescribed goals, objectives, or outcomes before actually starting out in real situations. The example in Figure 2.3 comes from Germany but applies in other contexts as well. Germany, like many countries, approached the development of climate-change-adaptation policies and accompanying actions with a typical 'rational' approach configured as a cycle. It included plans, targets, and the like. There is a great danger that such cycles are interpreted as a linear sequencing of steps despite being drawn as circles. This is part of the prevailing systematic tradition (see Chapter 6).

In our experience, little account is taken of the context and time-specific enactment of the practices that such a cycle demands – or what we might call policy performances that have to be created in real time, as emergencies and other surprise events unfold in a climate-change world. In this regard, a plan, no matter how well written, is a poor basis for creating the equivalent of a dance or a good piece of theatre, which is what situated climate-change adaptation will mainly have to be.

Consider what might be missing from Figure 2.3. We suggest the following: (1) building citizen stakeholding and choreographing adaptive routines, built-in

Policy Cycle

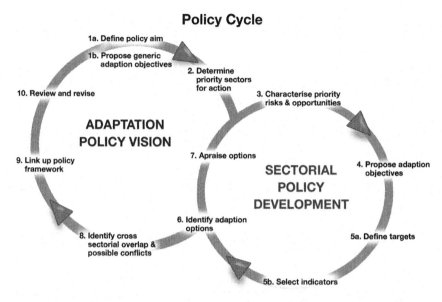

FIGURE 2.3   The systematic, essentially linear, policy process drawn as circles used in developing German climate change adaptation policies.[41]

feedback, learning, and adaptation about the policy itself, and (2) avoidance of lock-in to aims/objectives that may be kept in place despite an ever-changing context over a three-to-five-year project cycle.

The espoused 'lessons learned' for the future from this German process were:

1. The future is and will be uncertain.
2. An iterative policy process is needed.
3. Adaptation requires multilevel-governance.
4. Local and regional levels are most important for implementation of measures.
5. Mainstreaming is a key issue.
6. Integration into different sectoral policies must happen.
7. Adaptation needs broad commitment/participation/involvement of different governmental and non-governmental actors, essential for success of the strategy and its implementation.[42]

This list reflects some encouraging learning, but is it enough given the prevalence of siloed working in states?[43] We propose alternatives to this 'cycle' in Chapters 8 and 10.

Work from 2007 in the Australian Public Service Commission (APSC), and published research from Monash University's then SGRP (Systemic Governance Research Program), provide some pointers.[44] The APSC drew attention to consistent public policy failure in relation to 'wicked problems' such as obesity,

Murray-Darling River Basin reform, chronic disease prevention, and so on. Under Prime Minister Kevin Rudd, the term 'wicked problems' disappeared from the lexicon of ministers and public servants because the language of 'wicked problems' belonged to the other party, the previous government. Upon such political perversity rests the future of our world. The 2007 paper authors, as well as the scholars who coined the terms 'wicked' and 'tame' problems, argued for investment in systems thinking and practice capability. To date there has been little by way of meaningful response, despite continued policy failure that is systemic in nature. As it is known how to build systems thinking in practice capability, there are no rational reasons for this situation to continue (see Chapter 6).

2.3.3 Questions of boundary

Where does the state begin and end? This is not an easy question to answer. Any answer has to be contextual – is it a centralised state such as China, a despotic state like Russia, a state riven with 'state capture' such as South Africa, or the state you are living in now? There has always been a fluidity and contestation about state boundaries. In the past, as nation states emerged, wars and marriages were conducted as means to shape the boundaries of the state.

When the issue of governance reform arises, the question that needs to be posed is: what is the system of interest? These issues are exemplified in Anthony Barnett's sweeping analysis of the phenomenon of Trump and Brexit, summarised here by Fintan O'Toole:[45]

> every single region of England, without London, voted to leave the EU, from the green and pleasant hills to the scarred old mining valleys. This was a genuine nationalist uprising, a nation transcending social class and geographical divisions to rally behind the cry of 'Take back control.' But the nation in question is not Britain, it is England. The problem with this English nationalism is not that it exists. It has a very long history (one has only to read Shakespeare). The English have as much right to a collective political identity as the Irish or the Scots (and indeed as the Germans or the French) have. But for centuries, English nationalism has been buried in two larger constructs: the United Kingdom and the British Empire. These interments were entirely voluntary. The gradual construction of the UK, with the inclusion first of Scotland and then of Ireland, gave England stability and control in its own part of the world and allowed it to dominate much of the rest through the empire. Britishness didn't threaten Englishness; it amplified it.

In this analysis can be seen the relationship between structure (absence of an English parliament), agency (the active creation and re-creation of Scottish solidarity through the functioning of the parliamentary committees in Holyrood, the parliament of Scotland)[46] and identity (the loss of Britishness and absence of Englishness).[47]

2.3.4 Systemic reflections on the state

Many, if not all, state institutions were invented before it was accepted that humans were creators of an Anthropocene. As elaborated further in Part 3, questions concerning how the state responds to the Anthropocene are central to our times. Can China, for example, address its own 'environmental crisis' before deterioration becomes irreversible? Transparency may be key:

> History has shown that rigorous environmental protections are most likely to be instituted and enforced in open societies where an independent judicial branch, media, activists and public can freely challenge government and business interests. China has no such history, and its construction projects around the world have long been plagued by a troubling environmental record.[48]

China is not alone. The UK government approved the beginning of fracking in the week in 2018 when the IPCC said we had 12 years to avoid a climate catastrophe.[49] The institutions of UK government are evidently inadequate as well. What of failed, or failing, states? And what of the efficacy of institutions of the state, given the rise of powerful multinationals, global internet connectivity and financial flows that distort much of what we strive to do?

As evidenced by the many critiques (see Section 2.1), institutions of the state no longer function effectively in that they do not deliver on the primary purposes of the state and needs of the citizenry. These phenomena, we contend, are referred to when demands are made for whole system change. In a book of essays on Australian public-sector reform written in preparation for the Federal election of 2010, Ray proposed five agenda items for systemic reform:[50]

1. Expand the concept of reform to include the need to reinvent governance/governing as a systemic practice (see Chapter 8).
2. Initiate a process to reframe the issues of governance (the reform agenda as then framed was one of first-order change: better administration, service delivery, narrowly defined efficiency and enhanced command and control by the executive – a sure-fire recipe for poor governance).
3. Invest more in capability to use systemic approaches in the face of intractable policy issues (see Chapters 5 and 6).
4. Running in parallel with investment as described in the previous point, invent new institutional arrangements that are conducive to engaging with, and managing complex, 'wicked' situations.
5. Design and run new experiments in horizontal or citizen-engaged, emergent and self-organising governance.

How and why these systems-thinking concepts are needed in this task are taken up in Part 3.

2.4 The law, the legal or justice system

Rule of law is, for us, fundamental. The core idea in Thomas Hobbes' *Leviathan* (1651) was that 'the first duty of the state is to provide law and order ... the ultimate public good'.[51] The legacy from Hobbes' work is the notion of a 'social contract' between ruler(s) and ruled. The rise of Europe began because 'its states were in a sweet spot: powerful enough to provide order but light enough to allow innovation'.[52]

The word 'law' can be understood through its etymology. In Old English *lagu* meant 'ordinance, rule prescribed by authority, regulation; district governed by the same laws;' also sometimes 'right, legal privilege', or 'that which is set or established'.[53] In other words a law is an institution, which is invented, conserved over time, or not. Laws are usually created by the state, or by supra-states in the case of the EU, or by international bodies such as the UN. Laws fit within 'jurisdictions', from the Latin *ius, iuris* and *dicere* meaning 'law' and 'to speak'. A jurisdiction is the practical authority granted to a legal body to administer justice within a defined field of responsibility.[54]

According to the OECD, member states have more trust in their judicial systems than the state. Why might this be so? When the law is functioning well, it delivers justice and thus security to all citizens, regardless of wealth, gender, race, or class. The OECD concludes: 'on average, just over half (54%) of citizens reported having confidence in their country's judicial system and courts. Significant differences exist with 80% satisfaction in the highest-ranked countries and less than 20% in the lowest ranked'.[55]

Some nations have evolved cultures that place greater emphasis on the right and access to justice. Sometimes the written law may be good on paper but its enactment, monitoring, or control are subject to failure, whether by organisational dysfunction, coercion, or bribery. As with any 'system', the full range of activities that deliver the purpose have to be enacted in ways that are efficacious (i.e. they function) and effective (i.e. they achieve what they are designed to do).

In many countries it is only the law that holds back elective dictators. In South Africa (SA), 'the whole system of government and administration was simply unravelling under the weight of ubiquitous corruption, a ludicrously ill-equipped public service and a whole series of policy blunders'.[56] Extolling the virtues of its legal system, Mike Coleman said:

> only in South Africa could you see four different courts – Constitutional, Supreme Court of Appeal, High, and Land Claims – in such a short period give judgments based on such diverse arguments to the same end: strengthening rural land rights. Nowhere else in the world is there a legal system blending customary law, Roman–Dutch law, English law and modern democratic constitutional law.[57]

Despite its virtues, access to justice in SA, as with many countries, is still not equitable. Not all countries draw on the best of different legal systems.

Many challenges.have to be confronted to enable the law to deal with today's exigencies. Human-induced climate change is the most profound of them. Richard Lazarus said in 'Super Wicked Problems and Climate Change: Restraining the Present to Liberate the Future':

> Climate change may soon have its 'lawmaking moment' in the United States. The inherent problem with such lawmaking moments, however, is just that: they are moments. What Congress and the President do with much fanfare can quickly and quietly slip away in the ensuing years. This is famously so for environmental law. Subsequent legislative amendments, limited budgets, appropriations riders, interpretive agency rulings, massive delays in rulemaking, and simple non-enforcement are more than capable of converting a seemingly uncompromising legal mandate into nothing more than a symbolic aspirational statement.

When budgets for the law are determined by the government, powers are separated insufficiently. Other ways of determining and allocating budgets could, of course, be invented.

Lazarus observed insightfully that:

> Climate change legislation is especially vulnerable to being unraveled over time for a variety of reasons, but especially because of the extent to which it imposes costs on the short term for the realization of benefits many decades and sometimes centuries later. To be successful over the long term, climate change legislation will need to include institutional design features that insulate programmatic implementation to a significant extent from powerful political and economic interests propelled by short-term concerns'.[58]

How right Lazarus was: an Executive Decree by President Obama committing the US to the Paris Climate Accord was abandoned by his successor. In other words, the governance mechanisms and institutional designs used were inadequate for the task at hand.

2.4.1 Creating new legal institutions

Unlike many institutions, laws have specialised practitioners (lawyers, barristers, solicitors; prosecutors, magistrates, judges, justices, jurors) as well as all the institutions in which these practices are carried out: courts, commissions, inquiries, cases, etc. All of these can be understood to sit within the judiciary. This is:

> the system of courts that interprets and applies the law in the name of the state. The judiciary also provides a mechanism for the resolution of disputes. Under the doctrine of the separation of powers, the judiciary generally does not make statutory law (which is the responsibility of the legislature) or enforce law (which is the responsibility of the executive), but rather interprets

law and applies it to the facts of each case. However, the judiciary does make common law, setting precedent for other courts to follow. This branch of the state is often tasked with ensuring equal justice under law.[59]

Contemporary legal systems are generally based on one of four basic types:

civil law, common law, statutory law, religious law or combinations of these. However, the legal system of each country is shaped by its unique history and so incorporates individual variations. Both civil (also known as Roman) and common law systems can be considered the most widespread in the world: civil law because it is the most widespread by landmass, and common law because it is employed by the greatest number of people.[60]

As nation states have become more interconnected, international courts have been established. These will be of especial significance for the Anthropocene – which is no respecter of national jurisdictions. In 1945 and 1946 the International Court of Justice (ICJ) was set up under the UN Charter. This court can only act by consent of states:

the ICJ produces a binding ruling between states that agree to submit to the ruling of the court. Only states may be parties in contentious cases. Individuals, corporations, parts of a federal state, NGOs, UN organs and self-determination groups are excluded from direct participation, although the court may receive information from public international organisations. That does not preclude non-state interests from being the subject of proceedings if a state brings the case against another. For example, a state may, in cases of 'diplomatic protection', bring a case on behalf of one of its nationals or corporations.[61]

There are many examples of nations withdrawing from the court's jurisdiction when threatened with prosecution. As an effective institution it has a long way to go.

In 1959 Europe created the European Court of Human Rights (ECHR) which 'is a supranational or international court established by the European Convention on Human Rights. The court hears applications alleging that a contracting state has breached one or more of the human rights provisions'.[62] Other international courts have emerged, but more are needed.

2.4.2 Systemic failings of the legal/judicial systems

Why are contemporary legal systems inadequate? Here is a selection of their systemic failings:

• *Institutional complexity*: including the failure to abandon old laws and start again. In Figure 2.4 the 'sedimentary layers' of law that exist to govern

Victorian Legislation

Water (Commonwealth Powers) Bill 2008

FIGURE 2.4 Legislation passed and/or retained in the State of Victoria, Australia, between 1850 and 2008 relating to the governance of water and rivers.[63]

water/rivers have built up over 158 years and create a legal field impenetrable to all except those with high degrees of specialization.

- *Finding and not finding the truth*: in some jurisdictions the practice of law is consistently adversarial rather than conciliatory, learning and/or inquiry-based, and thus open to contingency and surprise. Family and children's law may be adversarial and not inquisitorial; its procedures may be held in secret with the presumption that a legal process can resolve the complexities of family life. European criminal procedural systems became hybrids of European and English, but they retained their defining feature, the principle that criminal courts must have the duty and authority to seek the truth. In England, by contrast, the well-meaning reforms of the 18th century that resulted in adversary trial had the effect of perpetuating the central blunder of the inherited system: the failure to develop institutions and procedures of criminal investigation that would be responsible for and capable of seeking the truth.[64]

- *Procedural justice is often confused with social justice*: practices differ within different legal systems and jurisdictions – positivistic 'black letter law' is a constraint as rules become ossified and not open to reinterpretation in ways relevant to contemporary circumstances.[65]

- *Laws operate ex post rather than ex ante*: the law/insurance combination has driven some progress where companies have become liable for environmental damage. But liability is limited to present degradation rather than the future. Carbon dioxide output is yet to be consistently incorporated into legal decisions. This same combination has also driven economic waste litigation aimed solely at transferring wealth or for reasons devoid of social value when societies turn litigious.

- *There is a loss of focus on, or a failure to regenerate, purpose in relation to particular laws*: rigorous examination of each law would throw into sharp relief where an overall field of law has gone astray. London is said to be the libel and divorce capital of the world. Does this tell us anything about the legislative health of these two fields? Employment law has become an expensive minefield, courtesy mainly of a judiciary without relevant knowledge. Chancery law is too complicated to be understandable (and is ultra-expensive to apply) – what is its purpose, and is it fulfilling it? Is there a better/cheaper way? We sign necessarily unseen contracts as long as the Bible to buy a piece of software. Why?

- *Privacy law is a burgeoning issue*: it is driven by the emergence of big data and data analytics, accompanied by breaches of data protection, widespread hacking and data theft. In work by the Australian Law Reform Commission:

> a major concern of stakeholders is the limited ability of the Office of Privacy Commissioner to address systemic issues. It requires a number of tools and strategies to enable it to discover, monitor and remedy systemic issues in agencies, organisations and industries; ideally before a breach occurs; and to act as a general deterrent to other agencies.[66]

This is an example of the need for praxis reform.

- *Historical praxis is failing*: innovations that are being prompted involve changing the system boundaries and the creation of hybrid institutions morphing between legal entities and civil society organisations. Systemic advocacy has emerged as a form of practice in the Oklahoma Disability Legal Centre, which:

> engages in systemic advocacy as a means of achieving [their] mission of protecting, promoting and expanding the rights of people with disabilities.

Through systemic advocacy, [they] seek to influence and change systems such as legislation, government or agency policy, services practices and community attitudes.[67]

In Victoria, Australia, under the auspices of the Federation of Community Legal Centres (CLC) capabilities are being built 'to identify and respond to systemic barriers to justice' through what they also call systemic advocacy work.[68] These examples show how innovation is increasingly prevalent within civil society.

- *Unenforced enforcement for the comparatively powerful is a theme running through much of the public sector:* it is a major cause of the endless differences between theory and practice, policy and delivery. The small people feel the brunt of the system that the powerful know how to play. Laws to stop a few bad people end up penalising good people with form filling whilst the bad people get free rein. The Menai Straits in Wales is rich in sea life, with extraordinary reefs and a significant mussel industry. It is a Mecca for canoeing, yachting and fishing. These interests compete for use. Recognising its value and ecological significance, the Countryside Council for Wales, through some proper public engagement, developed a plan of fair shared use. But some of the recreational users reacted strongly to the designation being enacted. Why, when agreement was apparently there? It emerged that none of them had faith that the public authorities would enforce the designation. Thus, the public would all play ball, but the big players – like some of the commercial mussel fisheries – would ignore the designation. So the good little people would be controlled, and the big would not be. The designation would in practice be worthless. We see a similar theme in planning – the little people get controlled, the big developers get away with it. The system of interest drawn up by the public authority was only an implicit plan, not its achievement, and as such purposeless.
- *The rule of law requires that justice be separated from politics:* governments seeing their role as making laws rather than achieving beneficial change on the ground is endemic to many jurisdictions. Legislators often find it easy to create new regulations but hard to sustain the budgets and workforce capabilities for monitoring, compliance, and evaluation. For criminal justice, the police are left to ration the application of laws. Headlines in 2018 exclaimed: 'The UK justice system is in meltdown'.[69] Simon Jenkins captures some of the systemic issues:

[The] criminal justice system is in disarray. The head of the crown prosecution service, ... is resigning amid rows over failed convictions. The head of the Parole Board has been forced to resign over [a] case.[70] London's murder rate has overtaken New York's, with fatal stabbings in Britain at their highest level since 2010. Prison violence and suicide are rising. The rule of law demands that justice be separated from politics. That is clearly not happening ... department Z has been inundated by pressure from politicians to take a tough line on sex cases, from domestic violence and rape to harassment and historical abuse. In some regions as much as one-third of court time is now consumed by such cases, which can be of intense complexity. The CPS has been trapped time and again by failing to follow rules of disclosure to defence lawyers. But it lacks competent staff. Its budget has been cut by a quarter since 2010, another political 'intervention'.[71]

What a system.

2.4.3 Systemic reflection on the 'law system'

The continued effective functioning of the 'law system' is vulnerable in many places. Von Bogdandy and Ioannidis propose a way of thinking and acting based on the concept of 'systemic deficiency in the rule of law'.[72] This can be understood as a form of systemic inquiry (see Chapter 8). They join others in claiming that the EU is in a crisis that is 'administrative and financial, but, most importantly, ...touches upon the ... principle that has served as the cornerstone of European integration ... the rule of law'. The systemic deficiencies, they claim, are 'due to endemic corruption, weak institutional capacities, or insufficient resources at the administrative or judicial levels'. As a result:

> some EU Member States present [such] grave deficiencies in guaranteeing the rule of law that their conformity with basic EU standards is seriously questioned. Although it is obvious that the EU cannot stay inactive in the face of such grave deficiencies, it remains unclear how potential responses fit with the overall EU constitutional framework.

These claims point to yet another case for systemic reform.[73]

The case for a wall-to-wall reassessment of areas of law is compelling. Many of these problems have existed for a long time. Essentially nothing changes. Four reasons can be postulated. First, periodically the judiciary has to fight off the government of the day attempting to reduce its independence. The judges become habituated to resisting change. They are obviously right to maintain their independence, but wrong to resist change. Second, many in the legal profession believe that all of life is reducible to a legal process. Often practitioners are unable to see beyond their own profession and ignore the many other ways of resolving a dispute. Third, the legal profession has a huge vested interest in the status quo. Law is a high-pay, high-status and high-power career with limited accountability. Fourth, few people outside the law understand it sufficiently to mount a credible challenge. Internal reform will not happen, particularly with so many representatives in government.

Are these systemic failings insurmountable? We hope not. The effective rule of law is essential to all governance and especially for the Anthropocene. The law does function well in some areas. If opened up to reform through contextual co-design and deliberation – a sort of emergent legal-reinvention through a global ecology of green-field sites – then new systemic relations ought to be possible. Major revision will be needed to make the rule of law efficacious for future governing.

2.5 The private, or business, sector

Writing in *The European Financial Review*, William Sun, Jim Stewart, and David Pollard argued there are 'fundamental problems in corporate governance practices' because:

> the corporate governance system not just failed to prevent the [2008] financial crisis and corporate collapses, but has actually incentivised corporations to manipulate share price and abuse corporate accounting principles and practices, to create and take excessive financial and business risks for short-term profit maximisation. … The underlying problems with corporate governance are not just some technical or implementation issues, but more about the issues of paradigms, governing approaches and the orientation of corporate governance systems, which are deeply ingrained in Anglo-American financial capitalism.[74]

It is this systemic mix that challenges our extant governance systems. In the Anthropocene, a period new to human history, the systemic malaise is exacerbated in ways few governments and private sector corporations seem prepared to acknowledge, at least publicly.

Just as in the case of the state and legal systems, institutions are pervasive: think of boards, shares, debentures, stocks, annual reports and shareholder meetings, and institutional complexity begins to surface. There are also different organisational forms: public, private and family companies, corporations, chambers, cooperatives, mutuals and partnerships. At the moment the 'company' or 'corporation' reigns supreme. In recent times these have taken new forms – multinational, supranational or meta-national companies or corporations. Parag Khanna poses the following question: 'Going stateless to maximize profits, multinational companies are vying with governments for global power. Who is winning?'[75] This list of the top 25 companies in Figure 2.5 does not include Google (which is now first or second), reflecting how dynamic their growth has been. 'The 10 biggest banks still control almost 50 percent of assets under management worldwide'. In 2015 the cash that Apple had on hand exceeded 'the GDPs of two-thirds of the world's countries'.

As *The Sunday Times*' Economics Editor observed in 2015:

> Despite the rise of China and of mega firms from Europe, Japan and other Far Eastern countries, US-based multinationals still dominate. The annual Fortune Global 500 list is a ranking of these big beasts in the world's

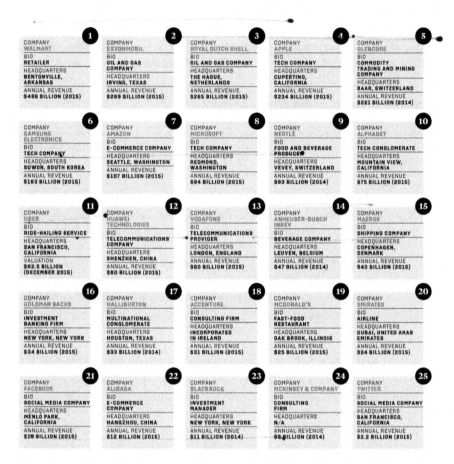

FIGURE 2.5 The top 25 'corporate nations' in 2015.[76]

corporate jungle, who between them account for $31.2 trillion of revenues – 40% of the world's GDP of $75 trillion. The two figures are not directly comparable [but sufficiently so to make the point]. These 500 companies employ more than 65 million people between them.[77]

Writing in 2012, Simon Caulkin makes many of the contextual points. We draw extensively on his journalism as we cannot say it better ourselves:

> Although many fall by the wayside, companies can be, and sometimes to all intents and purposes are, immortal. Their purposes can change and their ultimate allegiance is not to states or any other external power but to themselves. The irony is that for most of their history, corporations have been the instrument of other, senior sources of power – first religious (Stora's earliest recorded share transfer, in 1288, was between a bishop and his nephew [in what is now Sweden]), then state, when crowns 'nationalised'

religion during the Reformation and the nation state emerged as the primary unit of power. States granted charters to companies to further their economic ends. Britain outsourced the running of large parts of empire, including India, to the British East India Company.

Even when limited liability was generally adopted in the 19th century (to the disapproval of some who warned of the dangers of corruption) it was not of right but because of the expected collective, rather than individual, benefits.

But without our noticing, the boot has moved to the other foot. In a world where global markets are the ultimate arbiter of policy, the shadow banking system spews out derivatives and other money substitutes that dwarf official money supplies, and companies export employment, profits, and headquarters at will, few nation states can claim to be 'sovereign' in the conventional sense. In this world, around 2,000 private "supercitizens", as Rothkopf describes the largest multinationals, are fitter for today's purpose than all but 30 or 40 states.

Flourishing in the areas governments cannot reach, using their mobility to play off states against each other, companies have further tipped the scales in their favour by working to transform the privileges granted in the name of the common good – limited liability, immortality, unlimited size – into rights that regulators mess with at their peril.[78]

The story Caulkin tells is of the growing power and declining accountability of corporate giants. These stories continue with the revelations in 2018 about Cambridge Analytics, Facebook, the growing size and power of Amazon, and the ubiquity of Google and Twitter. All of these companies and others, including the large tobacco, oil and coal companies, pursue strategies to maintain their power and reach whilst exploiting whatever social licence to operate they have. Often the state colludes in facilitating or maintaining corporate power. This has become all too apparent in the rampant finance sector. Reviewing Nicholas Shaxon's *The Finance Curse: How Global Finance Is Making Us All Poorer*, Oliver Bullough points to Shaxon's demands for: 'radical transparency to reveal who owns what, as a core defence against kleptocratic capital flowing in from China, Russia and elsewhere, as well as land-value tax to defang the tax havens, and outright bans on some hot money'.[79] Bullough goes on to say that the big four accounting firms are part of the problem and that 'tech giants would need regulation to act in our interests rather than their own'.

How has this situation come about? As Caulkin argues:

The spearhead of the corporate transformation from servant to master has been the increasingly aggressive assertion of corporate personhood. Its apotheosis was the 2010 Citizens United case in which the US Supreme Court not only allowed companies the same right to free speech as individuals but also ruled that to restrict that right was unconstitutional.

The entire notion of the shareholder has to be rethought. In an age when a listed company's share register suffers 90% churn each year, the very concept of 'the shareholder' dissolves.[80] Calling for a 'cultural and behavioural transformation', Bob Garratt declared that the first duty of directors was not to shareholders, but to the company itself. Organisations have to move from agency theory to stewardship theory, he believes – restoring the original concept of the board's role from the 17th century.

The notion that the private and public sectors are distinct forms merits rethinking too. There are no absolute boundaries, and many organisations now are 'hybrids': some universities have become full or quasi-corporations even while still receiving funding from the state. Are they private- or public-sector bodies? The emergence of hybrids challenges old assumptions and tests historical institutional designs and governance systems.

Caulkin poses the key questions in the following terms:

the shifting interface between public and private power raises many more questions. How, for example, can "loose" centres of corporate power be reconnected to the world they affect so deeply? Can the markets be "greened" so that growth can be achieved without using human lives or the environment as fuel? Business school theories have played a part in bringing this new world about: how does the academy theorise – and teach – what is happening now? How, for example, do we think about leadership in a post-sovereign world where countries are only partially in charge of their own fate and companies have grown not just too big to fail but possibly also too complex to manage?

From Caulkin's perspective, it is the business-as-usual commitments across the private (and perhaps public) sectors that is the aberration. He draws on *The Rise and Fall of Management* by Gordon Pearson, 'who shows how corporate law, including the 2006 Companies Act, takes a much more enlightened approach to governance than current practitioners want to admit'. For example:

contrary to common assumptions, shareholders do not own companies (how could they and benefit from limited liability at the same time?), and directors owing their duty to the company can't be 'agents' of shareholders – indeed, they are charged with acting fairly as between all company members. It's a measure of how much present governance has lost its way that resurrecting such ideas should now seem so radical – and so urgently necessary.

Systemic deficiencies in the financial sector are beginning to be addressed in some relatively powerful circles:

Corporate Australia has been warned. The changing climate is something they can no longer ignore ... an executive member of the Australian

Prudential Regulation Authority (APRA), told businesses climate change posed a material risk to the entire financial system. His message was that boards and directors had a fiduciary duty to their shareholders to take it into account ... directors who failed to consider and disclose climate risk could be in breach of the Corporations Act. [Organisations] that fail to adequately plan for this transition put their own futures in jeopardy, with subsequent consequences for their account holders, members or policy holders.[81]

In other words, the sites of resistance to current mainstream practices can be found both in history and (re)invention or re-crafting. How to do this is the praxis we explore in later chapters.

2.5.1 The changing media ecology

The term 'the fourth estate' comes from continental Europe; it augments the three estates of the realm: the clergy, the nobility, and the commoners. The 'fourth estate' is the idea that the press and mass media through critical and public scrutiny hold governments, other organisations, and individuals to account by reporting on their activities. Although normally not considered an 'official' part of the state, in the course of the twentieth century, the news media or press, and then television, became the most commonly recognized part of the fourth estate.[82] With the rise of bloggers and independent journalists, and users of social media platforms, some people now refer to the fifth estate (though the term has existed since the counterculture days of the 1960s).[83]

What is undeniable is that for several centuries the media has been a key element in our governance model. Pamphlets were among the first printed materials; they were used widely in England, France and Germany and were often political or polemical in their content. The first great age of pamphleteering was inspired by the religious controversies of the early 16th century.[84] For a long time, political power has come with access to the printing press, and then other forms of media. There are many examples: Goebbels during the Nazi era, under other dictatorships in Spain, Argentina, Chile, etc., and in centrally planned countries like the former USSR and the Republic of China. In the latter, the term 'state media' usually applied.

The media is sometimes part of the state, often embedded in the political system, part of the private sector through the global tech titans, and increasingly part of civil society. But for much of the last 150 years media has been controlled by barons (think of Randolph Hearst and Rupert Murdoch), often with enough power to make or break governments. With the advent of a 24-hour news cycle, voracious in its demand for content and 'news', and the seeming inability of politicians to resist, the whole nature of politics changed. Currently the world lives vicariously on daily tweets from the President of the most powerful country in the world.

Few public broadcasters 'speak truth to power' these days; authentic language and the ability to call things what they really are have gone missing under pressure from media lobbyists and weak governments.[85] Rather than be a true 'fourth estate' holding power to account, the media have often become integral to governments and politics, happy to be courted by the powerful and for its editors and owners to rejoice in their influence. Much of it has become part of the status quo, which is not what a flourishing society needs, especially at a time of such great uncertainty and when the status quo is rotting. Social media has become a means for frustrated, effectively muzzled citizens to express their views publicly. Some have contributed to the barrage of unsubstantiated and fake news, so it has come under criticism. Sources of news are diversifying with the internet, but so too is 'fake news'. This is an area where further systems thinking is needed to resolve this dilemma.

To play its 'fourth estate' role effectively, the media must be independent of the state, free from concentration in the politics of their owners, and primed to speak truth unto power if their contribution to governance is to be effective. This should provide a source of political pressure, particularly when reporting on corruption, mismanagement or fraud. This has largely happened in South Africa, where the media ecology has fulfilled most of the fourth estate functions.

In Figure 2.1 we place the media close to the private sector – which is where its power and impact have been in recent times – but acknowledge that it will likely continue to dissipate across the four nodes of our governance model. It is part of a moving ecology of institutions, interests and practices. This happens even within the 'private sector' where there have been different organisational forms, which in turn give rise to different ethics, ethos and practices – or social purpose. Take *The Guardian*, run by a not-for-profit trust, and compare it with the outlets controlled by Murdoch's News Corporation, Fox News and the like.

Regulation is tricky. This is controlled by the state at present, but the media should be independent of it. In practice, freedom of the press comes to mean freedom for media owners and editors.[86]

In media ecologies controlled by powerful interests, governance can be undermined by (1) direct manipulation by owners, editors, and the like; (2) self-censorship by journalists who know how the political land lies and know what they have to do (and not do) to continue to find stories and jobs; and (3) data manipulation by specialist firms such as Cambridge Analytics or nation states like Russia or groups of other hackers who may operate by various means, including creating malicious internet bots.

2.5.2 Systemic reflections on the private sector

There can be no doubt that the biggest challenge to our governance systems comes from unconstrained private sector power. It has taken the power of a superstate, the EU, to start to curb those of Google's practices which are not in the public interest. The rise of supranational corporations, the changing media ecology and changing state–private sector dynamics have provided the most significant perturbations to the historical arrangements that are our governance systems. The question is how to move forward and deal with these perturbations? Where, in the Foucauldian sense,[87] are the sites of greatest possible resistance and change? For some potential answers we turn to civil society.

2.6 Civil society[88]

Civil comes from the Latin *civis*, meaning 'citizen'. Civil society is what relates to human affairs. In England, the term also applied to the 'civil service' – that which is not the monarchy or the church. In the governance model of Figure 2.1, civil society comprises all that is not the other - not the state, the law, the private sector or corporate media. Civil society is:

> [T]he aggregate of non-governmental organisations and institutions that manifest interests and will of citizens, or individuals and organisations in a society which are independent of the government. Civil society includes the family and the private sphere, referred to as the 'third sector' of society, distinct from government and business.[89]

For clarity, we include community-based organisations, social enterprises, and professional societies, including guilds, lodges and the like.

Earlier writers saw three main features of civil society: 'its autonomy from the state, its interdependence with the state, and the pluralism of values, ideals and ways of life embodied in its institutions'.[90] According to Robert Putnam, the capacity to create *social capital* through self-organising relationships amongst citizens is central to the creation and sustaining of a society.[91] Sometimes these relationships will be formalised and take organisational form; at other times they may be informal.

A legacy to be overcome is 50 years of neoliberalism and the creation of the individual, group, family, and 'social segment' as consumers. In the latter part of the twentieth century, governments believing they had to cut costs, or were not best at delivering services, outsourced or privatised much provision. Business, as well as civil society organisations, responded, sometimes to good effect but often with loss of service quality or to the detriment of the civil service organisation. Co-option, control and manipulation by the state was prevalent. Despite a sense that neoliberalism has had its day, modern capitalism has generated institutions and practices that relentlessly construct and reconstruct the consumer, whether through celebrity culture, click-bait technology, manipulation of 'big data', research and journal rankings, bidder for government contracts, or the co-option of some of the brightest people in our society into spurious selling, marketing, advertising and culture-creation roles. The Australian TV panel show *Gruen Planet* offered a compelling example of how to spin a nation and buy off a community, and thus subvert civil society (see Box 2.2).

BOX 2.2 SYSTEMIC INSIGHTS IN UNLIKELY PLACES

Apropos of the new Australian 'national conversation' about vested interests – most of them mining – I was struck last year by an episode of The Gruen Nation,[92] which went behind the green-washing of the mining and resources industries. If only Australian Treasurer Wayne Swan had shown this clip to the nation at his Press Club address we would have seen it for how it really is – a nation that can easily be spun. For example, Australians have come to believe through massive expenditure in advertising and spin that mining constitutes 30% of the economy and 10% of the work force when it is actually more like 10% and 3%.

An insider reveals how communities who oppose are approached by developers:[93]

> How do you buy off the community Toby, is there a checklist? I reckon a check (cheque) is always better than the checklist. ... I worked on a major, major, major infrastructure project years ago and we had some particularly difficult people up against us and we developed a six-point checklist:

1. Forge local relationships.
2. Understand local concerns.
3. Create local opinion leaders.
4. Klaim the middle ground.
5. Employ activists as consultants.
6. Marginalize the remainder.

Now that's hard to remember so as an aide memoire we took the first letter of each of those strategies as an acronym which is of course fuck'em.[94]

Insidious, systemic undermining of civil society is probably much more widespread than is realised. The basic governance model depicted in Figure 2.1 began before the emergence of the Web – a connectivity that sits on a fulcrum between the emergence of solidarity and/or fragmentation. Concerned about the failings of traditional governance, we have joined citizens across the globe who choose to petition and donate to new forms of civil society organisations. Avaaz – voice or song in many languages – is a 46-million-person campaign network working to bring the views and values of the people to influence global decision making. Its members live in every nation of the world. The employed team is spread across 18 countries on six continents and operates in 17 languages.[95]

What emerges is solidarity between like-minded groups across nations whilst division becomes stronger within nations. Organisations such as Avaaz did not exist before the rise of global connectivity. In other words, the context and design possibilities for our governance arrangements have changed irrevocably since the simple 'diamond' model came into existence. Some nation states have proposed legislative censorship of web-literate civil society organisations like environmental NGOs and, in Australia, the activist organisation GetUp.[96] Others appear to have resorted to state-sponsored murder to silence legitimate critique.

Our view is that if governance reform is to happen, then much of the thinking and practice for change will have to come from within civil society.[97] It is more active in this field than many appreciate. But as citizens we are still, by and large, poorly equipped conceptually and methodologically to enact our citizenship responsibilities effectively, to negotiate otherness:

> other will be born out of an encounter between two opposing trends that form the culture of the modern world – one that is globalising our reality, and another that is preserving our dissimilarity, our differences, our uniqueness. He will be their son and heir, and that is why we should seek dialogue and communication with him.[98]

Our concern, like Kapuściński's, is that 'perhaps we are tending towards a world so completely new and different that the experience of history to date will prove inadequate for understanding it and moving about in it'.

2.6.1 Systemic reflections – civil society and the 'diamond'

In respect of civil society, the thesis of our book is threefold:

- That it is being constrained by the ways in which the state, the law, the media, and the corporate sector are configured;
- It is possible to create enabling environments, with conducive institutional ecologies and systemic governing praxis, that foster and sustain civil-society-led governance innovation and change; and
- A principal part of the enabling of all forms of purposeful human action is systemic sensibility + systems literacy + systems thinking in practice capability, as discussed in Chapter 6.

Writing in his 2014 book, *Stand and Deliver. A Design for Successful Government,* Ed said:

> The system of government has more wrong with it than you can possibly imagine. It groans under the weight of its own contradictions, but is shored up by the weight of opinion of its beneficiaries – from the adversarial industries of political parties, the news media and the law, to the senior Civil Service and some large public service organisations, to the banks, pension funds, corporates, and others who win more than their fair share of the cake through lobbying. This is not a system for you and me.[99]

In this chapter we have provided a generic, heuristic model (Figure 2.1.) and used it to explore the systemic failings in each of the main elements. We have posed arguments as to why the current governance system is not for you or me. Of course, not all is failing. But acceptance of the Anthropocene and failure to respond will escalate the likelihood of more systemic failure. This is particularly true when inadequate interactions between elements give rise to emergent, unintended consequences, the subject of Chapter 3.

Notes

1 For example, Lyons, M., ed. 2010. *More than Luck: Ideas Australia Needs Now.* Sydney: Centre for Policy Development; Straw, E. 2014. *Stand and Deliver. A Design for Successful Government.* London: Treaty for Government; Kelly, P. 2014. *Triumph and Demise. The Broken Promise of a Labor Generation.* Melbourne: Melbourne University Press; Ringen, S. 2014a. Is American democracy headed to extinction? *The Washington Post.* 28 March 2014. (Accessed 12 March 2015); Ringen, S. 2014b. *Reflections on the Counter-Revolution in America.* Letter intended to have been sent to a gentleman in Washington. Lecture delivered to the Rothermere American Institute, University of Oxford, 29 January 2014; Tingle, L. 2015. *Political Amnesia. How We Forgot How to Govern.* Quarterly Essay, vol 60. Melbourne: Black Inc.; Johnson, R.W. 2015. *How Long will South Africa Survive? The Looming Crisis.* Cape Town: Jonathan Ball; Scranton, R. 2015. *Learning to Die in the Anthropocene. Reflections on the End of Civilization.* San Francisco: City Light Books; Ison, R.L. 2017. *Systems Practice: How to Act. In Situations of Uncertainty and Complexity in a Climate-change World.* 2nd ed. London: Springer.

2 Ison, R.L, and Schlindwein, S.L. 2015. Navigating through an 'ecological desert and a sociological hell'. A cyber-systemic governance approach for the anthropocene. *Kybernetes* 44 (6/7): 891–902.

3 Micklethwait, J. and Wooldridge, A. 2014. *The Fourth Revolution: The Global Race to Reinvent the State.* London: Penguin.

4 Micklethwait and Wooldridge. 2014. op. cit.

5 Ringen, S. 2009. *The Economic Consequences of Mr Brown. How a Strong Government was Defeated by a Weak System of Governance,* p. 64. London: The Bardwell Press.

6 Ison, R.L. 2010. Governance that works. Why public service reform needs systems thinking. In: Lyons, M., ed. 2010. op. cit.; also Phillips, S.D. 2004. The limits of horizontal governance. Voluntary sector-government collaboration in Canada. *Society and Economy* 26: 383–405.

7 Kelly. 2014. op. cit., p. 497.

8 Tingle. 2015. op. cit., p. 68.

9 Ball, P. 2016. *The Water Kingdom. A Secret History of China,* pp. 302; 308; 313 London: Vintage.

10 Johnson. 2015. op. cit.

11 https://en.wikipedia.org/wiki/State_capture (Accessed 14 March 2017).

12 https://en.wikipedia.org/wiki/Eskom (Accessed 16 April 2019).

13 Shapiro, M. 2016. *The End of Stationarity. Searching for the New Normal in the Age of Carbon Shock.* Vermont: Chelsea Green Publications.

14 Churchman, C.W. 1967. Wicked problems. Guest editorial. *Management Science* 14 (4): 141–142; Rittel, H.W.J. and Webber, M.M. 1973. Dilemmas in a general theory of planning. *Policy Science* 4 (2): 155–169. The distinctions between wicked and tame problems, terms coined in the late 1960s, are explored in Chapter 7 and in the Glossary (Appendix 2).

15 APSC (Australian Public Service Commission) 2007. *Tackling Wicked Problems. A Public Policy Perspective*. Canberra: Australian Government/Australian Public Service Commission.

16 https://en.wikipedia.org/wiki/Separation_of_powers (Accessed 3 April 2018).

17 Ibid.

18 Adapted from Ison 2016, *Systems Research & Behavioural Science*.

19 https://www.sciencedirect.com/journal/environmental-science-and-policy/vol/53/ part/PB (Accessed 2 May 2018).

20 Mulgan, G. 1997. *Connexity: How to Live in a Connected World*. London: Chatto & Windus.

21 These can be understood as a set of subsystems, or in the case of the media, a sub-subsystem.

22 https://en.wikipedia.org/wiki/The_Crown_(TV_series) (Accessed 23 March 2018).

23 Based on Wallis P. and Ison, R.L. 2011. Appreciating institutional complexity in water governance dynamics: A case from the Murray-Darling Basin, Australia. *Water Resources Management* 25 (15): 4081–4097.

24 https://www.etymonline.com/word/institute (Accessed 2 May 2018).

25 With staff, consumers, and communities contributing, it would have been an even richer diagram.

26 Tingle, Laura. 2015. op. cit.

27 http://www.oecd.org/governance/public-governance-a-matter-of-trust.htm (Accessed 2 May 2018).

28 OECD. 2017. *Government at a Glance*. Paris: OECD,

29 Riggirozzi, P. 9 November 2018. Democracy is at risk in Latin America and the far right is moving in – here's how it went wrong for the left. https://theconversat ion.com/democracy-is-at-risk-in-latin-america-and-the-far-right-is-moving-in-her es-how-it-went-wrong-for-the-left-106025? (Accessed 16 April 2019).

30 Samuel, Sigal. 28 August 2018. China Is treating Islam like a mental illness. *The Atlantic*. https://www.theatlantic.com/international/archive/2018/08/china-pathol ogizing-uighur-muslims-mental-illness/568525/ (Accessed 13 October 2018).

31 The survey methodology used reveals that in the UK those satisfied with the system of governing stood at only 29% in 2018 compared to a high of 36% in 2004. https://www.hansardsociety.org.uk/projects/research/audit-of-political-engagemen t (Accessed 16 April 2019).

32 The Cukierman index. See Cukierman, A. 1992. *Central Bank Strategy, Credibility, and Independence: Theory and Evidence*. Cambridge, MA: MIT Press.

33 A greenfield site strategy for institutional reform involves key stakeholder groups around an issue coming together and designing a new set of institutions, which when agreed to by the state are used to get rid of all the old institutions. In the process new 'initial starting conditions' – see Glossary – are created.

34 https://en.wikipedia.org/wiki/Bureaucracy (Accessed 23 March 2018).

35 The distinctions between systemic and systematic are explored in more depth in Chapter 6.

36 http://www.environment.gov.au/about-us/esd (Accessed 15 September 2018).

37 Sagoff, M. 1988. *The Economy of the Earth*. Cambridge: Cambridge University Press.

38 Ringen, Stein. 2009. op. cit., p. 64.

39 https://www.independent.co.uk/news/uk/politics/brexit-latest-staff-numbers-new-hmrc-jobs-employ-david-davis-a8030281.html (Accessed 3 April 2018).

40 Some months later more evidence of failure emerged with the UK government announcing that it will stand down 6,000 no-deal Brexit staff – after spending £1.5bn. This followed Parliament passing legislation to avoid the UK crashing out of Europe with no deal. What a mess. https://www.theguardian.com/politics/2019/apr /11/uk-stands-down-6000-no-deal-brexit-staff-after-spending-15bn (Accessed 2nd May 2019).

41 Adapted from Harley, M., Horrocks, L., and Hodgson, N. 2008. *Climate Change Vulnerability and Adaptation Indicators*. ETC/ACC Technical Paper.

42 Vetter, A. 2014. *Experience and Lessons in Integration from the German Adaptation Strategy* https://unfccc.int/sites/default/files/germany_andrea_vetter.pdf (Accessed 18 April 2019).

43 A silo is a compartmentalised structure – usually used for grain storage – but also pervasive in organisations where strong boundaries between parts are common.

44 Ison, R.L. and Wallis, P. 2011. Planning as performance. The Murray-Darling basin plan. In Grafton Q. and Connell, D., eds. *Basin Futures: Water Reform in the Murray-Darling Basin*, pp. 399–411. Canberra: ANU ePress. APSC. 2007. Tackling wicked problems: A public policy perspective. https://www.apsc.gov.au/tackling-wicked-problems-public-policy-perspective (Accessed 11 April 2019).

45 O'Toole, F. 2017. Brexit's Irish question. *The New York Review of Books*. p. 28.

46 Ison, R.L. and Watson, D. 2007. Illuminating the possibilities for social learning in the management of Scotland's water. *Ecology and Society* 12 (1): Art-21.

47 Later in the same article O'Toole argues that Northern Ireland has to be in the EU *and* the UK (i.e. both). This will require institutional innovation that is systemic. Such a strategy increases the choices available to citizens of Northern Ireland, which we argue is the basis of ethical action/governance because it keeps options open for citizens into the future.

48 Ortolani, G. 2018. China's Belt and Road poised to transform the Earth, but at what cost? https://news.mongabay.com/2018/04/chinas-belt-and-road-poised-to-transform-the-earth-but-at-what-cost/ (Accessed 2 May 2018).

49 Taylor, M. 2018. Top climate scientist blasts UK's fracking plans as 'aping Trump'. https://www.theguardian.com/environment/2018/oct/13/top-climate-scientist-james-hansen-attacks-uk-fracking-plans (Accessed 13 October 2018).

50 Ison, R.L. 2010. op. cit.

51 Micklethwait, J. and Wooldridge, A. 2014. op. cit., p. 37.

52 But this space also opened up because of the decline of the Ottoman Empire, and the introspection that had begun in China and Japan. Gradually throughout Europe monarchs began to see themselves not as THE state, but servants of the state. There is no entry for law, legal, courts, rule of law in the index of Micklethwait and Wooldridge's book. Thus, whilst law and order are central, they claim, to the rise and sustaining of the nation-state, they do not explore it as a fully integral subsystem of a governance system.

53 https://www.etymonline.com/word/law (Accessed 5 April 2018).

54 https://en.wikipedia.org/wiki/Jurisdiction (Accessed 5 April 2018).

55 OECD. 2017. op. cit.

56 Johnson, R.W. 2015. op. cit.

57 Coleman, Mike. 13 December 2018. A triumph for rural land rights holders. *The Daily Maverick*. https://www.dailymaverick.co.za/article/2018-12-13-a-triumph-for-rural-land-rights-holders/ (Accessed 14 December 2018).

58 Lazarus, R. 2009. Super wicked problems and climate change: restraining the present to liberate the future. *Cornell Law Review* 94: 1153–1234.

59 https://en.wikipedia.org/wiki/Judiciary (Accessed 5 April 2018).

60 https://en.wikipedia.org/wiki/List_of_national_legal_systems (Accessed 25 April 2018).

61 https://en.wikipedia.org/wiki/International_Court_of_Justice (Accessed 25 April 2018).

62 https://en.wikipedia.org/wiki/European_Court_of_Human_Rights (Accessed 25 April 2018).

63 Wallis, P. and Ison, R.L., unpublished.

64 Langbein, J. 2003. *The Origins of Adversary Criminal Trial*. Oxford: Oxford University Press.

65 'In common law, the informal black letter legal doctrine includes the basic principles of law generally accepted by the courts and/or embodied in the statutes of a particular jurisdiction. The letter of the law is its actual implementation, thereby demonstrating that black letter laws are those statutes, rules, acts, laws, provisions, etc. that are or have been written down, codified, or indicated somewhere in legal texts throughout history of specific state law. This is often the case for many precedents that have been set in the common law. An example of such a state within the common law jurisdiction, and using the black letter legal doctrine is Canada'. https://en.wikipedia.org/wiki/Black_letter_law (Accessed 25 April 2018).

66 Australian Law Reform Commission. https://www.alrc.gov.au/publications/45. %20Overview%3A%20Office%20of%20the%20Privacy%20Commissioner%20/su mmary-recommendations-address-syste (Accessed 25 April 2018).

67 Oklahoma Disability Law Center. http://okdlc.org/?page_id=604 (Accessed 25 April 2018).

68 The Change Toolkit. http://www.thechangetoolkit.org.au/why-do-law-reform/ (Accessed 25 April 2018).

69 Jenkins, S. 2 April 2018. The UK justice system is in meltdown. When will the government act? https://www.theguardian.com/commentisfree/2018/apr/02/uk-cri minal-justice-system-meltdown-violence-rising-government (Accessed 25 April 2018).

70 A reference to the Worboys case – the 'black cab rapist'.

71 Jenkins, Ibid.

72 von Bogdandy, A. and Ioannidis, M. 2014. Systemic deficiency in the rule of law: What it is, what has been done, what can be done. *Common Market Law Review* 1: 59–96.

73 Systems theory has been used as means to understand and conceptualise the law by some scholars (e.g. Richard Nobles, David Schiff. 2012. *Observing Law through Systems Theory*. London, Hart Publishing). Whether such work has resulted in better systemic function of the law per se, or as part of a system of governance, is beyond our scope.

74 Sun, W., Stewart, J., and Pollard, D. 2012. A systemic failure of corporate governance: Lessons from the ongoing financial crisis. *The European Financial Review*. http: //www.europeanfinancialreview.com/?p=2042 (Accessed 25 April 2018).

75 Khanna, P. and Francis, D. 2016. *These 25 Companies Are More Powerful Than Many Countries*. http://foreignpolicy.com/2016/03/15/these-25-companies-are-more-p owerful-than-many-countries-multinational-corporate-wealth-power/ (Accessed 26 April 2018).

76 Khanna, P. and Francis, D. 2016. op. cit.

77 Smith, D. 2015. Who runs the world? https://www.equatex.com/en/article/who-r uns-the-world/ (Accessed 11 April 2019).

78 Caulkin, S. 2012. On management. A big problem. *The Financial Times*. https:// www.ft.com/content/92778fd8-fbc2-11e1-87ae-00144feabdc0 (Accessed 26 April 2018). Used with permission of *The Financial Times*.

79 Bullough, O. 2018. Review of the finance curse: How global finance is making us all poorer. *The Observer*. 21 October. p. 52.

80 Caulkin cites corporate governance expert Professor Bob Garratt from a meeting of the Human Capital Forum.

81 https://www.apra.gov.au/media-centre/media-releases/apra-step-scrutiny-clim ate-risks-after-releasing-survey-results (Accessed 2 May 2019). This perspective is now being backed by the Australian Reserve Bank governor, putting him and the bank at odds with the government of the day. Similarly, the head of the Bank of England has made public statements aimed at the financial sector – see 'A new horizon' – speech by Mark Carney to European Commission High-Level Conference: A global approach to Sustainable Finance, Brussels. 21 March 2019. https://www.ban

kofengland.co.uk/speech/2019/mark-carney-speech-at-european-commission-high
-level-conference-brussels (Accessed 17th April 2019).

82 https://en.wikipedia.org/wiki/Fourth_Estate (Accessed 26 April 2018).

83 Newman, N., Dutton, W.H., and Blank, G. 2012. Social media in the changing ecology of news: The fourth and fifth estates in Britain. *International Journal of Internet Science* 7 (1): 6–22.

84 The Editors of Encyclopaedia Britannica. https://www.britannica.com/art/pamphlet (Accessed 26 April 2018).

85 Bennett-Jones, O. 20 December 2018. Can't afford to tell the truth. *London Review of Books* 40 (24): 29–32. https://www.lrb.co.uk/v40/n24/owen-bennett-jones/cant-afford-to-tell-the-truth (Accessed 21 December 2018).

86 https://en.wikipedia.org/wiki/Concentration_of_media_ownership (Accessed 26 April 2018).

87 https://en.wikipedia.org/wiki/Foucauldian_discourse_analysis (Accessed 21 October 2018).

88 https://en.wikipedia.org/wiki/Civil_society (Accessed 27 April 2018).

89 Ibid.

90 De Wiel, B. (no date). https://journals.library.ualberta.ca/pi/index.php/pi/article/viewFile/1422/963 (Accessed 29 April 2018).

91 Putnam, R.D., Leonardi, R., and Nanetti, R.Y. 1994. *Making Democracy Work: Civic Traditions in Modern Italy*. Princeton, NJ: Princeton University Press.

92 https://en.wikipedia.org/wiki/Gruen_(TV_series)#Gruen_Planet (Accessed 14 October 2018).

93 https://www.youtube.com/watch?v=qHWso24nzgE (Accessed 14 October 2018).

94 Blog by Ray Ison March 6 2012, https://rayison.blogspot.com/search?q=Gruen.

95 https://secure.avaaz.org/page/en/ (Accessed 29 April 2018).

96 O'Rourke, C., Oosting, P., Ritter, D., Bose, S., and Ryan, H. 13 June 2018. Trusting the government to protect civil liberties? That's a sick joke. *The Guardian*. https://www.theguardian.com/commentisfree/2018/jun/13/trusting-the-government-to-protect-civil-liberties-thats-a-sick-joke (Accessed 14 October 2018).

97 See the special issue of the journal, *Planning Theory and Practice* 16, 2015 - Issue 4 entitled: *The transformative potential of civic enterprise* with articles by Hendrik Wagenaar, Patsy Healey, Giovanni Laino, Geoff Vigar, Sebastià Riutort Isern, Thomas Honeck, Joost Beunderman and Jurgen van der Heijden.

98 Kapuściński, R., Ascherson, N., and Lloyd-Jones, A. 2008. *The Other*. London: Verso.

99 Straw, Ed. 2014. op. cit.

3

PREFERENTIAL LOBBYING AND EMERGENT FAILURE

3.1 Relational dynamics of the governance model

Governance failure can usually be attributed to a breakdown in the systemic relations between structure and process or between structure and practice. If an election cycle is too short to deal with complex, long-term issues, then it is essentially a structural element of governance that is in need of reform. Preferential lobbying, on the other hand, is an emergent practice that arises from the current, inadequate structures and the practices and processes they enable (see later in this chapter). Examination of failure can be taken deeper by looking at the limitations in the design of institutions that create a pervasive scaffolding structure to our living (see Chapter 8).

'Unintended consequences' are an emergent property of contemporary governance. Sometimes there's a fine line between emergent surprise and purposeful manipulation of the 'rules of the game'. This includes design by ideologues and narcissists. The late twentieth and early twenty-first century provide numerous examples of how theoretical and methodological ideas combine to shape ways in which the state manages itself as well as its relations with other elements in the governance system. Sometimes theory, method and practice combine to create a paradigm or an ideology. Marxist–Leninism was the intellectual, later ideological, tradition that gave rise to the USSR, and later (with filters through Maoism), the Chinese state. Influence and control over these and other lineages and their future trajectories have generated wars, violence, rewards, misery, starvation and release from poverty – a whole spectrum from very bad to pretty good. Other examples include Stalinism, Trotskyism, Perestroika, Deng Xiaoping-style capitalism[1] and Xi Jinping thought.[2]

Ideas cross ideological lines. New variations in governance arrangements emerge. Take the claims made in John Keane's book, *When Trees Fall, Monkeys*

Scatter, in which he shows how the one-party Chinese state draws heavily on *democratic* tools and techniques.[3] In our lifetimes we have encountered, or experienced, the effects of Keynesian Economics, Roosevelt's 'New Deal', Monetarism, Reaganomics, Thatcherism, New Public Management, Neoliberalism, Austerity, The Third Way, Digital Era Governance, New Public Governance and Ecologically Sustainable Development.

All models carry within them certain framing assumptions with significant systemic implications. And unless these framings are made explicit in situated ways, we run the risk of using the same words but talking past each other because we carry different conceptual models in our heads.

Systems approaches have within their repertoire various ways to explore emergent relationships. Influence and causal-loop diagrams can be used and help to make thinking explicit. For those involved, their process of development can be very illuminating (and a far more powerful learning experience than a diagram that is the end product of someone else's learning – as we are doing here, restricted by the designs of a traditional book).[4] Figure 3.1 is one such example that highlights some of the emergent 'global risks' contemporary governance systems have to deal with. Are they capable of engaging with, and steering through the complexity and uncertainty? Or, as we discuss below, are governance systems generating emergent dysfunctionality?

At the centre of Figure 3.1 is profound social instability. Governance failure at multiple levels is identified among the key drivers. The challenge is to know where purposeful action is possible, in order to generate leverage for systemic change.

3.2 Relational dynamics getting in the way

How do these relations between the elements in the governance model (Figure 2.1) produce the wrong actions and prevent the right? The principal culprits – the business, or private sector and state subsystems – are examined here within a critique of how an 'economic system' has been designed and granted privileges.

3.2.1 Business and the state

Companies are not wholly detached from the natural environment. They are run by people, some of whom care a lot and some not at all. The wise have spotted a huge business opportunity. Many industries are not sustainable if climate change carries on as forecast. It cannot be ignored in their longer-term planning. They study the science. Unlike politicians, company executives do not have the luxury or misfortune or the option of ignoring it.

At the same time, businesses operate according to the rules set for them. These arise from the prevailing economic system and the laws made by governments to direct or limit their behaviour. It may come as a surprise, but companies, like any organisation, do not necessarily behave as they do because the people within

The Global Risks Interconnections Map 2018

How are global risks interconnected?

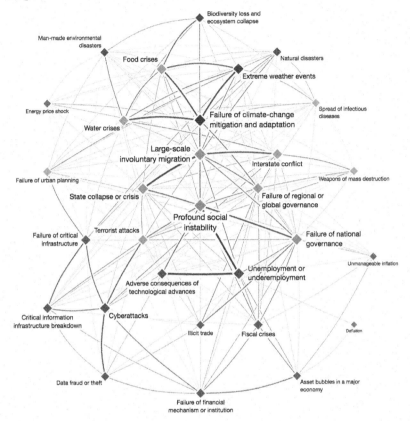

FIGURE 3.1   An 'influence diagram' to show the dynamic set of influences affecting global risk. The usual convention is that the thicker the connecting line, the greater the influence.[5]

them are either good or bad. If the law allows people to be employed with few rights, which means unit labour costs are lower, then competition will result in this form of employment becoming the norm. Countries that have maintained employee-centric rights have seen some industries migrate employment to low cost/rights countries to maintain competitiveness. Businesses do bad things because the rules direct them to.

Typically company law is interpreted in terms of the primacy of management's responsibility to the shareholders (see Section 2.5). They have no responsibility for the biosphere. Separate regulations constrain acts like dumping some forms of toxic pollution. But the shareholder is notionally pre-eminent. The financial markets are short term in their behaviour because the rules allow and, by default, encourage huge sums of money to be made in the very short term. Nature does not feature in the calculations for these profits – indeed, it is an obstacle. Such is the laxity of company law that in practice the interests of top management have become dominant in company decision making. While the system undoubtedly encourages those without ethics, top management are just humans who find they can pay themselves very large sums of money by manipulating legally lax corporate governance, and so do. Some do not and can make a difference, but it is hard work for an enlightened CEO to steer a sustainable course when all around choose not to subject themselves to this 'handicap'.[6]

However, if the rules are changed, then business will and does behave differently. This is not difficult. Give 11 people the rules for football, and they will play football. Give the same 11 the rules for basketball, and they will play basketball. If you watch a sport, what you will see will be very different. People running companies are the same. They need a different rulebook – as well as better refereeing.

In 1966, atmospheric research revealed that the ozone layer was being depleted by chemicals released by industry, mainly chlorofluorocarbons (CFCs). In 1968, the United States, Canada and Norway banned their use in aerosol cans, a mere two years after the problem was identified. Compared with today's slothful response to climate chaos, the US reacted with remarkable speed. Further research found the hole in the ozone layer over the Antarctic in 1985. The US Environmental Protection Agency estimated a big increase in deaths from skin cancer. Perhaps fearing court action as a result, DuPont acted faster than their European counterparts. A high propensity to litigate does occasionally have collective benefits. Further regulation followed. The latest evidence is that ozone depletion has slowed or stopped. But do take care when sunbathing.

Established companies do take action, under the right conditions. For the ozone layer, only one industry was affected, and only one part of it. The science was clear-cut, the human risks specific and incontrovertible, the communications through metaphor masterful. Perhaps, most significant of all was that an alternative, less harmful chemical became available quickly, followed later by others. The industry saw the writing on the wall, knew *how* to change and did. Despite all these advantages, most of the industry still had to be forced to do so by international regulation. For governments, operating between powerful industry lobbies on the one side and strong public opinion (and future votes) on the other, this was not too difficult a choice to make – in this case. It took the EU, which feels almost no democratic heat whilst industry lobbies are integral to its decision making, nearly 20 years to act. These are critical lessons that need to be heeded in governing, not for neoliberal economics or existing business or established elites but for people and the Anthropocene.

It is instructive to recall what proved to be highly successful communications with individuals in support of new regulations. They were based on easy-to-understand bridging metaphors (ozone shield, ozone hole) derived from popular culture which related to immediate risks with everyday relevance. Compared to climate change, the ozone case was seen as a 'hot issue' with imminent risk. The 'celebrity effect' had an impact too: President Reagan twice had skin cancer removed from his nose.

> The idea of rays penetrating a damaged 'shield' meshes nicely with abiding and resonant cultural motifs, including 'Hollywood affinities'. These range from the shields on the Starship Enterprise to Star Wars … It is these pre-scientific bridging metaphors built around the penetration of a deteriorating shield that render the ozone problem relatively simple. … That the ozone threat can be linked with Darth Vader means that it is encompassed in common sense understandings that are deeply ingrained and widely shared.[7]

We see here Jeremy Lent's understanding of myths and metaphors of Chapter 1 being put to good use.

3.2.2 The power of neoliberalism over business and the state

Today, business behaviour is determined principally by the dominant neoliberal economic (NLE) system in which it operates and by the emergent property of preferential lobbying. The former system was designed; the latter has emerged as a result of the former but is itself enabled by weak systems of governing. In this socially constructed system, business and profit come first, elites immediately second, most people far off in third place, and the biosphere nowhere. Preferential lobbying secures business and elite interest as a matter of course. These two systems in combination prevent a change in business behaviour (and much else).

The sheer power of whatever system we are in to direct or control our behaviour is rarely observed. At a camp for children, one 11-year-old said this was a real holiday as his family was not there. He was free to be himself for two weeks – a break from his ordained family role as the clever one, the naughty one, the sporty one or whatever his close relatives had unwittingly designated for him.

NLE is a very clever system: one can become a member without knowing. Once a member, points are earned, again without knowing. Its trick and, according to some, its very design and purpose is to trap sufficient people into full membership. Members receive significant privileges as the cake is divided in their favour. So long as they are well enough off, members will go along with it. We asked an Irish friend how the similar prevailing economic order is regarded there. He thought 20% in favour, 60% agnostic and 20% against. The agnostic members rule – and so it goes on.

We may think that we are exercising free choice when buying our next computer – and that it will provide many opportunities for learning, socialising and entertainment. But we are being *farmed* for profits. The more people who see their self-interest to be in NLE (for example, from the free movement of people), the more sustainable and secure it is. Such is its grip that history says only a plague, a violent revolution, state collapse or a major war can break us free.[8]

One day you wake up and realise you have become a consumer of whatever you have surreptitiously been told to buy. You do not quite know how this happened, but happened it has. Now you face a choice: you could exit this club, lose its benefits and risk the alternative being worse – although better for less-well-off others and the biosphere. Or you could remain a member. Most people do. The external conditions – in this case, the politically constructed economic system – determine the behaviour of individuals.

NLE spends a lot of time on promoting the myth that it is the *only* way, or that it is the only *true* way, or that the *alternative* is dire. The system is so beautifully designed that this promotion is built in. No budget line or separate fund exists: both companies and political parties follow it as part of their everyday workings. The UK Conservative Party has become a national marketing department for NLE. It was once a political party with some values and the capacity for thought. It now uses PR and spin, turning over whatever is left to NLE – forests, universities, health services, genes, death. The party is substance-free. It cares not that the Thatcher-privatised national telecoms company BT has been left to fall into disrepute, only that it is private. Beneficiaries of NLE have profited first from BT's monopoly, its over-pricing, and freedom to 'farm' consumers, and will then make further money picking over BT's carcass once it has become insolvent.

However, as with all forms of fascism – when defined as a tendency toward or actual exercise of strong autocratic or dictatorial control – NLE is pre-programmed for destruction. It is a monoculture, and monocultures don't endure, for two reasons. The first is that diversity is essential for survival. A single strain of wheat may produce the highest yield, but is always susceptible to attack by a rapidly mutating virus, one form of which will succeed someday. Then there is no wheat. The second is that a single strain may flourish in today's climate – but not in tomorrow's – it is damaged by too much rain or sun. Coffee growing is going this way. Biodiversity equals resilience. The more strains of crops in existence, the greater the chances one or more will survive the unknown future, and with it our food supply. In organisations this means having inbuilt redundancy – a capacity to meet emergent variety or surprise within the environment with internal variety.

This is also true for lifestyle and economic system diversity. We do not know the future, what challenges it will throw up and how circumstances will change. All of our eggs are in one economic-system basket. As 50 shades of market capitalism, public sector bodies and charities have been either converted or outsourced or have come to behave according to NLE precepts,[9] so diversity has been lost. NLE is as totalitarian in its svelte way as Soviet communism. The certainty is that it will implode, and that little will be left to fill its formerly rapacious void.

NLE's capacity to influence and direct behaviour is extraordinary. When, at its inbuilt command, billions of people all jump in one direction all at once, the effect could be enormous and its collapse could ensue. The financial crash of 2008 took the global economy close to the edge.

NLE determines much of business behaviour in its pursuit of profit at any price, to the detriment of both nature and most people. Economically, it is inefficient, as income transfers, not original wealth creation, generate so much of its profits. It is a system that no one has ever voted for. Given the chance, would you?

If that is not enough to distort the allocation of wealth and power, preferential lobbying is its perfect partner.

3.3 The emergence of preferential lobbying

Preferential Lobbying (PL) has become the norm in decision making in democracies around the world – from Brussels to Washington to Westminster to Lagos and Brasilia (see Box 3.1). Some governing systems have a stronger immune system than others. But the practice whereby an industry, company or profession secures its interests through a government decision – usually at the expense of a section of the public – is common and sometimes rife. When the practice is observed through the medium of a hidden camera and a frank explanation by a consummate politician, it feels wrong. It is within the rules, but our interests are not represented. Whether the decision is good for you or me, the economy, society or the country is irrelevant. Your interests/needs/preferences will take second place, or no place at all.

Lobbying is a process that transfers real money from consumers and taxpayers to companies and elites. Whenever regulation is bent to allow predatory pricing, higher tariffs paid by consumers to regulated utilities, externalised costs, maintenance of monopoly trades and professions, tax 'avoidance', environmental degradation, harmful chemicals, dodgy financial instruments, fat cat or unprotected pensions, you, me and the biosphere are footing their bill.

In the US, where its effects are blatant and obscene,[10] a 2009 study estimated that for every dollar a company spent lobbying for targeted tax benefits, the expected return was between $6 and $20. On one bill, the American Jobs Creation Act (despite its name, really just a corporate tax cut), researchers from Washington and Lee University and the University of Kansas calculated that 'the return on investment to lobbying' was 22,000%.

BOX 3.1 HOW PREFERENTIAL LOBBYING
TAKES GOVERNMENT DECISIONS

In the US, even people with very simple financial arrangements – say, a single woman with no dependents whose only income comes from her wages – often pay several hundred dollars a year for help with filling out their tax returns (there are more than a million professional tax preparers in the US), or spend around $60 a year on computer programs (for example TurboTax) that guide them through the forms. This is because American tax returns are long and bewildering, and people are scared of getting into trouble by screwing them up.

In 2005, the agency that collects state income tax in California began a pilot programme called ReadyReturn, a voluntary, 'simple, easy-to-use service that offers free, direct to government e-filing', similar to the British system. It saved the people who used it money and time, and was projected to save the state half a million dollars a year in administrative costs. The programme was so popular that both Republicans and Democrats wanted to take the credit for it. What could go wrong? Enter Intuit, the Silicon Valley software company that owns TurboTax. During the 2006 race for state controller (who oversees tax collection), Intuit funnelled a million dollars to the candidate who said he opposed ReadyReturn because it would hurt 'private enterprise' – that is, Intuit. The company also gave more than a million dollars in campaign contributions to the state's legislators, who promptly killed off ReadyReturn. The state government had to change before the tax board could bring the programme back. More than a million Californians now use it. So why not expand it to the rest of the country?

A report from National Public Radio and the news organisation ProPublica suggests that Congress has consistently blocked bills that would make it easier for people to file their federal taxes because of political donations from commercial tax preparers, particularly Intuit. In all, according to the Sunlight Foundation, commercial tax preparers have spent more than $28 million lobbying Congress to oppose any changes that might cut into their business. So far they've prevailed because the people who would benefit most from having easier tax forms can't afford to do their own lobbying. But there's no need for a congressman even to meet with a lobbyist for the tax preparers: he knows – because this is the way the system works – that if he opposes legislative changes that might hurt Intuit, he'll attract their campaign contributions.[11]

Many people and organisations lobby – it has been a sound part of an open democracy (although unnecessary under better governing). Preferential lobbying is different. At its conclusion, when governments have taken decisions, PL gives preference to the interests of big companies and powerful individuals, invariably at the expense of a section of the public in the standard of products and services and the price paid. That expense can accumulate to slow down the development of a national economy. PL is integral to neoliberal economics; it is essential to widening wealth and power disparities. It is essential, too, to the development and influence of elites, and it has kept nature's interests at bay. A systemic understanding of how PL happens is necessary to be able to craft new institutions, particularly new constitutional forms that create new constitutional knowledge and knowing.

You might think that preferential lobbying is inevitable in modern government, a fact of life, the price we pay, as its exponents might rationalise. But the extent and power of such lobbies is a function of the system of government. Lobbyists behave as they do because the system they operate in at least allows and usually encourages it – albeit unwittingly.

PL is not restricted to the private sector. Large public-sector bodies, trade unions, professions, NGOs and others can be effective lobbyists too. London black cab drivers form one of the most effective. But because they are the sources of greatest inequality, we are going to concentrate here on big companies.

3.3.1 How preferential lobbying arises from the system of governing

PL either starts or stops something. It could be a law, regulation, tax change or other ministerial decision. Companies oppose regulations that limit their behaviour or increase their costs – environmental protection, for example. Conversely, they promote and support a regulation that is a barrier to market for smaller competitors – the banning of some alternative remedies by the European Commission at the prompting of the pharmaceutical industry is one of many examples. Several books analyse lobbying in Washington and Brussels in some depth – they make for apoplectic reading.

To understand why the system of governing determines the extent and power of lobbying, consider two extremes. In a dictatorship, the only way to influence decisions is through inside negotiation, and only the approved rich and powerful have access. The interests of the citizens feature only by coincidence for a Joseph Stalin, or a Robert Mugabe.

At the other extreme is Athenian 'direct' democracy of the fifth century BC, when the rule of the people had replaced a dynasty of tyrants.[12] Participating citizens had the right to speak out and be heard and consulted on matters of common interest, debating and voting individually on issues great and small, from matters of war and peace to the proper qualifications for ferry-boat captains. The various interests were not just represented in the vote but were physically *present*. The lobbying playing field was more or less level. Where would an ancient Greek telecoms company go to secure its hold over the broadband distribution network in order to minimise its investment in fibre, limit competition and thus maintain higher prices and profits and lower service standards? To the Citizen's Assembly of course, where the company would find the very same citizens expected to foot this bill making the decision. As a citizen at the Assembly, would you vote for the company's preferences? With institutional arrangements to prevent corruption, your answer would be no. Your overriding interest would be to get a highly functioning network at a competitive price. There's very little preferential lobbying with direct democracy, then.

Nowadays, the system of governing determines lobbying power, in the case above, near binary. On the democracy scale, modern states fall variously in between the two extremes of dictatorship and direct democracy – as does their susceptibility to preferential lobbying. But none of their systems were developed when companies were as large and powerful as they are today, nor as global. The equivalents of Esso, Google or Goldman Sachs were not around in Athenian days, or when the US, French or UK constitutional architectures were being designed. If they were, given the foresight they showed, their 'founding fathers' would have built in safeguards against these essentially undemocratic forces. Unfortunately, they were not.

3.3.2 Why do preferential lobbies flourish?

In today's governing systems, eight conditions enable preferential lobbying:

1. Policy determination in private.
2. Exclusive access to policy makers.
3. Low subject knowledge of ministers and civil servants.
4. Few restrictions on political party funding.
5. Availability of patronage.
6. Only two parties for government.
7. No direct or participative democracy.
8. Weak checks and balances, especially feedback.

The more these conditions are present, the more influential will be the lobby, often conclusively so. A system of government is optimum for preferential lobbying when it contains all eight conditions, as in Westminster (UK).[13]

These contributory conditions are not mandatory. Some are absent from some countries – such as disproportionate party funding, patronage and first-past-the-post voting. They can all be changed. But unless they are, power and wealth, along with the biosphere, will continue to be drained away.

3.3.2.1 Decisions in private

The first condition is perhaps obvious in its value. When a policy is being determined in private, then public interests are absent, a policy can be manoeuvred easily in a particular direction, the political 'line' set before it becomes public, and briefings of journalists begun. There are no multiple perspectives here.

3.3.2.2 Exclusive access

This is where access to the relevant ministers and civil servants is essential. Access is borne of relationships. Former MPs and civil servants will get through on the phone or receive a positive reply to a lunch invitation, when most will not. Deborah Friedell reports that in the US it is rare for retired congressmen/women not to become professional lobbyists, such is the huge dollar value of their relationships.[14] Many London 'Public Affairs' companies have been set up by a party threesome of former advisers – they know both the game and the personalities. Companies pay handsomely and the 'exes' remain more or less in the thick of it.

Where does a sugar hedge fund go to change regulations in the Ukraine and the EU – since these regulations are obstacles limiting its business? To someone with access to these governments and relationships with the decision makers is the answer – in this case to a former minister.

Access can be from the outside in, or by gaining entry through secondment, from the inside out (see Box 3.2).

BOX 3.2 FRAMING THROUGH SECONDMENTS

Secondments are a form of access where the civil service or a political party swaps one or more staff with a large company. This is good learning for the secondees – and a means to plant ideas and frames of analysis beneficial to an industry. In 2010 during the so-called 'wash-up', the UK government squeezed through the Digital Economies Act (DEA) intended to protect established movie studios from the competition of peer-to-peer digital distribution. If they could, they might have introduced the death penalty for infringement. This laundering term – wash-up – of legislation, not money, is used once an election is called, when opposition and government agree what legislation-in-progress can be passed, on the nod, without further discussion.

The DEA was the product of long-term industry lobbying. In 1998 and until 2010, the British Recorded Music Industry representing the record and music companies, seconded a lawyer to the Department for Culture, Media and Sport. This sort of connection between industry and government can work well in transferring knowledge both ways. But here, over a long period, the civil servants bought the protectionist arguments of the secondee, whose principal job was to lobby, not directly, but by the gradual seeding in of industry views and analysis. The head of a digital film company also influenced the minister promoting the Bill.

Access is automatic where a profession is well represented in Parliament. In the UK the legal profession has long had the most representatives. Framing a case is then unnecessary as the recipients' minds come ready-framed through their own career experience – broadly all of life is amenable to a legal solution. The way in which the various 'justice' systems work, and often not work, is held back by this conditioning and by the desire of the profession to not be unduly disturbed in its business. To take the most obvious example, the sentencing regime for criminal justice prescribes the 'treatment' for an offender but never assesses its result. Why would a lawyer change, when the living is too good to risk and preferential argument so accessible to maintain the status quo?

3.3.2.3 Low subject knowledge of ministers and civil servants

The professional lobbyist will be most effective if the knowledge of the subject under development – pension funds, for example – is limited or superficial. The people in government with responsibility for unravelling this Gordian knot were not equipped to do so. In the 13 years of New Labour, eight pension ministers came and went; they hardly had time to get to grips with the problem before being shuffled off. They were appointed not for reasons of expertise or performance, but to maintain the power of the prime minister through patronage. (By and large, the nearer the prime minister is to ejection, the higher the rate of reshuffle – a leading indicator for resignation.) None of these eight ministers had any significant expertise in pensions, relying on a cadre of civil servants – who make it a matter of principle to stay in one policy area for three years or less. As the leading civil servant on pensions of his time said as his third year started, it was time to move on, otherwise his career would get stuck. Imagine then that you are the pensions minister, where will *you* go for advice?

As one former minister put it rather robustly: 'What's the alternative to listening to the industry – talking to daft academics and superficial civil servants?' This was in response to a question as to why industry lobbies tend to dominate policy making. Better the useful devil you know, albeit with a vested interest, than the ignorant devil, might be the rationale. At least the industry is real, is producing employment and economic activity, has genuine practical expertise and has the discipline of a profit-and-loss account to face once the decisions are taken.

UK civil servants transfer into vastly different roles – from weapons procurement to public engagement in science and technology, or from pensions to climate change. Mastering the brief is the term used by incoming staff to demonstrate prowess in policy making. They may often be clever people, but there is a gulf between this and a deep, experiential understanding of how an industry really works, the real determinants of its behaviour and thus how to change it successfully. Very few people outside the financial services industry, for example, know how it really operates (and not so many inside).

This situation is fertile ground for the sort of economic or market analyses big consultancies provide to make a company's case. Independent, yes (in a way), but all this analysis is prey to its assumptions, interpretations and caveats. A report is thus written to make the best case for its funders. Key is establishing a 'credible threat' to the stability and growth of an industry or company. This usually scares the minister.

Lobbyists come with the best advice. Their recipients, light on knowledge, eagerly digest it – and so their 'mastery' is extended. In the light of the usual absence of counter knowledge, the policy makers' minds are shaped by what they have learnt – or in effect been taught. When making decisions, we are all prisoners of our knowledge base and who is in the room.

3.3.2.4 Few restrictions on political party funding

The lobbyist's hand is further strengthened if his or her client is free to make donations to political parties. In the US, such donations are often made in flagrant exchange for a specific policy – although the sin is to make this explicit. In the UK, the exchange is more subtle – an expectation that favourable treatment will follow: newspaper support for your party for future television rights, for example. For as long as donations remain unlimited, the lever exists if operated with a little care.

3.3.2.5 Availability of patronage

Further exchange is available where government has patronage to dispense in the form of honours – like knighthoods or similar – or top jobs in return for financial or other endorsement. Wealthy donors cement the 'virtuous' circle of: preferred policy – party donation – honour/job. At the time of the UK 'cash for honours' scandal of 2006–2007 and subsequent revelations, this lever became more difficult to pull. But normal practice has resumed. As long as a prime minister has honours to distribute, the temptation and incentive exist.

3.3.2.6 Only two parties for government

First-past-the-post voting results in two parties only able to form or dominate a government. The lobbyist's hand grows yet more powerful. Consider the run-up to an election when a media company head seeks to trade a technical monopoly in newspaper ownership or full ownership of a monopoly satellite distributor in return for the electoral support of his media. First, this support is too valuable electorally to forgo, and second, should one party be resistant, a usually conclusive incentive can be applied by threatening to transfer support to the other potential governing party. It should be stressed that such deals are unstated yet crystal clear to the negotiators.

With proportional voting, the composition of the future governing coalition is difficult to forecast. As a consequence, the lobbyist's pre-election life is harder. Shuttling between several parties – with the added prospect of leaks – may still obtain the 'right' policy, but far less often.

Two party government has a further, unintended consequence: a free reign for ideology. With proportional representation, the moderating influence of another party or parties limits ideology as the principal justification of a decision. Without this moderation, and with the voting system promoting adversarial policy, redundant but activist-appealing ideology can flourish. In the UK, both the Labour and Conservative parties bring this to government. That ideology is then available in some areas for the lobbyist to use in support of their business – privatisation, outsourcing and 'private finance initiative' being obvious examples.

3.3.2.7 No direct or participatory democracy

The absence of informed direct or genuinely participative decision making is essential to lobbyists. Where, as in Switzerland, decisions ranging from the free movement of people to installing a new park-and-ride facility in Geneva are put to the citizens and expert, balanced technical papers are attached to the voting slip, preferential lobbying is mainly neutered. The Swiss culture is largely one of inquiry and finding the best decision.[15]

Short of riot, the effective diminution of public influence between elections is a further consequence of the absence of direct democracy. The electorate is only in the decision mix before and immediately after an election – the public's experience might be characterised as 'vote and go away'.

'We won a majority and we expect to be listened to'. That was the introduction from Lord Lucas, representing the UK government at a CBI/Pearson 2015 education and skills seminar. An education specialist in the audience asked if perhaps they should also be prepared to listen. Lord Lucas was clear that was not necessary: 'Will the government listen? No. We are too full of ourselves at the moment and we have our own ideas' was his response.[16] For most of a government's term, the field is clear for just a few people to determine policy in private – just what the lobbyist ordered.

3.3.2.8 Weak checks and balances, especially feedback

Finally, having secured the right policy in private, the lobbyist is best served by a system with weak checks and balances. The UK Parliament seeks to be useful in the scrutiny of legislation, with extensive review in committees and both houses of Parliament. Media and sometimes public debate may rage. Occasionally a government accepts an error has occurred, and the Lords retire to the tearoom puffed up with a triumph. But such is the Westminster system, all this is for naught if the government wants to have its way.

The majority of government decisions do not face any Parliamentary scrutiny. It is only through sharp eyes and a powerful publicity campaign that they can be challenged. This does happen. The online campaigning groups were enabled by the internet and born out of frustration at the exclusion of the public's various interests. Perhaps, too, they had read Professor Gerry Stoker's *Why Politics Matters. Making Democracy Work.*[17] He suggested that democracy – and the political class – must create a new politics, making it as easy as possible for as many people as possible to express and debate their political preferences, as a solution to disenchantment with government and disengagement from politics.

These online counter-lobbies have salvaged/retrieved some power and burdened many an elected representative (MP) with an overflowing email inbox. These are vastly more effective than going to an MP's surgery or sending a letter to a government department. But their funding and the public's 'cause' capacity limit them. In practice, most policies are still determined by a very small group, and governments are free to take decisions in any way they want – on no information, flawed analysis, prejudice or an anecdote on the 10.46 train from Pitlochry. Currently, political pressure is the only restraint.

The result of a preferential decision may be felt quickly by its immediate losers, or it may take ten years or more before a groundswell of public objection is heard. The 'flash to bang' time – the period between a decision being made and its results being felt back in government is occasionally short for big decisions and up to never for most. The absence of credible, independent feedback on the *results* of government decisions means accountability by a company for its lobbies is rarely felt, and certainly not by today's ministers.

We hope that this explains why preferential lobbying is ubiquitous. Its participants are not evil. Straight bribes rarely change hands. Taking a 'conspiracy line-of-sight' is not only wrong; it also produces ineffective solutions.

As we've said elsewhere, if we were in these 'systems' the chances are we would behave similarly – or spend our working lives knocking our heads against an immovable cushion. So, too, for every other player in this game, from senior civil servants to former political activists. It is a conspiracy of interest, not of people. But it can be changed.

3.3.3 How to stop preferential lobbying

So what would stop it? The short answer is to change those eight conditions that enable it now – although it must be borne in mind that these changes fall within the existing model, and the model itself must also be changed in its privileging of the state over civil society. Some of this is obvious, some less so. These are the main solutions:

1. Establish fair and limited political party funding.
2. Ensure powers *are* separate (i.e. no politicised judiciary). In the US, that means not having Supreme Court judges appointed by the president and Congress. In theocracies, it means removing religions and their institutions from governance of the state.
3. Remove political patronage. In the UK that means honours being awarded free of political control or influence.

4. Introduce effective proportional representation for all elections – ensure any group receiving 5% or more of the vote nationally gains a voice in the legislature.
5. Introduce participatory and deliberative forms of decision taking.[18]
6. Change *how* government decisions are taken (see Chapter 10)
7. Invent institutions and practice that vet these decisions.
8. Vet the *results* of these decisions to highlight their consequences and to establish accountability for them, principally through feedback (see Chapter 10).
9. Eliminate institutionalised bribery (explained in Chapter 11).

In our quest for fresh thinking, it is worth noting that the first four of these reforms are common currency amongst constitutionalists – but none have been tied to the causes of PL. The last five require the application of new understandings.

Some might see the answer to PL as making the lobbying playing field level – that is, to make the lobby of interested citizens as powerful as an industry, for example, if that is possible. This would, however, still leave final decisions to be made in private by the minister, who would be free to pick and choose from the lobbies, would provide no feedback or vetting, and would continue with the existing system of governing dominated by the processes of party politics. This would be far from systems thinking in practice, as we seek to demonstrate in the rest of this book. In many respects, STiP is the alternative to failed party politics. These only continue in operation for want of knowing how else to run government.

At this point, you might conclude that the job is done. The deleterious effects of preferential lobbying have been outed, the causes identified and solutions described. Surely now, this enlightenment is available and all that needs to happen is for politicians and civil servants to get on with it. Sadly, that is not what happens. PL is far from the only problem we face that emerges from the interacting elements of systems of governing (see Figure 2.1).

3.4 The systemic trap

The governance systems we have can be understood as a nested hierarchy of systems – ranging from the organisation of local or regional governance to national or transnational levels. At each of these levels there are vertical and horizontal dimensions. In the Westminster system, vertical accountability moves power towards the Minister and away from local people, except for the one moment of voting (or by joining the Party). By and large horizontal governance operating across the citizenry is underdeveloped or does not have mediating institutions to prevent undermining by the state (see Chapter 8). From the interactions emerge the economic, political (authoritarian, democratic, deliberative) and cultural practices that dominate our lives. At the moment, all are deficient in decision making, implementation and human and environmental democracy.

Some may liken the (electoral) competition to a three-legged race with ailing parties and politicians tied to each other for dear life, desperately trying to stave off so-called populist upstarts. The fact is: the status quo engineered by elites no longer cuts the mustard.[19]

There is no doubt that these systems are the major obstacle to action, and without their radical overhaul, all is lost.

Unfortunately, the insiders who run governments have not the time nor interest to change them. They have expended great energy, single-minded determination and usually an oversized ego to jump all the hurdles to get there. They are hardly likely to draw up a new rulebook requiring them to reapply for their jobs. Power and status are addictive. Few in *any* organisation have the independence of mind and education to see it for what it is. Just living in one of these work-intensive systems is sufficient to blind all but those with unframed minds.

You might expect the news media, think tanks and academics to mount a challenge. Some do, but many are as much part of the established system as those elected to it. They depend on it for stories, leaks, commissions, funding – and jobs. Mutual interest relationships are strong. Little governance-challenging thought can be expected from here.

The World Economic Forum has 1,000 company members typically with turnover of $5 billion or more. It is best known for its invitation-only annual meeting at Davos in Switzerland. Traditionally this has been where elites gather in luxury to congratulate themselves. It is the perfect setting for preferential lobbying. Its mission is cited as 'committed to improving the state of the world by engaging business, political, academic, and other leaders of society to shape global, regional, and industry agendas'.[20] The Transnational Institute describes the WEF's main purpose as being 'to function as a socializing institution for the emerging global elite, globalization's 'Mafiocracy' of bankers, industrialists, oligarchs, technocrats and politicians. They promote common ideas, and serve common interests: their own'.[21] A study, published in the *Journal of Consumer Research*, which investigated the sociological impact of the WEF, concluded that it does not solve issues such as poverty, global warming, chronic illness or debt. It has simply shifted the burden for their solution from governments and business to 'responsible consumers' – you and me.[22]

Recent years have seen a shift in tone. The WEF's current public papers exude concern for the state of the world:

The world has spun out of control. We have to rebalance the global system.
Inequality is not inevitable. Here's what we can do differently.
Workers are no longer equal consumers: *Time* for a 'New Deal' for the digital age?
Green bonds and green QE: Public & private finance can fight climate change. The Internet pollutes more than air travel: Time for low-carbon computing.

My word, this all appears as terribly enlightened. Why had this change occurred?, we wondered. Have they developed ethics? No, replied long-time commentator on Davos – Simon Caulkin – they're running scared. They know their world is failing, that people are revolting, that economically and environmentally the world is unsustainable. But they are stuck in the systems that cause this, continue to be its major beneficiaries, and have not a clue how to change them.

The change has to come from crafting new systems, and from the emergence of new political entities – collectivities enabled through Systems Thinking in Practice (STiP) – to put the craftwork of governing in place. Future political fights should not be over marginal changes in tax, health services, education, employment rights or whatever morsels traditional parties seek to tempt voters with but over the ways in which the world is ordered and run. This is war, but not as we know it. Our aim is to secure peace and live in harmony with the biosphere – and each other. Our enemies are the historical systems that are destroying it, and diminishing the lives of most people. The challenges are twofold. The first is time and the delay between the causes of destruction and that destruction becoming sufficiently apparent to motivate action. The second is that the enemy is in disguise, rarely seen, melts away into the night and is expert at avoiding all responsibility.

To change the trajectory evident from the OECD data (Chapter 2) is a compelling task in the face of globalisation, the exigencies of the Anthropocene, growing inequality and technological distortions to human well-being. A change in trajectory does not just happen, though unplanned, emergent surprise does occur a lot. There is, however, the possibility that we can act collectively to change it. But first to change our governance systems we need to understand what is missing – the subject of Chapter 4.

Notes

1 https://theconversation.com/capitalism-with-chinese-characteristics-52638 (Accessed 3 April 2018).
2 https://www.nytimes.com/2018/02/26/world/asia/xi-jinping-thought-explained-a-new-ideology-for-a-new-era.html (Accessed 3 April 2018).
3 Hartcher, Peter. 2016. How China Retains Power. *The Age*, Tuesday November 28.
4 See, for example, Blackmore, Chris, Natalie Foster, Kevin Collins, and Ray Ison. 2017. Understanding and developing communities of practice through diagramming. In Oreszczyn, Sue, and Andy Lane, eds. 2017. *Mapping Environmental Sustainability: Reflecting on Systemic Practices for Participatory Research*, pp. 155–182. London: Policy Press.
5 Burrow, S. 17 January 2018. It's time for a new social contract. *World Economic Forum*. https://www.weforum.org/agenda/2018/01/time-new-social-contract-inequality-work-sharan-burrow/?utm_content=bufferbbc53&utm_medium=social&utm_source=twitter.com&utm_campaign=buffer (Accessed 18 April 2019). Used with permission.
6 Consider Unilever and their attempts to change their model of operation in relation to sustainability only to be subjected to a hostile takeover bid from venture capitalists, which in turn exposed some of the 'reality' under the sustainability hype

– see Dupont-Nivet, Daphné. 2016. Inside Unilever's sustainability myth. *New Internationalist* 13 April. https://newint.org/features/web-exclusive/2016/04/13/inside-unilever-sustainability-myth (Accessed 21 October 2018).

7 Ungar, S. 2000. Knowledge, ignorance and the popular culture: Climate change versus the ozone hole. *Public Understanding of Science* 9 (3) 296–312.

8 Scheidel, Walter. 2017. *The Great Leveller.* Princeton, NJ: Princeton University Press.

9 Barnett, Anthony. 2016. *The Lure of Greatness.* London: Unbound.

10 Friedell, D. 2015. Corruption in America: From Benjamin Franklin's snuff box to citizens united by Zephyr teachout. *London Review of Books* 37 (6): 31–33.

11 Friedell, D., ibid.

12 In ancient Athenian democracy, sortition was the traditional and primary method for appointing political officials, and its use was regarded as a principal characteristic of democracy. Sortition (also known as selection by lot, allotment or demarchy) is 'the selection of political officials as a random sample from a larger pool of candidates, a system intended to ensure that all competent and interested parties have an equal chance of holding public office'. https://en.wikipedia.org/wiki/Sortition (Accessed 12 May 2019).

13 Straw, Ed., 2016. Unpublished paper. 'Why Preferential Lobbies Flourish and How to Stop Them'. Milton Keynes: Open University.

14 Friedell, Deborah. 2015. op. cit.

15 The culture is 'cemented' together in a network of relationships that arise from annual compulsory military service, which cuts across wealth and class lines. The effect is a shadow network that is used to good effect – though it may hold and conserve a form of patriarchy. A government commission in 2016 recommended the inclusion of women in the draft. A referendum in 2013 to abolish conscription fell with 63% voting against, showing continuing strong support.

16 Stewart, H. 2015. The arrogance of government. *Local Schools Network.* https://www.localschoolsnetwork.org.uk/2015/07/the-arrogance-of-government (Accessed 14 March 2019).

17 Stoker, Gerry. 2006. *Why Politics Matters. Making Democracy Work.* Basingstoke: Palgrave Macmillan.

18 The 2018 Irish referendum on abortion provides an excellent model as to how to run this form of deliberative democracy (see Chapters 4 & 9).

19 Elliot, Nicole. 8 March 2018. Elections Ahoy! *Investors Chronicle.*

20 http://www3.weforum.org/docs/GETR/2014/GETR_BackCover_2014.pdf (Accessed 10 February 2019).

21 Marshall A. 2015. *World Economic Forum: A History and Analysis.* https://www.tni.org/en/article/world-economic-forum-a-history-and-analysis (Accessed 10 February 2019).

22 Giesler, M. and Veresiu, E. 2014. Creating the responsible consumer: Moralistic governance regimes and consumer subjectivity. *Journal of Consumer Research* 41 (3): 840–857.

4

WHAT IS MISSING FROM GOVERNANCE MODELS?

4.1 The missing elements

This chapter is concerned with an alternative, three-dimensional governance 'diamond'. The 'biosphere' sits at the centre of this new model; other new elements are the 'technosphere' and 'social-purpose' (Figure 4.1). These new elements are introduced and explained, along with some rationale for their inclusion. In each part we set the scene for later chapters concerned with how to move from the old to a new model. What is proposed is a governance system with a new organisation in the sense described in Box 2.1. A changed organisation will also require new structures, especially new institutions.

Our proposal does not involve inventing global governance or creating a 'one model' fits all. These are recipes for disaster in our view. Instead, we favour variety-creation and variety-maintaining based on practices that are self-organising in nature, allow for emergence and are contextually and historically grounded. A feature of the biosphere that we have now created is that localised capacity to generate innovations and practices able to deal with surprise and localised variation will be in great demand.[1] Sociologist Bob Jessop argues that all governance systems fail at some time. If this is the case, then redundancy and residual variety are needed to bounce back, to be resilient in the face of shocks and breakdown. Versions of biosphere, technosphere and social-purpose governance should be invented at multiple levels and scales. There is no existing blueprint. In the Anthropocene, bouncing back requires systemic crafting and recrafting abilities and these need to be widespread throughout societies. These are issues taken up in Part 3.

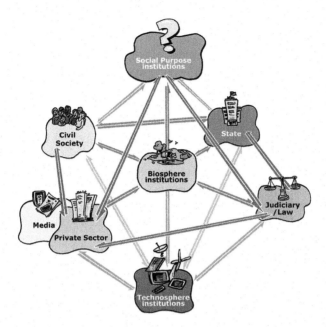

FIGURE 4.1   A three-dimensional 'governance diamond': a heuristic that situates three new elements into the systemic relations that generate the praxis of governing, viz. the *biosphere*, the *technosphere* and institutions that generate *social purpose*.[2]

4.2 The biosphere – the central missing element

For the first missing element, we use the term 'biosphere' (see Box 4.1). What we mean by this is all those biological and physical processes that operated under self-organising or self-governing dynamics before the onset of the Anthropocene (i.e. that period in earth's history when humans had not become the major force of nature that has changed whole-earth functioning). This was introduced in Chapter 1.[3]

BOX 4.1 THE BIOSPHERE

The term 'biosphere' comes from the Greek for 'life' (and 'sphere'), also known as the ecosphere (from the Greek *oîkos* 'environment'). It is 'the worldwide sum of all ecosystems. It can also be termed the zone of life on Earth, a closed system (apart from solar and cosmic radiation and heat from the interior of the Earth), and is largely self-regulating. By the most general biophysiological definition, the biosphere is the global ecological system integrating all living beings and their relationships, including their interaction with the elements of the lithosphere, geosphere, hydrosphere and atmosphere. The biosphere is postulated to have evolved, beginning with a process of biopoiesis (life created naturally from non-living matter, such as simple organic compounds) or bio-genesis (life created from living matter), at least some 3.5 billion years ago'.[4]

For the purposes of this book, and for thinking about a new governance model, we will reframe this explanation of 'biosphere' to extract (remove) human beings from our use of the term. This is, of course, a sleight of hand, because humans are inextricably part of the biosphere and will remain so unless we become extinct. But if we want to think about, or conceptualise, the human activity of governing, then it makes sense to speak of two systems – a social system and a biophysical system in mutually influencing co-evolution. In this framing, the state, law, civil society and the private sector/media are all subsystems in a social system (see Figure 4.2).

This reframing enables us to talk more easily about the 'natural cycles' of water, carbon, nitrogen, phosphorus, oxygen and the like, as well as the dynamics of other non-human species with which humans are in constant interaction, plus the feedback dynamics (both positive and negative feed-back – see Glossary in Appendix 2) between the 'two systems'. The impact of humans, the human condition of living in language, human development and use of technologies, and being able to be purposeful, create a rationale for the distinctions we are making.

Despite intense expressions of concern about the fractured relationship between humans and the biophysical world for over 70 years, governance has failed to deal effectively with the biosphere. Instead, the 'environment', or its proxy 'the ecologi-cal system', became a framing choice treated as an 'add-on' rather than as something central to our governance concerns. Two choices were particularly unhelpful. The first centred on the dualism of humans and nature. The second was the three pil-lars metaphor – the social, economic and ecological 'triple-bottom-line' associated with sustainable development discourses. Both need to be abandoned.

In their illuminating book *The Fourth Revolution. The Global Race to Reinvent the State*, John Micklethwait and Adrian Wooldridge (then with *The Economist*) completely omit the centrality of the biosphere.[5] The terms environment, climate change, Anthropocene and sustainable development do not make it into the index – nor do natural resources or mining. One has to ask why. Is it because as economists the environment exists only as an externality – out of conceptual sight, out of con-ceptual mind? So it is in governments of the world in which the most powerful min-istry is usually the Treasury or Finance Ministry, which employ a lot of economists.

Awareness of a burgeoning environmental crisis has grown in particular since the 1950s and 1970s, when economic thought and professionalism and the arms race took off. Several key influences can be identified. Ecology emerged as an area of study and concern in the nineteenth century but only became well estab-lished in academic and policy circles in the latter half of the twentieth century.[6] In 1933, Arthur Tansley formulated the term 'ecosystem' which was taken up by the Odum brothers and made popular as a key element of the study and practise of ecology and 'ecosystem science' in post WW2.[7] Unfortunately, this line of study which started out holistically took a scientistic turn: the outcome was excessive belief in the power of scientific knowledge and techniques, including turning the concept 'ecosystem' into 'real things' in the world.[8]

Much has been written about the unfolding of environmental and/or ecological consciousness. Although now widespread, these understandings have been constrained by early framing choices and the limitations of an 'environmental discourse' in the face of vested interests, a citizenry largely without systemic sensibility and eco-systems literacy, and governance systems comprising institutional arrangements that preceded this emerging consciousness. Alternatively, taking a systems view of the 'environment' is consistent with its etymological origins from the old French word 'environner', a verb meaning to envelop, surround, enclose, wrap, conceal or encircle. As a noun, environment thus means the state of being environed or the action of being environed. The verb–noun distinction has important practical and conceptual implications. As indicated in the microbiome case study in Chapter 6, we are never independent of that which surrounds us – we are in fact interdependent. In many ways we carry our environment on our backs, much like a tortoise carries its shell. In practical terms, whenever the term 'system' is used, then something that is 'not system' is created. This is called the environment of the system – that which surrounds and is mediated by a boundary choice.

This framing failure of 'the environment' can be seen in how the term/concept has been treated in education and popular culture. Too much environmental education has been concerned with learning about an abstracted, detached, disembodied, external environment – something to be protected, saved, exploited or plundered depending on perspective – rather than that which surrounds each of us. This has the effect of separating understanding from practice, especially from taking actions that have the potential to transform situations of concern that arise from our learning.

Governments have established new institutions designed to deal with climate change and other biosphere concerns. Despite good aspirations, many designs are failing because they do not produce the right actions. This is both a design and an enactment problem, made worse by the governance systems in which these innovations sit.[9] Enactment is a systemic issue associated with practice, language and institutional design: '[I]nstitutions are systems of public language themselves. They originate and then preserve the conventions under which a given community addresses issues, reaches decisions, defines and polices boundaries of the sayable … if things are to improve, our institutions must change fundamentally', claims Mark Thompson.[10]

By global standards, the UK Climate Change Committee (CCC) is an innovative institution set up in legislation enacted in 2007 with, unusually, bipartisan support across political parties. But Lockwood has found that the CCC's assumed basis in governance is flawed:[11]

> [W]hile the Act might appear to lock-in a commitment to reducing emissions through legal means, this does not guarantee political lock-in.

The assumption, made by some proponents of the Act, that accountability of political leaders to a public concerned about climate change, via Parliament, would provide the main political underpinning to the Act, is not justified.

Lockwood argues that:

the Act has helped create major institutional transformations, although the degree to which new institutions have displaced the power of existing ones is limited. The Act has produced some policy feedback effects, especially in the business community, and some limited investment effects, but both have been insufficient to withstand destabilisation by recent party political conflicts. The Climate Change Act remains at risk'.

In other words, the failings of state functioning outlined in Chapter 2 mean that the design for the institution is not fully effective because corruptible political processes control appointments to the committee and limit action on its findings and recommendations. Creation of a new, written constitution with the biosphere as central would address this issue (see Chapter 9).

We are also hiding truths, failing to tell it how it is, as exemplified by the flood threats in London, along with the intractable descent into living with life-shortening air quality that greatly exceeds WHO guidelines. Headlines exclaim that 'more than 2,000 GP surgeries and hospitals in UK are in areas that breach WHO air pollution guidelines',[12] but nothing substantial happens. In 20 or so years there will be significant rises in morbidity, an 'epidemic', as there was in London during the smog of the mid-twentieth century.

Air quality is part of the commons (see Chapter 8); it is also a key component of the biosphere, which is yet to be at the centre of our concerns. This is another example of state capture by vested interests – especially the car industry, the taxi lobby, the road industry and others. The system of power sustains itself because challenges to the sense of self, to identity and well-being in the citizenry have yet to reach a tipping point. Citizens are still trapped in reinforcing habitual thought and action,[13] as is the runaway role of technology in our world.

4.2 The technosphere

Whilst humans are not the only developers and users of technology, they have excelled at technological innovation.[14] In the process, we have expanded the human potential for good and bad. What is important to understand is that, as with the biosphere, our governance arrangements have been equally inadequate; much of what we humans do is mediated by technology, and it has become a foundation to what it is to be human and do what we do in relation to the biosphere. The technosphere as a focus of concern must be added to the new governance model (see Figure 4.1).

FIGURE 4.2 A way of understanding human social systems coupled with the biosphere. Each is in an unfolding co-evolutionary dynamic with the interactions mediated by human-invented technologies and institutions.[15]

The following claim is now made: 'Technology is hijacking our minds and society. …. deeply concerned former tech insiders and CEOs intimately understand the culture, business incentives, design techniques, and organizational structures driving how technology hijacks our minds'.[16, 17] The internet, developed with such altruistic purposes in mind, is a case in point. Tristan Harris argues:

> I'm an expert on how technology hijacks our psychological vulnerabilities. That's why I spent the last three years as a Design Ethicist at Google caring about how to design things in a way that defends a billion people's minds from getting hijacked. When using technology, we often focus optimistically on all the things it does for us. But I want to show you where it might do the opposite. Where does technology exploit our minds' weaknesses?

He says:

> 'I learned to think this way when I was a magician. Magicians start by looking for blind spots, edges, vulnerabilities and limits of people's perception, so they can influence what people do without them even realizing it. Once you know how to push people's buttons, you can play them like a piano.[18]

There are now health, environmental, ethical and equity issues associated with how technology functions in our society. The challenge is to make technology governable.

The technosphere has grown in concert with the rise of the Anthropocene. It is a term coined in the 1970s and refers to the sphere, or realm, of human technological activity. It is the technologically modified environment in which humans exist (see Box 4.2).

BOX 4.2 THE TECHNOSPHERE

According to Jan Zalasiewicz, the term 'technosphere' 'is the brainchild of the USA scientist Peter Haff' and refers to:

> all of the structures that humans have constructed to keep them alive, in very large numbers now, on the planet: houses, factories, farms, mines, roads, airports and shipping ports, computer systems, together with its discarded waste.

He continues: 'The technosphere is the novel ecosystem created by technologies interacting with the natural ecosystem, or biosphere. It's a term that is finding traction with some researchers as hardware proliferates, but its meaning remains slippery'.[19] It is claimed that 'the technosphere is a major new phenomenon of this planet – and one that is evolving extraordinarily rapidly'.[20] It is estimated that 'the bulk of the planet's technosphere is staggering in scale, with some 30 trillion tons representing a mass of more than 50 kilos for every square metre of the Earth's surface'.[21]

Unlike the authors of the articles on which Box 4.2 is based, we exclude humans from our conception of the technosphere, but do admit human-invented organisations, institutions or what can be called social technologies.[22] For reasons outlined below, we also want to think about the technosphere in relational terms and in terms of how it functions to mediate relations between all elements of a new governance system (Figure 4.2).

All technology requires human invention or human activity to sustain it, yet we have also created a world where technology has developed a life of its own. Williams says:

> The technosphere can be said to have budded off the biosphere and arguably is now at least partly parasitic on it. At its current scale the technosphere is a major new phenomenon of this planet – and one that is evolving extraordinarily rapidly. ... Compared with the biosphere, though, it is remarkably poor at recycling its own materials, as our burgeoning landfill sites show. ... If technofossils were to be classified as palaeontologists classify normal fossils – based on their shape, form and texture – the study suggests that the number of individual types of "technofossil" now on the

planet likely reaches a billion or more – thus far outnumbering the numbers of biotic species now living.

The excesses of technology have been with us for some time. Martin Heidegger, writing in the 1930s, railed against the dangers of technology: 'losing our essential humanness, by becoming totally subservient to what he called "calculative reason"[or] the instrumental rationality that is directed towards the control of … nature'.[23] One only has to think of the long lineage of technologies of war. Perhaps more significant is that many have become seduced by the idea that technology is a saviour and that human ingenuity can innovate or invent our way into a bright future. Some commentators reject 'sustainable development' ideas in favour of 'progressive development' (i.e. the exploitation of the biosphere in the belief that technology will be invented in time to overcome the losses and emergent problems). Many economists employ a similar framing for the future. Despite the pervasiveness of technology and the rise of the technosphere, few people have a deep appreciation of how technology functions in systemic terms (see Figure 4.3) or how it should be governed and/or used in governing.[24] To respond needs discourses, practices and institutions able to deliberate on and articulate social purpose as part of a governance system.

Sometimes it is easier to spot technologies that don't work. A set of *social technologies* that can offer the wrong affordances in terms of what we currently do includes projects, targets, framing choices, aspects of artificial intelligence and information systems.[25] As with Talbot, we are of the view that 'our crisis today

hammered

hammer

hammerer

FIGURE 4.3   All technology mediates human practices, understandings and relationships. A hammer has certain affordances that enable the practice of hammering by a hammerer and in the process something is hammered (in this case the computer).[26]

is a crisis of conviction about the primacy of our conscious powers of devising'.[27] New institutions that inhabit the new governance model as structures are needed. These will have to be devised, monitored and sustained (or changed) through a new social-purpose subsystem.

4.3 Social purpose

Blue Zones is the description given to a handful of regions of the world where communities have very long life expectancies,[28] with a high proportion of people who live to 100+. These are natural pockets of evolution, the features of which have now been adopted to create purposeful change in other communities through social action. This leads to changed understanding, new practices and new institutional and technological features (what is described as social learning in Chapter 8). Food and drink, or more correctly, manners of eating and drinking, are important elements. Longevity happened to these people – so longevity is not something you adopt but something you become immersed in as a way of living. It is claimed that the overarching criteria is that of purpose – living a life that is purposeful.

Having a sense of purpose is 'a common thread across the Blue Zone communities. The Okinawans call it "Ikigai" and the Nicoyans call it "plan de vida"; for both, it translates to "why I wake up in the morning"'. Melissa Eisler continues: '[k]nowing your sense of purpose is worth up to seven years of extra life expectancy'.[29] Some of the claimed benefits of having a purpose in life from the Blue Zones research are:

- It gives you direction. It's easy to fill your life with a bunch of tasks and plans, but if you don't get clear on your purpose, you may head down an unfulfilling, unhappy or painfully wrong path. When you have a clear purpose—a reason to get you up and excited every morning—you can then take the right steps to create your most meaningful life.
- It reduces mortality risk. Studies have shown that having a purpose is an indicator for healthy ageing.
- It increases your resilience. Having a purpose may motivate you to reframe stressful situations to deal with them more productively. In the long run, this will help you facilitate recovery from stress and trauma.
- It improves quality of sleep. Studies have shown that a higher level of meaning and purpose among older adults is related to better sleep. It can also be protective against symptoms of sleep apnoea.
- It helps you achieve success (in your terms). When you discover your purpose, you will have the motivation to pursue it. All your successes, however you define them, will be a direct result along the way.
- It cultivates a positive outlook. For Nicoyan centenarians, their reason to live propels a positive outlook among them and helps keep them active. '[They have] a strong sense of purpose; they feel needed and want to contribute to a greater good'.

We have been remarkably lucky in our professional lives to be associated with organisations that, for the main part, have a strong sense of purpose, which has, in turn, satisfied our own sense of purpose. Many are not so lucky. There have been times when organisations we were in seemingly lost their way – their own sense of purpose and ethical compass. When this happened, our sense of purpose, our day-to-day enthusiasm, was significantly weakened. Having sufficient autonomy of purpose in the workplace, a marriage or a family is, we suggest, an important aspect of human well-being. The same is true of any grouping, including the nation state, a region, city or town – anywhere where identity rests and needs ongoing social creation for its expression. Our book is, in part, a response to the crisis of social purpose, which exists across multiple levels of organisations and which extends to the whole human race. The state and our modes of governance are no longer adequate arbiters/negotiators of social purpose.

Social purpose[30] has different meanings in different contexts. Within the context of law, social purpose is a scheme declaring that a statute should not be construed in a way that would violate normal societal values or good.[31] In the business world, the term has been associated with brand:

> If a Brand Purpose is finding out what a brand is good at and aligning it with their users' needs, then Social Purpose goes further. It expands on the user focus to look at how a brand can solve societal issues that affect users' lives.[32,33]

Another tradition of social purpose can be found in adult education. This concerns itself with what Johnston calls 'the changing nature and widening scope of adult learning within a developing Learning Society' and attempts to foster:

> the idea of Adult Learning for Citizenship as a way of maintaining and reconstructing social purpose learning within a Risk Society and as a necessary challenge and counter-focus to the dominant discourse of Lifelong Learning shaped by the economic imperative and framed very much in terms of human capital'.[34]

Johnston argues for 'four different but overlapping dimensions of social purpose learning: learning for inclusive citizenship, for pluralistic citizenship, for reflexive citizenship and for active citizenship'. He also concerns himself with 'new rationales for social purpose adult learning linked to instructive examples of practice'.

It is important to note that we are addressing issues of governance and not democracy. They are clearly closely related, but they are best considered as two different systems-of-interest (i.e. a *system to deliver governance/governing* compared with a *system to enact democracy*). Arend Lijphart in his book *Patterns of Democracy* provides a comprehensive overview and analysis of 36 countries in terms of their espoused democracies. He makes the important claim that 'consensus democracy may not be able to take root and thrive unless it is supported by a consensual political culture'.[35] We interpret this as evidence that praxis is pivotal. Lijphart's claim is backed by the evidence that 'consensus-oriented culture provides the basis for and connections between institutions'. Another way of saying this is that consensus democracies, in contrast to majoritarian democracies, exhibit more connectivity and strive to build greater citizen stakeholding by engaging them with major issues of concern and, in the process, negotiating and renegotiating social purpose (i.e. moving beyond a simple majority-based governance achieved by infrequent voting and crude instruments like Yes–No referenda).[36] Compare what happened in the UK's referendum of 2016 on leaving or remaining in the EU with the Irish one of 2018 on abortion (see Box 4.3).

BOX 4.3 TWO REFERENDA COMPARED

Irish journalist Fintan O'Toole, writing after the UK Brexit and Irish abortion referenda, offers insightful analysis that supports a central argument of our book. It is the simple insight that one person's referendum is not another person's referendum. As an institutional form, a referendum has little meaning unless (i) its design, especially how the questions are formulated, and (ii) the system of rules and processes within which it is run are considered. In this example, the differences are striking, as were the outcomes. O'Toole says of the Irish referendum: 'A brave experiment in trusting the people helped defeat tribalism and fake "facts", which is not something that could be said of the UK referendum'.[37] How did this happen?

According to O'Toole, Irish voters 'were subjected to the same polarising tactics that have worked so well elsewhere: shamelessly fake "facts"; the contemptuous dismissal of expertise; deliberately shocking visual imagery; and a discourse of liberal elites versus the real people'. But 'Irish democracy had an immune system that proved highly effective in resisting this virus. Its success suggests a democratic playbook with at least four good rules'.

Our interpretation of O'Toole's four rules could be seen as a strategy for pursuing social purpose as part of a new governance system. The rules are:

1. **Trust the people.** 'A crucial part of what happened in Ireland was an experiment in deliberative democracy. The question of how to deal with the constitutional prohibition on abortion – a question that has bedevilled the political and judicial systems for 35 years – was put to a Citizens' Assembly, made up of 99 randomly chosen (but demographically representative) voters. These so-called ordinary people – truck drivers, homemakers, students, farmers – gave up their weekends to listen to 40 experts in medicine, law and ethics, to women affected by Ireland's extremely restrictive laws and to 17 different lobby groups. They came up with recommendations that confounded most political and media

insiders, by being much more open than expected – and much more open than the political system would have produced on its own'.

Importantly, the Irish parliament listened to the outcomes: 'an all-party parliamentary committee essentially adopted the proposals of the Citizens' Assembly. So did the government. And it turned out that a sample of "the people" actually knew pretty well what "the people" were thinking. If the Brexit referendum had been preceded by such a respectful, dignified and humble exercise in listening and thinking, it would surely have been a radically different experience'.

2. **Be honest.** 'The Yes side in the Irish debate handed its opponents a major tactical advantage but gained a huge strategic victory. It ceded an advantage in playing with all its cards turned up on the table'.
3. **Talk to everybody and make assumptions about nobody.** This rule is essentially about avoiding the creation of dualisms, a them-and-us binary divide. It requires getting out and listening without prejudice.
4. **Personalise the political.** Understand that trust emerges when people meet others as legitimate others telling their stories.

Governing in the Anthropocene will need much more of what the Irish did than what the British have done. In the end it is about effectiveness in negotiating trajectories of living driven by the articulation and re-articulation of social purpose.

Purpose is something we humans are capable of talking and organising about.[38] Within systems scholarship, Russ Ackoff and Fred Emery are seen to have written the classic text on purposefulness.[39] A key distinction for them was that between purposive and purposeful behaviour. Purposive action denotes action by another (including non-human others), to which purpose is attributed. By contrast, purposeful action is that which is willed by someone – an individual or a group. These distinctions operate in daily life when we attribute purpose to someone, or to a group, without involving them in the process(es) of attribution of purpose (e.g. in reaction to the actions of a politician involved in Brexit decision making in the UK). For this reason purposive behaviour is open to misinterpretation as to its purpose. On the other hand, engaging in reflections and/or conversations about purpose is, according to Anne Khademian, critical to 'identifying ways to realize more flexible, decentralized, and networked approaches to engage our big collective problems' which 'is the intellectual challenge' of the future.[40] For public organisations, she argues that 'the clear[er] we are about the organizing purpose, the more decentralized and immediate the accountability processes can be'. This shift is urgently needed for effective governing; the evidence according to Khademian is consistent – 'there is an urgent need for a more flexible, decentralized, and networked approach to organizing in order to effectively engage our most challenging public problems'.[41] These distinctions are useful and important in STiP understandings and practices as we will elaborate in Chapter 8.

Our concerns with purpose are very practical. We are less concerned with the attribution of purpose to others, nor do we claim any teleological purpose for the biosphere, technosphere or human existence. Responsibility for purpose sits with us as thinking-doing beings operating at the individual and collective levels.

The biosphere, technosphere and social purpose are now added as additional elements in a new governance system. This is also a new organisation. The relations between these elements must create something that is functional. New structures, though necessary, will not be enough unless accompanied by new ways of thinking and acting. In the next part we ask: How can systemic functioning of new governance systems be crafted and improved? We focus on the importance of systems praxis, the actual doing of governing, within which sit a range of other practices such as leading, managing, strategising, forecasting, coordinating, evaluating and allocating – to name but a few.

Notes

1 As indicated in Figure 1.1 (and Box 1.1) the Anthropocene will deliver greater variation in temperature and rainfall or drought and most of this will be unpredictable. This will require capacity to act in the face of variation, which is likely to be relatively localised.
2 Adapted from Ison 2016, *Systems Research & Behavioural Science.*
3 According to Yuval Noah Harari, humans have had major impacts on life on Earth for much longer than we have imagined. As evidenced by extinctions of megafauna, these actions have changed whole ecologies, but not until much later did they create sufficient impact to warrant coining the term Anthropocene – see Harari, Y.N. 2014. *Sapiens. A Brief History of Mankind.* Harmondsworth: Penguin.
4 https://en.wikipedia.org/wiki/Biosphere (Accessed 25 May 2018).
5 Micklethwait, J. and Wooldridge, A. 2015. *The Fourth Revolution: The Global Race to Reinvent the State.* London: Penguin.
6 Bramwell, A. 1989. *Ecology in the 20th Century: A History.* New Haven, CT: Yale University Press. Also Wulf, Andrea. 2015 *The Invention of Nature. The Adventures of Alexander von Humboldt. The Lost Hero of Science.* London: John Murray.
7 Tansley, Arthur G. 1935. The use and abuse of vegetational terms and concepts. *Ecology* 16 (3): 284–307.
8 See Wulf. 2015, op. cit. The process of turning a concept into a thing is called reification – think of all the feminine statues reified as the embodiment of justice. There are also distortions introduced through the rise of ecologism – see http://www.worldwidewords.org/turnsofphrase/tp-eco1.htm (Accessed 20 December 2018).
9 https://climate-adapt.eea.europa.eu/countries-regions/countries/germany.
10 Thompson, M. 2017. *Enough Said: What's Gone Wrong with the Language of Politics?*, p. 317. New York: Vintage.
11 Lockwood, M. 2013. The political sustainability of climate policy: The case of the UK Climate Change Act. *Global Environmental Change* 23 (5): 1339–1348.
12 https://www.theguardian.com/environment/2018/oct/25/patients-at-thousands-of-hospitals-and-gp-practices-breathing-toxic-air (Accessed 25 October 2018).
13 Duffy, D.N. 2017. *Evaluation and Governing in the 21st Century. Disciplinary Measures, Transformative Possibilities.* Basingstoke: Palgrave Macmillan.

14 See Harari, op. cit.
15 Developed by Ison for the CADWAGO Project http://www.cadwago.net/- Accessed 10 May 2018; also published in Godden and Ison 2019, *Australasian Journal of Water Resources*. https://doi.org/10.1080/13241583.2019.1608688.
16 The Centre for Humane Technology, which came into existence based around the experiences of many within the 'high-tech' fields.
17 Harris, Tristan. 2018. How a handful of tech companies control billions of minds every day. http://humanetech.com/ (Accessed 18 April 2019).
18 Harris, Tristan. 2016. How Technology Hijacks People's Minds—From a Magician and Google's Design Ethicist. https://observer.com/2016/06/how-technology-h ijacks-peoples-minds%E2%80%8A-%E2%80%8Afrom-a-magician-and-googles-des ign-ethicist/ (Accessed 15 April 2018).
19 Medrano, K. 2016. WTF Is the Technosphere? The Anthropocene? There's No Word for the Manmade World. https://www.inverse.com/article/16853-wtf-is-the-techno sphere-the-anthropocene-there-s-no-word-for-the-manmade-world (Accessed 16 April 2019).
20 Professor Mark Williams, University of Leicester. https://phys.org/news/2017-11-earth-technosphere-trillion-tons.html (Accessed 4 May 2019).
21 See: Zalasiewicz, J. Williams, M., Waters, C.N. et al. 2016. Scale and diversity of the physical technosphere: A geological perspective. *The Anthropocene Review*, November 28. https://doi.org/10.1177/2053019616677743.
22 See Ison, R.L. 2017. *Systems Practice: How to Act. In Situations of Uncertainty and Complexity in a Climate-Change World.* 2nd ed. London: Springer and The Open University.
23 See https://en.wikipedia.org/wiki/Martin_Heidegger (Accessed 4 May 2019); Snodgrass, A. 1993. Hermeneutics, universities, and the letting-be of technology. *Proc. Universities as Interpretive Communities.* 23–24 November, pp. 75–94. Sydney: University of Sydney.
24 Cross, N., Elliot D., and Roy, R. 1974. *The Man-Made World.* Milton Keynes: The Open University. Ison, R.L. 2017. op. cit.
25 Ison, R.L. 2017. op. cit.
26 Ison, R.L. 2017. op. cit.
27 Talbott, S. 2014. Technology and Human Responsibility. *Netfuture* 125. http://www .netfuture.org/2001/Nov1501_125.html (Accessed 8 April 2019).
28 Talbott, S. 2007. *The deceiving virtues of technology.* In *Devices of the Soul.* O'Reilly Media see https://www.oreilly.com/library/view/devices-of-the/9780596526801/ ch01.html (Accessed 18 April 2019).
29 Eisler, M. (n.d.) *3 Lessons in Having Purpose from Those Who Live to 100.* The Chopra Centre. https://chopra.com/articles/3-lessons-in-having-purpose-from-those-who -live-to-100 (Accessed 18 April 2019).
30 Not to be confused with social value – http://www.socialvalueuk.org/what-is-soc ial-value/.
31 https://en.wikipedia.org/wiki/Social_purpose (Accessed 18 April 2019).
32 Mindshare. 2016. *What is social purpose?* https://www.mindshareworld.com/uk/a bout/what-social-purpose (Accessed 18 April 2019).
33 Rodríguez, O. and Bharadwaj, V. 2017. Competing on social purpose. *Harvard Business Review.* https://hbr.org/2017/09/competing-on-social-purpose (Accessed 18 April 2019).
34 Johnston, R. 1999. Adult learning for citizenship: Towards a reconstruction of the social purpose tradition. *International Journal of Lifelong Education* 18 (3): 175–190.
35 Lijphart, A. 2012. *Patterns of Democracy: Government Forms and Performance in Thirty-six Countries.* New Haven CT: Yale University Press. 2nd ed. He makes a distinction between majoritarian and consensus democracies and concludes that consensus democracies have the better record – '[T]hey clearly outperform the majoritarian

democracies with regard to the quality of democracy and democratic representation as well as with regard to … the kindness and gentleness of their public orientations' (p. 295).

36 According to Lijphart (ibid.): 'The majoritarianism-consensus contrast arises from the most basic and literal definition of democracy—government by the people or, in representative democracy, government by the representatives of the people—and from President Abraham Lincoln's famous further stipulation that democracy means government not only by but also for the people—that is, government in accordance with the people's preferences' (p. 1).

37 O'Toole, F. 2018. If only Brexit had been run like Ireland's referendum. *The Guardian* Wed, May 30. https://www.theguardian.com/commentisfree/2018/may/29/brexit -ireland-referendum-experiment-trusting-people (Accessed 18 January 2019).

38 Pursuit of purpose can be linked to *phronesis* – as it ' involves not only the ability to decide how to achieve a certain end, but also the ability to reflect upon and deter-mine good ends consistent with the aim of living well overall'. https://en.wikipedia. org/wiki/Phronesis (Accessed 28 October 2018).

39 Ackoff, R.L. and Emery, F.E. 1972. *On Purposeful Systems*. Chicago: Aldine-Atherton.

40 Khademian, A.M. 2010. Organizing in the future: Pursuing purposefulness for flex-ible accountability. *Public Administration Review* 70: S167–S169.

41 Checkland, P. and Poulter, J. 2006. *Learning for Action*. Chichester: John Wiley & Sons; Blackmore, C., Cerf, M., Ison, R.L., and Paine, M. 2012. The role of action-oriented learning theories for change in agriculture and rural networks. In *Farming Systems Research into the 21st Century: The New Dynamic*, pp. 159–177. Dordrecht: Springer; Bateson, G. 1972. Social planning and the concept of deutero-learning. In *Steps to an Ecology of Mind*, pp. 159-–176. Edited by Bateson G. Chicago: The University of Chicago Press.

PART 2

What is systems thinking in practice?

5

SYSTEMS THINKING IN PRACTICE IS NOT HARD

5.1 The cobra effect

The story is told of a plague of cobra snakes in Delhi when India was still subject to British rule. The authorities set up a control programme under which they paid a bounty for each dead snake. That seemed to work OK, until local entrepreneurs discovered they could supplement their earnings by breeding snakes and slaughtering them for the bounty. Hmmm. So the authorities wagged their fingers and stopped the payments. Whereupon the snake breeders loosed their now valueless quivers back into the city, which ended up with a bigger population of venomous cobras than ever before.

Despite this archetypal example of unintended consequences being sufficiently well-known to have its own name – the cobra effect – governments around the world continue to fall into this trap.[1]

The cycle goes as follows. A problem occurs. Public pressure mounts. The news media leads the self-righteous demand that 'something must be done', joined by populist politicians. The government must show its teeth and act. It casts around for a solution – 'something' or 'anything'. A bright adviser or civil servant comes up with a novel idea in the bath. Action is taken, the news interest moves on and success is declared. Except the wider economic system swings into play and the problem gets worse or another, worse, problem arises.

By contrast, the Singaporean government seeks to avoid the unintended by putting 'all their legislation through a decision-treeing and simulation process to eliminate as many unwanted and unintended effects of proposed legislation as possible'.[2] In 2003, the Singapore Government began to move 'from a traditional hierarchy into a new-age system of governance characterised by a Whole-of-Government approach' that recognised the complexity of 'wicked problems'.

In many corners of the world, future-proofed examples of applied systems thinking can be found. We have selected three from our experiences, which we have probed to bring out some of the significant aspects of applying systems thinking. The first has been run by two people with a strong education in, and empathy for, this way of approaching a problem, who then joined with two others who just think this way but use no explicit systemic tool bag. The second is an example of the way 'multiple perspectives' produce a systemic solution. The third sees a STiP specialist apply the rules very carefully to make meetings energised and productive. As the under-achievement of governments becomes endemic, stories such as these will, we hope, give more and more people the courage to 'just do it'.

5.2 Cutting costs and improving health

Our first example is set in the context of health systems in the midst of the longevity-technology fix. In more-developed countries, life expectancy has increased from 67 to 78 years since 1960, extending the average retirement to death period from 5 to 16 years (depending on the standard retirement age). This is good news but comes with a price tag as health service and state pension costs increase with each extra year of life. At the same time, medicine is progressing at speed, along with many other fields of scientific research. More conditions can be treated successfully. This is also good news, but comes with a further price tag.

Where health funding is closely coupled with its consumption, then the system has the flexibility to increase organically. If you want to buy more oranges, then you could choose to spend more of your income on them. If health services were a simple market item, then we could each choose to spend more on them, and less, for example, on clothes. For those that pay for each procedure directly, this is how they have to behave. This is entirely rational: you cannot take a foreign holiday or watch television if you are dead.

But for many people, health is a collective provision, a sharing of costs – the less fortunate health-wise benefit from the more fortunate income-wise. It is a form of insurance. Some countries' health services are almost entirely funded from *general taxation*. They are thus competing with everything else governments spend money on. Tax increases are unpopular, especially with the levels of ineffectiveness experienced in most modern countries. The greater the distance between the funder and the consumption, the harder it is for people to value that taxation and for governments to raise it. Its value or purpose gets lost in the noise of competing priorities, party politics, anecdote, disinformation and news media concoction. This gives rise to Straw's law of derivative taxation: the greater the distance between the pound collected and the pound spent on public services, the less effectively it will be used.

The simple answer to increasing health funding is to move from general taxation to direct payment, offset by state reimbursement, as in France and several other countries. But those health services where people can enter them anywhere without worrying about the cost are highly valued. Demand cannot be managed through the direct payment mechanism, so supply is restricted by rationing operations, numbers of beds and doctors and making the service harder to access. At the same time, efficiency measures and cost controls are pursued. Ministers adopt the usual method of 'expert' solutions from the centre, either trialled in the press to assess 'public reaction' or introduced quietly in the background, hoping no one will notice.

The tools are procedures, key performance indicators, internal markets, outsourcing and privatisation. Their ideological inspiration is the notion that the private sector operates more efficiently. Thus if routine operations, GP services, cleaning and so on are competed for and run by the private sector, they will, of themselves, be more efficient. Despite this, or perhaps because of it, costs continue to rise disproportionately, and efficiencies are limited, at best.

'Managerialism' has become common too. This presumes all organisations can be run according to a pre-programmed set of techniques. These are the controlling, bureaucratic, form-filling, 'performance management' demands of so-called 'leadership teams' and their corporate police forces of HR, procurement, finance and others. Managerialism may also pick up on good concepts like the quality improvement methodology of 'lean', hire consultants to apply it, and tick that box as completed. But in practice, little changes, except to give the concept a bad name. Managerialism is also characterised by a lack of understanding of and feel for the unique qualities of a particular organisation. Whilst needing to change, many organisations have been ruined by the standardised application of 'the only answer I know'. As staff are treated with less and less appreciation of the human condition, so their behaviour towards customers and patients comes to resemble their treatment by managements.

5.2.1 Somerset, England

This is the story of four people who thought and did differently. It is an inspiration for people everywhere to get on and sort out a local problem or two, without waiting for permission. Through his work on compassionate communities,[3] an academic influenced a medical consultant, who improved end-of-life care, and then found a doctors' practice using similar means to reduce demand at their surgery. They came together and thought it wise to run the data to see what was happening quantitatively. Jaws dropped as they found that from their district, emergency admissions to hospital had dropped 14% over the 44-month study period of 2013–2017, whilst across Somerset County it continued to rise, being 28.5% higher. Costs of unplanned admissions from the town of Frome fell by over £1m, or 20.8%.[4] In a resource-capped service, these are the admissions that squeeze out the routine operations and boost waiting lists. Suddenly, compassionate communities had become much more than a human value but a major therapeutic tool and an incisive cost-cutter. How did this happen?

Allan Kellehear is a 50th Anniversary Professor (End-of-Life Care) at the University of Bradford, UK, and a medical and public health sociologist. He founded the world's first academic public health palliative care unit in Australia in the 1990s. He has researched this field for over 30 years.[5]

Drawing on Allan's work, Compassionate Communities[6] is a social marketing term for organisations engaged in community development (Box 5.1). They help care for a dying person through small acts of compassion, supporting the dying person during their end of life, often enabling them to die well and, if possible, at home. The community could be family, neighbours, local organisations, faith groups, local businesses or people living in a particular area.

Jean Jones' husband had had cancer for five years. Once he became really ill, Jean gave up her job to become a full-time carer. She had some support from a local cancer support scheme. Neighbours in Jean's street rallied round her at her lowest ebb, popping in, offering to do the shopping, ironing – everyday tasks to make life easier, and to support them both.

BOX 5.1 COMPASSIONATE COMMUNITIES: WHAT HAPPENS?

Compassion was found in the street, and they came to me and supported me when I needed it most. One neighbour came round, and said 'Do you need any help?' and I said, 'No', but she said 'I'm coming in anyway' and came in and took the ironing away to do.

Jean now hopes to give back what she received. She makes efforts to connect and support others, and counter the feeling of isolation. 'We are all responsible, it's everyone's business. It's in everyone's grasp to get to know their neighbours, and there is nothing like saying "Good Morning..".' Jean organised a street party to help people to get to know one another.

She has since made two films, one with Compassionate Communities Sandwell, telling her story, and another which she uses to start dialogue with nursing staff in the local hospital.

Compassionate Communities spends much of its time simply explaining and promoting this approach to local people, hospices and hospitals. Just being reminded of the real benefits and joy in helping one another is often all that is needed.

A feature of a machine close to breaking point is its tendency to thrash. As it works harder, so its components wear, connections loosen and noise rises. The machine thrashes until it literally falls apart as first one component snaps and the rest follow. Organisations do the same.

Fed up with being housed in a health service thrashing for its life, and worn down by the barrage of initiatives from the centre that usually made the situation worse, a 'disruptive innovator' stepped out of the perpetual 'reform' dystopia of the National Health Service (now into its fourth decade), and looked elsewhere.

Julian Abel was a consultant in palliative care in Somerset, a county in the west of England, where health services are funded from general taxation. He read Allan's book. During a quiet reflective moment he asked himself: 'What's the most important thing to people at the end stage of their lives?' The answer, which may be obvious, but not to machine-like organisations and standardised professions, is to be at home amongst their loved ones. He aimed for a 50% home death rate by using a compassionate community programme – from a then current rate of 25%.

Inspired, he started reading up on the research. He was immediately struck by the finding[7] that the most important factor in reducing mortality and its associated improvement in health, is *social connectedness*. This is better than stopping drinking, smoking or overeating, or more screening. Social relationships improve health. Face-to-face contact is vital. It may all start with the newborn baby and her/his first experience of the eyes of the loving parent.

A colleague of Julian's had spent a year with the Institute for Health Improvement (IHI) in Boston, USA.[8] Founded in 1991 it is 'an independent not-for-profit organisation, a leading innovator, convener, partner, and driver of results in health and health care improvement worldwide'. Its aim is that everyone should get the best care and health possible.

The IHI's early years were spent mainly developing the means to achieve this aim. Much was learnt from other industries as to how they had improved safety, reliability and quality. IHI observed the potential in reliability programmes for oil exploration and in quality improvement methodology for the manufacture of cars. Enormous strides had been made in these industries, as anyone who recalls driving the 'old bangers' of the 1970s will know.

This willingness to look outside one's own employer, industry, country or profession for analogies and applicable practice is a hallmark of systems thinking. It is easy to ridicule management jargon and business school cookbooks, but it is not by chance that technology of enormous complexity and use can, today, be bought so quickly and cheaply. Supply chain planning, just-in-time procurement, total quality, self-directed work teams, decision trees, are concepts with universal application. 'System reliability' is an established science in industry, with wide applicability and the professional province of systems engineers.[9]

But it is one thing to know what to do and another entirely to put it into practice. The IHI therefore developed change methodologies, including the PDSA cycle of Plan, Do, Study, Act: develop a plan for an improvement, test it out on a small scale, study the results and adjust as necessary and apply across the whole organisation. It avoids the top-down disasters common in centralised systems. Good ideas have value, not hierarchy. Training in the change methodologies and mentoring the health staff applying them are key to expanding their coverage.

Julian used compassionate communities as a therapeutic tool for end-of-life care, but this needed the Weston hospital staff and local communities to adopt the approach as well. The IHI methodology was applied. Data to track results was essential. Without this, they would not have known where they were going, and why, and whether this new approach was working. It was.

5.2.2 Frome, Somerset

Meanwhile in Frome, a quaint town of nearly 29,000 people in Somerset, its new medical centre was constrained by its funding and available staff, so it could not employ enough doctors and nurses to cover patient appointments and visits. Its lead GP (doctor), Helen Kingston, unable to expand the supply side of the equation, pondered whether it would be possible to reduce demand.

In 2014, Helen employed an inspired community development worker – Jenny Hartnoll – as part of the clinical team. She set up the community development service inside the GP practice, called Health Connections Mendip.[10] One of its four key components has been the extensive mapping of over 400 local resources, including community groups, peer support networks and volunteer support. She built up a list of all the voluntary groups – from knitting, to dog walking, to book clubs and model railways. Where gaps existed, new groups were started – a macular degeneration group, a leg ulcer club and a bereavement group. 'Health Connectors' worked with patients on goal-setting and care planning, and on building their naturally existing networks.

Many people were isolated, and just found comfort in the next biscuit or cigarette, and absorbed their day in bed or in front of the television, whilst their health continued to decline. Volunteer 'Community Connectors' introduced them to the voluntary groups, got them interested and many joined. Social isolation decreased, as did visits to the surgery: classic prevention rather than cure. Demand reduced, and more doctors were not needed.

The Frome leaders, and this is a point we like to emphasise, had no especial grounding in systems thinking but just thought that way. Plenty of people do. You do not have to be a fully fledged systemic thinker, analysing every act you observe, to work systemically and to apply such concepts as framing, emergence and affordance intuitively (see Glossary in Appendix 2). Good systems of organisation promote this space. Many systems eliminate it.

People who work this way exhibit an independence of thought, a desire to improve whatever it might be, a willingness to change their minds, an openness to and enthusiasm for fresh ideas, a thirst for learning and knowledge. They are not taken in by the pressure of accepted practice, the toxic orthodoxies of an organisation, climbing the pole of promotion for its own sake, or corporate politics. They also have egos open to learning, saying 'I don't know but let's try to find out' rather than allowing fear, defensive routines and pursuit of control to dominate their lives.

Consequently they identify a problem – especially a persistent problem subject to all sorts of conventional measures – and look around, spot connections, observe patterns, seek practice and experience of similar problems from anywhere, look from the bottom up from the users' and citizens' perspectives, and seek out the difficult people who often know exactly what is wrong. From all of this standard human behaviour a systemic improvement, sometimes a solution, will emerge. It can be the attitude and orientation of those involved that makes systems thinking – not just the approach that comes out of the toolkit.

5.2.3 Working together

As part of his end-of-life care initiative, Julian was introduced to Frome Medical Practice, and found that they had been applying the principles he had been advocating. They joined forces. This was a real eureka moment, as they realised the similarity and complementarity of what they were doing, having started from different places and having used different methods. They joined up secondary and primary care and integrated this powerful therapeutic tool of compassionate communities into routine clinical practice. The cost savings arising could then be spent on non-emergency health care. Feedback of results has driven the initiative further forward as they have expanded it to other areas of Somerset, using Quality Improvement methodology of the IHI (see above). A critical aspect of this is allowing people to make mistakes – otherwise how will they learn? This is the opposite of managerialist practice where mistakes are penalised.

5.2.4 Reflections

It helps to be an intelligent, motivated, experienced maverick, with some power. The mavericks in this example have done this themselves, with limited funding, and largely without any management involvement (or support). Their answer is systemic.

Julian comments that:

> the question becomes how to change the system in the long term. This is where Allan has particular strength, because public health medicine looks at societal behavior change as one of its key components. This means that we are using many of the techniques for building the longevity of our projects, including community development, social marketing, policy support, education, engagement, etc. We are planning to make sure this does not disappear.[11]

The cultural context may be significant too, in that Frome attracts diverse lifestyles. All of the councillors on its town council are 'independents' – political party representation has been voted out. The town has confidence in its own capacity to get things done.

At this moment of optimism, it would seem churlish to add a note of caution. But experience says that when the change founders leave, then the organisational norms will, like memory foam, reassert themselves and a great innovation will disappear. If in this, and many other cases, this is not to happen, the question then arises as to what kind of governance of this health service would sustain and develop these changes? The answers are to be found in the following chapters.

In the meantime, we have to reflect that modern government is becoming less and less useful. It cannot overcome its systemic obstacles (see Chapters 2 and 3). In this void, we are seeing local groups fixing things for themselves, a trend to be encouraged. The challenge and opportunity for us as citizens is to assume authority wherever we can. Don't wait, expect or ask, just do it. If in these circumstances we act systemically, then good results will flow. Governments will become even more irrelevant. Ignoring politicians is the surest way to wake them up. They may then do what has to be done and accept their own transformation.

5.3 Flood defences in Shaldon

Flooding is a problem around the world. New flood measures are needed as the ice melts and the oceans rise, as rainfall becomes more concentrated and as changing use of land reduces its capacity to absorb water. The Environment Agency (EA) in England identified the small seaside town of Teignmouth, sitting on the edge of the mouth of the river Teign, as at risk. Other than a devastating invasion by France in 1690 and air raids during the Second World War, this small town has led a relatively quiet life.

As these 'expert' public bodies do, the EA developed a flood prevention scheme behind closed doors and took it to the town for 'consultation'. Scale models were displayed in the local library and a public meeting convened. Here all the obstructions, concrete walls, road diversions needed during construction, lost business and general disruption were on display. Few people were aware of any flood risk. Without access to the sea for their boats, the fishermen especially could see their livelihoods disappearing. Shocked – this was the first most residents had heard about it – the meeting became rowdier and rowdier. The community rejected the scheme. The EA staff retired emotionally bruised and mentally battered.

The EA's approach is known as Decide-Announce-Defend, or DAD. You will have experienced it many times. A public authority or company decides in private what it wants to do, announces it with greater or lesser élan, hopes that no-one will notice, is surprised at the strength of feeling it has aroused and goes into full 'crisis management' mode with its 'PR' advisers, defending for all its worth with whatever tactics it deems fit. These vary from salvos of massaged statistics, repetition of claimed benefits, sledging of opponents, to calls to bow to their 'democratic' or 'market' mandate. Such defences can and do last for years:

> When we get things wrong with communities, it is hideously inefficient (in terms of staff time) and expensive, and we don't set any limits on that expense – we just react to the problem until it stops or is resolved. Therefore, we must adopt this new approach to stop that kind of expense and inefficiency.
>
> *Environment Agency technical manager*[12]

With its fingers burnt in Teignmouth, the EA turned to the town on the opposite side of the estuary, Shaldon. Although it had not flooded 'in living memory', the existing informal defences offered a low standard of protection. Housing is in a 'basin' behind the defences, which would begin to fill were it to be flooded to life-threatening first floor level; this area includes a primary school. Wave action and the number of gaps in the existing defences – which were present to provide people with direct access to the beach – could exacerbate this risk. Existing defences also affected the ability of some of the minor tributaries and surface water drainage systems to discharge. This could cause localised flooding from surface water and sewage.

Determined not to repeat the Teignmouth tiff, the EA employed a professional facilitator[13] to pilot the EA's 'Building Trust with Communities' aspiration. The approach was to be Engage-Deliberate-Decide, or EDD. This was based on several insights. The first is that if people are not aware there is a problem, then they are unlikely to look kindly on a solution that brings, seemingly, only disbenefits. The second is that if people are involved through a transparent and fair process, not only will a more effective solution be found but the people will be more likely to support it, even if it is not their preference. Third, as implementation is felt as more of a shared task, construction will not be disrupted by angry objectors and will proceed smoothly and at lower cost.

Least observed but most important, a fourth insight is that multiple perspectives will be brought to the table. 'Expert' authorities never have *all* the knowledge, despite their customary confidence. Local people actually experience floods and their source. The person in the street has wet shoes. The person in the office does not. The person in the street may also be a highly qualified scientist or engineer, well able to understand complex models or with detailed local knowledge of drain hole covers. The person in the street will challenge conclusions that do not fit with lived experience. Simply by bringing multiple perspectives to the table, both the nature of the problem and its potential solutions are crafted systemically. Two or ten heads really are better than one.

The perspectives in this case ranged from the EA's project manager and engineering consultants, to residents, dog walkers, local authorities, business forum, boat owners, sandbag distributors, flood risk and emergency response groups, rowers, a school governor, Teign Estuary Partnership, hoteliers, lifeboat committee members, and the water carnival.

A liaison group was established, and agreed to this remit:

OUR AIM IS:

To work together with all interested parties in deciding how best to respond to all* flood risks in Shaldon and Ringmore. In particular to *insist on* an integrated response by the Environment Agency, South West Water, Devon County Council Highways and Teignbridge District Council (the responsible bodies).

*all = wave, tidal, fluvial, surface water run-off and sewage

---

Some of the knowledge unknown to the EA brought by the liaison group was a surprise. The EA has a statutory duty for tidal flooding only. Local people knew from their own wellingtons[14] that surface water run-off from high rainfall and the inadequate capacity of sewers was also a significant issue. This could be made worse by solid flood walls which kept the sea out, but the rainfall in. The local council's highways department and the South West Water company became parties to the solution. The finished works included drainage with innovative engineering features.

Flooding was a potential problem not just for Shaldon, but for the whole estuary. At the request of local residents, the area (i.e. the system of interest), was extended to the neighbouring village of Ringmore.

Remote experts working in private for the central government department, without any public discourse or review, produced the tidal surge models, which then defined the height of proposed sea walls. These figures did not match people's observations. Eventually these models and their predictions were amended and the proposed walls lowered by over a quarter of a metre. The multiple perspectives of local people had added significantly to the knowledge base.

To encourage creative problem solving and to allow deliberation to lead to the optimum outcome, all potential solutions were put on the table. These included a barrage across the estuary. The EA were terrified of its scale and cost and wanted to exclude it. The liaison group analysed it carefully. Residents came to realise that it would be far too costly. People are not stupid when informed with evidence in which they have confidence.

The EA did not want floodgates. Relying on their being closed *before* the sea rises increases risk. But without floodgates, access for boats would be prevented and walking limited. Through the process of engagement, locals gained a sense of ownership for the ongoing safety of the flood defences. Eight floodgates were added, linked to a warning centre by telemetry, and now local people have a 'civil society' role in their operation. People take this responsibility seriously – it is they who will drown.

In summary, public engagement at Shaldon led to:

- Getting a *mandate* for action from the community, based on agreement that the tidal *flood risk* is sufficient to justify finding ways to reduce the risk.
- Involving the community in *generating and scrutinising* all potential ways of reducing the flood risk, including a wall-based tidal flood defence scheme, barrage, individual property protection, doing nothing, awareness-raising campaigns and reducing wave action.
- Getting community input to maximise the community *utility* of a wall-based tidal flood defence scheme by advising on layout, height, finish.
- Responding to the community concern (ultimatum) about the need to tackle *all forms of flooding* by helping all relevant bodies to work together to

tackle surface, sewage and tidal flooding, rather than just focusing on the EA remit of tidal flood risk.

- Responding to community *identity and governance* by extending the scheme to cover Ringmore as well as Shaldon, despite its being an initially excluded and separate flood cell.
- Increasing *resilience* of the community by generating interest and creating a parish flood action plan. This included coverage of flood issues in parish newsletters and the local press.
- Generating community *ownership* of (and confidence in) the scheme's operation via the parish council.
- Improving *trust* in and respect for the EA staff and opening constructive channels of communication.
- Suggesting how to *speed up* the construction process without interrupting local events and the tourist season and maintaining *communication* with the wider community.
- Obtaining whole team buy-in to the solutions, with early value engineering reducing both the cost and the construction programme.

Such civil society benefits have seen other localities use this newfound connectedness and confidence to take up other challenges quickly – like community hydro schemes and cafes – without the need for external stimulus.

The scheme was built, without disruption, on time, and over £1.16m below its construction budget of £8.53m.[15] It gave an immediate reduction in flood risk from 6% to 0.33% Standard of Protection. It has worked too, surviving a major storm in 2014, although the weather has yet to test it to its design limits. The community has operated the gates successfully .

The EA then returned to Teignmouth, this time with EDD rather than DAD. A successful scheme has been built there too, but the time taken from when the EA first identified the need, to the scheme's completion was ten years, compared with five years at Shaldon. EDD invests more time up front with the result of less time overall. Military maxims stress reconnaissance. This makes a lot of sense. Without all of the available knowledge relevant to the forthcoming battle, the chances of losing and dying rise. The same is true of government, though usually without the deaths.

Reflecting on the engagement phase of this project, none of the key practitioners were aware of the words 'systems thinking' being uttered once. But systems thinking was there, because the engagement process adopted brought multiple perspectives to its analysis and solution. The angle of view was widened, further knowledge brought forth, and the solution emerged from the process. Citizens also sought successfully to have the boundaries of the 'system of concern' changed. And some of the practitioners brought with them their own systems literacy, ideas, techniques, methods and the like which were able to contribute to what was achieved.

5.4 Using systems thinking purposefully to improve

As the examples thus far show, arriving at 'system' improvements can be achieved with unconscious systemic thinking, and with 'joined-up' work that, on reflection, makes systemic sense (Frome). In other instances, the practitioners involved have systems thinking capabilities but, in the main, keep it to themselves (Shaldon). We could call these *intuitive* and *silent* systems thinking, respectively. Our challenge is to foster the circumstances for more of both. Investment and openness about using systems thinking are needed to have greater capacity and capability with transformative purposes in mind. In saying this, it is still possible to start in a relatively simple fashion in everyday organisational life, with this third example.

5.4.1 'I' statements and active listening: fostering autonomy, responsibility and ethicality[16]

Meetings, committees, briefings and online interactions can be debilitating. They often undermine the collective intelligence of those involved. They may lack clarity of purpose. People can talk past each other, conflating issues of what, why and how, without being aware of anything but the confusion and feelings of wasting time. Effective facilitation, group contracting and clarity of roles (who is note taking, for example) may be missing.

There is a tendency within our culture to perpetuate authoritarian communication by accepting the validity of statements of the form 'You are wrong/no good/unacceptable'. We may lose the ability to separate out an evaluation of our ability from an evaluation of who we are. Undermining an individual's self-confidence is the easiest way to make them open to control and manipulation. The first reason for using 'I' statements is to break this habit. The second is that 'You' statements are widely used as a defensive strategy, one that avoids declaring one's own thoughts and feelings about a situation. Making 'I' statements breaks this habit. 'I' rather than 'You' is a key skill of a systems practitioner, since it helps to clarify your own position and perceptions, insights and understandings (i.e. to take responsibility and to act ethically).

Another practical way to promote real communication is through active listening. As a practitioner, you have to be able to listen to people with sufficient care and understanding so that you can 'get' their perspective on the situation – and it will usually be very different from your own. The most common mistake is to assume you know what the other person has said. This assumption comes from one's own internal model of the other person, and will be most active when you have strong critical feelings and ideas about them. Active listening is a technique for correcting this propensity to misinterpret other people. The technique is very simple. In a conversation you listen to what they say, and before you give your own response you say back to them, in your own words, what you have understood them to say – and invite them to confirm or correct your understanding.

Because we humans live in language, it is only through conversation (from the Latin meaning 'to turn together') that we can communicate and get things done. It is for this reason that so much on-line comment is not effective communication. One of the reasons that Open University (UK) online teaching works is because attention is paid to the nature and quality of online interaction. All spaces are moderated. Learning can only occur when interactions involving feedback are heard and understood. We actively seek to avoid blaming and the use of 'you' statements. In our practice, we use theories about communication and learning, which entail systemic, relational dynamics to design and deliver 'learning systems' that are effective for their purpose.

5.5 Dealing with cobras in the future

What would multiple perspectives, changing boundary conditions and engaging in active listening have made of the proliferation of cobras in Delhi?

The first step would be the gathering of perspectives from all sources in one of the many deliberative processes now available. Experts and local people would bring a lot of specific information. What exactly is the scope and shape of the issue? Is it a problem for some but an opportunity for others? Why has the population of reptiles got out of hand? What has happened to the usual predators – boars and mongooses? Where, precisely, are the cobra's preferred hiding holes – in embankments, tree hollows, termite mounds, rock piles and small mammal dens? Are they drawn to the area by human food scraps? Indian cobras usually lay between 10 and 30 eggs in rat holes or termite mounds between the months of April and July, and the eggs hatch 48 to 69 days later. Are their nests the same in Delhi?

Is prevention rather than cure possible? Can the breeding cycle be disrupted? Or food supplies? Or more predators introduced? The answer in each case might be: Don't know! In which case, checking first for the interaction with the local economic system and local social norms, small-scale experiments would be trialled. As they progressed, adjustments would be made based on feedback of the effects and results. Those experiments that worked would be extended.

But all of this takes much more time and effort *up front* than producing a quick fix. The choice here, as so often in government, is quick and wrong or slow and right. Without built-in discipline for decision making, politics tends to the easy option, as do we all.[17] From time to time, someone will come to power who understands this truth and acts accordingly. But waiting for the messiah to deliver us is both lengthy and temporary. What dominates is the system around those in power and what it demands of them. If the system allows quick fixes and their results are left to fester or are spun out of existence, then the cobra effect is what will occur most often. The challenge is not just to think systemically but to *make* governments do this consistently. The way this is done is to put it into constitutional law and other institutional innovations.

In the next chapter we unpack what is entailed in the shifts from systemic sensibility to systems literacy and STiP capability. A case for investing in STiP capability cannot be made unless the basic elements are understood and included.

Notes

1 There are a number of well-known system archetypes, made popular in Senge, P. 1990. *The Fifth Discipline: The Art and Practice of the Learning Organization.* New York: Random House. These archetypes include: Balancing process with delay; Limits to growth; Shifting the burden; Shifting the burden to the intervenor; Eroding goals; Escalation; Success to successful; Tragedy of the commons; Fixes that fail; Growth and underinvestment – see https://en.wikipedia.org/wiki/System_archetype (Accessed 4 May 2019).
2 Bellinger, Gene (personal communication); see also: Ho, P. 2018. The future-of-government approach is important, but not easy to execute. *Today*, Wednesday 21 November 2018. https://www.todayonline.com/singapore/future-government-approach-important-not-easy-execute (Accessed 21 November 2018).
3 Kellehear, A. 2012. *Compassionate Cities.* Abingdon: Routledge.
4 Abel, J., Kingston, H., Scally, A., Hartnoll, J., Hannam, G., Thomson-Moore, A., and Kellehear, A. 2018. Reducing emergency hospital admissions: A population health complex intervention of an enhanced model of primary care and compassionate communities. *British Journal of General Practice* 68 (676): e803–e810. NB: the figures in the text above are reported as observational, not causal.
5 https://www.youtube.com/watch?v=Vs-2CvuuEqk (Accessed 15 November 2018).
6 https://www.compassionate-communitiesuk.co.uk/ (Accessed 16 April 2019).
7 Holt-Lunstad, J., Smith, T.B., Baker, M., Harris, T., and Stephenson, D. 2015. Loneliness and social isolation as risk factors for mortality: A meta-analytic review. *Perspectives on Psychological Science* 10 (2): 227–237.
8 http://www.ihi.org/about/Pages/default.aspx (Accessed 16 April 2019).
9 https://www.incose.org/ (Accessed 15 November, 2018).
10 https://healthconnectionsmendip.org (Accessed 15 November, 2018).
11 From a conversation with Julian Abel.
12 Straw, E. and Colbourne, L. 2009. Evaluation of the use of working with others-building trust. *Environment* 2. See http://documents.campaignstrategy.org/uploads/Colbourne%20Associates%20Report%20on%20Shaldon%20Evaluation.pdf.
13 Disclosure: Ed's wife, Lindsey Colbourne.
14 A form of rubber boot named after the Duke of Wellington.
15 Twigger-Ross, C., Bennett, T., Johnston, R., Papadopoulou, L., Sadauskis, R., and Orr, P. 2017. *Enhancing Ex-Post Evaluation of Flood and Coastal Erosion Risk Management Strategies and Schemes.* London: Collingwood Environmental Planning Limited. See https://www.cep.co.uk/2017-publications (Accessed 4 May 2019).
16 In this section we draw on teaching material from the Open University course *Managing Complexity. A Systems Approach (T306) Block 3* co-authored by Jake Chapman and Bob Zimmer.
17 Kahneman, D. 2012. *Thinking, Fast and Slow.* Harmondsworth: Penguin. Kahneman's thesis is that we assume certain things automatically without having thought them through carefully. He calls these assumptions heuristics. He lists many examples of how certain acquired heuristics lead to muddled thinking, giving each a name, for example the 'halo effect', 'availability bias', 'associative memory'.

6

INVESTING IN 'SYSTEMS THINKING IN PRACTICE' CAPABILITY

6.1 Systems thinking: learning from 50 years of systems education

What did the practitioners described in Chapter 5 do when they did what they did? On what basis can we claim that they did systems thinking? Equally, in the vignettes drawn from Ed's and Ray's experience (Appendix 1), what was it that justifies claiming that they lived with systemic sensibility? And how is effectiveness understood, or claimed in all of this? Our answers to these questions come from several sources. We start with experiences drawn from designing and presenting systems thinking courses at the UK OU (Open University) since 1972.[1]

Students of OU systems courses study at a distance. They are all of mature age. Most work, in diverse fields, while they study. This enables an active pedagogy to be developed which means that the learning based on systems concepts, methods, theory etc., can be applied in the student's own context. This is not learning in the abstract, but grounded and used by students to improve and change situations of concern using STiP.

Over time, experiential insights have emerged about the character of OU systems students (who now number over 40,000).[2] A 'rule of thumb' is recognised: about one-third of students come with a strongly held systemic sensibility. For this cohort, discovering systems thinking through formal study offers solace and gives credibility to the way in which they intuitively understand the world. It is a great relief for them to know that they are not alone, that there is a language and concepts that make sense of the way they think. For another third, study of Systems creates *Aha! moments*. These are when realisation dawns that you can appreciate your own thinking and act to change it. For the final third, the courses lead to a sort of personal precipice, a challenge to their sense of identity, because systems thinking challenges what they are good at or how they have succeeded in their world. Fear undoubtedly plays a part. Exposed to systems literacy, some of these students may change over the long term as they become more open to their experiences (i.e. become more reflexive).[3] The world to which students return after study does not usually sustain this shift. This has to change.

For simplicity, let's give these three student groups a name: *resisters, revivalists* and *remainers*.[4] Why these names? This requires an explanation of the phenomena that sit behind each grouping. Our argument here is that we humans are born imbued with systemic sensibility that arises from our evolutionary past, our biology and, for the fortunate, their manners of living experienced as children.[5] Some resist losing this sensibility (the 'resisters'). Others lose it over time when subjected to the prevailing paradigms, practices and institutions of Western civilisation. For the limited numbers that do formal study of Systems, there is a chance they will become the *revivalists*. Others, as in the case of Frome (Chapter 5), being open to their circumstances and asking the right sort of 'why' questions brings them to a similar place. The *remainers* have too much invested in the status quo – both personally and in the world in which they operate. Chapter 1 has already outlined some phenomena that probably apply to *remainers*. This category could also be applied to change-deniers like big tobacco and big oil, who organise and invest to prevent change in the face of experience and evidence. *Remainers* may be purveyors of fear or immobilised by their own fear.

In seeking to govern effectively, the first challenge is to know what systemic sensibility is and how to retain, foster, or recover it. With further investment, systems literacy and then STiP capability can be built so that the exigencies of the technosphere and the biosphere can be drawn into our capacities and capabilities for governing (Figure 6.1).[6] The OU's provision of systems education shows that what we envisage is possible. It is also scalable with will and investment.

Investing in STiP capability to increase the probability that new forms of governing can be made to work effectively is not just a problem of engineering. New structures, particularly institutions, are needed (see Part 3) but must go hand in hand with sophisticated awareness of *what* one is investing in and *why*. This chapter addresses the former, *what*. Different traditions of contemporary systems and cybernetic scholarship inform the narrative.

6.1.1 Systems thinking: thinking in terms of relationships

The life of a baby human is replete with practices that cultivate a systemic sensibility. A cuddle; mouth to nipple; response to a cry; mobility through rolling, crawling, then walking; the ecology of words and sounds that invite responses, particularly word and name training; triggering and responding to emotions; and the gradual emergence of self in relation to others. All of these phenomena have relational dynamics in common. Living in a relational world is an evolutionary context into which we are born. Becoming conscious that this is our birthright is another thing, it seems. This is a challenge, as coming to be aware of relational dynamics is the essence of a systemic sensibility needed for our living and flourishing.

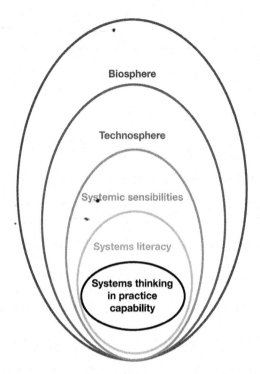

FIGURE 6.1   A systemic framing to move towards systems thinking in practice (STiP) capability. Acknowledge the primary roles of the biosphere, then the technosphere, recover systemic sensibility, invest in systems literacy and STiP capability.[7]

As experiences of OU systems students show, only a limited number of us retain our systemic sensibilities. Getting everyone into such programmes, desirable as that may be, is unlikely to achieve the shifts needed in the time frames that matter. What are some other possibilities? One is to foster a global discourse that challenges prevailing paradigms about what it is to be human, to be an individual, to have freedom and autonomy. To abandon, in effect, *Homo economicus*.[8]

Recent shifts in science and medicine should make this easier, particularly in view of the rapidly expanding knowledge about how 'our second genome, the vast and diverse array of microbes that live on and in our bodies, is driving our metabolism and our health' (Box 6.1). The emerging story is about our microbiomes, how the ecology of organisms we carry mainly in our guts has the potential to reshape how we think about ourselves. It is now known that human cells make up only 43% of the body's total cell count. The rest are microscopic colonists. This emerging field raises questions of what it means to be human.[9] Collectively we will come to realise that we each carry within us an ecology of other organisms such that who we are is a product of our dependence on our interdependencies with other organisms and other elements of the biosphere.

Just as it seems possible to intervene and make systemic change for the better in relation to the organisms that share our body, so we are proposing systemic change in relation to the organisations and institutions that share and shape our lives. As human understanding of the interdependencies that conserve our existence come to be appreciated more fully, our appreciation of ourselves as situated permanently in various 'systems' may develop too. This may aid the recovery of systemic sensibility.

BOX 6.1 HUMAN DEPENDENCE ON OUR INTERDEPENDENCIES[10]

Recent research reveals a hitherto relatively unknown, or underappreciated, set of relationships that make us who we are: 'the 'vital relationship between the healthy bugs we accumulate in our gut and our immune system'. This work reveals a type of systemic failure we have orchestrated for our own health:

> we have over the past 50 years done a terrific job of eliminating infectious disease [but] we've also done the same to many good bacteria and as a result we're seeing an enormous and terrifying increase in auto-immune disease and in allergy [and] in later life the delicate balance between our body and bugs gets skewed, leading to inflammatory diseases such as irritable bowel syndrome or frailty in old age.[11]

The research also suggests that our gut microbiome has a major role in the development of chronic conditions such as obesity.

What is becoming clear is that those organisms that are in relationship with us (bacteria, archaea, fungi and viruses) make and sustain who we are: this is our evolutionary legacy. It has been described as our second genome – a source of huge genetic diversity, a modifier of disease, an essential component of immunity, and an 'organ' that influences not just our metabolism but also our mental health. Unlike the human genome that is fixed at birth, this 'second genome' can be manipulated in many ways. There is the possibility not just to 'read our microbiome and look at predispositions, but to change it for the better'.[12] This means intervening to put our living into a new co-evolutionary trajectory with these organisms. This agenda for innovation and change, for human purposefulness, is analogous to what we need to do with our governance systems at multiple levels, such as a work group, a department, an organisation, a nation or amongst groups of nations.

Research into the gut is also reframing its role in human cognition. The gut is as powerful, perhaps more powerful, than the brain. This new understanding brings into question the biological and conceptual basis of much now done under the auspices of AI, mistaken attempts to recreate the cognitive power of humans in machines. 'Should we now think of ourselves not as self-sufficient organisms, but as complex ecosystems colonised by numerous competing and health-giving microbes?'[13,14]

There are certain cultures and professions that sustain one's systemic sensibility. Anyone visiting the National Museum of the American Indian in Washington DC[15] will be rewarded with awareness of extensive systemic sensibilities across the different tribal groups. The same is true of many indigenous cultures. There were other contexts that favoured systemic sensibilities, which are no longer experienced. The shift from nomadism to sedentary urban life was a critical turning point. In the shift, the relationship humans had with the landscapes they traversed was lost (see the writing of Bruce Chatwin).[16] As outlined in the Preface, growing up on or managing a mixed farm – one concerned with the relationships between people's livelihoods, weather, climate, soil, animals, plants and microbes – fosters systemic sensibility, without which it is difficult to thrive.[17] The same is true for good 'relationship' counsellors and therapists. Urban residents, now over 50% of the world's population, when lacking understanding of their ecological interdependencies with the biosphere, risk undermining the recovery of citizen systemic sensibility.

When someone accepts a new explanation, their world changes. Acceptance of the explanation of what it is to be human in Box 6.1 may change your world. After reading it, perhaps it merely reinforced how you already thought – so you're a resistor. Or you may have had the Aha! moment of the revivalist. Perhaps you consider it not to have any profound implications – a remainer. But what next? What do we do with a new explanation of this sort? The challenge is to make new explanations part of who we are – to embody the explanation so that what we do also changes. The next section is designed to enable you to explore your own levels of relational or systemic thinking.

6.1.2 Testing your systemic sensibilities through relational thinking

Here are four questions to test whether you think in relational terms, the core of a systemic sensibility:

1. How does crawling/walking arise as a form of practice?
2. What relationships can our hand enact which have evolutionary significance?
3. Why do illusions/magic tricks work?[18]
4. If someone takes a whiteboard marker and places it on the board following an arc that eventually brings the pen back to the starting point, then what have they done?

The systemic answer to question 1 is that walking happens because of the ongoing relational dynamics between two entities (which we could call systems). In the first there is a person (with a body, and a past) in relation to a floor (or path or field) – remove the relationship and walking does not happen. Imagine in the midst of walking you are whisked up into the sky, and as happens in the circus, you keep moving your legs but walking does not happen. It does not happen because the relationship between a body and the floor has broken down, it no longer exists. Walking as a phenomenon should not be confused with a causal explanation of what leads the legs to move.[19] Experience shows that the first inclination for most will be to provide answers that are systematic in nature (i.e. linearly causal; see Figure 6.2), such as the motivation of the child causes them to move their legs. But this in itself does not explain the practice of walking.

Question 2 was often posed by Gregory Bateson.[21] The question is stimulated by the propensity we have to talk in terms of things – like four fingers and a thumb – rather than in terms of relationships – between an opposable thumb (an important evolutionary trait) and each of four fingers (i.e. a set of four relationships).

Illusions work, primarily because our biology works so that in the moment we are unable to distinguish between perception and illusion. It is only upon reflection that we can clarify what was what. Illusionists understand the brain has adapted to take short cuts. It operates by imposing onto the world historical patterns built into our nervous system rather than by being open to deterministic, causal signals from outside. For the most part, this does not constrain us, but being aware that this is the case ought to trigger an alert button. It is dangerous to engage in practices that do not value multiple perspectives or rely totally on our own perspective. Failure to be alert is to fall into a cognitive trap: the mistaken belief that our relationship with the world is based on sound, objective foundations. Humans are closed systems with respect to information: it is our own history that determines what we do and don't admit as information.

Most people answer question 4 as 'You have drawn a circle'. In other words the answer is given in terms of the creation of an object, a thing. This is a common understanding. An alternative answer is that a distinction was created by making a boundary, with a relationship between the inside and outside. Thus a

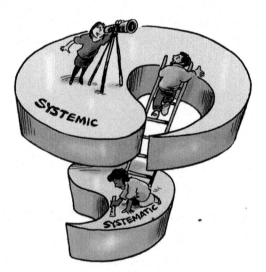

FIGURE 6.2 The systemic-systematic duality, read like you would yin and yang. The two adjectives which come from the word system, systemic-systematic, are related types of thinking and practice. Effort is needed to climb out of the dominant, systematic paradigm, but not abandon it.[20]

circle was brought forth. Distinction is the basis of what is experienced – without distinction there is no experience.

These questions are posed for two reasons. The first is an attempt to trigger a gestalt-like moment, to take the reader out of the seductive embrace of the dominant paradigm. The challenge is to make relational, systemic thinking the natural default. You can practise when you read Part 3.

The second reason is to add a note of caution to enthusiasts for systems methodologies, techniques and tools. Unless the users embody systems thinking as relational thinking, then there is a great likelihood they will use methods, knowingly or not, within the prevailing systematic paradigm.[22] By doing this, effectiveness is lost. The same argument could be extended to the users of the rules in a constitution or any other institutional innovation.

6.1.3 Making sense of your systemic sensibilities through dualism and duality

Having become aware of systemic sensibilities, the next step is to cultivate them and embark on building systems literacy, or your sense about systems (Figure 6.1). Jane Austen's novel *Sense and Sensibility* provides insight into the relational dynamics between these concepts: for Austen *sense* means good judgment, wisdom or prudence, and *sensibility* means sensitivity, sympathy or emotionality. The sisters in the novel had both, but the balance (preferences, predilections) differed.[23] Elinor had great 'sense', whilst her sister Marianne had great 'sensibility'.

By endowing her characters with both, Austen did not treat them as a dualism – in which one element negates the other – but as a duality, two concepts that when together form a whole, or unity. To see pairs as a duality or a dualism is a choice we make. Some pairs are commonly understood as dualities: predator/prey, yin/yang, responsibility/response-ability, organisation/structure, growth/development.[24] In the West we live in a world dominated instead by dualisms: right/wrong; subjective/objective; fast/slow; public/private; left/right; good/bad; body/mind; centralisation/decentralisation. Dualisms restrict choice. Seeing pairs as systemic totalities, dualities, opens up choices. If one thinks systemically, then one also acts systemically (theory/practice). Over time this duality slips into the background so that one could claim to intuit systemically, or to have developed a systemic aesthetic. Unfortunately, we do not live in one of Jane Austen's novels where sensibility and sense nurture each other such that both flourish. This failing has profound implications for what we humans do, the governance systems we inhabit and the changes we might seek to make.

In some minds, Austen's duality has become interpreted as a dualism: sense as rationality versus sensibility as emotion. This is, of course, a trap that has created an 'apartheid of the emotions', a condition that does not acknowledge that *emotioning*[25] is central to being human and is largely banished from consideration in work and professional life.[26] Being rational is but one of many ways of being emotional. A main concern underlying this book is to invite awareness of sensibility, that quality of being able to appreciate and respond to complex emotional or aesthetic influences.

For those in touch with their own systemic sensibilities who have developed some systems literacy through life experience or study, such as in ecology, systems science, practical holism or systemic family therapy, the new microbiome research (see Box 6.1) will not come as a surprise. It will make sense if it explains what is already thought, or intuited. Some people will be relieved – after a lifetime of being critical of medical research and practice for not being systemic – that what seems obvious is at last being taken seriously. Being open to systemic *sensibility* is necessary for transformative change.

6.1.4 Harnessing the concept 'system'

The word 'system' is widely used. But not often in the sense introduced earlier of an integrated whole, distinguished by an observer, whose essential properties arise from the relationships between its parts. Unfortunately – or fortunately? – the word system has gone feral – it has escaped from its historical and scholarly lineage and has acquired an everyday sense that connotes:

- An entity (with unspecified boundary, elements and thus relational dynamics) that prevents or resists change – as in '*THE system*'.
- Some form or set of (usually unspecified) elements with more, or less, connectivity.
- Some elements that have something in common – again often unspecified.[27]

Unfortunately, in the last 50 years there has been a failure to institutionalise 'systems' narratives, conceptions and praxis effectively except as 'things' (e.g. computer systems or ecosystems). The metaphor of 'system as feral' implies untamed escape and could suggest a lack of utility or worth. However, we seek good use of the escaped, feral nature of the term to enhance practices that facilitate transformative actions in today's world.

To make good use of the concept *system* we use the two English adjectives that come from the word system, *systemic* and *systematic* (Figure 6.2). Being systemic refers to the understanding of a phenomenon within the context of a larger whole and the nature of the internal relationships. The vignettes in Chapter 5 told of success that came from the purposeful creation of new sets of relationships. The new relationships released a new dynamic which could be understood as a new system. Importantly, in the cases that worked, change was not systematic, or linearly causal. The most effective change is emergent and non–deterministic.

This opening section has set out to explore and present a simple logic: we humans are born into an enabling world that brings forth our systemic sensibilities. Accepting a new explanation of what it is to be human and to fully internalise our dependence on our interdependencies (with the biosphere) offers a unique opportunity to place recovered systemic sensibility at the heart of governance reinvention and re-enactment. Relational thinking is synonymous with systems thinking which combines systemic and systematic thinking as a duality (Figure 6.2). Embarking on this path is not always simple; there is a need to clear the mind and get rid of obstructions if we are to succeed.

6.2 Clearing a path towards systems thinking in practice capability

Through cultural and institutional misalignment we have subjugated, or undermined, our natural systemic sensibilities. These have been displaced by commitments to a systematic paradigm that promotes thinking and acting in terms of linear cause and effect, a focus on objects, 'things' or elements rather than the relations between them and us, and a naïve, destructive, set of beliefs founded on what Lakoff and Johnson[28] describe as 'classical faculty psychology' (Table 6.1).[29]

TABLE 6.1 Some contrasting features between the traditional Western conception of the disembodied person with that of an embodied person.[30]

Traditional Western conception of the disembodied person	*The conception of an embodied person*
The world has a unique category structure independent of the minds, bodies or brains of human beings (i.e. an objective world).	Our conceptual system is grounded in, neurally makes use of, and is crucially shaped by, our perceptual and motor systems.
There is a universal reason that characterizes the rational structure of the world. Both concepts and reason are independent of the minds, bodies and brains of human beings.	We can only form concepts through the body. Therefore, every understanding that we can have of the world, ourselves, and others can only be framed in terms of concepts shaped by our bodies.
Reasoning may be performed by the human brain, but its structure is defined by universal reason, independent of human bodies or brains. Human reason is therefore disembodied reason.	Because our ideas are framed in terms of our unconscious embodied conceptual systems, truth and knowledge depend on embodied understanding.
We can have objective knowledge of the world via the use of universal reason and universal concepts.	Unconscious, basic-level concepts (e.g. primary metaphors) use our perceptual imaging and motor systems to characterize our optimal functioning in everyday life – it is at this level at which we are in touch with our environments.
The essence of human beings, that which separates us from the animals, is the ability to use universal reason.	We have a conceptual system that is linked to our evolutionary past (as a species). Conceptual metaphors structure abstract concepts in multiple ways, understanding is pluralistic, with a great many mutually inconsistent structurings of abstract concepts.
Since human reason is disembodied, it is separate from and independent of all bodily capacities: perception, bodily movements, feeling emotions and so on.	Because concepts and reason both derive from, and make use of, our perceptual and motor systems, the mind is not separate from or independent of the body (*and thus classical faculty psychology is incorrect*).

Classical faculty psychology holds on to the destructive Descartian mind-body dualism, but human cognition is a whole-of-body phenomenon and not restricted to the brain. A three-brain model that includes the gut, the brain and the heart is now providing new insights into the human condition.[31] Intellectual straightjackets need to be removed to design and enact future governance systems.

There are further intellectual and paradigmatic constraints that prevent systems thinking from flourishing. Some of the main ones are addressed now.

6.2.1 Reliance on 'magic bullet' or systematic thinking

The 'magic bullet' metaphor reveals much of what is wrong with our current ways of thinking (e.g. that there is a single trigger, and that a linear trajectory is pursued towards some target). There is a single person who decides when to fire, no deviation is expected, and so on. Figure 6.3 (left) depicts this dominant systematic paradigm in which we live and from which we practise governing. It can be understood as the expression of a problem in terms of an event for which a solution as a fix, grounded in the mistaken belief of simple causality, is proposed. But most governance situations are not like this. Rittel and Webber describe this practice in terms of trying to tame a wicked problem prematurely, and inappropriately.[32] It rarely works.

A STiP alternative is shown in Figure 6.3 (right); this shows how the issue of road congestion can be understood as a 'wicked problem' so that systemic improvement possibilities are offered – what Donella Meadows described as leverage points or points to intervene in a system.[33] Systems dynamics modelling, the STiP tradition from which this figure is derived, draws heavily on circular causality and the dynamics of positive and negative feedback (see Appendix 1). When investment in new roads is analysed in isolation from other forms of transport, more are built, making car travel more attractive, leading to the freeways filling up, and often back to congestion. The circle then repeats. Analysing transport as a whole, including how demand arises and may be reduced, plus alternatives for moving people and goods – trains, buses, cycles, airplanes, alongside roads – produces more balanced investment with improved de-congestion over time.

One can be systems literate but poor at using the concepts in practice. Having a concept with the potential to help you do what needs to be done is little use unless you can employ it in practice. To do this well requires change in how practice itself is understood.

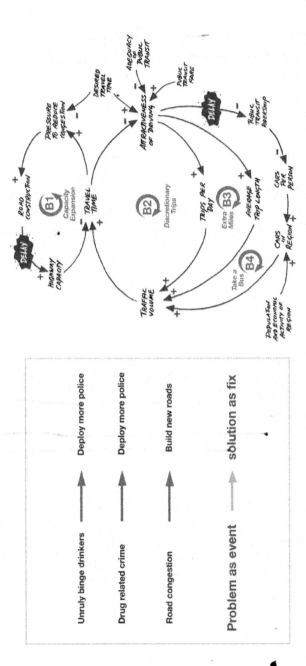

Systematic

Unruly binge drinkers	→ Deploy more police
Drug related crime	→ Deploy more police
Road congestion	→ Build new roads
Problem as event	→ solution as fix

Systemic

FIGURE 6.3   Examples of the systematic (left) and systemic (right) traditions/paradigms compared in relation to public policy and governance.[34]

6.2.2 Understanding the political ecology of practice[35]

6.2.2.1 Use of language

We humans live in language. Those who speak more than one language consistently report that they feel and act differently when living in different languages. Languages have evolved different structures and as a result have different effects on the user of a language. Because we are born into one or more languages, there is usually a taken-for-grantedness about how language operates – that is how it is! It requires a special effort to contemplate how language might use us without our awareness. This is a big topic that is not discussed nearly enough. The examples that stand out as a constraint in moving towards STiP capability are the major metaphors of human communication.

All language is metaphorical and our use of metaphor changes all the time. Metaphors reveal, conceal and carry theoretical entailments. Klaus Krippendorff, the Gregory Bateson professor for Cybernetics, Language and Culture at the University of Pennsylvania's Annenberg School, recognises six major metaphor groups for human communication:

1. Container metaphors
2. Conduit metaphors
3. Control metaphors
4. Transmission metaphors
5. War metaphors
6. Dance-ritual metaphors.[36]

The first five groups are built on systematic, mechanistic understandings of human communication, more akin to signal transfer. The only one that is systemic, linked to how communication functions biologically, is the dance-ritual metaphor group, the idea that human communication is a turning together as in a conversation. The metaphor you use determines what you do, your practice.

If practice is thought about at all in everyday life it is probably connected to what is done in learning a new skill such as playing a violin, or becoming an adept football player. The English language distinguishes between practice and practise – the former is a noun with several meanings, including 'the habitual doing or carrying out of something'. Practise is a verb and means 'to perform, do, carry out' or 'work at, exercise or pursue ... a profession, occupation etc'.[37] A practitioner is someone who is involved in a form of practice – a form of practice that can be named, classified, distinguished – such as a bricklayer or barrister. But what they do is practise their practice. In daily life we ignore these subtleties of meaning at our peril.

We are living with the wrong uses of language and failing to construct stories or narratives relevant to our circumstances. One could claim that too little use of language and narrative construction is founded on and extends to a systemic sensibility. The lack of systemic diagrams in major publications, the prevalence of systematic, rather than systemic metaphors and concepts, and an over-reliance on narrative text that cannot deal with complexity are part of this problem. A missing capability is the ability to read, construct and use systems diagrams (i.e. to use languages other than words).[38]

6.2.2.2 Traditions of understanding

As humans we have much in common from our evolutionary history, including our ability to use, or live in language, but thereafter we grow apart in our developmental trajectory. We are born into a culture (or tribe) operating at several levels, from family to nation or diaspora, a particular language community and a complex institutional ecology that is rarely perceived as a product of human invention. This can be summarised by saying that the 'traditions of understanding out of which we think and act' are unique to each of us.[39]

Traditions of understanding:[40]

- are important because our mental models or models of understanding grow out of traditions
- can be defined as a network of prejudices and empirical experiences that provide possible answers and strategies for action
- can also be defined as a network of pre-understandings because the word prejudices, literally understood, means 'pre-understanding'
- are ways to see and act but also ways to conceal
- embed what has, over time, been judged to be useful practice in a culture
- can become a blind spot when it evolves into practice lacking any manner of critical reflection being connected to it: this is a risk for any culture
- create blind spots that can be observed at the level of the individual, the group, the organisation, the nation or culture, and in the metaphors and discourses in which we are immersed.

Our traditions of understanding are inescapable – in the moment they govern much of what we do before rationality (sense), purposefulness and/or reflexivity kick in. We can, however, strive to be open to our own traditions of understanding and appreciate how these both enable and constrain us. The way to do this is by becoming reflexive, or being able to carry out the second-order process of reflecting on our reflecting, as in exploring the question: What do we do when we do what we do? The following points apply to all forms of practice:

- All practice is embodied and situated (in an ever-unfolding present).
- All observations require an observer.
- Everything said is said by someone.
- All knowing is doing.
- All being, knowing and doing is relational.
- All observers, practitioners and actors have a history, a tradition of understanding out of which they think and act.

Consider how Donald Trump practises being President of the USA compared with Barack Obama. Both operate within the same institutions (rules of the game), including the Constitution. But all institutions have to be enacted and what we see is how enactment of the same rules follows a different trajectory because of the different traditions of understanding of the two central players and their entourages. It is for this reason that we need to look to deliberative and embodied forms of practice to make future governance systems function. This involves accepting new explanations (including theories and metaphors), engaging in new practices (including listening), experiencing differences and building and sustaining new social relations. Collectively these actions are given the term praxis.

6.2.2.3 Understanding praxis and reflection-in-action

Not many people in academic, administrative and political life think of what they, and others, do in terms of practice or praxis. Praxis is purposeful action which acknowledges that all of our actions, our practices, are infused with history and that history comes in terms of explanations, including theories that we have internalised, or embodied throughout our life. Praxis failure is one of the main reasons why our governance systems are failing (see Box 6.2).

BOX 6.2 THE SYSTEMIC FAILURE OF 'JOINED-UP' GOVERNMENT IN THE UK[41]

In the 1990s, New Labour in the UK was elected espousing what Anthony Giddens had called the 'third way'.[42] How to do this was never clear. In the absence of an effective praxis, the third way sometimes became conflated with, or ran in parallel with, attempts to do joined-up government.[43] Ensuring different agencies worked together was part of New Labour's *Better Government* agenda, intended to reduce cost and improve quality and effectiveness of public services.

Systemically, joined-up government is essential, but it became a cliché. Traditional hierarchical structures and organisational silos limiting cooperation created 'the impression of dancing together while actually standing still'.[44] These institutionalised settings did not support its enactment (i.e. practice) and they failed to become conserved as a discourse coalition. According to Martin Hajer, discourse coalitions are characterised by practitioners whose ideas became elements of political practice moulded 'because of political ideology or choices for a particular organisational form'.[45] Praxis is central to how discourse coalitions operate. They constitute 'an ensemble of notions, ideas, concepts, and categorisations through which meaning is allocated to social and physical phenomena, and which is produced and reproduced'.[46] For example, the aspiration of this book is to contribute to the building of a discourse coalition for crafting governance systems fit for the Anthropocene. The shift we seek could fail as well. But our book does deliver an explication of praxis and a rationale for investing in systems praxis within new governance systems.

In contrast, as New Labour became more and more frustrated by the existing government machinery, it alighted on systematic means with targets[47] and other defining attributes of the new public management paradigm prevalent in government agencies at this time.[48] These had some effect for a while, but not being institutionalised, this waned with the passing of their sponsors. The 'targets culture' became endemic at considerable social cost.[49] In his book *The Whitehall Effect*, John Seddon examines the systemic consequences of the use of 'targets' by successive Conservative and Labour governments. The main unintended consequence was to distort behaviour and produce gaming of the targets, rather than employing a governance model that allowed localised interpretation of the phenomenon of concern and the generation of action that led to improvement (i.e. localised co-design).

Simon Caulkin[50] observed that:

> pursuing targets to the detriment of patient care may have caused the deaths of 400 people at Stafford [hospital] between 2005 and 2008. ... Put abstractly, targets distort judgment, disenfranchise professionals and wreck morale. Put concretely, in services where lives are at stake targets kill ... target-driven organisations are institutionally witless because they face the wrong way: towards ministers and target-setters, not customers or citizens. Accusing them of neglecting customers to focus on targets ... is like berating cats for eating small birds. That's what they do.

Using Caulkin's cat to explain how organisational targets operate exemplifies a *structure determined system*[51] – a cat does what it does because it is 'structured' by its evolutionary history. Those in government, or any organisation, also do what the organisation is structured to do. Behind the rising popularity for 'whole system change' is, we suggest, a desire to break out of the traps of structure determinism in governance by creating new organisational elements (as in Figure 4.1) and constituent structures (as discussed in Part 3).

Improving praxis, whilst necessary, is on its own not enough to break out of the traps described in Box 6.2. Let's explore a particular form of praxis to uncover the systemic dynamics involved. In choosing *research practice* or praxis we do so with a small *r* in the sense that anyone trying to act purposefully in relation to a situation of concern is involved in *research* practice. Enlightened, reflexive policy makers and politicians who practise governing need to see themselves in this light.

Purposeful activity that is undertaken with a view to exploring, understanding and acting to improve a situation must be done within 'a political ecology of

Understanding practice...?

P = practitioner
F = framework of ideas/theories:
framing choice for S
S = situation
M = method or methodology
◯ = tradition of understanding

FIGURE 6.4 A heuristic model designed to explore the systemic elements of a generic practice based on *researching*. The heuristic is based on awareness that all practice is situated, embodied and rarely done alone, and that to understand the relational dynamics of how practice functions, the practitioner (P) is extracted from the situation of concern (S).[52]

practice'. This demands certain skills – such as reflection in and on action, and reflexivity (the capacity to reflect on your own reflections, a second-order process) in order to remove from background to foreground awareness of one's own traditions of understanding so that they can be articulated, considered, explained and changed. Purposefully setting out to make the circumstances of practice more conducive to a beneficial outcome we will refer to as 'taking a design turn': acting with awareness that one can operate reflexively at the level of one's practice and also at the level of the context of practice, where enabling or constraining structures come into play (the 'design turn' is taken up again in Chapter 8).

Figure 6.4 is a way to explore practice in relational terms. Little *r* research differs from big **R** research in that it is not a specialised form of practice with its own culture and rules; it is more a sensibility with added capability.

To begin on a journey towards the design turn, to be engaged in genuinely reflexive praxis, *r*esearch has to be appreciated as involving: (i) the researcher/practitioner (P) with their traditions of understanding; (ii) a situation of concern (S) which is engaged with through a framing choice (F), whether knowingly or not, and/or a purpose-driven theoretical lens; (iii) choices about methodology or method (M); and (iv) the possibility of learning about S, M, F, P and the extent to which an effective 'researching performance' emerges from the interactions of these different elements.

Not many researchers (especially big R researchers) think of their practice in systemic terms. It can be claimed, however, that systemic appreciations of practice are well developed in some other fields, even if systems concepts and language are not used explicitly. For example,[53] according to Magnus Ramage, Donald Schön explains how a description of his musical experience, or practise, illuminates his most celebrated concept, that of 'reflection-in-action':

When good jazz musicians improvise together, they similarly display reflection-in-action smoothly integrated into ongoing performance. Listening to one another, listening to themselves, they 'feel' where the music is going and adjust their playing accordingly. A figure announced by one performer will be taken up by another, elaborated, turned into a new melody. Each player makes on-line inventions and responds to surprises triggered by the inventions of the other players. But the collective process of musical invention is organized around an underlying structure. There is a common schema of meter, melody, and harmonic development that gives the piece a predictable order. In addition, each player has at the ready a repertoire of musical figures around which he can weave variations as the opportunity arises. Improvisation consists in varying, combining, and recombining a set of figures within a schema that gives coherence to the whole piece. As the musicians feel the directions in which the music is developing, they make new sense of it. They reflect-in-action on the music they are collectively making – though not, of course, in the medium of words.[54]

According to Schön, we can both 'think about doing [and] … think about doing something while doing it'.[55] It is this process, where professionals improvise in the moment based on their past experience, that he terms reflection-in-action. One who reflects-in-action 'is not dependent on the categories of established theory and technique, but constructs a new theory of the unique case'.[56] This will become a vital competence in the Anthropocene, which will demand new levels of openness to surprise, uncertainty, complexity and 'not knowing'.

Building on Schön's example, we suggest that the praxis at the core of future governance must move to the idea of orchestrating, improvising and choreographing effective systemic performances. The rules can exist in a constitution or other institutions, but in an Anthropocene-world the exact same music can no longer be played unless accompanied by improvisation. In Chapter 5 when, after the 'Teignmouth tiff', the EA moved to Shaldon and from a DAD (Decide-Announce-Defend) approach to an EDD (Engage-Deliberate-Decide), they were engaged in reflexive praxis that choreographed an effective systemic governance performance. No doubt the new facilitator with their traditions of understanding was crucial, as understanding and use of systems concepts and methodologies, even if not espoused as such, were needed (i.e. systems literacy was needed to invent new forms of governance in that situation).

To be effective on a greater scale will require the capacity to reflect on the practice performances so that designs, choreographies and conducive institutions can scale-up situated governance effectiveness. These new 'governance systems' will need to be inhabited by capable systems thinking practitioners.

But to move in this direction, there is first a need to reframe another current mainstream impediment – that of knowledge.

6.2.3 From knowledge to knowing-based praxis

To make the shift towards STiP capability requires an embodied way of knowing about knowing. We live in a world that understands knowledge as a thing,
substance-like, that exists independently of the process, or praxis of knowing.
This is another failure to frame pairs as dualities, viz.: knowing/knowledge
like theory/practice. Alongside reflection-in-action, Schön developed another
important concept to address this conundrum: knowing-in-action is

> how we actually embody and work with knowledge: 'when we go about
> the spontaneous, intuitive performance of the actions of everyday life,
> [when] we show ourselves to be knowledgeable in a special way ... our
> knowing is ordinarily tacit, implicit in our patterns of action and in our
> feel for the stuff with which we are dealing. It seems right to say that our
> knowing is in our action'.[57]

The 'systematic paradigm' as we articulate it, is aligned with what Cook and
Seely Brown[58] call 'knowledge as possession' because it treats knowledge as
something people, groups or organisations possess. Instead, they argue, 'this
epistemology [theory of knowledge] cannot account for the knowing found in
individual and group practice'. They hold that 'knowledge is a tool of knowing,
that knowing is an aspect of our interaction with the social and physical world,
and that the interplay of knowledge and knowing can generate new knowledge
and new ways of knowing'.[59] They call this a generative dance between knowledge and knowing. They argue with evidence that this movement is a powerful
source of organisational innovation.

The practical implications of this de-framing of 'knowledge' and reframing as
the duality of 'knowledge and knowing' are profound. They range from the recognition that context-sensitive action and co-design of public policy is needed
for effective governance and the realisation that commissioning of reports to
produce 'new knowledge' in no way guarantees the generation and enactment
of effective policy. The Shaldon vignette in Chapter 5 exemplifies a shift from
knowledge to knowing-based praxis. In DAD, what is declared is articulated scientific, expert or political knowledge which leads to a need to impose or defend
this knowledge against other, localised and contextualised ways of knowing that
are revealed by the EDD approach. We say more about this in Part 3.

6.3 Towards STiP capability for governing

Central to systems thinking – and thus praxis – is being able to move between
levels of understanding, or abstraction. A classic systems diagram such as Figure 6.1
depicts a layered structure of nested systems or subsystems. Interpreting such a
diagram requires a systemic sensibility, plus some systems literacy, so that the form
of the relational dynamics between elements can be appreciated. The Romans

realised this phenomenon through their god, Janus, who expressed the idea of seasons passing, or going from inside to outside through a door or gate.[60] Remaining focused on, or overinvested in, the systematic at the expense of the systemic is a recipe for despair.

6.3.1 Ashby's Law on variety

An apt vignette about coming to systems literacy is from Ed's consultancy career. This began in a jam factory in 1977, identifying and correcting the causes of low productivity. Later, arriving in 'the centre', Whitehall (UK), he thought he would finally find where it all happened: the Cabinet Office, the Department of Environment, Food and Rural Affairs, the Ministry of Justice, amongst others. Surely, the closer he got to the top, the more the errors below would be corrected. Someone would be making a decision, pulling on a large lever, and real improvement would be occurring in some distant place. It is not called the 'government machine' for nothing, he thought. With a few exceptions, the reverse was the case. He learnt that it is not possible to run much when dealing with 50 million people. Contrast this with, say, a Scotland of 5 million or comparatively high-functioning governments like Finland, Singapore and Switzerland of about 7 million. Much later, he found out why: *Ashby's Law of Requisite Variety* formulated in the 1950s.[61]

John Naughton claims that Ashby's Law is the scientific concept that should be more widely known. In colloquial terms he describes Ashby's Law as a simple proposition:

> if a system is to be able to deal successfully with the diversity of challenges that its environment produces, then it needs to have a repertoire of responses which is (at least) as nuanced as the problems thrown up by the environment. So a viable system is one that can handle the variability *of its environment. Or, as Ashby put it, only variety can absorb variety.*

So if a control system like senior management, or a central government, is unable to deal with, respond to, learn from or decide for based on the feedback from within an organisation and its operating environment, or from the governed, then control begins to fail. The only antidote is to match variety with variety, such as pushing down decision making in an organisation, or with citizens, to allow timely feedback to function in the face of localised surprise and uncertainty.[62]

Knowing about Ashby's Law comes with systems literacy. Using it to good effect moves from literacy to STiP capability. For example, understanding that to control the criminal justice system for 50 million people means that those in the centre need to know as much as is known in all its components of prisons, police forces, courts and so on. Otherwise there will never be sufficient capacity to understand the nuances of operation and performance in each of the many components. Knowing Ashby's Law enables insight and makes more effective decisions and designs possible (Part 3). At the moment, it does not get much of an airing in government offices, nor is it acknowledged by leaders with high control needs. The urge for power is too great to understand that centralisation has very substantial limits. It is a spurious form of control. In the Anthropocene, central control cannot work, no matter how it is done.

6.3.2 Struggles to build a STiP praxis •

In 2015 in the encyclical *Laudato Si*, Pope Francis claimed that 'nothing in this world is indifferent to us [human beings]'. He went on to say that

> More than fifty years ago, with the world teetering on the brink of nuclear crisis, Pope Saint John XXIII wrote an Encyclical which not only rejected war but offered a proposal for peace. He addressed his message *Pacem in Terris* to the entire "Catholic world" and indeed "to all men and women of goodwill". Now, faced as we are with global environmental deterioration, I wish to address every person living on this planet.

He said:

- Given the scale of change, it is no longer possible to find a specific, discrete answer for each part of the problem. It is essential to seek comprehensive solutions which consider the interactions within natural systems themselves and with social systems.
- We are faced not with two separate crises, one environmental and the other social, but rather with one complex crisis which is both social and environmental.
- When we speak of the 'environment', what we really mean is a relationship existing between nature and the society which lives in it.
- Nature cannot be regarded as something separate from ourselves or as a mere setting in which we live. We are part of nature, included in it and thus in constant interaction with it. Recognising the reasons why a given area is polluted requires a study of the workings of society, its economy, its behaviour patterns and the ways it grasps reality.

At the same time as Pope Francis was preparing his encyclical, the Chinese Communist Party was preparing its *13th Five-Year Plan for Ecological & Environmental Protection* (2016–2020). This plan said:

'The plan … supports the "wars" against air, water and soil pollution. The plan has three core missions – to raise the quality of the environment, to strengthen holistic management solutions and to speed up the amendment of environmental issues'.

Water is again a key aspect of the plan. Here are the six general aims for improving China's water resources' quality from 2016 to 2020:

1. 'Establish unit-based management of water resource quality.
2. Establish holistic, basin-wide strategies to tackle pollution.
3. Prioritise protection of good-quality water bodies.
4. Establish holistic strategies to tackle groundwater pollution.
5. Strongly improve polluted urban water bodies.
6. Improve water quality of river mouth and nearshore areas'.[63]

Both of these documents reveal an intrinsic systemic sensibility and authors with some systems literacy. Each offers helpful and necessary systemic understandings. What is missing are references to, or strategies for, deploying systems thinking in practice capabilities (STiP). In both cases, the question arises as to whether capability exists to do what the authors seek to have done.[64] What lessons have been learnt that can inform strategies such as these?

6.3.3 Lessons from STiP education: concepts to work with

As discussed earlier, the Open University (OU) has been designing and delivering 'learning systems' about Systems for mature age students since the early 1970s. A lot has been learnt about recovering systemic sensibility, building literacy and fostering STiP capability.[65] At the same time as the concept system has gone feral, systems literacy in the general population, especially in the UK, less so in Germany, seems to have declined.[66] For many people a computer and its connections became THE system. As we write, there is a resurgence in interest across the globe in 'whole system change'. This creates possibilities but also danger if the capacity and capability to do 'system-change' fails for want of investment in praxis capability and conducive institutions.

In the OU model for learning systems thinking, the term 'system-of-interest' is employed as a means of taking responsibility for 'the system anyone is seeking to develop. This means that any system has to be seen, designed or imagined by someone or some group because they hope to understand, change or improve a situation by using the concept system. Thus, a system-of-interest is the product of distinguishing a system in a situation, in relation to an articulated purpose, in which an individual or a group has an interest (a stake). A constructed or formulated system-of-interest to one or more people is used in a process of inquiry. It is a term used to avoid confusion with the everyday use of the noun 'system'. Like the example of how a circle happens when 'taking a line for a walk', a system-of-interest is formulated when someone makes a boundary judgment that distinguishes, or mediates a relationship between a system and its environment (that which surrounds). Following this logic opens up a creative path of practice. For example, for the purpose of learning, we could perceive the current Conservative Party in Britain *as if* it were

- a system to deliver Brexit (departure from the EU)
- a system to impose right-wing ideology

- a system to generate dysfunctional government
- a system for the Conservative party to maintain political power.

or myriad other possible systems-of-interest. The point here is not to start out by claiming *ex ante* that a system exists. Doing this is a system-as-ontology, or systems-are-real choice that is central to the mainstream systematic tradition. The practice response in this pathway is to produce knowledge about systems. The alternative, complementary and less common path is to ask: In the complex and uncertain situation of governing, what might we learn if we were to create or imagine some purposeful systems-of-interest? The product of this design, or co-design, is an epistemological device, a way of knowing systemically about a situation of concern. Having started, we could look at what a given system-of-interest does and how this contrasts with what those in the situation say they do. Systemic improvements can be identified and if the key people are involved in the process, what is culturally feasible changes as a result of joint learning. Pursuing this line of inquiry will reveal elements and relations, or non-relations, between elements. This systems praxis approach can be adopted in any situation of uncertainty, complexity, mess or 'wickedness' where gaining systemic insights for effecting understanding and change might be useful. It can even be used to explore how *a system to understand and change existing power relations in situation X* might function.

Choosing between the systemic pathways (seeing systems as epistemological devices, ways of facilitating knowing about situations) and the systematic pathway of acting as if systems were real is not an either/or choice but is best regarded as a duality as depicted earlier in Figure 6.2. Treating systemic/systematic praxis as a duality makes sense because in certain circumstances, linear cause and effect thinking is needed and is exceptionally powerful in the right settings. Unfortunately, we have overinvested in the systematic at the expense of the systemic.

Experience at the OU based on the actions of their mature-age, generally work-based, students evidences just how useful STiP can be. Some lessons learnt include:

- There is a need to provide students with as many systemic pathways to effect action for change as possible; the adage followed is that being ethical involves acting to keep open as many choices as possible, so ethics is part of what we do, not a code to follow, and can be connected to the idea of maintaining our evolutionary possibilities, a key to governing.
- OU systems academics have had to look at their own ethics of action when feedback indicated that systems students sometimes suffered for their new-found enthusiasm for STiP. Some reported having to be silent about their learning in the workplace, or that their new understandings meant they could no longer tolerate their organisations. Stories of students choosing to change career became common. New OU modules thus take a second-order approach in their design so that students learn about their own STiP, but also, through committing to a 'design turn', learn to consider the purposeful design of situations in which they and their own STiP can flourish.

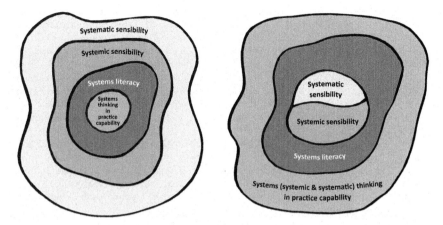

FIGURE 6.5 Where we are (left) – where the systematic dominates, and where we need to be (right), with the shift to a wave-front of individuals with expanded systems thinking in practice capability.[67]

We can choose to think of humans as being naturally endowed with systemic sensibility (as depicted in Figure 6.5 – left), which has become subsumed in, or overwhelmed by, a more encompassing systematic sensibility. The great challenge humanity faces is to flip this situation so that all citizens become aware of, and in touch with, both a systemic and systematic sensibility at the core of our being (Figure 6.5 – right). To enable this shift, investment is needed in systems literacy and a citizenry endowed with STiP capabilities. Moving along this pathway to develop and enact new systems of governance will require adeptness in using the concept 'system' and all that it entails.

Sometimes systems is described as a meta or trans-discipline. Mike Jackson once said systems was 'a handmaiden to all other disciplines' (as is, perhaps mathematics).[68] Like all intellectual fields, there are many lineages with commonalities and differences and a myriad of methodologies, techniques and tools with which to take advantage of systems concepts like those used in this chapter and included in the Glossary. Having sharpened your systemic sensibilities and opened a pathway towards systems literacy and STIP capability, in Part 3 we offer STiP-informed improvements for governance systems.

Notes

1 The UK Open University (OU), established in 1969, is Britain's largest university, with 68,000 full-time-equivalent students in 2019. This equates to over 150,000 part-time, mature-age students, as well as about 500 research and full-time doctoral students. Production of a module, formerly called a course, entails investment of £250–750K.

2 This is the number of students who have studied some systems in one of their courses since 1972.

3 More needs to be known about the experiences of these OU students through empirical investigation; these claims are consistent with a limited number of empirical studies, such as the work of Marcia Salner: see Salner, M. 1986. Adult cognitive and epistemological development, in systems education. *Systems Research* 4: 223–232.

4 Labels are given to these three cohorts with some trepidation, as they are open to misinterpretation; these are chosen to convey the sense of 'resistance' to power and the dominant discourses that Foucault articulates. 'Revivalists' has a born-again feel – though in the sense used here it is an intellectual awakening and the emergence of reflexive capabilities; use of the term 'remainer' is not taken from the UK Brexit/Remain dualism, but to imply the more general desire to stay or defend where one is at.

5 Some claim that evolution functions by conserving lineages of manners of living; a young human is born into one or more languages and conditions which have, or do not have, love, food, attention, reciprocity, etc. The argument here is that children born into a world rich with relational stimuli that are experienced as positive emotions (e.g. love and acceptance rather than fear, abuse), favours systemic sensibility expression and expansion.

6 In Chapter 4 the terms technosphere and biosphere were explained in detail.

7 Adapted from: Ison, R.L. 2018. Governing the human-environment relationship: systemic practice. *Current Opinion in Environmental Sustainability* 33, 114–123. https://doi.org/10.1016/j.cosust.2018.05.009.

8 A term for 'economic man' which rests on the ideology that by using rational assessments *Homo economicus* attempts to maximise utility as a consumer and economic profit as a producer.

9 https://www.bbc.com/news/health-43674270 (Accessed 30 November 2018).

10 To exemplify the argument, we draw on a BBC Discovery programme devoted to the latest research into humans' second genome.

11 https://www.bbc.co.uk/programmes/w3csxgw4#play (Accessed 16 April 2019).

12 https://www.bbc.co.uk/programmes/w3csxgw3 (Accessed 16 April 2019).

13 https://www.bbc.co.uk/programmes/w3csxgw5 (Accessed 16 April 2019).

14 Enders, G. 2015. *Gut. The Inside Story of Our Body's Most Under-Rated Organ.* Vancouver: Greystone Books.

15 https://americanindian.si.edu/visit (Accessed 11 October 2018).

16 https://en.wikipedia.org/wiki/Bruce_Chatwin (Accessed 11 October 2018).

17 But most agriculture is sedentary and some farmers do not look over the fence and see the broader landscape in which their farming functions; versions of acting locally whilst thinking globally are still required.

18 Kuhn, G. 2016. Tricking the brain: how magic works. *The Conversation.* https://theconversation.com/tricking-the-brain-how-magic-works-56451 (Accessed 16 April 2019); https://www.youtube.com/watch?v=-_2mj1pwveo (Accessed 16 April 2019).

19 These questions have been inspired by Humberto Maturana apart from question 2, which was inspired by Gregory Bateson.

20 Ison, R.L. 2017. op. cit.

21 https://en.wikipedia.org/wiki/William_Bateson (Accessed 16 April 2019).

22 There is a track record of this happening when SSM (soft systems methodology) was designated by the government of the UK for use in large IT project commissioning – which in terms of effecting better governance failed through poor practice and weak institutions.

23 Austen, J. 1811. *Sense and Sensibility.* London: Penguin Classics.

24 See Ison, R.L, and Straw, E. 1 March 2018. Duality, dualism, duelling and Brexit. *OpenDemocracy* https://www.opendemocracy.net/can-europe-make-it/ed-straw-ray-ison/duality-dualism-duelling-and-brexit (Accessed 17 February 2019); O'Brien, K. 2016. Climate change and social transformations: Is it time for a quantum leap? *WIREs Climate Change* 7(5): 618–626.

25 Emotioning was coined by Humberto Maturana as a means for 'releasing a dynamic from "thingness"; the word "emotioning" is a neologism, it is not (yet) found in the dictionary. However, it follows a perfectly standard grammatical rule that enables what is usually a verb (e.g. run) to be used as a noun (running). Thus it implicates that "emotion" should have been a verb, and we now have a noun form "emotioning" so we can refer to the general case of that happening'. http://www.sympoetic.net/Emoti oning/emotioning.html (Accessed 12 October 2018).

26 Ison, R.L. 2017. *Systems Practice: How to Act. In Situations of Uncertainty and Complexity in a Climate-change World.* 2nd Ed. London: Springer, and The Open University.

27 Ison, R.L. 2016. Governing in the Anthropocene: What future systems thinking in practice? *Systems Research & Behavioral Science* 33 (5): 595–613.

28 Lakoff, G. and Johnson, M. 1999. *Philosophy in The Flesh: The Embodied Mind and Its Challenge to Western Thought.* New York: HarperCollins Publishers.

29 For a contemporary overview of how human cognition works see the following Ted Talk – https://www.ted.com/talks/anil_seth_how_your_brain_hallucinates_your_c onscious_reality#t-1008861.

30 After Lakoff, G. and Johnson, M. 1999. op. cit., pp. 552–557.

31 https://spinalresearch.com.au/three-brains-head-heart-gut-sometimes-conflict/ (Accessed 17 February 2019).

32 Rittel, H.W.J. and Webber, M.M. 1973. Dilemmas in a general theory of planning. *Policy Sciences* 4 (2): 155–169.

33 Meadows, D. 1997. Places to intervene in a system. *Whole Earth.* Winter.

34 Adapted from: Morecroft, J. 2010. Systems dynamics. In *Systems Approaches to Managing Change: A Practical Guide.* Reynolds, M. & Holwell, S., eds. London: Springer, and The Open University. The system dynamic model is derived from Sterman, John D. 2000. *Business Dynamics: Systems Thinking and Modeling for a Complex World.* McGraw Hill. No. HD30. 2 S7835 2000.

35 https://en.wikipedia.org/wiki/Political_ecology (Accessed 11th October 2018).

36 Krippendorff, K. 1993. Major metaphors of communication and some constructivist reflections on their use. *Cybernetics & Human Knowing* 2 (1): 3–25.

37 Brown, L. ed. 1993. *The New Shorter Oxford English Dictionary.* Oxford: Oxford University Press.

38 Blackmore, C. and Ison, R.L. 2007. Boundaries for thinking and action. In *Research Skills for Policy and Development: How to Find Out Fast.* Eds. Thomas, A. and Mohan, G. London: SAGE Publications.

39 In this sense we are cognitively autonomous but not cognitively independent, as the relational dynamics with our surroundings are highly influential on our overall cognitive development, especially through childhood.

40 Russell, D.B. and Ison, R.L. 2007. The research-development relationship in rural communities: an opportunity for contextual science. In *Agricultural Extension and Rural Development: Breaking Out of Knowledge Transfer Traditions.* Eds. Ison, R.L and Russell, D.B., pp. 10–31. Cambridge: Cambridge University Press.

41 Adapted from: Ison, R.L. et al. 2018. op. cit.

42 Giddens, A. 1998. *The Third Way. The Renewal of Social Democracy.* Cambridge: Polity.

43 See Ling, T. 2002. Delivering joined-up government in the UK: dimensions, issues and problems. *Public Administration* 80 (4): 615–642.

44 Mackie, D. 1999. Dancing while standing still. *Streetwise: The Magazine of Urban Studies* 37–68.

45 Hajer, M. 1995. *The Politics of Environmental Discourse, Ecological Modernization and the Policy Process.* Oxford: Oxford University Press; Hajer, M. 2009. *Policy Making in the Age of Mediatization.* Oxford: Oxford University Press; Hajer, M. and Dassen, T. 2014. *Smart about Cities. Visualising the Challenge for 21st Century Urbanism.* Sydney: naio10 Publishers/PBL Publishers,.20.

46 Hajer, M. 2009; ibid., 59–60.

47 Barber, M., Moffit, A., and Kihn, P. 2010. *Deliverology 101: A Field Guide for Educational Leaders*. Corwin: Thousand Oaks.

48 McLaughlin K., Osborne, S.P., and Ferlie, E. eds. 2002. *New Public Management: Current Trends and Future Prospects*. Abingdon: Routledge; Straw, E. 2014. *Stand and Deliver. A Design for Successful Government*. London: Treaty for Government.

49 Seddon, J. 2008. *Systems Thinking in the Public Sector*. Axminster: Triarchy Press; O'Donovan, B. 2014. The Vanguard method in a systems thinking context. *Systemic Practice and Action Research* 27 (1): 1–20; Pell, C., ed. 2012. *Delivering Public Services that Work*, vol 2. Axminster: Triarchy Press.

50 Caulkin, S. 2009. This isn't an abstract problem. Targets can kill. *The Observer, Business*. http://www.theguardian.com/business/2009/mar/22/policy (Accessed 22 Feb 2015).

51 A structure determined system is explained in the Glossary (Appendix 2).

52 Ison, R.L. 2017. op. cit.

53 Donald Schön (1930–1997), widely appreciated as the originator of the concept of the 'reflective practitioner', spent a lifetime providing insightful answers as to how individuals, groups, and organisations could become more reflexive. His work was grounded in urban planning and design but has been extremely influential in education, management, social work, law, and many other fields – see Ramage, M. 2017. Learning and change in the work of Donald Schön: Reflection on theory and theory on reflection. In *The Palgrave Handbook of Organisational Change Thinkers*, D.B. Szabla et al., eds. DOI 10.1007/978-3-319-49820-1_57-1.

54 Schön, D. 1987. *Educating the Reflective Practitioner: Toward a New Design for Teaching and Learning in the Professions*. San Francisco: Jossey-Bass. 30.

55 Ibid., p. 54.

56 Ibid., p. 68.

57 Ramage, M. 2017. op. cit. 49; Schön, D. 1983. *The Reflective Practitioner: How Professionals Think in Action*. New York: Basic Books.

58 Cook, S.D.N. and Brown, J.S. 1999. Bridging epistemologies: The generative dance between organisational knowledge and organisational knowing. *Organisational Science* 10 (4), July–August.

59 Just as the concept 'system' can be used as an epistemological tool for knowing.

60 Janus was sometimes called the God of Doors. Arthur Koestler in his book *Janus. A Summing Up* employed Janus as his image of a duality, from which he argued that order and stability arise as 'an alternative to despair'.

61 See Naughton, J. 2017. *What Scientific Term or Concept Ought to Be More Widely Known?* for how Ashby's Law could be used more in many more situations of concern. https://www.edge.org/response-detail/27150 (Accessed 7 December 2018).

62 Ibid.

63 http://chinawaterrisk.org/notices/chinas-13th-five-year-plan-2016-2020/ (Accessed 16 April 2019).

64 For example, in China, as Philip Ball cogently argues, despite a new environmental law in 2015 there are strong arguments that this law fails to acknowledge a citizen's basic right to an environment fit for life (p. 313). In other words the environment is not yet 'afforded the highest level of priority on a par with laws directed at promoting economic growth and controlling population'. There is also widespread fear that failure to deal with water problems will destabilise the whole of society (p. 308). Ball, P. 2016. *The Water Kingdom. A Secret History of China*. London: Vintage.

65 See Ison, R.L. 2016. op. cit.

66 A reason for this is that the German secondary education system contains material about systems, especially the sociology of Niklas Luhmann. In contrast, one would find it hard to find systems and cybernetic understandings anywhere in the UK curriculum. In the US, the Waters Foundation has invested in developing systems

literacy in schools – see http://watersfoundation.org/wp-content/uploads/2017/07/STIS_Research.pdf (Accessed 12 October 2018).

67 Adapted from: Ison, R.L. and Shelley, M.A. 2016. Governing in the Anthropocene: Contributions from systems thinking in practice? *Systems Research and Behavioral Science* 33 (5): 589–594.

68 Jackson, M. (personal communication, 1996).

PART 3

Using systems thinking in practice for governing

Navigating our way into the future. Some of the 'oars' that will have to be used and renewed.

7

REINVENTING GOVERNANCE SYSTEMS

I have decided not to leave the country. The system has to leave.[1]

7.1 Governing in three dimensions

The challenge we have set in this book is to articulate how to govern in the Anthropocene in three dimensions. In Chapter 2 we introduced the four elements of the old model and pointed to dysfunctionalities within each of them. In Chapter 3 we explored the emergent properties arising from their relationships, and how and why the old governance model is failing. In Chapter 4 we proposed the addition of three new elements to our original model (Figure 4.1). These changes are akin to the atomic structures of elements, additions that change the whole configuration, create new relational dynamics and produce something new. A new chemistry emerges. In Chapter 5 we gave examples of local change being governed by systems thinking and in Chapter 6 highlighted the shift from systemic sensibility, to systems literacy and STiP capability.

Two challenges present themselves: how to move from the old to the new (Figure 7.1), and how to make the new model functional in ways that enhance, or do not restrict, the shift. In this chapter we consider some factors that might either constrain or enhance the shift. The next chapter (Chapter 8) is primarily concerned with practices and institutions that will make the new model more functional.

7.1.1 Reinvention takes second-order change

Adding the biosphere, technosphere and social purpose to our governance system sets the agenda for second-order change. Here we explore what it means

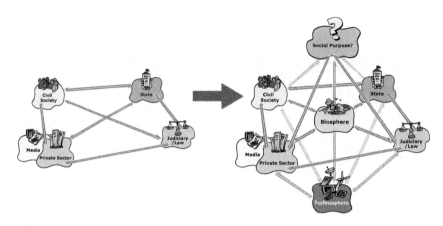

FIGURE 7.1   A key challenge – how to transform for governing in the Anthropocene: from an ill-prepared two-dimensional set of relationships (left) to a three-dimensional governance diamond (right).[2]

to realise that agenda. As with fish, the first step is to recognise the water you are in.[3] Awareness is necessary to recognise first-order change and then to ask: 'What about second-order change?'

Recent research from the OECD's Office for Public Sector Innovation (OPSI) suggests that reforms to governance based on systems thinking in practice (STiP) are possible. They say that: 'Governments are redefining the boundaries between themselves and their citizens in important ways [that] help to provide more inclusive, transparent and accountable governments, which can further amplify the power of innovation'.[4] Success has citizen engagement at its core:

> Innovative governments are enhancing citizen engagement and ensuring public involvement at every stage of the policy cycle: from shaping ideas to designing, delivering and monitoring services. The goal is not only to improve the type and quality of services that governments provide, but also to transform the culture of government so that citizens are seen as partners who can shape and inform policy and services.[5]

The OECD is facilitating a new set of relationships between the state and, mainly, civil society. Several themes have emerged from this work:

- Governments are pursuing multiple approaches to involving citizens in promoting innovation.
- Governments are renegotiating what it means to be an expert through active participation and co-creation of policies and services by their citizens.
- Governments are linking citizen engagement to other key initiatives.

Key recommendations from the OPSI studies include to

- Develop government-wide engagement strategies.
- Arm public employees and citizens with tools to connect and establish dialogue.
- Build evaluation into the innovation process.
- Take feedback into account and reconnect with citizens.
- Not accept the system as a given.
- Undertake systems analysis through an innovation lens.
- Invest in human capacity.
- Encourage cross-government networks.[6]

If imbued with systemic sensibility, systems literacy and – most importantly – STiP capability, these recommendations offer a formidable agenda for change. But what happens when civil servants and the like participate in OECD processes and leave knowing that the system they work in is no longer acceptable? Are they equipped to engage in second-order change or condemned to valiant efforts that ultimately make little difference? We raise this issue because there has been no shortage of recommendations in recent years as to how the dynamics between the state, business and civil society should play out. For example, in a paper outlining the public policy implications of 'wicked problems', the then Australian Public Service (APSC) Commissioner said:[7] 'Tackling wicked problems requires a broad recognition and understanding, including from governments and Ministers, that there are no quick fixes and simple solutions'.

The APSC paper authors assert that

> tackling wicked problems ... calls for high levels of systems thinking ... thinking [that] helps policy makers to make the connections between the multiple causes and interdependencies of wicked problems that are necessary in order to avoid a narrow approach and the artificial taming of wicked problems. Agencies need to look for ways of developing or obtaining this range of skills.[8]

This is a call for investment in STiP capability.

In a presentation entitled 'New modes of policy implementation call for new capabilities',[9] the same APSC head described the necessary capabilities as paying attention to problem framing and boundary setting; generating fresh thinking on intractable problems (i.e. generating multiple, partial perspectives); working across organisational and disciplinary boundaries; making effective decisions in situations characterised by high levels of uncertainty (see Chapter 10); being able to tolerate rapid change in the way problems are defined; and engaging stakeholders as joint decision makers, not just providers or recipients of services. She went on to say that not all public servants will need to work this way all the time (some may not be affected at all), but many will be confronted by ambiguous and complex problems at some point. She also emphasised that 'it's important for senior levels of the public service to exercise the kinds of leadership that these problems require'.[10]

If both the APSC and the OECD know what has to be done, how can it be enacted? How can their proposed reforms and those advocated by many governmental organisations, researchers and individual thinkers be made to happen and stick? First-order change – what some describe as doing the wrong thing righter – has not worked. Second-order change, a change-of-change that changes the 'whole system' is concerned with developing new ways of thinking and acting to break out of the traps we have created for ourselves – of learning how to do the right thing for current circumstances.

As early as 1969 Rittel and Webber had come to the view that

> the difficulties attached to rationality are tenacious, and we have so far been unable to get untangled from their web. This is partly because the classical paradigm of science and engineering--the paradigm that has underlain modern professionalism--is not applicable to the problems of open societal systems.[11]

Fifty years later, this 'high ground of technical rationality', as Donald Schön described the mainstream position, along with pervasive structural constraints, restricts second-order change.[12] Despite this awareness, and the active campaigning and actions of many well-informed and committed citizens and activists, it is difficult to discern if we are in a glass-half-full or glass-half-empty scenario. The challenge is to effect a shift from the old model to the new (Figure 7.1). We can't do this with an eyes-wide-shut strategy.

7.2 Overcoming ill-prepared governance systems

Overcoming denial requires constant critical scrutiny through public fora that are transparent and well managed. Creating self-organising civil-society institutions that can become progenitors of a new institutional ecology within the new social purpose node (Figures 7.1) seems the most likely innovation pathway to effect second-order change. One example would be a standing citizens' convention on the constitution (as an institutional reification of social purpose) so that it is open to adaptation and change when needed (see Chapter 9). Chapter 10 sets out forms and methods of operationalising feedback.

Crop plants may not flourish because of plants that we call weeds. The same analogy applies to governance. There are weedy institutions that must be removed or controlled if second-order change is to succeed. This involves opening space for change.[13] One way of doing this is to extend governance thinking and practice to the long term. China's Belt and Road initiative, which seeks to resume China's 2000+ year historical role in world affairs, is a case in point, though not without its limitations and detractors. Reframing the Tibetan Plateau and the associated Himalayas as the world's 'third pole', along with the Arctic and Antarctic and investing in a new 'Third Pole' research institute are examples of innovation in framing, language, discourse and institutional innovation, all with significant geopolitical strategic intent given the pressures on water and food emerging in the Anthropocene.

All systems of governing need institutions for the long term. Some exist but are poorly integrated into governance. Other possibilities can be invented, such as a 'Congress for the Future'.[14] A primary criterion must be to acknowledge, from the start, the uncertainty and complexity of situations. Systematic project conception and management – vital for fixed outcomes in construction – has no place for fuzzier situations where it should be replaced by systemic inquiry and co-inquiry (see Chapter 8).

Market mechanisms – having created much of the problem – have also the potential to break out of institutional rigidities. The insurance industry and prudential regulation authorities have read the writing on the wall – or the excess claims from climate extremes and pollution. Fossil-fuel phase-out strategies, well-orchestrated divestment campaigns and investment in climate solutions are making inroads. These involve 'removal of investment assets including stocks, bonds, and investment funds from companies involved in extracting fossil fuels, in an attempt to reduce climate change by tackling its ultimate causes'.[15] In some regards this is easy compared to technology, where we are on a steep learning curve.

7.2.1 Developing biosphere sensibility and literacy

The addition of the biosphere as central to governance systems is intended in part to address the 'hole-at-the heart' of our Western cosmology. This absence is explored by Knudtson and Suzuki in their book *Wisdom of the Elders*.[16] The biosphere takes many forms in different indigenous societies and, most importantly, it remains present in most. The Dreaming Laws of the Yarralin community on the edges of the Timor Sea in Northern Australia as interpreted by Deborah Rose-Bird suggest some possible transcendent rules:[17]

- Balance – a system cannot be life enhancing if it is out of kilter, and each part shares in the responsibility of sustaining itself and balancing others.
- Response – communication is reciprocal. There is here a moral obligation: to learn to understand, to pay attention and to respond.
- Symmetry – in opposing and balancing each other, parts must be equivalent because the purpose is not to win or to dominate, but to block, thereby producing further balance.
- Autonomy – no species, no group or country is 'boss' for another; each adheres to its own law. Authority and dependence are necessary within parts, but not between parts.

Developing practices and institutions that can invent and then enact such rules is the challenge moving forward.

The biosphere, as we have framed it, can speak for itself through volcanic eruptions, earthquakes, storms, hurricanes, tornadoes. and the feedback dynamics that are due to human impact on the biosphere (see Preface), but it is poorly equipped – at least within Western sensibilities – to be a deliberative, negotiating partner in generating new governing praxes and/or inventing new governance institutions. Of course, if humans ceased to exist, the biosphere would continue and the technosphere would stop developing (though for many years it would leave a significant footprint). As we humans are making and remaking the biosphere and the technosphere, then we must take responsibility for our actions and their systemic implications. Doing this could be understood as reawakening our systemic sensibilities in ways still functional in some indigenous societies.

Currently our relationship with the biosphere is given agency through investing in international conventions and agreements, environmental/sustainability education, sustainability science, environmental regulations, and some dedicated environmental courts; organisations such as environmental protection agencies (EPAs), environmental NGOs, social enterprises and advocacy groups, including divestment campaigns; commissioning and carrying out environmental assessments, EIAs, etc.; philanthropy; environmental activism and 'green' purchasing or consumption. Many dedicated individuals are 'greening' current activities such as corporate social/environmental responsibility.

Despite this impressive plethora of pathways, the biosphere still holds insufficient power in our governance arrangements. This arises because the biosphere does not feature at the next level up, and these pathways thus have insufficient power – they can be only first-order change. With the biosphere empowered, then the role and functioning of these and other pathways can become efficacious.

7.2.2 Taking responsibility for the technosphere

It is also unclear what institutions, and thus governance arrangements exist, or could exist, for governing the technosphere. Past attempts at governing technology have met with limited success, mainly because all initiatives were couched within a framing of accelerating or sustaining economic growth, or securing human progress through unfettered technological development. Too often when technology is mentioned, thinking stops at the thing, or artefact. Instead, a systemic appreciation is needed.

As Joseph Murphy argues: 'technology mediates the relationship between environment and society because it transforms the world in relation to the production and reproduction of our lives'.[18] Technology commentator John Naughton explains our predicament:[19] 'Corporate giants have created an entirely new surveillance capitalism. And we're too hooked to care'. He goes on to say:

> 'From the moment the internet first opened for semi-public use in January 1983, it evoked utopian dreams. It was easy to see why. Cyberspace—the term coined by the novelist William Gibson for the virtual space behind the

screen—really did seem to be a parallel universe to "meatspace," the term invented by Grateful-Dead-lyricist-turned-essayist John Perry Barlow for the messy physical world that we all inhabit. Cyberspace in the 1980s was a glorious sandpit for geeks: a world with no corporations, no crime, no spam, no hate speech, relatively civil discourse, no editorial gatekeepers, no regulation and no role for those meatspace masters whom Barlow called the "weary giants of flesh and steel." But then, gradually, the internet was commercialised and those two parallel spaces merged to create our networked world, in which the affordances of cyberspace combine with surveillance and corporate control.

Even this technology romantic (and technology writer for *The Observer*) now sees regulation as a good thing.[20] But is regulation enough? Yet another case of necessary, perhaps, but not sufficient.

7.2.2.1 How technology functions in a social system

To incorporate the technosphere into a new governance system one has to first appreciate what technology is, how it functions in a social system and the systemic relations between people, the biosphere and governance arrangements. Murphy referred to this as the people-technology-governance nexus.[21,22]

So, what is and isn't a technology? The word technology comes from the Greek *techne*, often translated as 'craftsmanship', 'craft' or 'art'. When we think of technology as a thing, then we corrupt its etymology, as the crafting dimension is lost, as is the 'ology' – the field of study or discourse. Today social technologies can be distinguished from artefactual technologies. The potential advantage of reframing institutions as social technologies is that it makes possible a move from seeing institutions as things to seeing them as mediators of human action (or non-action), as in the hammer example in Fig. 4.3.

An example of an artefactual technology is an iPhone. But iPhones had inventors, designers, engineers, marketers and institutional-arrangement users and creators such as pricing policy people before the phone was ever sold to a user. When it comes to a user, then the basic process is no different to when a chimp uses a handy stick to get termites out of a mound. A relational dynamic, a practice, is created between an artefact and a user. Sometimes we are conscious of this dynamic, sometimes it fades into the background, or is hidden. When hidden, the artefact can be said to have designs that use us rather than the other way around.

In other circumstances, what was a relational dynamic breaks down and the artefactual components become residual, a sort of detritus of the kind that has to be cleaned out after the death of parents in a family home. All this human-generated stuff is what now contributes to the technosphere (see Chapter 4). But whilst an artefact is in use, it can be said to have affordances. Affordances are not a property of the technology *per se* but arise in the relationship between a

design ← fit

technology and a user (e.g. an iPhone and its 'fit' into a hand). Affordances can be realised through good design or accidental fit.

7.2.2.2 Designing and regulating technology within a governance system

Incorporating the technosphere into a new governance dynamic, as depicted in Figure 7.1, requires two sets of understandings, understandings that are in short supply. The first is understanding based in the philosophy of technology, and particularly its phenomenological and hermeneutic traditions.[23] These traditions provide the rationale to see technology not as a thing in itself but as a mediator of relational dynamics. The second is recognition that regulation alone will not work; Heidegger felt that attempts at control of technology wouldn't work because it was an external manifestation of a deeper problem in human society – the hegemonic enframing of thought by techno-rationality.[24] Central to techno-rationality is the prevailing utilitarian basis of thought based on the principle of 'sufficient reason', manifest primarily as linear causation – or the systematic tradition. Heidegger was deeply pessimistic about humans being able to break out of their own enframings of thought and action, and thus from the grip of technological determinism.[25]

There are innovation possibilities. We need to better understand the affordances that new technology offers *before* committing to massive investment and designs that distort our social priorities in the face of the Anthropocene. Technology must serve a social purpose. This requires that the systemic benefits and disbenefits be brought into awareness and deliberation before major commitment of investment, including R&D funding, or approval for release. This will require something like *before the event* systemic awareness through, for example, scenarioing, to be institutionalised (Box 7.1). One such purpose is that it must improve, or be benign, with respect to relations with and within the biosphere. The means by which we govern relationships with the biosphere and the technosphere will be very sensitive to how we choose to frame situations of concern and pursue new ways of addressing and readdressing social purpose.

BOX 7.1 SCENARIOING·AS A PRACTICE· AND INSTITUTION

Scenarios are the product of scenarioing praxis. Scenarios are often glossy, end up between the covers of reports, and sit on shelves unused. As a planning device, scenarios are regarded as a way of not trying to get the future right but avoiding getting it wrong.[26] When the focus shifts from the product to the process, then scenarioing can be an effective means for deciding what has to be done and how it might be achieved within the constraints of uncertainty.[27]

> But it can be argued that scenarioing, as praxis, all too often falls between the incommensurable demands of different epistemological positions about the nature of knowledge/knowing and thus of evidence. Aware of these tensions, Ison and colleagues developed a heuristic model of praxis considerations (or activities) to enhance and develop the theory-informed practice of scenarioing within a systemic governance process.[28] This model could be applied informally or formally by technology developers, funders and/or regulators. It would be essential that the scenarioing process drew on participants with multiple perspectives and critically explored the systemic impacts of a technology on those likely to be affected but not involved in decisions.[29]

Being open to the language of technology can also help. As Stephen Talbott noted:[30]

> A 'device', for example, can be an objective, invented thing, but it can also be some sort of scheming or contriving of the mind, as when a defendant uses every device he can think of to escape the charges against him. The word 'contrivance' shows the same two-sidedness, embracing both mechanical appliances and the carefully devised plans and schemes we concoct in thought. As for 'mechanisms' and 'machines', we produce them as visible objects out there in the world even as we conceal our own machinations within ourselves. Likewise, an 'artifice' is a manufactured device, or else it is trickery, ingenuity, or inventiveness. 'Craft' can refer to manual dexterity in making things or to a ship or aircraft, but a 'crafty' person is adept at deceiving others.

Technology is always a product of our own devising; we thus have underexploited agency to change our design sensibilities and to bring the technosphere within the ambit or provenance of future governance systems.

7.2.3 Deframing and reframing situations

'Framing' situations is a choice we have, and one we always make, even though we may not be aware of what we do. Just as most paintings are framed, so are situations that we encounter throughout our daily lives. When we give phenomena names, then a framing choice is created.[31] For example, the 'wicked' and 'tame' problems of Rittel and Webber were terms they invented to frame their experiences. As George Lakoff notes: 'All thinking and talking involves "framing." Since frames come in systems, a single word typically activates not only its defining frame, but also much of the system its defining frame is in'.[32] Framing choices create initial starting conditions that become conserved as lineages (pathway dependencies) and as institutions. Paying attention to how situations are framed, and by whom, is the means of avoiding doing the wrong thing righter.

Deframing and reframing are the first critical steps of a sequence needed for starting out:

1 Take responsibility for framing choices applied to situations of concern and explore systemic affordances of framing choices.
2 Admit different actors, so that a starting conversation is populated with multiple partial perspectives of a situation of concern.
3 Formulate systems-of-interest as ways of knowing about a situation systemically (e.g. Figure 7. 3) but be critically reflexive about boundary choices.
4 Explore and design for purpose, revisit articulations of purpose regularly and know that purpose is what a system does.

Designed human activity systems to carry out these steps will come in many forms. Some relevant practices already exist and others are known about but not institutionalised. Here is a sample.

7.2.3.1 Moving the narrative: from environmental education to biosphere governing

Most environmental education and designs for environmental policy still treat the environment as an externality, or even more perversely, as a set of 'natural capital' assets to be counted and accounted. To succeed, environmental education should be reframed as 'biosphere governing' and approached through the lens of what the Americans call civics. A variation on the same phenomenon applies to investments in environmental programmes in the media. Take, for example, the very popular BBC environment/wildlife programmes fronted by Sir David Attenborough. The shows have high production values and have inspired many people, but until April 2019 they have presented a myth, rather than how things actually are.[33] The scenes can take weeks or even months to create and are thus of a 'nature' inaccessible to all in our lived, as opposed to virtual, worlds. The BBC and many other nature creatives deliver a pristine nature selectively collaged, rather than the 'real' nature heavily impacted by human activity. We experience a chimaera.[34] There is a strong case for citizen activism, for example, to bring pressure to bear on reworking the rules of operation for public broadcasters and moving control of their governance into the social purpose subsystem of the new governance model (see Figure 7.1).

Our critique of the ways in which we have come to use and accept the term 'environment' is an act of deframing. The challenge after deframing is to reframe in ways that are systemically desirable.

7.2.3.2 Working with the Anthropocene framing

We have chosen the Anthropocene as one of the main framing choices for this book. Being open to what 'the Anthropocene', as a 'framing choice', reveals and conceals seems a sensible strategy at present. Choice of the Anthropocene places all humans clearly in the frame. It reveals the power that humans have over our circumstances but conceals the fact that only some humans have contributed. It is also tied to particular ways of thinking and acting (e.g. the great expansion in capitalist activity after World War II where the 'econocene' is put forward as a more appropriate term, or framing choice, based on its ideological foundation in 'economism', the reduction of all social relations to market logic).[35] Also concealed are inter- and intra-species inequalities that are too often ignored.[36]

Some may claim that we are just attempting a re-versioning of Gaia as articulated by James Lovelock and Lynn Margulis: 'the mythological name [of the Greek goddess who was the personification of the Earth that] was revived in 1979 in *Gaia: A New Look at Life on Earth*'. The Gaia hypothesis proposes that:

> living organisms and inorganic material are part of a dynamical system that shapes the Earth's biosphere, and maintains the Earth as a fit environment for life. In some Gaia theory approaches, the Earth itself is viewed as an organism with self-regulatory functions.[37]

Our conception of the biosphere as part of a governance system is significantly different to Gaia, as we are using the 'biosphere' concept for a different purpose. We seek to make conceivable and operational new metaphors for governing with a systemic, relational, dynamic between humans (framed as a social system or multiple social systems) and the biosphere as central. Through the acts of governing, or navigating or steering, a trajectory of living unfolds with human biosphere and technosphere relations within the context of unfolding social purpose at its core.[38]

7.2.3.3 Situational framing: acting to maximise choices

Because we have agency in our framing choices, we can choose to frame a situation as 'a problem', 'an opportunity' or 'contested issue'. Framing choices, knowingly or not, directs thinking and practice. Systems scholars have coined particular neologisms (invented terms) as a means of describing and explaining the situations they experienced. Turkish-American cybernetician Hasan Ozbekhan introduced the idea of the 'problematique' to refer to the 'bundle of problems' that the Club of Rome wished to address in the late 1960s. This concept subsequently became central to 'The Limits to Growth' report[39] and to the special character of the problems it intended to investigate:

> First, these problems could not be solved within electoral cycles because of their long-term characteristics; second, they could not be solved within individual countries because of their global scale; third, these problems

could not be considered separately, because they constituted interacting 'clusters of problems'. The 'problematique' thus summed up this inextricable net of long-term and global-scale problems.[40]

We have already used several of these invented terms: 'wicked problems', 'messes', the 'swamp of real-life issues', 'complex adaptive systems'. What is important is to be aware that all choices are framings for praxis, not terms to classify phenomena or situations. All choices need to be approached in the spirit of 'what can be done if we frame this situation as X'.

In the OECD initiative described earlier,[41] the claim is made that 'complexity is a core feature of most policy issues today and in this context traditional analytical tools and problem-solving methods no longer work'. Their report:

> explores how systems approaches can be used in the public sector to solve complex or 'wicked' problems. ... identifies tactics that can be employed by government agencies to work towards systems change; and provides an in-depth examination of how systems approaches have been applied in practice.[42]

In other words, the OECD – in this report at least – has chosen to frame their situations of concern as 'wicked problems'. Being aware of this choice, and then embedding practice in a systemic, or knowing-based governance system, opens up more pathways for change (Figure 7.2).

All practice is situated (Figure 7.2a). In Figure 7.2b, practitioner 1, aware of the distinction wicked/tame, has a framing choice (pathway W1a or W1b). Practitioner 2, not aware of the distinction wicked/tame, has fewer choices and generally resorts to systematic governance mechanisms (pathway T2 in Figure 7.2c). Coupling a wicked framing with a systemic governance mechanism based on processes of knowing (not reified or objective, fixed knowledge) opens up further choices and possibilities for co-evolutionary adaptation of practice through feedback and, if needed, reframing (Figure 7.2c). Second-order change is much more likely so long as the initial implications of the framing choice are pursued consistently.

7.2.3.4 Using language and narratives fit for our times

Mark Thompson asks 'is there anything that the public themselves can do to better prepare them to be a good sovereign?'[43] The only answer is yes. Investment in recovery through narrative, better reporting, experiential learning that recovers nascent systemic sensibilities, together with the development of systems literacy, are all means of breaking out of this trap. There are some simple strategies available. A form of Metaphor Impact Assessment (MIA) could be instituted and mandated in organisational life, especially in governance conversations. MIA could take place in a few hours as part of group start-up, or it could last much

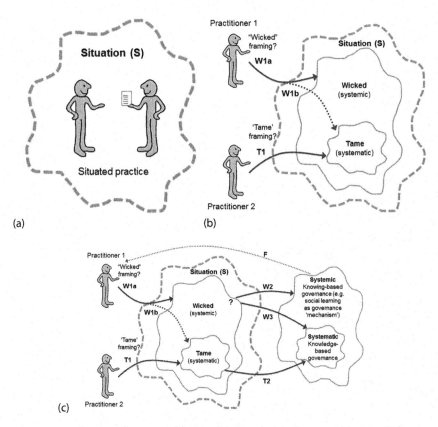

FIGURE 7.2 The consequences of framing choices (wicked or tame situations) for systemic governance.[44]

longer, producing deeper and more tightly held awareness. It could be carried out on an ongoing basis to effect better initial starting conditions – but also as part of an ongoing M&E (Monitoring & Evaluation) strategy.

Research led by the OU Systems group provides examples (Figure 7.3), as does the work of other systems scholars like Gareth Morgan in *Images of Organization* and the work of Mark Winter and Tony Szczepanek in *Images of Projects.*[45]

MIA is not difficult once a little understanding has been achieved. Figure 7.3 is a metaphor map of a pre-existing plan, the Thames Working Plan. When the document is analysed, then some major metaphor clusters become apparent. Some of these can be seen to be potentially disabling of effective systemic governance (e.g. the plan as fighting, the plan as teaching, the plan as blueprint). Done *after* the event, a space has to be opened up for reflexive consideration through MIA of the plan and its entailments. If done *before* a policy has become stabilised, then there is much more scope for effecting systemically desirable trajectory and outcomes.

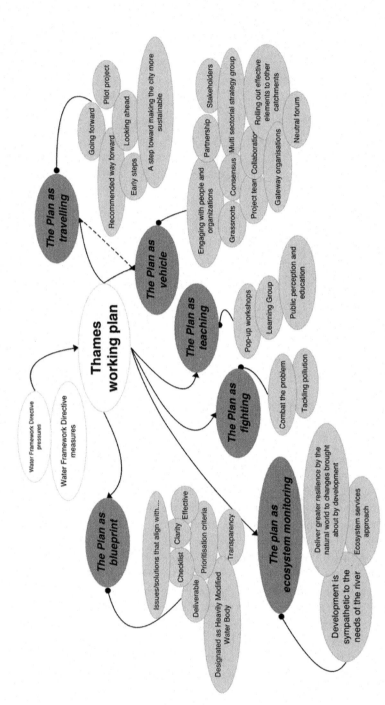

FIGURE 7.3 A metaphor map of the Final Project Report *Your Tidal Thames*.[46] Words in standard roman format are from the document, and the bold italicised word bubbles are root metaphors proposed to explore the systemic implications.[47]

7.3 New metaphors for governing

Governance is a much used and abused concept, and the praxis of governing is rarely spoken about. We offer four metaphors for governing that draw on systems and cybernetic thinking.[48] They reveal understandings that are 'missing in action' in current governance systems. Their purpose is to recast how we think of and act out governing, and thereby to release the innovations needed to move to the new governance model (Figure 7.1). We propose use of the duality governance/governing – what is done and its doing. Adopting these metaphors is central to the process of reinventing.

Governance encompasses the totality of mechanisms and instruments available for directing and influencing society, including the entire cycles of adaptive planning, designing, regulating, legislating, budgeting and managing. Matters of governance do not reside just with the functioning of states but with any form of organised human activity: an organisation, a project, program, inquiry or even a family. Governance is not an abstraction; it is something that is done, enacted in theory-informed and context-specific ways. Governance also enacts ideologies and power relations.[49] It is not management. One does not replace the other.[50]

7.3.1 A reformulated cybernetic metaphor for governing

Governance can be framed using the central metaphor of a helmsperson steering a boat, or charting a viable course in response to feedback from the biophysical world – mainly currents and wind – in relation to purposes that are negotiated and renegotiated within an unfolding context — that is, in repeatedly recalibrated responses to uncertainty (Figure 7.4).[51] In the sailing example, the dynamics between a social and biophysical system are mediated by artefactual technologies – such as the boat – and social technologies or institutions – like the rules of a sailing race. From this metaphor we take the term 'systemic or cybersystemic governance/governing' (i.e. the relational dynamics between doing the sailing and outcomes that unfold over time).

If an effective governance system is to emerge from the dynamics of the parts in the new 'governance diamond' (Figure 7.1), then a new metaphor like this 'sailing/steering/navigating' metaphor is needed. It can also be used by designers of human activity systems, including the new institutions to make the new governance model functional (Chapter 8). Advocacy of this metaphor has parallels with research into new organisational forms by Frederic Laloux. His three key reinventing metaphors are the organisation of:

1. Self-managing (not hierarchical or mechanistic).
2. Wholeness (enabling the functioning of whole people).
3. Pursuing evolutionary purpose.[52]

This governance/governing metaphor, whilst not new, has to be framed as a duality and enacted as a form of praxis (theory-informed practical action). It should

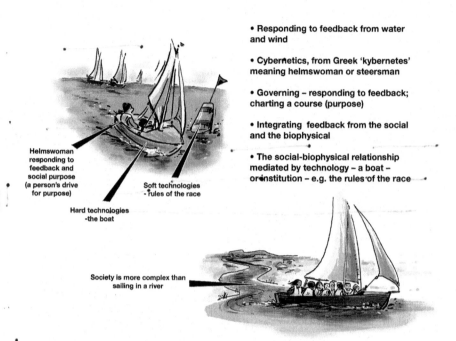

- Responding to feedback from water and wind

- Cybernetics, from Greek 'kybernetes' meaning helmswoman or steersman

- Governing – responding to feedback; charting a course (purpose)

- Integrating feedback from the social and the biophysical

- The social-biophysical relationship mediated by technology – a boat – or institution – e.g. the rules of the race

Helmswoman responding to feedback and social purpose (a person's drive for purpose)

Soft technologies - rules of the race

Hard technologies -the boat

Society is more complex than sailing in a river

FIGURE 7.4 A metaphor for the praxis of cyber-systemic governing based on the Greek verbs *kybernao/kybernan* meaning 'I steer/to steer'.[53]

not be interpreted as sailor-as-emperor or authoritarian ruler. Instead, new types of co-operative 'sailing' need to be developed at a range of systemic levels and with numbers, or requisite variety, that make the acts of governing functional in systemic, relational terms. Think of the Shaldon vignette in Chapter 5 and imagine that example multiplied across all English river-basin districts in terms of its design and process and ongoing levels of participation and deliberation (i.e. as an institutionalised form of governing).[54]

7.3.2 Governing as orchestrating a performance

The second metaphor for the praxis of governing is an orchestra, such as a prestigious one like the Berlin Philharmonic. Drawing on your systemic sensibilities and growing systems literacy, how might you characterise an orchestra? Well, it is a group of practitioners known generically as musicians – those who practise, or play, music. The playing is orchestrated by another practitioner called the conductor. There are different types of musicians who play different instruments, each of whom come from different musical backgrounds and traditions of understanding, as do conductors. The technology elements include the instruments and the composition and its score as well as the architecture and acoustics of the venue, and also more intangible elements such as 'the interpretation of a piece'. What emerges from this social and technologically mediated dynamic is called a performance. But the quality of the performance depends on one additional element, that of the audience. Thus, to be satisfying to an audience, the performance must meet certain technical and aesthetic requirements. These can be culturally specific – say the differences between a Vienna, Berlin and New York audience. To be successful, audiences must keep coming and paying. What an orchestra does is its form of praxis. It is a participatory, joint or collaborative practice and is a fitting analogy for what we mean by the process of social learning discussed in Chapter 8.

With reputation, continued investment and availability of practitioners with the requisite capabilities, reification (or institutionalisation) is possible. The result is an entity, an organisation, the Berlin Philharmonic, which attracts investment, patronage, dedicated venue, marketing and the like. This is the other part of the duality that makes up how we understand social learning – a governance mechanism, an institutional configuration that can be built into public policy and deployed in various domains as long as satisfying performances continue to emerge.

7.3.3 Governing as guided improvisation

The third metaphor arises from consideration of the differences between an orchestra where someone else's music is played and that of a jazz band where the form, or rules of participating, are laid out, but the individual contributions – and thus the whole performance – is open to the particular skills, histories and contexts of those contributing. The same duality exists between praxis and institution (even if jazz groups may be more ephemeral and investment significantly less). Self-organising, emergent performances are needed in some contexts, and the two forms – orchestration and improvisation – offer a complementary strategy when applied to governance.

Broadly, the role of the centre or national government is in orchestrating and the role of local and regional government and civic society is in improvising. This duality is taken further in Chapter 8.

A glimpse of the future through this metaphor can be gleaned from an old jazz favourite, 'It Ain't What You Do (It's the Way That You Do It)', slightly adapted:

- 'I thought I was smart but I soon found out … I didn't know what life was all about
- It ain't what you do it's why you do it
- It ain't what you do it's the way that you do it
- It ain't what you do it's the time that you do it
- It ain't what you do it's the place that you do it
- It ain't what you do it's who you do it with
- And that's what gets results!'[55]

7.3.4 Governing as trajectory-correcting co-evolution

The question of how walking arises as a practice which was posed in Chapter 6 illustrates a trajectory-correcting co-evolution metaphor. The human body that participates in the walking can be taken as an analogy for the human social system, made up of all that we humans do, including inventing, naming and enacting the institutions and technologies that proliferate in our world. These institutions and technologies can be understood as the shoes we put on to do our walking – sometimes we know that we are wearing them, sometimes not.

Some shoes make it easy to walk because of their design (affordances such as stretching, breathing, waterproofing). Others cause blisters or are just uncomfortable. But real comfort arises once we have worn the shoes in (i.e. when they adapt to our feet and our mode of walking). The shoes then disappear into the background.[56] The feet do not cause shoes to be comfortable, just as the shoes are not comfortable to start with. Comfort is the quality of a relationship that arises in the recurrent interaction between the foot and the shoe, termed co-adaptation. It is how co-evolution works.

The other element in the dynamic of walking is the medium of the path. This is analogous to the biophysical world (see Figure 7.5). Walking has an impact on the medium – think of tracks that arise spontaneously on new estates where people walk where they want rather than following paths laid out by the developer.[57] In metaphorical terms, the designs and extent of the use of the shoes manifest in impact. All impacts are imbued with certain qualities and consequences (e.g. wearing stiletto heels on parquet flooring).

Effective Anthropocene-governing responses, we argue, mean making a framing choice that places two intrinsically interrelated systems (social and biophysical) into a new co-evolutionary trajectory based on clear understanding about what is to be governed and how governing functions.[58] The new governance system that we propose (Figure 7.1) can be understood in these terms.[59] Figure 7.5 is one way of thinking about this co-evolutionary dynamic. In using these concepts, we employ a mode of inquiry outlined earlier for metaphors. One that asks (i) what might be revealed or concealed by considering governance situations *as if* they were structure-determined, co-evolutionary systems and (ii) through our governing, how can the ongoing viable coupling of social and biophysical systems be sustained, with particular qualities, into the future?

Given the good work being done by many, what needs to happen to clear the way so that these metaphors can be taken up, institutionalised faster, be more effective and can be sustained in systemically desirable and culturally feasible ways? As we have the advantage that we live in language, we can, through practices that facilitate systemic conversations, literally 'turn together' in new dances of responsibility, make second-order change happen. The purposeful design of human activity systems is one such practice.

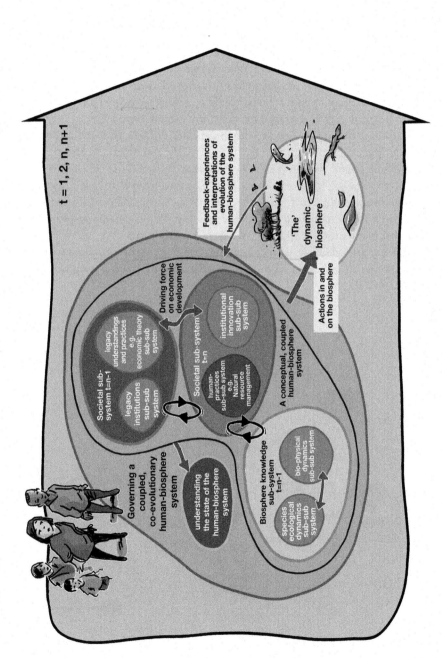

FIGURE 7.5 One conception of coupled social-biophysical systems governed as an unfolding co-evolutionary dynamic over time (t = 1, 2, n, n+1 etc).[60, 61]

7.4 Purposeful human activity systems

The new three-dimensional governance diamond that we propose can only come about through human action. The focus for human action has to be, in the first instance, on the arrows or flashpoints in Figure 7.6 that join other parts of the model with the biosphere, through invention and ingenuity and organised resistance. This is where developments such as the Extinction Rebellion and Schoolchildren Strikes have important roles to play.[62]

Ways to reframe thinking about our thinking are necessary to release second-order change at a rate and to a depth that has impact. To do this we must convert, conceptually at least, the new elements understood as subsystems into a set of what Peter Checkland called a 'human activity system' (HAS). HASs are systems that can be purposefully designed for transformation (Chapter 8).

What HASs require are people with understandings, practices and social relations who pursue purposeful actions. In essence, the rest of Part 3 concerns itself with the purposeful design of new human activity systems to effect particular types of governance transformation. This does not mean that systemic change does not arise serendipitously, but it does mean that we are collectively pretty bad at designing and conducting social processes capable of generating purposeful action that is systemically desirable. We have a lot to learn.

At the meta-level, purposeful designs for governance transformation will have to be enacted through articulations and re-articulations of social purpose within

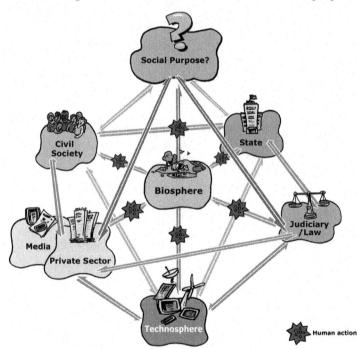

FIGURE 7.6 Focal points for human action in the three-dimensional 'governance diamond'.

the social purpose subsystem. This can be done through the design and testing of HASs (Figure 7.7). In the new governance model, the key locus of responsibility for the biosphere, technosphere and social purpose subsystems sits within the social purpose subsystem itself. STiP practices, such as the purposeful design of relevant HASs (Figure 7.7) will be needed.

Institutions and organisations have to be devised that act into the long term, that are capable of deploying STiP capability, and of providing inputs to, and responding to, feedback from all the subsystems of the governance model (Figure 7.6). If this sounds a bit abstract, then read on. The rest of Part 3 exemplifies how this could be done. Chapter 8 will explain systemic inquiry and other novel forms of STiP praxis as well as STiP-inspired institutional forms.

In practice, STiP-informed design and designers have important roles to play, along with citizens and people with expertise (but it is not expert-led). In general terms, inventing, designing, running and facilitating purposeful human activity systems will be the focus – for example, designing, negotiating and revising constitutions (Chapter 9). Praxis based on reflexivity and the capacity to generate novel framings, reframings and deframings will be important because these set initial starting conditions for any purposeful action.

7.4.1 Fostering trajectories of social purpose through governance innovation

To effect and sustain second-order change requires conversations about purpose. From this it follows that capability is needed to make novel choices in novel contexts with adjustment along the way. Setting fixed goals, aims or objectives gets

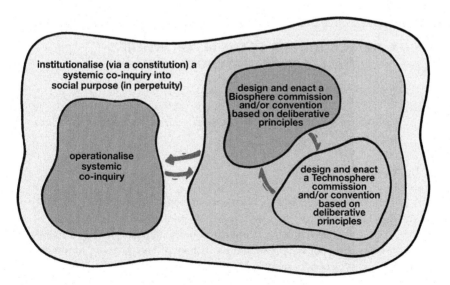

FIGURE 7.7 A conceptual model of a human activity system to effect governing of social purpose in relation to the biosphere and technosphere.

in the way of pursuing purpose. Understandings and behaviours based on goal-seeking limit practice and thus innovative possibilities.[63] In the Anthropocene, pursuit of economic performance (no matter how understood) can no longer be the de facto purpose of a governance system. Instead, economics, reframed as merely one aspect of being social, would be recast as an emergent property of human–biosphere relations, which includes human well-being.

Organisations should also aspire to be purposeful and to build their governing practices on articulations and re-articulations of purpose.[64] The purposeful pursuit of purpose fosters self-organisation and localised innovation when the encumbrances of goal-setting and goal-seeking behaviour are abandoned.[65] Social purpose, as a key element in a governance system, comprises fora, processes and institutions used for engaging in purpose articulation and re-articulation. These are also products of social processes that must be capable of generating accommodations between different interests/perspectives so as to design and conduct purposeful action that is systemically desirable and culturally feasible.

Whilst there are many candidates for developing and running new institutions within the social purpose subsystem of the new model (Figure 7.7), here we deal briefly with only one, the purpose of state-financed education.

7.4.2 Reclaiming social purpose from an ineffective state – education

We outline what innovation under 'social purpose' might look like by drawing on an essay about education policy written by Ed Straw (with James Park);[66] see Box 7.2.

BOX 7.2 SCHOOL FOR SCANDAL, OR WHERE'S THE LEARNING IN SCHOOLS POLICY?

Writing from within England, Ed asks:

How can we engage, deliberate and decide on what's best for our education system?

His response is:

As our government zigzags on yet another approach for schools, I wonder why, unlike most countries, we can't settle on a model and Get It Right.

Consider that in no other European country do politicians agree so little on how its school system should be managed. The incessant arguments here about secondary schools, their ownership and control, structure, testing, exam results and curricula we take as 'normal' surprise and confuse

---

visitors from abroad. Maybe we just like debating and disagreeing rather than doing.

[In contrast:]

The German (selective) system has been in place since its independence in 1949 (imagine that here). In Finland (comprehensive) – usually acknowledged to be Europe's top educational performer – the political parties went into the 2015 general election with a shared commitment to a policy document they had worked on with teacher and head teacher unions, parent groups and secondary school students.

Good grief, politicians agreeing for the greater good: how terribly backward, they must be foreign. But these countries know that education policy takes consensus to work – hardly surprising given the nature of the task: a collective social good; for a solid economy other children's education is as important to us as our own; and the penalty of a poor education is felt by us all – in taxes, crime, and social cohesion. Schools in Finland are the product of adult politics.

[In the UK] ... violent policy alterations cost an unquantified lot in taxes, in disruption to children's education, and in teacher stress. Having spent a working lifetime in and around governments and seen the waste endemic in our system regardless of the colour of the party in power. ... the nature of our political system has compelled successive radical secretaries of state for education – Kenneth Baker in 1988, David Blunkett in 1997, Michael Gove in 2010 (and PMs David Cameron in 2015 and Theresa May in 2016) – to go through a similar process: developing policy in private without engaging those essential to its operation; promising publicly that they will deliver major change; arguing that they alone know how this can be achieved; insisting that the urgency of the task requires them to direct things from the centre; directing people's energies towards a narrow range of test score targets; raising everyone's stress levels; ignoring the voices of those warning of dangers ahead; undermining the motivation of those responsible for making their policies work; and bringing forth legislation that, at root, mirrors their own experience of education – apparently believing that what worked for them some decades ago will work for everybody in very different circumstances.

It falls to each of their successors to point out the limitations of such a one-dimensional approach to managing a complex system. This leads to their re-opening a limited dialogue with the profession, trying to repair the damage done to trust and morale, working out how to broaden the focus of the curriculum, and sometimes re-inventing the systems that were designed with such care a decade or so previously, then torn down before they had a chance to reach maturity ... without of course confessing that this is what they are doing. (The National Health Service is another victim of zigzag government).

[As introduced in Chapter 5],

this approach to policy making is termed DAD – Decide, Announce, Defend. It has a long, costly, and conflict-inducing history. You will have experienced it many times. This 'expert, top-down' model of decision-making suits those that believe they know best for whatever reason: of their education, intellect, or ego. It saves the messy business of engaging with the public and comprehending the actual complexity of the real world. Being 'decisive' makes for good politics – even though 'strong' government is rarely what is needed.

For how much longer will we have to endure this circus where political whim is trumps, knowledge is disposable, and commitment a foreign concept?

The zigzag nature of policy-making has made it impossible to establish effective solutions. The waste of resources that results from 'reform' in perpetuity, and the damage it inflicts on the life chances of the young people caught up in the whirligig of change, are never measured. Running a system in a state of permanent revolution and high anxiety has significant downsides. It may seem extraordinary but Theresa May and the others are content to use children as guinea pigs. Politicians' ideologies are evidently more important than children's education. ... Ringaringapolicy.

In a world with no need for ideology, where everyone wants good education, it doesn't have to be this way. If it had worked then it would have stopped. But it has not, so it won't.

The net result of 30 years of this political contest is that some schools are educating to a very high standard and children flourish. At the other end are 'ASNLs' – at school and not learning – the classic adolescent boys I meet: bored, alienated and rich in testosterone, unable to make sense of the purpose of 5 GCSEs when their destiny is the vital jobs of hill farming or broadband network builders. The Children's Society has highlighted the levels of emotional distress experienced by large numbers of young people – traceable to schools? In *A Mindfulness Guide For The Frazzled*, Ruby Wax comments: 'Right now children are being hot housed for exams. But no-one's asking how much they can take before they burn their little brains out from the pressure'.

The CBI is a regular critic of the skill levels being produced by the school system. Martin Wolf in the FT [*Financial Times*] on coping with Brexit, states: 'The UK has to rectify longstanding supply-side failings. The list includes ... inadequate basic education of much of the population and the innumeracy of much of its elite.' I did enjoy that latter point.[67]

Those who recall Chapter 5 will know that the alternative to DAD is EDD (Engage, Deliberate, Decide). If education is reframed as an investment by citizens in citizens rather than as a private economic good, then it makes sense to build within the social purpose subsystem an institution or institutions capable of designing and enacting EDD over the long term. Think of the sailing metaphor (Figure 7.4) and ask who the best crew might be that is required to chart a course over the long term.

EDD means making policy in the open, accessible to all who are interested, gathering and promulgating a real fact base, looking at other countries' systems, and talking about it away from adversarial politics and ideologies. The final decision becomes relatively straightforward. Most significantly, all those involved in making the system work – teachers, parents, pupils, employers, governors and funders – are committed to it, a precondition for success. With stability, all can put their energies into its operation rather than into yet another argument. And guess what, you will find selective and non-selective systems that work well – it's not just the structure, it's the commitment, the stability and the system.

In his essay, Ed goes on to say that:

> to state the obvious, schools are all about learning. But learning should apply as much in the development of its policy: first to learn from previous mistakes, second from the waste of zigzag, third from all the real facts and information out there, fourth from all those engaged in schools, and fifth from other countries. This takes time and humility, but not anywhere as much time as has been consumed by our political process in the last 30 years.

In making these claims, Ed is espousing a purpose for education; 'a system to provide and deliver learning as an investment in its citizenry' may be the system-of-interest he has in mind. Many would agree with such a purpose, but in what he does, Ed attributes a purpose to those responsible for education, that may or may not be true. As outlined earlier, this is engaging in purposive, not purposeful, behaviour. If we checked it out, we might find that the systems description was more like 'a system to provide social care for the majority of youth at an age when they can generate many social problems', or a 'system to enhance economic performance of the nation' or 'a system to give the best chance to your children and those of your social class'. Without openness, transparency or co-design any of these system descriptions could be a possibility. EDD removes the possibility of distorted social purpose and builds confidence and trust (Chapter 8).

Given the story in Box 7.2, the question we use to draw this chapter to a close is: What institutional innovations based on Engage, Deliberate, Decide could be imagined and built into future governance systems? The answers would have to avoid the zigzag phenomenon, thus ruling out the current functions of the state that are wedded to short political and news cycles and ideological football. Citizens would require legal recourse through constitutional means to bodies charged with negotiating and navigating inquiries that formulated and reformulated social purpose. In turn, these would have to inform feedback-learning on the adequacy, or lack of adequacy of the constitution(s). We make further suggestions in the next chapters. The three new elements of the governance model are sites for reconfiguring power relations, practices and relational dynamics in our governance systems, freed from structure-determined configurations and ready to reallocate resources.

In concluding this chapter and preparing for the next, we note that in 1919, 100 years ago, the Bauhaus movement began:

> German architect Walter Gropius established Staatliches Bauhaus, a school dedicated to uniting all branches of the arts under one roof. The school acted as a hub for Europe's most experimental creatives, with well-known artists like Josef Albers, Wassily Kandinsky, and Paul Klee offering their expertise as instructors.[68]

As espoused in the new European School of Governance (EUSG), it is time for a *New Bauhaus* in which we all become experimental creatives crafting and fostering the emergence of new governing practices and institutions.[69]

Notes

1 Anonymous young woman speaking about Algeria on the BBC-OS, the World Service, 4.08 p.m., Friday, 8 March 2019.
2 Ison, R.L. et al. 2018. Adapted from Ison, R.L. (2016) Governing in the Anthropocene: What future systems thinking in practice? *Systems Research & Behavioral Science* 33 (5): 595–613.
3 It is unclear whether fish know they are in the water; if they do, then humans may very well emulate fish.
4 OECD Observatory of Public Sector Innovation. 2017. *Systems Approaches to Public Sector Challenges: Working with Change.* Paris: OECD Publishing.
5 Ibid.
6 OECD Observatory of Public Sector Innovation. 2017. *Embracing Innovation in Government Global Trends February.* Paris: OECD Publishing.
7 https://www.apsc.gov.au/tackling-wicked-problems-public-policy-perspective (Accessed 9 April 2019).
8 APSC (Australian Public Service Commission) 2007. *Tackling Wicked Problems. A Public Policy Perspective.* Canberra: Australian Government/Australian Public Service Commission.
9 Briggs, L. 2009. *Delivering Performance and Accountability – Intersections with 'Wicked Problems'.* Presentation to ISSS Conference, Brisbane, 15 July. See http://isss.org/world/brisbane-2009 (Accessed 9 April 2019).
10 There is no reason these same skills should not be required across all subsystems of the new governance model.
11 Rittel, H.W.J. and Webber, M.M. 1973. Dilemmas in a general theory of planning. *Policy Sciences* 4 (2): 155–169.
12 Kinsella, E. 2007. Technical rationality in Schön's reflective practice: Dichotomous or non-dualistic epistemological position. *Nursing Philosophy* 8: 10–113.
13 High, Chris. 2002. *Opening Up Spaces for Learning: A Systems Approach to Sustainable Development.* Unpublished, PhD Thesis, Milton Keynes: The Open University.
14 The Congress is as a way of giving adequate attention to the long-term in an overwhelmingly short-term political world. Developed by Lindsey Colbourne for the UK Sustainable Development Commission, it would be convened by Parliament every

year bringing together citizens and experts to debate scrutinise and pronounce on one or more long term issue. It would generate a sense of collective responsibility on issues that can't be solved by government alone and would act as a counterweight to short term and sometimes media inspired 'something must be done' quick fixes.

15 https://en.wikipedia.org/wiki/Fossil_fuel_divestment (Accessed 25 October 2018).
16 Knudtson, P. and Suzuki, D. 1992. *Wisdom of the Elders*. Sydney: Allen & Unwin.
17 Deborah Bird Rose (cited in Knudtson and Suzuki 1992), pp. 38–41.
18 Murphy, J. 2006. Conclusion. In Murphy, J., ed. *Governing Technology for Sustainability*, London: Earthscan, 208.
19 Naughton, J. January 19, 2018. The new surveillance capitalism. *Prospect*. See https ://www.prospectmagazine.co.uk/science-and-technology/how-the-internet-contr ols-you (Accessed 5 May 2019).
20 https://www.theguardian.com/commentisfree/2018/oct/21/think-the-giants-of-s ilicon-valley-have-your-best-interestsat-heart-think-again (Accessed 26 October 2018).
21 Murphy, J. 2006. op. cit., p. 212.
22 The word nexus presents certain challenges to systems scholars. The word means "a binding together' which could mean improving systemic or systematic relations or fusion. The main issue is to understand what the praxis elements are beyond the use of the word.
23 Phenomenology has influenced many fields of scholarship, including systems schol- ars like Peter Checkland whose development of SSM (soft systems methodology) was influenced by Edmund Husserl, the founder of the philosophical study of the structures of experience and consciousness. See https://en.wikipedia.org/wiki/ Phenomenology_(philosophy) (Accessed 5 May 2019). Hermeneutics is the theory and methodology of interpretation; there is a strong interpretivist school with systems scholarship. See https://en.wikipedia.org/wiki/Hermeneutics.
24 Snodgrass, A. 1993. Hermeneutics, universities, and the letting-be of technology. *Proc. Universities as Interpretive Communities*. 23–24 November, pp. 75–94. Sydney: University of Sydney; the term enframings is similar in meaning to that of 'traditions of understanding'.
25 Much has already been said about praxis in earlier chapters; phronesis is something lacking in public life; it is an 'Ancient Greek word for a type of wisdom or intelli- gence. It is more specifically a type of wisdom relevant to practical action, implying both good judgement and excellence of character and habits, or practical virtue'. https://en.wikipedia.org/wiki/Phronesis (Accessed 28 October 2018).
26 Schwartz, P., 1991. *The Art of the Long View: Planning for the Future in an Uncertain World*. New York: Currency-Doubleday.
27 Saliba, G. and Withers, G. 2009. Scenario analysis for strategic thinking. In *A Practical Guide to Evidence for Policy and Decision-Making*. G. Argyrous, ed., pp. 116–136. Sydney: University of New South Wales Press.
28 Ison, R.L., Grant, A., and Bawden, R.B. 2014. Scenario praxis for systemic and adap- tive governance: A critical framework. *Environment & Planning C: Government & Policy* 32 (4): 623–640.
29 There would be much to learn from the GMO (Genetically Modified Organism) technology debates across Europe and especially in the UK, including lessons about framing failure and contestations over the nature of evidence.
30 Talbott, Stephen. 2004. *In the Belly of the Beast. Technology, Nature, and the Human Prospect*. The Nature Institute. See http://natureinstitute.org/pub/persp/3/beast.pdf (Accessed 9 April 2019).
31 Schön and Rein offer the concept of 'policy frames' as ways to resolving 'intractable policy controversies'. Framing, reframing and frame-reflections are proposed as ways to clarifying the relationship between policy making and knowledge, and as ways how society and policy actors could better understand competing 'frames' within

which facts and evidence are constructed – see Schön, D.A., and Rein, M. 1994. *Frame Reflection*. New York: Basic Books.

32 Lakoff, G. 2010. Why it matters how we frame the environment. *Environmental Communication* 4 (1): 70–81.

33 Journalist George Monbiot was one of the first to criticise the BBC and Attenborough – see Monbiot, G., Wed 7 November. David Attenborough has betrayed the living world he loves. *The Guardian* https://www.theguardian.com/commentisfree/2018/nov/07/david-attenborough-world-environment-bbc-films (Accessed 4 May 2019). Attenborough and the BBC presented a much heralded turn-around in position – see https://www.bbc.co.uk/news/av/uk-47972979/sir-david-attenborough-presents-c limate-change-the-facts – but there is still much ground to make up.

34 In the sense that a chimera is an illusion or fabrication of the mind; especially an unrealisable dream.

35 Norgaard, R. 2015. *The Church of Economism and Its Discontents*. Great Transition Initiative. https://www.greattransition.org/publication/the-church-of-economism-and-its-discontents (Accessed 10 April 2019).

36 The framings centred on capitalism and economic activity are insightful and point to the significant failings of Western capitalism. These must be understood and over-come, but they are not, in and of themselves, central to reform. The key question we pose in this book is how to reinvent the social such that the centrality of current economic thought falls away to its rightful place in our governing concerns.

37 https://en.wikipedia.org/wiki/Gaia (Accessed 4 June 2018).

38 It is important to appreciate that for any why-what combination, there are multiple hows that can be pursued. In governance systems, the hows are best left to local con-textualised formulation and action.

39 Moll, P. 1991. *From Scarcity to Sustainability: Futures Studies and the Environment: The Role of the Club of Rome*. Frankfurt: Peter Lang Pub Incorporated.

40 Blanchard, E.V. 2010. Modelling the future: An overview of the Limits to Growth debate. *Centaurus* 52 (2): 91–116. (97).

41 https://oecd-opsi.org/projects/system-approaches/ (Accessed 9 March 2019).

42 OECD op. cit., Note 3. https://www.oecd.org/governance/systems-approaches-to-p ublic-sector-challenges-9789264279865-en.htm (Accessed 19 March 2019).

43 Thompson, M. 2017. *Enough Said: What's Gone Wrong with the Language of Politics?*, p. 321. New York: Vintage.

44 Ison, R.L., Collins, K.B., and Wallis, P. 2014. Institutionalising social learning: Towards systemic and adaptive governance. *Environmental Science & Policy* 53 (B): 105–117.

45 See, for example: Ison, R.L, Allan, C., and Collins, K.B. 2015. Reframing water gov-ernance praxis: Does reflection on metaphors have a role? *Environment and Planning C: Government and Policy* 33, 1697–1713. doi: 10.1177/0263774X15614466; McClintock, D. 1996. *Metaphors That Inspire 'Researching with People': UK Farming, Countrysides and Diverse Stakeholder Contexts*. PhD Thesis, Systems Department, The Open University, UK; McClintock, D., Ison, R.L. and Armson, R. 2003. Metaphors for reflecting on research practice: researching with people. *Journal of Environmental Planning and Management* 46: 715–731; Helme, M. 2002. *Appreciating Metaphor for Participatory Practice: Constructivist Inquiries in a Children and Young People's Justice Organisation*. PhD Thesis, Centre for Complexity and Change. Open University, UK; Morgan, G. 1997. *Images of Organization*. Thousand Oaks, CA: SAGE Publications; Winter, M. and Szczepanek, T. 2009. *Images of Projects*. London: Routledge.

46 Published in Ison, R.L., Allan, C. & Collins, K.B. 2015. Reframing water gov-ernance praxis: does reflection on metaphors have a role? *Environment & Planning C: Government & Policy* 33, 1697–1713, based on Thames21 and Thames Estuary Partnership, 2012. *Your Tidal Thames*. Final Project Report. London: Thames21.

47 Ison, R.L., Allan, C. and Collins, K.B. 2015. Reframing water governance praxis: Does reflection on metaphors have a role? *Environment & Planning C: Government & Policy* 33: 1697–1713.

48 See, for example, Blunden, M. and Dando, M., eds. 1994. Rethinking public policy-making. questioning assumptions, challenging beliefs. In *Special Edition of the American Behavioral Scientist*, Vol. 38, No. 1; Ison, R.L. 2010. Governance that works. Why public service reform needs systems thinking. In *More Than Luck. Ideas Australia Needs Now*, Davis M, Lyons M., eds., pp. 215–228. Sydney: CPD; Ison, R.L., Collins, K.B., and Wallis, P. 2014. Institutionalising social learning: Towards systemic and adaptive governance. *Environmental Science & Policy* 53 (B): 105–117; Rhodes, R.A.W. 1996. The new governance: Governing without government. *Political Studies* XLIV: 652–667.

49 Stirling, A. 2012. Opening up the politics of knowledge and power in Bioscience. *PLoS Biol* 10 (1): e1001233. https://doi.org/10.1371/journal.pbio.1001233.

50 Head, B.W. 2009. From government to governance: Explaining and assessing new approaches to NRM. In *Contested Country: Local and Regional Natural Resource Management in Australia*, Lane M.B., Robinson C., and Taylor B., eds. Melbourne: CSIRO Publishing: 15–28.

51 Little recent scholarship about governance retains the nuances of its roots. A.M. Ampere drew on the Greek for steering to formulate the science of civil government in 1834. From these roots Norbert Wiener reformulated the term cybernetics in 1948 (*Cybernetics: Or Control and Communication in the Animal and the Machine*), turning 'steering' into the 'science of steering'. The Greek also offers the term kubernêtês, the person who directed the oarsmen powering a trireme warship. The English word governor applies to the control mechanism in a steam engine, which operates on feedback. See Tsien, H.S. 1954. *Engineering Cybernetics*. London: McGraw Hill and for an overview and short history of cybernetics, see Medina, Eden. 2014. *Cybernetic Revolutionaries*. Cambridge, MA: The MIT Press.

52 Laloux, F. 2014. *Reinventing Organizations*. Brussels: Nelson Parker.

53 Adapted from Ison, R.L., Alexandra, J. & Wallis, P.J. 2018. Governing in the Anthropocene: are there cyber-systemic antidotes to the malaise of modern governance? *Sustainability Science* 13 (5): 1209–1223.

54 Another way to understand this is as a set of constantly unfolding self-organising governing 'experiments' – just as each sailing trip is different, so is each governing performance, but the ways of practising and the meta-rules can have a lot in common.

55 'It Ain't What You Do (It's the Way That You Do It)' is a calypso song written by jazz musicians Melvin 'Sy' Oliver and James 'Trummy' Young. It was first recorded in 1939 by Jimmie Lunceford, Harry James, and Ella Fitzgerald. We have added three lines.

56 The test of this phenomenon comes if you take a comfortable pair of shoes and put them in a cupboard for a year – then reuse them. The comfort usually disappears because your foot has changed or the shoes have become less plastic etc. See Collins, K.B. and Ison, R.L. 2009. Editorial. Living with environmental change: Adaptation as social learning. *Special Edition, Environmental Policy & Governance* 19: 351–357.

57 Some sensible planners and architects do not put in paths until local people have made the paths that are relevant to their living in a particular location.

58 Ison, R.L. 2018. Governing the human–environment relationship: Systemic practice. *Current Opinion in Environmental Sustainability* 33: 114–123. https://doi.org/10.1016/j.cosust.2018.05.009.

59 This can also be understood in terms of structural coupling and the functioning of 'structure determined systems', concepts coined by Humberto Maturana (Maturana and Varela 1987); http://www.sympoetic.net/Systems/structural_determinism.html (Accessed 4 May 2017).

60 Adapted from: Wei, Y., Ison, R.L., Western, A.W., and Lu, Z. 2018. Understanding ourselves and the environment in which we live. *Current Opinion in Environmental Sustainability* 33: 161–166.

61 An implication of this model is that the biosphere is never fully knowable in advance in a way that can guide action deterministically.

62 Ison, N. Thursday 2 May 2019. After Extinction Rebellion, Australian politicians are on notice – change is coming. *The Guardian*. https://www.theguardian.com/co mmentisfree/2019/may/02/after-extinction-rebellion-australian-politicians-are-on -notice-change-is-coming (Accessed 5 May 2019).

63 See the SDGs (Sustainable Development Goals) as discussed in Chapter 8.

64 Ison, R.L. 2018. op cit.

65 Alexander, V. 2011. *The Biologist's Mistress: Rethinking Self-Organization in Art, Literature, and Nature*. Litchfield Park, AZ: Emergent Publications.

66 Straw, E. 2016. https://www.localschoolsnetwork.org.uk/2016/12/school-for-scan-dal-or-wheres-the-learning-in-schools-policy (Accessed 9 January 2020).

67 In the UK there is compelling evidence that the education system is failing, even in terms of a purpose framed in economic terms: The Centre for Cities' new report *Competing with the Continent* presents an in-depth picture of how UK city economies compare to 330 European cities from across 17 countries. It concludes that UK cities play a bigger role in the national economy than in other countries, yet UK cities are lagging behind in terms of productivity. Poor skills levels are likely to be the biggest cause of low productivity.

68 https://mymodernmet.com/what-is-bauhaus-art-movement/ (Accessed 29 October 2018).

69 https://europeanschoolofgovernance.eu/ (Accessed 29 October 2018).

8

NEW PRACTICES AND INSTITUTIONS FOR SYSTEMIC GOVERNING

8.1 Taking a systemic design turn

The aim of this chapter is to harness innovations to change the relationship between practice and institutions so as to enact *systemic governing*. We shall be imagining how to make the new governance model functional. The examples used are tools for crafting new governing systems, or for designing new tools-for-governing-practice. Crafting is a practice of the 'design turn' and is dependent upon systems thinking in practice (STiP) capability. We can call this systemic designing.

When a plane or car is designed and built within an engineering human-activity-system, then its *why* and *what* and *how* are *relatively* simple. A design is created and a product that meets design specifications is delivered. But relative is a relative concept. Plane and car industries have not reconfigured the boundaries to their systems-of-interest in the light of Anthropocene imperatives. In other words, they perpetuate a system that now delivers the wrong transformations (first-order change).[1] Reinvention, or redesign of novel systems for personal and social mobility, for example, are needed with designs that prioritise biosphere, technosphere and social purpose considerations (Chapter 4).

Car and plane manufacturers are interested in cars and planes – their production is *what* their system does. But in a personal/social mobility system, cars and planes would be just some of many possible *hows* (including dampening demand for social mobility). This example is axiomatic: what is understood as a wicked or tame problem is a matter of boundary choice. Change the boundary and the system-in-focus changes, as does its purpose. Boundary expansion (i.e. adopting a wicked [or similar] framing) is an imperative in all future governance/governing innovation. Putting this axiom into effect involves embracing a *design turn* using systemic design capabilities to craft new institutions and social or 'soft' technologies and relationships between them (i.e. making the new 'governance diamond' functional as a meta-system delivering multiple transformations); see Figure 7.1.

equity

Transformation relates to *why* questions, to questions of purpose. To deliver a transformation a system also has to work: this is *what* the system does – it must be efficacious. Other questions – measures of performance – can be asked of a system: is it ethical, equitable, efficient, stable, resilient? More measures are possible, but purpose must be related to effectiveness. Systemic designing involves exploring why, what, how relationships in situated ways.

Systems and design scholar Peter Jones says

> systemic design is distinguished from service or experience design in terms of scale, social complexity and integration. Systemic design is concerned with higher order systems that encompass multiple subsystems. By integrating systems thinking and its methods, systemic design brings human-centered design to complex, multi-stakeholder service systems as ... found in industrial networks, transportation, medicine and healthcare.[2]

Systemic design is also as much about the attitude and predisposition of the designer as what is designed.

Taking a design turn is a second-order process involving the design of institutions, tools or practices as well as the affordances of the situations for use of an institution or tool or for the doing of practice.

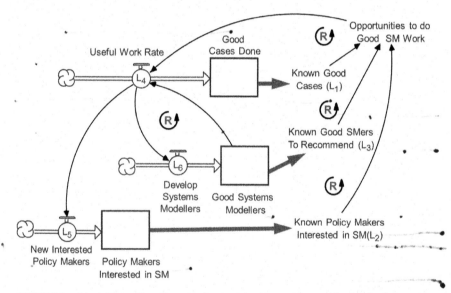

FIGURE 8.1 Stock/flow diagram representing the interconnected levers for improving the use of systems modelling (SM) in the policy arena. Squares represent stocks; arrows, flows. Four reinforcing (R) loops are depicted.

Box 8.1 provides an example of being reflexive and taking a design turn to both improve situations through systems dynamics modelling as well as providing affordances that enhance this form of STiP praxis.

BOX 8.1 DESIGNING A SYSTEMIC STRATEGY TO ENHANCE SYSTEMS DYNAMIC (SD) MODELLING IN POLICY FORMULATION. WHAT POTENTIAL LEVERS EXIST?[3]

Professor David Lane writes:

Potential leverage points overlap and are connected – naturally. They can be illustrated using a systems (causal loop) map (see Figure 8.1).

The levers (L) can be understood as two sets of three. The first set creates instantaneous effects (note how they all use active verbs).

L1. Know good cases to cite. It is important to be able to give an example of previous situations in which systems modelling has been of practical use to a policy maker. It is an obvious question for a potential client to pose: Where has this systems stuff worked before? A ready answer, brief but with telling detail, can be critical in making an opportunity to do more systems work (e.g. David's work was very influential in the UK as part of the Munro Review of child protection – which both took, and recommended, a STiP approach).[4]

L2. Know about policy makers' interested in systems modelling. Identify and remember whom to keep in contact with and whom to spend time approaching. Try to know who will champion systems-based work.

L3. Know good systems modellers to recommend. Many will want to do the work themselves – and that may be the answer. But confronted with the question 'Where can I get people to do system modelling?', you might find that you are busy or that skill in another system approach is what is really needed.

The second set of three levers creates accumulated effects. These have the potential to endure.

L4. Make sure that useful work is done and grasp every opportunity to do so. This flow of work then adds to the stock of good cases of systems modelling having been used (L1).

L5. Work on getting more policy makers interested in systems modelling – by doing good work and helping policy makers to get the best from it. That experience adds to the stock of those who have been helped and who become champions (L2).

L6. Develop systems modellers. The experience of doing useful work is a critical element. You may become more experienced yourself or it may be others who improve. This adds to the stock of good systems modellers (L3).

Creating the three stocks is important, but they are invisible unless we do something about it. That is why it is equally important to make sure that the bold links are created, to make sure that the stocks are visible. Now we can see that the two sets of three are not separate … but mutually supportive, indeed,

> reinforcing. Levers L1 and L4 reinforce each other, as do L2 and L5, as well as L3 and L6.
>
> There is more. That middle stock of good systems thinkers helps make sure that good systems modelling gets done and then creates another reinforcing loop because more good system thinking experience is created. We now have a system with at least four positive feedback loops. The overarching logic to get it started says shout about who and what are out there, communicate successes. This will help bring systems modelling further into the policy arena.

David Lane's example is of a practitioner walking their talk. It is pragmatic and demonstrates how STiP capability can be used and developed in everyday professional life.[5]

8.1.2 Some systemic design principles

A number of systemic design principles have been articulated in earlier chapters. These include:

- Foster systemic sensibility; think and act relationally/systemically, reverting to the systematic in appropriate cases only (Section 6.1.1).
- Pay attention to initial starting conditions; start off systemically especially through deframing, framing and reframing praxis (Section 7.2.3).
- Work with dualities in preference to dualisms – especially the knowledge/knowing, systemic/systematic, governance/governing dualities (Sections 6.2.3; 6.1.4; 6.3.3; 7.3).
- Appreciate the political ecology of practice/praxis (Section 6.2.2).
- Use awareness of the implications of living in language in systemic designing (e.g. Metaphor Impact Assessment [Section 7.2.3.4]).
- Be reflexive; reflect in and on action (Section 6.2.2.3).
- Create new distinctions, new experiences, that expand the traditions of understanding from which you and other actors/stakeholders think and act (Section 6.2.2.2).
- Foster situational understanding and boundary judgments based on multiple, partial perspectives (Chapter 5).
- Act so as to maximise (rather than close down) future choices (Section 7.2.3).

Other principles are emerging from conversations about systemic design and its close relation, transformation design.[6] Jones proposes the following set of principles:[7]

- _Idealisation_, identifying an ideal state or set of conditions that compel action towards a desirable outcome or signifies the value of a future system or practice (based on _Idealized Design_ as formulated by Russ Ackoff).[8]
- _Appreciating complexity_ – acknowledging 'the dynamic complexity of multi-causal wicked problems and the cognitive factors involved in understanding the relationships that indicate problem complexity'.[9]
- _Purpose finding_ – purposes can be determined by agreement and therefore designed or redesigned.
- _Boundary framing_ – each boundary judgement carries significantly different values, actions, and possible effects (deframing, framing and reframing are forms of boundary framing).
- _Employ requisite variety_ – the citizens chosen in the panel before the Irish referendum exemplify this feature, as they encompassed the variety in the broader population (see Box 4.3).
- _Coordinate feedback_ – see Chapter 10 and the literature on single, double and triple-loop learning.
- _System ordering_ – 'ordering defines the relationships of objects, system components, or abstract concepts to each other in a systematic way. The ordering of relations within a system set creates a compositional unity'.[10] This principle demonstrates the need for both systemic and systematic practice.
- _Generative emergence_ – designed wholes are more than the sum of the parts – it is possible to design, or manage for emergence (e.g. the various attributes _brought forth_ as depicted in Figure 8.2b).
- _Continuous adaptation_ – 'social systems may be self-organizing, but they are not self-ordering systems'; thus, purposeful action is required to stay adapted to a constantly changing system environment (i.e. coevolution).
- _Self-organising_ – which:

> serves a positive feedback or reinforcing process that enables creative organization of social systems by its participants. The cybernetic feedback processes of negative feedback (guidance) serve a self-adaptation capacity, the regulation of behaviors within preferred or sustainable limits. The systems principle of self-organizing enables the design of actions that increase awareness, incentives and social motivations to accelerate organizing behaviors.[11]

Transformation design is based on 'open communication processes for creative enquiry into new potentialities ... realized through new organisational structures and cultures, systemic innovations, or collaborative educational forms'.[12] Holzner focuses on only three design principles for transformation: cognition, communication, and cooperation.[13] Von Anshelm articulates an imperative for systemic and transformation design: it is about 'daring to initiate and perform experiments in social coexistence'.[14] Some examples are now given.

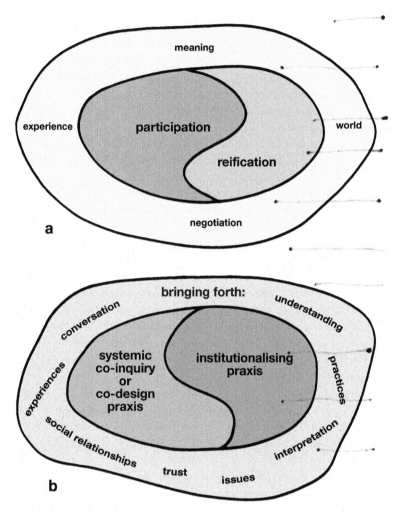

FIGURE 8.2 (a) The duality of participation and reification in the context of experience, meaning construction, negotiation, and the inhabited world; (b) A praxis duality of systemic co-inquiry and/or systemic co-design with institutionalising.

8.2 Participating and institutionalising

8.2.1 Participation and reification

Participation in governing, or any practice for that matter, is the means by which multiple partial perspectives are brought to bear on a task. Substantial research has shown that participation is necessary but not sufficient in responding to complex, uncertain issues, especially in a climate-changing world characterised by increased variation and surprise. Participation in and of itself changes little unless the participation brings forth all or some new experiences, new conversations, new stakeholdings, agreement about what is at issue, acts of interpretation, changes in understanding, new practices, breakdown of power relations, new social relations and the emergence of trust (see Figure 8.2b). The ultimate test is that through participation, committed stakeholder groups are effective in transforming a situation of concern for the better. Effective transformation usually requires some form of stabilising, or institutionalising, of the gains that are made from participatory governance processes. This is an ethical imperative; otherwise, those involved experience being *participated*. Without institutionalisation, a treadmill effect is created which leads to burnout and disillusionment of those engaged.

Etienne Wenger[15] and his colleagues concerned with social theories of learning use the term 'reification', or making something into a thing, to describe what happens when a concept, idea, or set of rules is stabilised and given an alternative form (Figure 8.2a). Converting the concept justice into a female statue outside a courthouse is one form. The reification of rules into a regulation is another. In other words, institutionalising, making outcomes into an institution, is a form of reification. In Wenger's theories relating to the function of communities of practice (CoPs), participation is the antidote to reification – the way of getting no-longer-useful reifications dissolved, done away with, deframed or reframed.

In Figure 8.2b, Wenger's conception is reframed in terms of a duality between two types of praxis: systemic co-inquiry and/or systemic co-designing praxis (discussed below) and institutionalising praxis.[16] When operating, this duality brings forth a set of emergent phenomena, none of which can arise deterministically through participation understood as simple cause and effect. The praxis elements must also include STiP capabilities (including systemic institutional design – birth as well as death of institutions – and systemic inquiry, design and evaluation). Together these constitute the elements of *systemic governing*. Think of lawmaking done through co-inquiry or co-design. But when laws are hung onto for too long, they go stale or create too much complexity (e.g. Figure 2.3). This then requires more co-design lawmaking that undoes the old – discarding what is no longer needed.

Praxis can, of course, be solitary or carried out with others, either purposefully or accidentally. We use the prefix 'co' as in co-design, co-inquiry and co-evaluation to refer to practices that are done purposefully in collaboration with others. There are diverse accounts of such practices in the literature, but few are effectively institutionalised.

8.2.2 Social learning: a praxis plus institution

Having learnt that participation was always necessary but never sufficient in complex, uncertain governance situations, members of the Open University's ASTiP Group have been researching and facilitating social learning for over

20 years, alongside other scholars. A rich literature and body of evidence have built up. The cases described in Chapter 5 are replete with elements of social learning. The term _social learning_ has taken on multiple interpretations. This is OK, as long as responsibility is taken for explaining how it is conceptualised and put into action. Explained in this section is, first, how social learning has become an alternative to naïve participation, and second, a governance model designed to extend and complement current mainstream approaches.

The test bed for ASTiP social learning research was in the governing of rivers, which across Europe are subject to a policy created as an EU 'directive', the WFD or Water Framework Directive.[17] The work began with an innovative reframing: choosing to see the sustainability of river catchments as an emergent property of social processes. A body of evidence-based scholarship now exists to show how social learning operates as both process (praxis) and institution (governance mechanism) in river catchments understood, or framed, as co-evolutionary social-biophysical systems (as in Figure 4.2). There are no reasons why the findings cannot be applied in other domains: cities, organisations, projects, and national, regional, and local governments.

Having another look at Figure 8.2b is likely to be helpful in understanding the ASTiP conception of social learning. At its core is a duality – process and institution. Social learning is a means of putting into effect either the orchestra or jazz-ensemble metaphor for governing discussed in the previous chapter. As with social learning, orchestras and jazz ensembles are institutional forms, things, in which someone invests money, time, effort and other resources. On the other hand, they are nothing without the capacity to create effective performances, which involves different players, instruments, scores etc., all of which are engaging in collaborative practice, practice that requires practice.

Effectiveness, as outlined earlier, is a measure of purpose, why a system exists. In the case of an orchestra, it may be to satisfy audiences, to deliver prestige and tourist income to a city, or to satisfy the desires of a benefactor – or some version of all of these.

For governing, the way social learning works is relatively straightforward. It can start in a number of ways:

- A group of people form who want to understand and do something about an issue of concern – not all may agree on what is at issue or what constitutes an improvement.
- As in the case of flood defences in Shaldon (Chapter 5), where a public-sector body confronts an issue relevant to a community and decides to use a social learning approach.
- In the conduct of innovation or change laboratories in which participants jointly build new stakeholdings in an issue or situation.
- As a framing and set of practices for sustained activist campaigns
- By policy makers who recognise the 'wickedness' of an issue or situation and realise that social learning is the only approach that can work.

When an issue emerges or a need arises that involves multiple stakeholders with varying histories and understandings, who commit, either from the start, or during the process, to transforming the *situation-of-concern*, then it is possible to design and facilitate processes that foster changes in understandings and practices of those participating. Over time, with sustained work, a trajectory emerges that leads to concerted action (Figure 8.3a). In many ways, it is like learning, over time, the rules for playing jazz and working together to create an improvised performance that changes the situation of concern to something agreed to be better. There is an additional significant change that happens with those involved – a change in social relations, including the emergence of trust and accommodations of difference (Figure 8.4).[18]

The ASTiP research conducted in Europe, China, South Africa and Australia established five main factors that enabled or constrained actions that give rise to social learning as a process (Figure 8.3b). These are:

- History, of both the situation and those involved (i.e. initial starting conditions and avoidance of pathway dependence).
- Institutions, including policies (as discussed in Section 2.2.1).
- Stakeholding, particularly the ability to build stakeholding in an issue where none was present before.
- Facilitation (by people and process designs) and mediation (by technologies and mediating objects).
- Epistemological politics – the question of whose knowledge counts and the power plays between different ways of knowing.

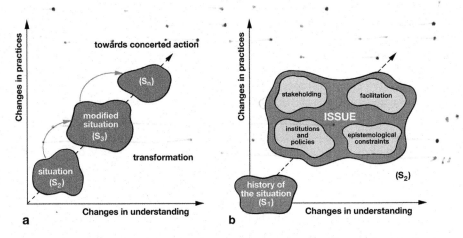

FIGURE 8.3 Left diagram (a): the situational (S) transformation dynamic affected when stakeholders work together around an issue of common concern, and experience changes in understanding and practices as the process unfolds. Right (b): the factors identified through case study research, which impinge on social learning as a dynamic process and thus the success of transformational action.[19]

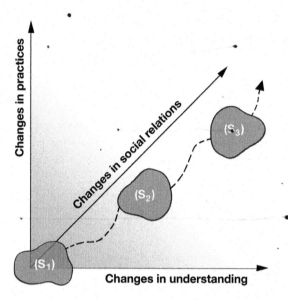

FIGURE 8.4 The added dimension of situational (S) change effected through social learning (i.e. changes in social relations as well as practice and understanding). The pathway of change/transformation is never purely linear.[20]

As outlined in Figure 8.5, the intellectual basis of most mainstream governance arrangements is to name the problem, assume that it is fixed, and that a fixed form of knowledge applies. The classic policy responses combine each or all of fiscal or market mechanisms, education or information or regulation, to normalise or control practice/behaviour. Social learning has different epistemological assumptions, assumptions much more suited to the surprise, uncertainty and complexity of an Anthropocene world.

Investment in social learning, like the orchestra/jazz band analogy, offers an opportunity for centralised negotiation and articulation of a society's priorities in relation to phenomena it seeks to address, *and* localised, improvised, co-designed 'performances' to meet higher-level purposes. Such a strategy builds citizen engagement (stakeholding) and cultivates variety that is creative and adapted to context. It is a governance mechanism for enacting Ashby's Law of Requisite Variety.

Just as an orchestra might be bullied by its conductor or exploited by its sponsor, so too can the social relations that build over time through social learning be undermined and destroyed, losing in the process that rare commodity, 'relational capital'.[21] Institutional arrangements are thus needed, including constitutional backing, to maintain the ethicality and viability of social-learning functioning in the face of the command-and-control practices of the mainstream systematic paradigm.

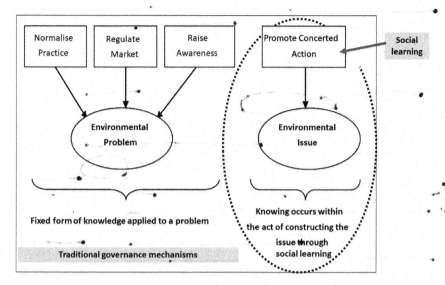

FIGURE 8.5 The intellectual and epistemological foundations of social learning as a form of governance (right) differ from the mainstream approach in relation to problems/issues.[22]

8.2.3 Systemic inquiry or co-inquiry

Systemic inquiry and co-inquiry are institutional and praxis innovations designed as antidotes to 'projectification'. Projects permeate and pollute our world mainly when they are, as institutions, used in the wrong ways and wrong contexts. For the most part their affordances facilitate systematic rather than systemic praxis. Contemporary projects are often designed for certainty, regularity, and in the mistaken belief that all wicked problems can be tamed within a project.

Systemic co-inquiry is a particular means of facilitating movement towards social learning (see above). As an institutional form it can be seen as a meta-platform (boundary expansion) or process for 'project or program managing' in that it has a focus on:

- Understanding situations in context and especially the history of the situation.
- Addressing questions of purpose.
- Clarifying and distinguishing 'what' from 'how' as well as addressing 'why'.
- Facilitating action that is purposeful and which is systemically desirable and culturally feasible.
- Developing a means of orchestrating practices across space and time which continue to address a phenomenon, or phenomena, of social concern when it is unclear at the start as to what would constitute an improvement.

Projects start out with an underlying emotion of certainty – of knowing or pretending to know what will be done. Systemic (co)-inquiry begins in a different emotional space – one of not knowing, admitting to uncertainty and complexity. ASTiP researchers have used systemic (co)-inquiry in a range of settings in several countries.[23]

Systemic (co)inquiry builds on, and extends C. West Churchman's concerns with the design of *inquiring systems.* He reflected on the tendency to bolster science and its research as the paradigmatic exemplar of an inquiring system. He rejected this and observed that 'reflective learning in the literal sense ... is the thinking about thinking, doubting about doubting, learning about learning, and (hopefully), knowing about knowing'.[24] He defined inquiry as an activity which produces knowledge.[25] Put another way, inquiry facilitates a particular way of knowing which, when enacted, makes a difference. As Churchman observed, when exploring the metaphor of a 'library of science', the common definition of science as a systematic collection of knowledge is 'almost entirely useless for the purposes of designing inquiring systems. ... in other words knowledge resides in the user not in the collection. ... it is how the user reacts to the collection ... that matters'.

Systemic (co)-inquiry is an institutional form designed for use in the Anthropocene (i.e. when confronted by uncertainty, complexity, systemic interdependencies, and surprise). For example, it would make much more sense for each nation's equivalent of the UK Climate Change Committee to conceptualise and conduct itself as an ongoing systemic co-inquiry with citizen involvement. This would create a commitment to learning in the long-term. Systemic co-inquiry could also be used in the building of *commoning* praxis.

8.2.4 Commoning

Elinor Ostrom received the Nobel Prize for economics on the basis of her work on elucidating the institutional dynamics of governing the commons or, as it is now sometimes called, 'commoning'.[26] Despite the Nobel Prize, she was not popular amongst mainstream economists.[27]

The 'commons' refer to resources that are shared or generated by a group of people – this may include rangeland (pastures), water, air etc. Commoning is central to the discourse of ecological democracy being advocated by Tim Hollo.[28] He notes that the commons is:

> an ancient concept, imbued with deep understandings of connection, ...
> the commons is better understood as a system than a form of property. It is a system by which a community agrees to manage resources, equitably and sustainably. As commons theorist David Bollier describes it in *Think Like a Commoner*, it is 'a resource + a community + a set of social protocols'.[29]

Ostrom recognised eight principles for running and/or designing commons.[30] These are:

1. Specifying clearly defined boundaries – especially who is entitled access to what. Unless there's a specified community of benefit, it becomes a free-for-all, and that's not how commons work.
2. Rules should fit local circumstances. There is no one-size-fits-all approach to common resource management. Rules should be dictated by local people and local ecological needs.
3. Participatory decision making is vital. There are all kinds of ways to make it happen, but people will be more likely to follow the rules if they had a hand in writing them. Involve as many people as possible in decision making.
4. Commons must be monitored. Once rules have been set, communities need a way of checking that people are keeping them. Commons don't run on goodwill but on accountability.
5. Sanctions for those who abuse the commons should be graduated – the commons that work best don't just ban people who break the rules. That tended to create resentment. Instead, they had systems of warnings and fines as well as informal reputational consequences in the community.
6. Conflict resolution should be easily accessible. When issues come up, resolving them should be informal, cheap, and straightforward. That means that anyone can take their problems for mediation, and nobody is shut out. Problems are solved rather than ignored because nobody wants to pay legal fees.
7. Commons need the right to organise. Your commons rules won't count for anything if a higher local authority doesn't recognise them as legitimate.
8. Commons work best when nested within larger networks. Some things can be managed locally, but some might need wider regional cooperation – for example, an irrigation network might depend on a river that others also draw on upstream.

Systemic design principles also apply to commoning. New communications technologies may play a role in some commoning functions (e.g. item 8, above) if not subject to manipulation. Designers of the Web originally saw it as a global commons to be used by all for the good of all. However, the institutions for governing this commons are still in their infancy (as for much of the technosphere – see Chapter 7).

Hollo goes on to argue that:

> this raises a central question for a system of governance based on the commons. How does government support what needs to be led from within the community itself? Indeed, how do we reclaim politics, re-enfranchise ourselves, when the very concept of politics is currently on the nose?

His response is to claim that:

> Essentially, the task is two-fold: to switch government from undermining communities to institutionally supporting and enabling them, and to build around genuine prefigurative politics, demonstrating leadership, showing what can be done. Where currently governments are allowing corporations to enclose our public and democratic space, we need to make the community, the commons, the focal point of government by building participatory democratic processes and institutions at every level. This doesn't mean postal votes; it means citizens' juries for major issues, participatory budget processes, participatory planning in local areas – proactively, rather than only as a reaction to developer proposals.[31]

A concurrent recovery and development of a citizen's systemic sensibilities would be a worthy addition to Hollo's vision, whilst also investing in activity that builds systems literacy and STiP capability.[32] As Hollo says:

> A vital part of the equation here is to ensure that local community activities are linked to the systemic, political goal.[33] Participating in a local Buy Nothing Group, for example, is a non-capitalist act which supports the local community and reduces environmental pressures. But it only becomes a truly transformative act when explicitly and directly connected to the greater whole.

We interpret this as requiring institutions to provide relationships across horizontal and vertical governance vectors as well as innovations that allow the articulation and rearticulation of social purpose by an active, engaged citizenry. This process can no longer be delegated to the state and the inadequate procedures used to enact democracy (Chapters 2 and 4).

8.2.5 Systemic enacting: the SDGs (Sustainable Development Goals)

The great achievements thus far of the UN's new SDGs are that they are agreed, are broader in focus, and apply to all nations, unlike the predecessor MDGs (Millennium Development Goals), and now have significant backing through investment by China. Having been agreed, the SDGs constitute a new institution. Agreement on the 17 goals and 169 targets now focuses attention on the implementation of the goals. Goal 17 specifically addresses the challenge of implementation. As articulated, the SDGs invite the creation of 'an integrated, holistic, multi-stakeholder approach'. This implies the need for STiP capabilities and conducive governance conditions.[34]

Thinking about the SDGs as a social technology enables the following question to be asked: 'What affordances do the SDGs offer to a user?' We know from experience that a good computer mouse offers affordances to a hand that makes the hand–mouse interaction fall into the background. Well, the affordances the SDGs offer are mainly a new language and talking point. Countless words will be written about them and meetings held. Multiple users of the SDGs can be imagined: a government, a Minister, a policy maker, a citizen, an agency, an NGO, and thus different affordances will emerge. The SDGs may remain out of sight, out of mind, for many unless made actionable and speakable in locally contextualised ways. There is also the question about their design affordances; remembering that the concept of affordance is not a property of one thing or another, but one of the relationships between a (social) technology and a user.

On one of her Australian visits, Naomi Klein said: 'Climate change tells us we need to get out of our silos and build the movements we know we need'.[35] Working from Australia, Thwaites and Kestin draw attention to a key issue of affordance:

> Perhaps the most important recommendation of the [stakeholder] workshops was the need to look for linkages between the goals and to recognise the synergies and trade-offs between them. For example, the use of first-generation biofuels might reduce carbon emissions and provide energy security but could have a negative effect on agriculture and food prices.[36]

How can the SDGs work for the good of all? Is it even possible, given some of the inherent design flaws? Not according to Jason Hickel, who argued that:[37]

> The core of the SDG programme for development and poverty reduction relies precisely on the old model of industrial growth — ever-increasing levels of extraction, production, and consumption. Goal 8 calls for 7% annual GDP growth in least developed countries and higher levels of economic productivity across the board.

There are also what he calls 'big unaddressed issues' like the SDGs offering 'little by way of solutions to many of the biggest known drivers of global poverty'.

In addition to these design concerns, the unintended effects of goals and targets have to be acknowledged. In the 1980s, systems scholar Peter Checkland pioneered a move away from goal-oriented thinking towards thinking in terms of learning, changing, adapting, and contextual designing using STiP (see Figure 8.6). Given the affordances associated with the history of use of the concepts of goals and targets, how can the implementation of the SDGs be made systemic? A lot will depend on how their implementation is framed and how they are institutionalised nationally, regionally, and within particular organisations and sectors.

Answers in contextually relevant ways to these questions will govern the sorts of practices that emerge. They will have to embrace the systemic design principles articulated earlier and avoid (i) becoming a tick-box exercise conveying administrative rather than transformative effectiveness; (ii) a narrow framing choice that subjects many years of well-intentioned effort to the affordance limitations that goals and targets carry; and (iii) non-reflexive scientism. Social innovation labs, of which there have been a profusion in recent years, if designed and enacted well, with the right practices and appropriately institutionalised, appear to hold considerable promise (Figure 8.6). Systems educators/researchers in the OU STiP group have been designing and running effective labs (as summer schools, or short- and medium-term events or workshops) for many years.[38] With investment in capability, a wide range of deliberative praxis can be incubated or cultivated in lab-forms, including a watershed or river catchment, framed as a governance unit.[39] The evidence is that these work well for those engaged in the learning and transformation process – but they work less well in effecting broader change unless (i) the key decision makers are in the room the whole time, and (ii) the outputs are translated into new institutional arrangements that secure, over time, the desired outcomes (Figure 8.2a).

A 2017 report poses, and partially addresses, the challenge arising from an explosion in social innovation labs that:

> have emerged around the world with the premise to provide alternative and effective approaches for tackling systemic problems and bringing about positive social transformation. These labs have grown rapidly in number and popularity alongside the social innovation movement, and have gained the attention of practitioners, researchers, and policy makers.

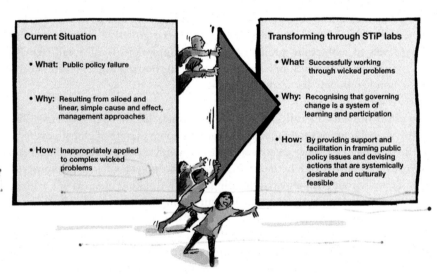

FIGURE 8.6 Designing to avoid public policy failure: a move from tame to wicked framings that demands a shift from speaking and acting in terms of goals and targets, and that can be facilitated by investment in STiP learning labs: doing systemic design, inquiry and evaluation.[40]

This report asks: 'What exactly are they and how do they function? What are the most effective methods they use? What are the challenges they face? Have they delivered the promise on which they were built?'[41] These are all questions worthy of ongoing attention, especially in the context of effectively enacting the SDGs. More opportunities would be created if new SDG labs were subsumed into the new social purpose arrangements outlined in Chapter 7.

8.2.6 Innovation through systemic action research

Systemic action research (SAR) happens when researchers see themselves as part of the research system and seek, with others, to act through their practice to transform situations in which they practice. The OU ASTiP Group has a history of conducting this type of research. They do not regard teaching and research as a dualism, so SAR is applied across all domains of practice, in both internal and external contexts. The OU SAR has STiP *praxis development* at its core and has application within groups, organisations and in the design and conduct of new governance systems. Cybernetic and systems, or cyber-systemic understandings, are central to this program of research. Some of the innovations include:

- *Systems diagramming*: This can provide a powerful means to explore or communicate different understandings of the world around us and of the potential outcomes of actions. Diagramming has become an important ingredient of how STiP has been taught at the OU. The process of creating a diagram is an important means for individuals and groups to 'reveal' how they understand a situation, particularly the different elements, patterns of causality and the nature of influences they perceive. Eventually they can propose what 'systems' might usefully be seen as part of an inquiry or learning process (i.e. the diagram captures someone's thinking and mediates communication about this thinking with others).[42]
- *Staff induction as systemic inquiry* into an organisation, for *relationship making* and providing *feedback* to senior management: Most induction is something done to someone, usually poorly. Based on the idea of rapid organisational appraisal, a group of inductees paired with an equal number of longer-term employees explores an organisation through having conversations (semi-structured interviews) along preselected transects (a sample of the organisation as a whole) and assimilating their learning for an end-of-week presentation to senior management.[43]
- *Contracting in group processes*: Poor group function can be headed off by beginning with contracting. An innovative way of working is to ask those present to nominate all the ways they can think of to make it a bad process. These can be flipped into a set of positive actions that will act as a basis for the group contract, which is overseen by the group itself and revisited regularly. Done well, contracting aids purposefulness.

- *Is/ought-based inquiry*: This is based on critical systems heuristics (CSH), a particular systems approach, and involves inquiry, usually with others, into how a 'current system' is perceived and then how they think it ought to be perceived; the CSH framework allows answers to a set of critical questions to be generated in both the *is* and *ought* modes.
- *Creating mediating organisations*: New institutional forms are being explored to mediate between the arms of vertical governance (the state) and horizontal governance (civil society) in coupled social-biophysical systems like rivers, cities etc. This is particularly the case where the state is failing, as in water governance in South Africa.[44]
- *Governing fear*: As Simon Bell writes: 'We are all victims of fear. Project Fear has been with us for hundreds of years. So far, we have made little attempt to map fear or understand how it is used'. Simon has used STiP approaches to find out how fear is weaponised and targeted and how to avoid making things worse.[45]

Other praxis examples have already been touched upon in this book. These include systemic design; systemic evaluation; adaptive SSM; adaptive boundary critique; reflexive learning through metaphor; and triggering/facilitating enthusiasm, including active listening and narrative (see Appendix 1).

8.3 The purposeful pursuit of social purpose

The longevity of groups that function effectively is closely related to the extent to which members have a common sense of purpose. A sense of common purpose does not just happen – it requires articulation and rearticulation. This is not hard. It can be done using mechanisms such as institutionalising an agenda item at an AGM (annual general meeting) of a group or organisation that asks 'Should we continue to exist?' Discussion of this as a first item of business enables the negotiation and renegotiation of purpose or a decision to allow 'death' – the expiration of purpose. Governance fails where organisations do not have a sense of common purpose. Groups ranging from project teams to whole nations lose their way when there is insufficient sense of common purpose.

Praxis in pursuit of purpose can operate effectively in all domains. A colleague leading a systemic inquiry into how to facilitate the Open University's becoming a 'learning organisation' was asked to meet with the OU Council's Staff Strategy Committee. The rationale for the invitation was that the committee, over two years old, had no idea about its purpose. Using a technique called 'snappy systems', adapted from Soft Systems Methodology, this colleague delivered a presentation to committee members with a built-in exercise that explored purpose. In half a day, this use of STiP enabled the committee to be clear about its role and purpose for the first time.[46] Other systems concepts and methodologies enable the design of purposeful systems.[47]

As outlined in Chapter 2, the current model of the state is incapable of enacting a 'social purpose articulating and pursuing system'. As argued in Chapter 4, we seek reform to education and other complex and uncertain domains such as well-being – two major areas of human activity that require significant reframing with concomitant institutional innovation. A starting point is to think how effective it has been to take the setting of interest rates out of the hands of the elected government of the day, and to decide explicitly and transparently what areas of life are best governed outside of party politics and executive government.[48] Thus what works in relation to the economy and international financial flows can also work in other domains. In the first instance, these new social purpose institutions/organisations would have responsibility for two prime functions (i) education, reframed as 'eco-literate citizen-building and enacting', and (ii) well-being – understanding, improving, and monitoring it. In this reframing, education becomes an investment by a society in itself through building the eco-literacy of its citizens and the expectation, with enablement, to engage in lifelong learning, including the diverse and evolving skills needed for work. In other words, to abandon the neo-liberal conception of education as a private good solely in service to the economy.

Well-being has many interpretations. We emphasise the need to avoid an anthropomorphic framing and include within it a health, as opposed to sickness, focus. This shift is consistent with attempts to move health services towards a localised well-being (and/or liveability) model, as in the example from Frome, discussed in Chapter 5. But building on Figure 7.6, we go further and argue that human relations with other species and the biosphere itself are integral to human well-being and our ethos of living. Thus, oversight for biodiversity, in fact all interspecies relations, should reside here. Like central banks, these new institutions/organisations should have employees with expertise (they should not rotate), a committee of expertise, but each with an additional citizens' assembly which convenes periodically and is run as a deliberative process, like the Irish referendum (see Chapters 4 & 9).

The UK Climate Change Committee (CCC) could be part of the innovation we seek. Justifiably, it could be a subsystem of the new well-being organisation, with a mandate to conduct an ongoing systemic inquiry into what it means for the country and its citizens to 'adapt' to human induced climate change. At the moment it can only do part of what is required, as it is an 'arm's-length organisation' responsible to the government (and politicians) of the day. Such bodies should be accountable to, and work through, citizens.

Another example is the UK's NIC (National Infrastructure Committee), set up by the then Treasurer in 2015. As described by its former Executive Officer (EO),[49] it is 'an independent, strategic advisory body'. Eight commissioners, supported by 40 civil servants, provide the government with impartial, expert advice through published reports and public statements. As an arm's-length body, it can do two things that a government department cannot. First, it can say politically contentious things, which gives ministers cover to make difficult decisions.

In its report on connectivity in the North of England, the Commission explicitly identified those transport corridors that are most in need of expansion (versus those that are not), which allowed the government to prioritise their limited funds. Second, it can act surgically and strategically. Established government departments are focused on the day-to-day, all-consuming operational functions. They have neither the time nor the perspective to step back, look at the big picture, identify needs, and propose solutions. The NIC's work on digital connectivity is a case in point. Whilst the regulator focused on the market for 5G, the NIC pointed out that ensuring broad 4G coverage should be the priority.

The CCC and NIC examples point to important functions that the new institutions would need to carry out. But those involved and at the core of current arrangements still frame change in first-order terms. The NIC officer frames his concerns very much in an improving business-as-usual model. He advocates better consultation:

> France, Germany and Switzerland are much better [than the UK] at public consultation. Leveraging their more federalised government structures, everyone from local councillors upwards consults their constituents both in person and online. Constituents' fears about disruption are mollified, and they are educated about a project's benefits.[50]

In today's circumstances, consultation is a poverty-stricken approach. Participation is better, but still not sufficient. Social learning, incorporating systemic inquiry, is the next frontier.[51] But more radical moves to ecological democracy are needed. There is nothing transparent about purpose – national infrastructure for what? Clearly there is a need for the locus of power in our governance systems to change radically around several key areas of human endeavour.

8.4 Institutionalising STiP in organisations

Increasingly, experiments with STiP are emerging in different contexts. These include innovation and co-design labs of different sorts, organisations that include local governments, foundations, NGOs, think tanks, banks, technology R&D groups, public-sector bodies such as police forces and international bodies such as the OECD. In the UK, a new MSc-level apprenticeship for the 'systems thinking practitioner' has been formulated by a committee of employers and approved by government. Here is a brief example drawn from this wave of innovation.

Lankelly Chase (LC) is a smallish London-based Foundation.[52] It has a long-term focus for its work, which it calls 'severe and multiple disadvantage'. This term 'was intended to cover the interlocking nature of social harms such as mental illness, offending, homelessness, abuse, drug misuse, and the poverty that appears to generate them'. What is relevant here is that with STiP at its centre, they have reinvented the organisation, how they think about and practise what they do. Three concepts are central: systems, place and action inquiry. Here is a sample:

When we say systems we mean "a set of things"—people, cells, molecules or whatever—interconnected in such a way that they produce their own pattern of behaviour over time.[53]

The systems which support people facing severe and multiple disadvantage are complex and rooted in particular places. These systems are not the same in Newcastle, Blackpool, Cardiff or Glasgow. In each of these places, the systems have their own patterns and behaviours. These systems include people who are getting paid to design and deliver projects, as well as people who live and act within places.

Clarity about the place they are working in is an essential starting condition:

> We will need to work at different levels within a place – for example, across the local authority, at ward or street level. The tension between communities of interest and communities of place is something that we will have to continually pay attention to. Each place will define the relevant boundaries for the systems they are seeking to improve. The boundaries of these places will be drawn in relation to the particular challenges that each place is responding to.[54]

This framing can be understood as recognising the primacy of place-based appreciation of systemic complexity and design, or co-design through action inquiry with new systems-of-interest.[55] These are some of the systemic design concepts introduced in Chapter 7 and above.

Importantly, the LC staff are engaged in processes across the organisation to articulate and rearticulate core assumptions and their underlying theory of change. The current articulation is:

- We are all part of the system.
- It's not our role to make change; we build conditions for change to flourish.
- No one person holds the whole truth.
- Everyone needs to recognise and acknowledge their own need to change.
- Systems produce outcomes, not organisations or projects.
- Everyone within such a system must have a voice in how the system works.
- Everything and everyone exists in relationships. To fully understand a person or thing, you have to understand their relationships to other things.
- Emotions are present in all of this work. We need to acknowledge and work with this.

In their practice, they adopt the perspective that:

> there are systems everywhere from your family as a system through to public service systems addressing severe and multiple disadvantage like homelessness, criminal justice and domestic violence. This means we've had to

think about how to start somewhere. How to draw a boundary around the systems in which we're interested.[56]

Their approach is to initiate co-inquiries with those they agree to fund:

> [the] inquiry will work to support a small number of places to build the desired system behaviours and to support those places to make changes to improve the way that those systems function for people who face severe and multiple disadvantage.[57]

But what is perhaps more exciting is that they have reframed all that they do as a form of 'action inquiry'. They call this meta-inquiry 'Building the Field', which pertains to the domain of their concerns. In undertaking this inquiry, they seek to address questions like:

- Where do our actions have the greatest leverage?
- How do we remain open to different approaches?
- How do we build the systemic capability/authorising environment?
- How do we ensure that these opportunities are available to everyone regardless of role, ethnicity, class, sector?
- What networks exist already that we can support? Or do we need to support the emergence of a new self-sustaining network?
- How do we ensure that learning spreads across the UK, and what are the best mechanisms for this?
- How can a foundation best govern itself in ways that are ethically defensible and systemically desirable?

In doing what they do, they have created favourable starting conditions, made explicit their framing choices, and invested in praxis development. For example, they:

- Frame situations of 'severe and multiple disadvantage, climate change, poverty, gender inequality, and so on' as intractable or wicked problems facing society.[58]
- Appreciate the limitations of traditional responses to wicked problems, which are in identifying what works. This leads policy makers to mistakenly think that they can 'create ever more elaborate and evidenced interventions to address an issue or support people to lead socially and economically functional lives'.[59]
- Engage with potential grantees, by asking them to think about their application in terms of how it will change systems.
- Support collaborative capability-building by funding initiatives, such as the New Philanthropy Capital (NPC) report: *Systems Change: A Guide to What It Is and How to Do It.*[60]

There is a growing body of evidence and experience in using and institutionalising STiP in organisational contexts across both the private and public sector. What limits uptake at the moment is lack of investment in capability building, strengthening and making coherent a STiP discourse, and further institutional innovation. The experiences of Lankelly Chase can be drawn upon to reframe and reinstitutionalise the public policy process, and to force companies into practices that constitute a new social license to operate.

8.5 Possibilities and constraints for systemic governing

The focus of this chapter is the systemic relations between practices and institutions, but not just any old practice or institution. Taking the 'design turn' requires systemic sensibility and systems literacy that can be turned into effective STiP capability. Institutions need affordances that enable STiP to flourish. There is sufficient evidence to be confident that, with more ongoing investment and innovation, new cadres of practitioners able to do creative, situated systemic designing, inquiring and evaluating can create a wave of innovation in systemic governing. Part of the responsibility of these new cadres will be to do double work. They will be innovating in their own practices, as well as working towards making the contexts of their practice more amenable and long-lasting. Walking a fine line between participating in systemic practices and institutionalising their innovations will be called for. What Lankelly Chase has set out to do, and sustain, as a means to tackle persistent social disadvantage typifies what will be required.

What must be appreciated to advance ongoing innovation? Fortunately, examples are emerging all the time. On the other hand, most citizens are oblivious to these developments and discern no emerging patterns that might make things better. The burgeoning failure of our current governing practices is what the media reports and is front-and-centre for most folk. There are many well-intentioned people trying to make a difference, and much of this is located in civil society and the not-for-profit sector. Examples include events like 'hacking the Anthropocene'.[61,62]

More creativity with systemic designs will be needed. Giving rivers legal status through institutional innovations is relatively new in terms of contemporary governance, though not new within indigenous societies nor in the history of European cultures. Place names like Holywell speak to a past in which wells were considered holy and thus revered for the water they offered.[63]

Tim Hollo writes that the obvious action, in the context of rebalancing rights, is to grant legal rights to nature. Why should BHP Billiton have legal rights but the Great Barrier Reef should not? In an ecological democracy, the concept that the natural world has rights should be embedded at each level, from the local to the global. Examples of how this can be done are emerging rapidly around the world, from New Zealand and India declaring certain river systems to be legal persons to Bolivia enshrining the rights of Mother Earth in its constitution.

There is even a Draft Universal Declaration of the Rights of Mother Earth that was presented and discussed at the Cochabamba World Conference on Climate Change and the Rights of Mother Earth in 2010. Introducing and implementing such laws at various levels, including the global level, should be a priority.[64]

Taking a design turn, new institutional forms can be designed, such as constitutions, with the right affordances for particular types of practices to be enacted. New practices and new institutions demand new governance systems mediated by constitutional reforms, the subject of the next chapter.

Notes

1 Examples of first-order change are fuel economy, emissions reduction and materials innovation; even hybrid and fully electric cars exemplify first-order change.
2 Jones, P. 2015. Systemic design principles for complex social systems. In *Social Systems and Design*, G.S. Metcalf, ed. Kyoto: Springer Translational Systems Sciences 1: 91–128.
3 Material in Box 8.1 draws heavily on: Lane, D.C. 2016. 'Till the muddle in my mind has cleared away': Can we help shape policy using systems modelling? *Systems Research and Behavioral Science* 33 (5): https://doi.org/10.1002/sres.2422.
4 https://www.gov.uk/government/publications/munro-review-of-child-protection -final-report-a-child-centred-system (Accessed 5 March 2019).
5 In the revised governance model presented in Chapter 4, government-based policy makers would not be the only recipients or users of systems-modelling expertise.
6 Another potentially relevant form of practice is dialectical design, a form of design based on creative contradictions – 'the design and its environment, including the people involved, are assumed to form an inseparable whole. The whole and its parts are subject to interaction and change throughout the entire design process.. See Taxén, Lars. 1995. *The Dialectical Approach to System Design, First World Conference on Integrated Design and Process Technology*, Austin, TX. https://www.researchgate.net/ publication/242576032_The_Dialectical_Approach_to_System_Design (Accessed 7 March 2019).
7 Jones, P. 2015. Systemic design principles for complex social systems. In *Social Systems and Design*, G.S. Metcalf, ed. 1, pp. 91–128. Tokyo: Springer Translational Systems Sciences.
8 Ackoff R.L. 1993. Idealized design: Creative corporate visioning. *Omega, The International Journal of Management Sciences* 21 (4): 401–410.
9 Jones, P. 2015. op. cit., p. 109.
10 Ibid., p. 116.
11 Ibid., pp. 116–117.
12 Jonas, W., Zerwas, S., and von Anshelm, K., eds. 2015. *Transformation Design: Perspectives on a new design attitude*. Berlin, Heidelberg: Birkhäuser Science/Springer.
13 Ibid.
14 Ibid., pp. 15–16.
15 Wenger, E. 1989. *Communities of Practice*. Cambridge: Cambridge University Press.
16 This duality can be seen as a variation on the stability-change duality described so effectively by Donald Schön in his Reith Lectures and in his book *Beyond the Stable State* (1971; New York: Random House).
17 Beginning in 2000, this was also a time of testing 'directives' as a new institutional form. They have not worked that well, as each creates a policy-context silo.
18 Accommodations between different perspectives create more possibilities than consensus seeking; consensus positions are lowest common-denominator and lead those participating to lose their enthusiasm (see Glossary in Appendix 2).

19 Ison, R.L., Steyaert, P., Roggero, P.P., Hubert, B., and Jiggins, J. 2004. *Social Learning for the Integrated Management and Sustainable Use of Water at Catchment Scale* (EVK1-2000-00695SLIM) Final Report. See http://slim.open.ac.uk (Accessed 6 May 2019).

20 We are indebted to Patrick Steyaert for this version of the heuristic.

21 SLIM. 2004. *The Role of Conducive Policies in Fostering Social Learning for Integrated Management of Water.* SLIM Policy Briefing No. 5. SLIM. See http://slim.open.ac.uk (Accessed 6 May 2019).

22 Ison, R.L., Röling, N., and Watson, D. 2007. Challenges to science and society in the sustainable management and use of water: Investigating the role of social learning. *Environmental Science & Policy* 10 (6): 499–511.

23 For example, Foster, N., Collins, K.B., Ison, R.L., and Blackmore, C.P. 2016. Water governance in England: Improving understandings and practices through systemic co-inquiry. *Water* 8, 540; doi:10.3390/w8110540; Collins, K.B. and Ison, R.L. 2009. Jumping off Arnstein's ladder: Social learning as a new policy paradigm for climate change adaptation. *Environmental Policy and Governance* 19: 358–373.

24 Churchman, C.W. 1971. *The Design of Inquiring Systems*, p. 17. New York: Basic Books.

25 Ibid, p. 8.

26 https://en.wikipedia.org/wiki/Elinor_Ostrom (Accessed 21 November 2018).

27 https://blogs.wsj.com/economics/2009/10/12/economists-react-nobel-award-sends-message-about-economics/ (Accessed 5 March 2019).

28 https://griffithreview.com/articles/commons-and-commonwealth-enclosure-rebirth-tim-hollo/ (Accessed 5 March 2019).

29 https://makewealthhistory.org/2018/01/15/elinor-ostroms-8-rules-for-managing-the-commons/ (Accessed 5 March 2019).

30 Ostrom, Elinor. 1990. *Governing the Commons: The Evolution of Institutions for Collective Action.* Cambridge: Cambridge University Press. See also Williams, J. 15 January 2018. *Elinor Ostrom's 8 rules for managing the commons.* https://earthbound.report/2018/01/15/elinor-ostroms-8-rules-for-managing-the-commons/ (Accessed 6 May 2019).

31 Tim is actively walking his talk – see https://greens.org.au/act/person/tim-hollo (Accessed 5 March 2019)

32 Helfrich, Silke. 2016. *We Can Bring About a Language of Commoning,* October 19, 2016. Available at: https://blog.p2pfoundation.net/patterns-commoning-can-bring-language-commoning/2016/10/19. (Accessed 5 March 2019).

33 We would not speak of political goals but of social purpose articulating and rearticulating.

34 Reynolds, M., Blackmore, C.P., Ison, R.L., Shah, R., and Wedlock, E. 2018. The role of systems thinking in the practice of implementing sustainable development goals. In *Handbook of Sustainability Science and Research,* pp. 677–698. Cham: Springer.

35 Naomi Klein. See https://www.youtube.com/watch?v=a5LuIAJEFUc (Accessed 10 April 2019).

36 Thwaites, J. and Kestin, T. 2015. Sustainable development goals: A win-win for Australia. *The Conversation.* https://theconversation.com/sustainable-development-goals-a-win-win-for-australia-47263?utm_medium=email&utm_campaign=Latest+from+The+Conversation+for+September+24+2015+-+3483&utm_content=Latest+from+The+Conversation+for+September+24+2015+-+3483+CID_d9e0f4f016982d58ead7baad1ed51f1b&utm_source=campaign_monitor&utm_term=just%20for%20developing%20nations (Accessed 10 April 2019).

37 https://theconversation.com/why-the-new-sustainable-development-goals-wont-make-the-world-a-fairer-place-46374 (Accessed 5 February 2019).

38 See Foster, N. et al. 2017. op. cit.

39 Ison, R.L. 2018. op. cit.

40 Figure source: Reynolds, Martin et al. 2018. op. cit.
41 Papageorgiou, K. 2017. *Labs for Social Innovation*. Institute for Social Innovation. ESADE and Robert Bosch Stiftung.
42 From Ison, R.L. 2018. op. cit.; see also Blackmore et al. 2017. op. cit.
43 Armson, R., Ison, R.L., Short, L., Ramage, M., and Reynolds, M. 2001. Rapid institutional appraisal (RIA): a systemic approach to staff development. *Systems Practice & Action Research* 14: 763–777.
44 Some of this work is being carried out in a co-inquiry with AWARD in South Africa in a large project concerned with the resilience of the Limpopo River system – see http://award.org.za/index.php/projects/usaid-resilm-o/ (Accessed 7 March 2019).
45 https://www.open.edu/openlearn/project-fear (Accessed 7 March 2019).
46 See Armson, R. 2011. *Growing Wings on the Way*. Axminster: Triarchy Press.
47 Reynolds, M. and Holwell, S., eds. 2010. *Systems Approaches to Managing Change: A Practical Guide*. London: Springer & Milton Keynes: The Open University.
48 In using this example we are not endorsing the place that interest rates hold in our society but pointing to an institution that can effect important decisions through its design.
49 https://www.centreforpublicimpact.org/five-reflections-national-infrastruct ure-body/?utm_source=Centre+for+Public+Impact&utm_campaign=8587536 892-EMAIL_CAMPAIGN_2018_08_21_08_38&utm_medium=email&utm_ term=0_3b8694e112-8587536892-&utm_source=Centre+for+Public+Impact& utm_campaign=8587536892-EMAIL_CAMPAIGN_2018_08_21_08_38&utm_ medium=email&utm_term=0_3b8694e112-8587536892-187126449 (Accessed 5 February 2019).
50 Ibid.
51 Collins, K., and Ison, R.L. 2009. op. cit.
52 https://lankellychase.org.uk/our-work/place/ (Accessed 6 February 2019).
53 In this, Lankelly Chase draws on the work of Donella Meadows.
54 Collins, K., and Ison, R.L. 2009. op. cit.
55 Fearing some governing board negativity to the idea of systemic inquiry, the alternative framing as action inquiry was used.
56 Collins, K., and Ison, R.L. 2009. op. cit.
57 Ibid.
58 Ibid.
59 Ibid.
60 https://www.thinknpc.org/publications/systems-change/ (Accessed 3 February 2019).
61 https://hackingtheanthropoceneiv.wordpress.com/ (Accessed 14 March 2019).
62 A list can only be very partial and thus selective; some to highlight include: (i) the UK-based Incredible Edible initiative – see https://www.incredibleedible.org.uk/ (Accessed 15 April 2019); (ii) Seeds of good Anthropocenes – see https://goodan thropocenes.net/; (iii) Buurtzorg, the Dutch model of neighbourhood care that is going global – see https://www.theguardian.com/social-care-network/2017/ma y/09/buurtzorg-dutch-model-neighbourhood-care; (iv) the Green New Deal initiative in the USA – see https://en.wikipedia.org/wiki/Green_New_Deal (Accessed 13 April 2019).
63 The market town of Holywell takes its name from the St Winefride's Well, a holy well surrounded by a chapel. The well has been known since at least the Roman period. It has been a site of Christian pilgrimage since about 660, dedicated to Saint Winefride who, according to legend, was beheaded there by Caradog, who attempted to attack her. The well is one of the Seven Wonders of Wales and the town bills itself as The Lourdes of Wales. Many pilgrims from all over the world continue to visit Holywell and the Well. Source: https://en.wikipedia.org/wiki/Holywell (Accessed 15 April 2019).

64 Tim Hollo Griffith Review, Hollo, T. 2018. https://www.griffithreview.com/articles/commons-and-commonwealth-enclosure-rebirth-tim-hollo/ (Accessed 6 January 2020); also O'Donnell, Erin, and Talbot-Jones, Julia. 2017. Three rivers are now legally people – But that's just the start of looking after them. *The Conversation,* March 24. http://theconversation.com/three-rivers-are-now-legally-people-but-thats-just-the-start-of-looking-after-them-74983; also Vidal, J. 2011. Bolivia enshrines natural world's rights with equal status for Mother Earth. *The Guardian* 11 April. https://www.theguardian.com/environment/2011/apr/10/bolivia-enshrines-natural-worlds-rights; Draft Universal Declaration of the Rights of Mother Earth. https://www.iucn.org/content/draft-universal-declaration-rights-mother-earth.

9

WHY AND HOW
CONSTITUTIONS MATTER

9.1 Tale of two referenda

To explore why constitutions matter, we expand the earlier comparison of the Irish and UK referenda to understand why and how what happened, happened. The UK has no constitutional provisions for calling and running referenda. Its government decided to hold one – mainly to appease the anti-EU faction in its own party. It was conducted entirely without any requirement for cool-headed discussion on a level talking field, advice, expert opinion, or facts. It was a classic political free-for-all, with the news media operating, in effect, as political parties. Only once the result was declared, did the demands of turning a narrow decision into practical action call for some reality. Obstacles – notably the Irish border – known for years before the referendum was announced, came into public consciousness. In negotiation with the EU, the Prime Minister and influential ministers and others then made substantive choices as to the form of exit that should have informed the decision. At the time of writing (mid-2019), no solution has been found. Roughly half the country is facing one way and half the other, each hoping to impose its majoritarian will on the other, leaving a lot of sore losers. The sort of robust public deliberation essential for considering such a divisive issue was and is entirely absent.

What might that robust deliberation look like? Abortion in a historically Catholic country – its 1937 constitution was submitted to the Vatican for review and comment – is as divisive as it gets. A large majority of the country still identify as Catholic in the census. The Irish constitution makes explicit provision for a referendum when a 'Bill contains a proposal of such national importance that the will of the people thereon ought to be ascertained'. The referendum is called by a joint petition of a majority of the members of the Senate (the upper house) and not less than one-third of the members of the House of Representatives addressed to the non-executive President. The method of election of full proportional representation (PR) through single transferable vote for 49 of the 60 members of the Senate, and partial PR for the House, ensured diversity of opinion in these chambers and thus acceptance that this was of 'such national importance'. This petition followed a long campaign to change the provision prohibiting abortion. The Irish constitution can be changed only by the people.

A Fine Gael-led coalition government took office in 2016 with a program that promised a randomly selected Citizens' Assembly to report on possible changes to the Eighth Amendment of their constitution, which forbade abortion. Such processes have become culturally accepted in Ireland since their use to remove their territorial claim to Northern Ireland, as part of the peace agreement in 1998. As a historically divided country, Ireland has had to learn how to cohere.

At first mention, pro-choice activists saw the Citizens Assembly as 'kicking the can down the road'. Many perceived that Enda Kenny did not want to be the Taoiseach (Prime Minister) who brought in abortion. A large number of politicians were very afraid of the topic, feeling the country wasn't ready for it. But they underestimated the Irish people and the power of expertly organised public deliberation:[1]

> In all the excitement, we should not lose sight of what did not happen. A vote on an emotive subject was not subverted. The tactics that have been so successful in the UK, the US, Hungary and elsewhere did not work. A democracy navigated its way through some very rough terrain and came home not just alive but more alive than it was before. In the world we inhabit, these things are worth celebrating but also worth learning from.[2]

9.2 Personal ethics, national culture and constitution

In these two referenda we can hear the interplay – or relational dynamics – between the constitution and the people operating within it. The tighter or more prescriptive the constitution, the less wiggle room for the politicians and administrators, and the more the informed conclusions of the people pertain – as in Ireland. The looser the process, the more the politicians make hay and an uninformed half-decision results – as in the UK.

The culture or ethos of a nation plays a significant role in the decisions a government takes and in their enactment by us all, but only to make them more or less good for their peoples. A good constitution embodies an ethos and restricts the space for its abuse.

This helps explain why, under an identical constitution, Presidents Trump and Obama could act so differently. Despite his liberal and democratic intent expressed in many speeches, Barack Obama entered a 'Wall Street government', preprogrammed by unlimited party donations and preferential lobbying. The US system of governing has become a system for wealth appropriation. His hands tied, he was unable to translate his intent into fundamental economic and social change (other than Medicare). Having been let down by someone as a Democrat perceived traditionally on their side, many on the wrong end of neoliberalism saw their only chance in someone who reportedly did not even intend to win.[3] Donald Trump has pushed constitutional limits to challenge the status quo and indulge his prejudices. An inadequate constitution has neutered one president and facilitated an odd one. If the US constitution had the protections proposed in Chapter 3 to prevent preferential lobbying, Obama would have been able to pursue the social and economic justice program he had been elected for.

More than this, if today's constitutions already had the means to balance modern power, then Trump would never have been elected or even been a candidate in the first place. Trump, as much as Margaret Thatcher, is a product of these broken systems – not their salvation. Mrs Thatcher came to power at a time when Britain was still in the grip of class warfare. Whilst in most more developed countries this battle had long ceased, especially after the leavening effects of World War II, the electoral system in the UK maintained a two party state. Those parties represented the haves and the have-nots, managers and workers, upper and lower classes. The two parties maintained an increasingly redundant class struggle into the 1980s and, even now, a 'civil war' that was already well over in the rest of Europe, where proportional representation gave voice and power to more diverse and less divisive parties. In the UK, trade unions were, typically, obstructive and striking for more money regardless of its fundability, and managements were typically unprofessional and uneducated. Mrs Thatcher was needed to bring them into the latter half of the twentieth century. Under proportional representation, this 'class struggle' would have taken its place long ago at the margins of political value. The Labour party remains mainly funded by trade unions and the Conservative party by wealthy business people.

Figures 9.1 and 9.2 are a simplified means of showing the relational dynamics between individual or personal ethics, the prevailing culture of a society and its constitution. The description here is sequential. In practice it will be recursive, as one factor affects the others. The model applies to all organisations from the UN to a local sewing club.

Figure 9.1 shows (1) a distribution of the individual prevailing ethics of a nation's citizens, from weak or effectively none on the left to strong on the right. This distribution in total moves left or right over time as society's social norms and culture (2) alter. Attitudes to democracy, for example, may harden or soften, strengthening or weakening where the distribution sits. Within this distribution, the constitution (3) then sets the limits on the behaviour of institutions and organisations. In a dictatorship (Figure 9.2), almost no limits are set and here leaders behave without reference to ethics, only to power. At the top end of the scale, Switzerland has probably the tightest constitutional limits and institutional affordances are thus far better, but the economic still dominates and institutions of the biosphere do not feature. With the right institutions, the three-dimensional governance model would set more precise limits on the behaviour of people in power.

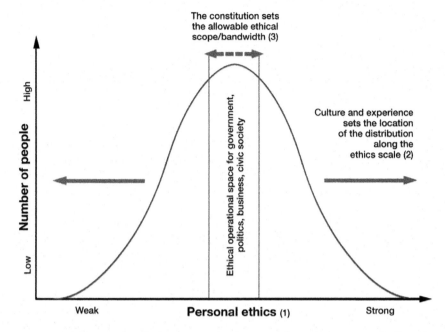

FIGURE 9.1 How personal ethics, national culture, and the constitution set the boundaries on behaviour, decision and action.

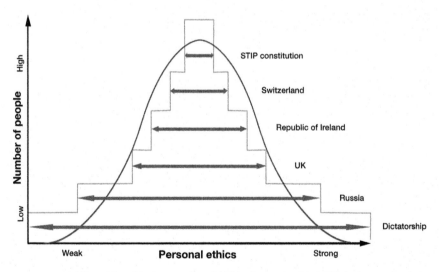

FIGURE 9.2 Allowable ethical scope/bandwidth determined by different constitutions.

9.1.1 Beware people in power

Politicians should not be here to demonstrate their 'rightness' or for their psychological flaws to dominate, but to make beneficial change. Those in power will not, at least initially, take to tighter constitutional controls. That is a sure sign they are needed. Research in neuroscience has demonstrated what many people have observed for years – that power damages the brain. Those, in whatever walk of life, who exercise power for long periods change as people. 'When power is unconstrained by democratic controls or good systems of governance, then power-holders may show undesirable distortions in judgment, cognition and behaviour as a result of its drug-like effects on the brain'.[4] Leaders receive a psychological hit to their brains' reward systems from making an important decision. Government should not be a 'freak show' in private. This is the point where ego confronts democracy, where the psychopathology of leaders confronts the needs of the people and where the constitution should mediate between the two.

Beware anyone who seeks absolute power or to loosen the controls over their actions. National constitutions and company governance have always been there to limit the remit of leaders' egos. Nelson Mandela seems to have been one of the very few powerful leaders who recognised this, but he had a most unusual life journey.

9.2 Constitutions matter

Aristotle described a constitution as creating the frame upon which the government and laws of a society are built. A constitution may be defined as an organisation of offices in a state, by which the method of their distribution is fixed, the sovereign authority is determined, and the nature of the end to be pursued by the association and all its members are prescribed. A constitution is the 'meta-law' under which all the institutions of governing operate. It is essential that the 'constitutioners' – the people – decide what is to be fixed in this meta-law and thus kept beyond the politics of the day, and what is left to government and other institutions to amend. In some jurisdictions with loose constitutions, electoral boundaries, voting ages and voter registration are amendable by government. Consequently, gerrymandering[5] is rife. Where the role of local and regional government is not prescribed, then centralisation will occur. If a government can change the 'constitution' then it is not a constitution.

The 'invisible hands' of constitution are everywhere. As you read and we write, a good one will be adding to your life and a bad one deducting. The reasons your train is or is not running on time, you are or are not being treated well in a hospital, your bank is or is not looking after your money securely, can often be traced back to your country's constitution. Trust in government is highest in Switzerland. Its constitution is probably the best in the world. By contrast with today, in the nineteenth century the constitution of the US was far ahead of its competitors in Europe in democracy and thus the motivation of citizens and the performance and accountability of government. The twentieth became America's century as it led and dominated the world. How much of the US's primacy was attributable to its constitution? Although the statistical relationship has not been established – yet – the systemic relationship has: constitutions matter.

By contrast, what proportion of climate change is attributable to the US constitution? The connections are quite obvious. The US is the world's largest greenhouse gas producer and leading exporter of the biosphere-destructive economic system. Big companies and industries have prevented GHG limiting legislation and its effective enactment, except at the margin. As we saw in Chapter 3, preferential lobbying has been its means and is pervasive. The now-inadequate US constitution has allowed and enabled this through unlimited political party donations, a two-party state, gerrymandering of elections and political appointment of Supreme Court judges. It would be instructive to estimate the GHG effect of each relevant law, regulation and executive order – passed or prevented – and to total their effect. How much of the rise in the Earth's atmospheric temperature has the US constitution produced? Arguably, its constitution and those of other super polluters are potentially killing us all – raising the question as to whether global rules should be applied to national constitutions.

The reason preferential lobbies by big companies succeed and transfer income from you to their controllers and funders is to be found in the interstices of most constitutions. The reason elites arise and grow is there, nestling in their folds. The reason neoliberalism has been allowed to become the dominant form of capitalism is that many constitutions are such that they cannot prevent or contain it.

We have read countless papers, books and articles from the four corners of the world on how to improve decision making through systems thinking.[6] But only by exception is this thinking applied, and then for the limited period of an enlightened minister's term of office. Otherwise, like memory foam, the existing norms and imperatives of government machines return behaviour to its unenlightened form. The nine changes proposed to prevent preferential lobbying cannot be wished or proselytised into existence.

The UN has Sustainable Development Goals – good. But its meta-organisational process for their achievement relies a lot on 'urging' – as in 'UN rights experts urge Member States to go beyond statements'.[7] Advocacy has some effect sometimes. But delivering these goals will take much more than an urge. An effective system of governing cannot rely on politicians and government officials doing the right thing. The reason constitutions exist is to make the right things happen.

The national founders (the 'founding fathers' in the US) of the eighteenth and nineteenth centuries would have grasped all this and built in safeguards against business power and biosphere degradation, just as they did to prevent leaders becoming de facto dictators, political parties behaving as fascists, and populist majorities pillorying minorities. There is nothing radical or out of the ordinary in the proposals made in this book. The abuse of power, which is what preferential lobbying is, is a must for constitutional rectification. Of course, those benefiting from it now – some of whom own the traditional media, which might be expected to do its job in supporting these changes but which does not because of their owner's personal interest – are those who dominate the political platforms. Politicians have allowed the media cycle to own them, not least because – operating within a broken system – they find themselves largely powerless. The best they can hope for is a positive headline and making their way towards a top job. There are exceptions of course. But many are unable to see the faults of the system in which they have been brought up. This is usual, although, at times such as these, unacceptable.

9.3 What do constitutions do?

The design of modern constitutions for democracies can be traced back to the replacement of absolute monarchs and tribal structures as sources of state power. Their intent was to establish the rule of law, human rights and democratic representation. Their starting point is the electoral system – who can vote, with what system, through which constituencies, when and for whom. With their representatives in place, political authority is then assigned to various institutions intended to provide for sound administration of government, to keep the new rulers in check, and to prevent the 'tyranny of the majority'. The means are the separation of powers into the legislature, executive, and the judiciary. The legislature is the parliament, assembly or congress with – usually but not always – a second chamber to act as a check and balance, the composition of which is also specified either through election or regional representation. As introduced in Chapter 2, the executive is divided into the head of government (who can be directly elected as an executive president), an executive council, or cabinet, departments or ministries, and the civil service or administration. The form and powers of central, regional and local government are defined. Rules to form and control the armed forces and the police and security services, and how to enter into international treaties are set. The rules for constitutional change are defined. 'Entrenchment' determines who has the power to change which parts of a constitution, either by the electorate as a whole or some combination of higher authorities. Some constitutions include 'direct democracy' in the form of rights to call and hold referendums. A constitutional court is established to police adherence to the rules. This is an overview, but that is basically what you get.

At their time of origination, this was a whole system of governing, systemic in design. A point to stress is that government is but one room in the house of the system of governing. Think of it, perhaps, as the sitting room – devoted to talking, and sending instructions to the kitchen and shed, where useful things are produced for consumption elsewhere. The difficulty governments have today is twofold. The instructions are formed only through family debate and the preferences of close friends. Second, no means exist for the consumers to give feedback to the sitting room about whether one thing is always running out whilst others are left on the shelf, what would be more useful, what is convoluted to use, what has no effect, what has the opposite effect, and so on. The occasional message gets through in garbled form, but the house is not connected to the telephone and broadband networks. It lives in quite splendid isolation, conversing only with its well-heeled neighbours-with-strong-views-thought-to-be-influential. As a consequence, less and less of what comes out of the house is useful, although the consumers still pay the same price.

Current constitutions mix and match from the principles and elements established over millennia up to and including the US constitution of 1788 and the French revolution of 1791. Since then, developments have taken place in many countries – typically to reassign political authority between institutions – but only to improve their functioning *within* this framework. Meantime the world has moved on in the last two centuries, whilst most constitutional thinking and frameworks have not kept pace (see Chapter 4).

That today's constitutions do anything well – and some do for some problems – is a testament to their original construction. But they are all creaking, some are broken and *The Collapse of Complex Societies*[8] looms. Some have been constructed or substantially changed during the modern era (e.g. South Africa, Switzerland). But the principles on which they are based have remained the same.

Constitutions around the world vary considerably, even between established democracies. What they have in common is that *none* have been designed for the modern role of governments and for the modern lives of their peoples. None have been designed explicitly to spend effectively 40% or more of a nation's money on a host of widely varying functions, in the process becoming major doers and deliverers. Some are better at this than others, but they have failed to solve the many 'wicked' problems of life – migration, child neglect, violence, enduring hardship, crime, poor schooling. None have been designed to counter the power of large companies, and to handle the decision complexity wrought by globalisation, information mountains, and technology proliferation (as discussed in Part 2).

Current constitutions were not designed with extending lifespans in mind. As these have increased, the issue of intergenerational fairness has come to the fore. The tendency of governments is to avoid the unpopularity of making current generations pay for their current lifestyles. Other than those paid for by a solvent fund, costs of pensions are picked up by the working population, some of whom find themselves fully funding their own future pensions *and* paying for the unfunded pensions of government employees. The EU is a prime example of the latter. This is a straight transfer of wealth from one generation to another, without the former being in any way asked or involved in the decision.

Governments that run continual deficits to fund today's expenditure are deferring this cost for future generations to pay. The clean-up costs for the exploitation of our natural habitat will be paid for by the young and unborn for many decades to come. At the same time, future generations benefit from the huge investment in infrastructure and buildings funded by past and present taxpayers. Frank Ramsey published a paper in 1928[9] that involved 'a strategically beautiful application of the calculus of variations' to determine the optimal amount an economy should invest (save) rather than consume so as to maximise future utility, or in Ramsey's words 'how much of its income should a nation save?'

Expanding the boundaries of concern, Dan Bromley said that 'those of us now living stand as dictators over the environmental assets to be inherited by future persons and in the standard economic approach to that problem we act in our interest, not in the interests of future persons'.[10]

Deciding who should pay for what intergenerationally is not a matter covered in any constitution. A fairness test would stipulate that this could not be left to a political process, dependent for its power on an unfair representation of generations. That is the tyranny of the majority. These sorts of issues have to be deliberated and the 'deal' lodged in a safe place far from immediate budgetary grasp. Some countries (Germany, France, Italy, Spain) have grasped this in part with the introduction of a 'golden rule' that stipulates over the economic cycle, government will borrow only to invest and not to fund current spending.

Ancient constitutional principles were established, too, when people's relationship to the natural world was one of deep connection – they knew they depended on it – and of curiosity and enquiry. But very few foresaw either its limitations or human capacity to exhaust the biosphere. Until recently, no constitution incorporated the biosphere as an essential participant. The good news is that some are now – for example, in Peru, Wales, Slovenia, Ecuador and Colombia. In 2017, Colombia's constitutional court awarded rights to the Atrato, a river that flows through the globally recognised biodiversity hotspot of Colombia's northwestern Pacific rainforest[11]. The river has these rights because of what it provides for human life – not because it should be equated with human life. Its bio-cultural rights now include the river's 'protection, conservation, maintenance and restoration'.

In following 15 other countries[12] across the world, Slovenia has made access to drinkable water a fundamental right for all citizens and stopped it being commercialised (i.e. it belongs to the commons). Its constitution now says:

> Everyone has the right to drinkable water. Water resources represent a public good that is managed by the state. Water resources are primary and durably used to supply citizens with potable water and households with water and, in this sense, are not a market commodity.[13]

The Slovenian example demonstrates that changing the rules of the game can bring social and environmental change as well, as long as the constituent institutions operating at lower systemic levels are enabling of the practices that deliver on the constitutional intent. These countries are leading the way in acknowledging that constitutions are no more than human invented artefacts, to be reinvented by humans.

The opportunity now opens up to reinvent constitutions to contain the means to run complex public sectors, solve wicked problems, control elites and corporate power, assure intergenerational fairness, harness the technosphere, and represent and protect the biosphere, both for our future and for the biosphere itself. As a consequence, excessive wealth and power disparity would recede, enfranchisement would return, public services become of consistent quality, companies accountable, the banking system operate as part of our world, and our habitat secured.

9.4 How to make a constitution

Now you might expect there to be reams of study by constitutional academics and thinkers identifying ways to rectify these gaping holes. But there are not. Inquiry by those – in universities and elsewhere – who might be thought to have the necessary learning is absent. Science was in much the same position about 500 years ago. Then the Scientific Revolution took hold:

> During the last five centuries, humans increasingly came to believe that they could increase their capabilities by investing in scientific research. This wasn't just blind faith – it was repeatedly proven empirically.
>
> People throughout history collected empirical observations, but the importance of these observations was usually limited. Why waste precious resources obtaining new observations when we already have all the answers we need? But as modern people came to admit that they did not know the answers to some very important questions, they found it necessary to look for completely new knowledge. Consequently the dominant modern research method takes for granted the insufficiency of old knowledge. Instead of studying old traditions, emphasis is now placed on new observations and experiments.[14]

As humankind left behind the fixed so-called 'beliefs' of religions in which the unknown was simply an 'act of God', it embarked on this thing called science. Science is all about acknowledging our ignorance and embracing our capacity to enlighten it. In other fields with manifest and deep-seated challenges – medicine being one obvious example – you would find research institutes endlessly experimenting and testing 80,000 different molecules to find the two that worked, for example. What ambition.

Regrettably, this same shift has not occurred in the field of constitution. Arend Lijphart in comparing majoritarian with consensual democracies,[15] Gulcin Ozkan and Richard McManus in comparing presidential with parliamentary systems,[16] and 'Team Populism' in correlating populist governments with falls in inequality[17] are, with others, showing the way. As yet, no one is testing the equivalent of 80,000 systemic molecules to isolate those that work. But governance is a field of study that has at least as much to offer the health and contentment of humankind as medicine. A typical constitutional professor is a deep expert on the past – a priest quoting from their bible, knowing all that there is to know – but never having *considered* that the existing body of knowledge no longer makes the grade.

Rudimentary processes, adorned with the oxymoron 'political science' and operating at the absolute limits of constitution, are considered to be the best people
can use to take contested decisions. We should no more be expecting a professor of modern history to be researching genetic cures for cancer than cures for
today's diseases of government. But typically that is what we have – intelligent
people in high-status jobs being paid to rearrange the deckchairs on the *Titanic*
whilst the band plays on. Some metaphors endure.

The 'founding fathers' of the constitutions we have now, ranging from the
authors of the Magna Carta to such as Thomas Hobbes, Jean-Jacques Rousseau
and John Locke, were all in search of new knowledge. They chose not to rest
on an apparently immutable body of knowledge. A principal task of this book
is to stimulate the equivalent new knowledge for societies, nations, and the
Anthropocene to work successfully. Much of this can be found in the fields of
organisation and systems thinking. These *have* made very considerable strides in
understanding over the last 60 years or so, and this is where constitutional thinking should go for fresh inspiration.

Most constitutions have inbuilt provisions for their amendment. Some are
effective – Switzerland is probably the best, and we see the example of Ireland
above. Some are hard – the US is trapped at least until their situation worsens.
Some countries have none – as in the UK. In some cases, enlightened leaders or
establishments see the need for change and set up a small expert group, which
then develops proposals.[18] In most cases, citizens have to campaign to start the
process. Typically, this would then lead to a citizens' assembly, extensive public
deliberation, and eventually a vote. Herein lies a very big message for us as citizens – if we want constitutional change we will have to campaign for it.

Here is how Iceland went about it:

> Following the economic collapse in 2008, the crowdsourcing of a writ-
> ten constitution began with people sitting down to talk about the basic
> values they shared with their neighbours. By and large, the Icelandic draft-
> ing was not done by constitutional law experts – members of the public
> were selected by ballot and included a farmer, a truck driver, a pastor, a
> film-maker, a student and the director of an art museum. Conversations
> took place in town halls, on social media and even in knitting circles. The
> resulting Icelandic Constitutional Council opted to give legal personal-
> ity to nature itself. This in turn was based on the Ecuadorian concept of
> Pachamama (world mother).[19]

Bruce Ackerman describes how typically leaders, lawyers, and academics have
made constitutions since World War II.[20] In the interconnected and informed
world of today, we have no need to rely on enlightened leaders and their specialist advisers. Given the major shifts in power that new systems of governing entail,
the populace has to be at the centre of the process. Without this, only first-order
change will result.

It is useful to consider what a citizens' assembly for a national system of governing would deliberate on. After freeing the mind and framing the process as systemic inquiry – appreciating a lack of knowing what might be best (Chapter 8), it would examine how ancient constitutions, representing great advances at the time, now work in contending with the current world, where and how they fail and the new principles and mechanisms to be added. The various experiments in governance around the world, from China and Wales to Slovenia and Iceland, would be explored. When running a workshop, Ray starts by asking how this could be made a bad experience for each other, and then asks what rules we would have to make to get rid of the bad. This is the praxis of constituting how we will act/be together.

Next, would come purpose – what it is the assembly is aiming to do – followed by understanding how beneficial improvement is made. This would lead into the fourth separation of powers (see Chapter 10) and cybernetic feedback, institutional forms and their accountability to citizens, decision-specific democracy and tiers of government, as well as rules for elections and deliberation. This may feel like an overwhelming agenda, but experience says a soundly constituted citizens assembly would work its way through. Importantly, because they are confronted by the unfolding uncertainty and complexity of the effects of the Anthropocene, future constitutions would build in adaptability. Alongside the fundamental new set of rules, 'constituting' will be an ongoing, adaptive, learning process, with constitutions stabilised for shorter periods than has happened historically.

9.5 Time to change the rules

We hope that the analysis in Chapter 3 of a major systemic failure in government that has enabled and allowed preferential lobbying – and its undemocratic, socially unfair, economically inefficient, environmentally destructive, and essentially corrupt consequences – is sufficient to demonstrate both the urgent need for new thinking and for reinforced constitutions. The Irish referendum, incorporating parts of the biosphere as in Slovenia and Colombia, and other innovations around the world, show what is possible.

It is only by changing the rules by which governments and other elements of a new governance system operate that lasting and consistent improvement will occur. That rulebook is the constitution. Think of a game. If the rules are wrong, the game does not work. If one player cheats, the others lose interest. If – as in a casino – the rules are biased, one player always wins. We can see all these faults at play in our constitutions: enduring problems never solved, soft corruption where the protected species cheat and the non-voters opt out, and lobbying where the benefits are biased to large companies and others. But a constitution is an institution which we humans can redesign, and in doing so, populate it with other new institutions that enable it to work differently. Its design would offer citizen responsibility in exchange for government response-ability, not as a demand but as an ethos of living.

At the same time a major investment in the thinking and practices of this book will make the enactment of constitutions perform efficaciously, effectively, efficiently, and ethically. Shakespeare was a brilliant playwright but, for the performances to work and excel, effective actors are essential. Competent future governance actors will combine systemic sensibility, systems literacy and systems thinking in practice capability.

The time is upon us to consider seriously what a constitution could do for the future of our countries and for the future of the biosphere. The following chapter examines how to make beneficial change in government and the provisions in future constitutions to realise this.

Notes

1 The design and operation of a Citizens' Assembly was recommended in Appendix A of the Houses of the Oireachtas, Joint Committee on the Constitution, Fourth Report, Article 16, Review of the Electoral System for the Election of Members to Dáil Eireann, Final Report, July 2010. It intended through these means to depoliticise the issue. It drew upon the experiences of similar bodies in the Netherlands and the Canadian provinces of Ontario and British Columbia.
2 O'Toole, F. 29 May 2018. If only Brexit had been run like Ireland's referendum. *The Guardian.*
3 Wolf, Michael. 2018. *Fire and Fury: Inside the Trump White House.* New York: Henry Holt and Company.
4 Robertson, I. 2013. How power affects the brain. *The Psychologist* 26: 186–189
5 Gerrymandering is a practice to establish a political advantage for a particular party or group by manipulating district boundaries. The term is named after Elbridge Gerry, who, as Governor of Massachusetts in 1812, signed a bill that created a partisan district in the Boston area that was compared to the shape of a mythological salamander.
6 https://www.oecd.org/governance/observatory-public-sector-innovation/library/28.02%20systems%20thinking%20schedule%20FINAL.PDF (Accessed 30 March 2019).
7 UN News. 2017. https://news.un.org/en/story/2017/09/567172-un-rights-experts-urge-member-states-go-beyond-statements-take-action-help (Accessed 5 January 2019).
8 Tainter, Joseph A. 1988. *The Collapse of Complex Societies.* Cambridge: Cambridge University Press.
9 Ramsey, Frank Plumpton. 1928. A mathematical theory of saving. *The Economic Journal* 38 (152): 543–559.
10 Bromley, Dan. 2006. *Sufficient Reason: Volitional Pragmatism and the Meaning of Economic Institutions.* Princeton, NJ: Princeton University Press.
11 Mount, Nick. 6 October 2017. Can a River Have Legal Rights? *The Conversation.* http://theconversation.com/can-a-river-have-legal-rights-i-visited-the-jungles-of-colombia-to-find-out-84878 (Accessed 6 January 2020).
12 Rampedre (the online Permanent World Report on the Right to Water) http://www.rampedre.net.
13 Cooke, L. 2016. *Inhabitat.* https://inhabitat.com/slovenia-becomes-first-eu-nation-to-enshrine-human-right-to-water-in-their-constitution/ (Accessed 6 January 2020).
14 Harari, Yuval Noah. 2011. *Homo Sapiens: A Brief History of Humankind.* New York: Vintage Books.
15 https://sites.hks.harvard.edu/fs/pnorris/DPI403%20Fall09/12%20DPI403%20%20Constitutions.pdf (Accessed 15 April 2019).

16 Ozkan, Gulcin. 11 February 2019. Parliamentary Systems Do Better Economically than Presidential Ones. *The Conversation*. https://theconversation.com/parliam entary-systems-do-better-economically-than-presidential-ones-111468 (Accessed 6 January 2020).
17 https://www.theguardian.com/world/2019/mar/07/revealed-populist-leaders-lin ked-to-reduced-inequality (Accessed 15 April 2019).
18 One such non-governmental group is the Independent Constitutionalists UK. http:// icuk.life/declaration.html (Accessed 15 April 2019).
19 https://www.theguardian.com/commentisfree/2019/sep/03/prorogation-crisis-uk -written-constitution (Accessed 27 September 2019).
20 Ackerman, Bruce. 2019. *Revolutionary Constitutions: Charismatic Leadership and the Rule of Law*. Boston: Belknap Press.

10

MAKING BENEFICIAL CHANGE

10.1 Institutionalising STiP in government through feedback

Our task now is to apply systems thinking to the way governance, and particularly governments, works through institutional innovations. How can governments make, or enable, beneficial change consistently and with the reliability and pace the advent of the climate and biodiversity crisis now demands? What design turns will make this happen?

10.1.1 Cybernetic feedback

Children are like scientists. What looks like play is actually experimentation. They formulate explanations, test them, collect and analyse the results, and revise their world view accordingly.[1] To learn is to change. Feedback is knowing what has happened as a result of what has been done. Then the doing can be changed to improve the done. Or, if the result is poor, stop the action altogether. The faster the feedback, the quicker response can happen, and vice versa. The more accurate the feedback, the better the correction. In systems theory this is called cybernetics. This is the steering metaphor of Section 7.3.1 in action.

Cybernetics is the study of the communication and control through feedback in both living and lifeless systems (organisms, organisations, machines). Cybernetics seeks to understand and design the functions and processes of systems that have a purpose and that participate in circular, causal chains that move from action to sensing to comparison with espoused purpose, and again to action. First-order cybernetics focus is on how anything processes information, reacts to information and changes or can be changed to better accomplish the first two tasks. Reliable information is obviously essential. Second-order cybernetics introduces humans as controllers and communicators, immersed in capacities for interpretation, deliberation, holding multiple, partial perspectives and able to articulate and pursue purposes (unlike machines). Governance innovation will require both strands of cybernetics (see the Glossary in Appendix 2, where the differences are explored in more detail).

The point of cybernetic feedback is to improve results in relation to purpose. The feedback information does not just sit there, being ignored or spun away. Corrective action follows. This process is especially important for the biosphere, a system of high complexity and perpetual change that is dependent on drastically reducing the delay and attenuation of the feedback signal in relation to taking control action (i.e. to make the model of Figure 7.5 functional).

Human beings would not exist without feedback. Cells possess an extraordinary self-organising capacity. Over millennia they have developed to become complete human beings and every other living being.[2] The mathematical equations that govern this self-organisation are quite simple and yet result in order and chaos, patterns and the unpredictable, from the spots on a cow to the ridges on desert sand dunes, from the fractals of a lung to storms and tornadoes. To create order and beauty and *function*, feedback is essential. At each stage of development, in mathematical terms, the output from one equation forms the input for the next cycle. The organisms monitor, self-correct and self-develop.

The same principle is true of organisations: the greater the feedback, the more it, and each person in it, will respond and self-correct. But here is where the biosphere and automated control systems have huge advantages over governments – they respond to the signals received without further prompting. The organism is a whole. Today's systems of governing are not whole. Our aim is to create self-correction in governance. For society-wide transformations to low carbon living to occur, transformations will be needed in the way in which knowledge is produced and used (see Chapters 6 to 8).[3]

10.1.2 The fourth separation of powers

Governments do collect results and data to inform results – statistics on employment, economic output, crime, debt, tax yields, health and immigration, for example. The OECD publishes comparisons on attainment at school, amongst much other useful data. But, as with mobile phones, the coverage is patchy and quality variable. Some governments do apply some of them, some quite well and some badly. The extent to which this occurs is dependent on the degree of democracy and accountability, the diversity of education and experience of those in government, and the prevailing ethos. None is cybernetic. Feedback should not be an optional extra but instrumental. Thorough feedback is so fundamental to governance systems that it has to be required by the constitution.

Independent fact checkers and 'feedbackers' – representing civil society – have sprung up in recent years to fill this institutional void, but their resources are limited. Independently of government, scientists are providing extensive feedback on climate change, pollution and biodiversity.

In economic transactions, people experience the results of their decisions directly – if they buy a defective product, they soon discover their mistake – but in the case of political decisions there is no such immediate feedback mechanism. As a result, politicians may lose touch with reality and behave irresponsibly. You may have noticed.

The three established separations of powers – legislature, executive and judiciary – have stood for a long time. They are essential. A fourth separation of powers[4] is necessary to bring reality to the work of governments, by providing the institutional means for the independent collection and publication of the results of all that they set out to do. We have called this fourth separation the 'Resulture'. Organisations cannot work effectively without feedback on their decisions and actions. Without results they are flying blind, in flight but not knowing where to. This is as true for governments as it is for companies that use and depend on a huge amount of feedback. Without it they would go bust, aircraft would fall out of the sky, and cars would crash.

The Resulture is not as much of a constitutional leap as it may at first appear. The Audit Branch is specified in many constitutions. Its role is the *financial* auditing of government and its many bodies through, typically, a national audit office, with constitutional independence from government. This may also extend to aspects of efficiency, effectiveness and corruption. We are proposing a substantially widened role for this branch.

10.1.3 Feedback on what?

There is a lot to find out. Have changes in the ownership or governance of water resources led to their sustainable use? Is the enforcement regime working for deep-sea trawling? Just what are the results of agricultural subsidies in the round? Are the regulations for new construction producing 'zero carbon' housing? Are the markets for internet access and search competitive? Are the seven principles of the EU's General Data Protection Regulation being met? Are children safer with 'safeguarding' measures, and what does 'safe' mean? How much does this or that law cost to run? What has changed this year as a result of the existence of national environmental agencies? What is the result of all that money spent on the many parts of the criminal justice system? For each health and safety regulation, has the number of people injured or killed reduced, stayed the same or gone up? How do we know if a regulator is being successful, however success is measured?[5] Has 'homeland security' in the US improved with the vast Department of Homeland Security? And so on.

On a much smaller scale, the purpose of constructing a fence along a river bank to keep out the sheep is to keep water clean and allow new vegetation to grow for CO_2 absorption and species diversity. In assessing its result, we would want to know whether the natural habitat **is** being regenerated. A proxy for this is the presence of the fence. We might think that this is too trivial to bother assessing, but then consider the counterfactual. Within weeks of its erection, the fence is broken, sheep are everywhere, there is no regeneration. In terms of its purpose, nothing has been achieved. Are we to say that this does not matter? Should government just be ignorant of or ignore this? What is the point of passing a law that, in practice, has no effect; or promising to plant a million trees, many of which will then die; or introducing a regulation that has the reverse effect; or operating a scheme to incentivise renewable heating that incentivises fuel use; or an aid program that promotes corruption and incentivises leaders to retain power for as long as possible? Are we content that governments spend money on pure waste? The results of all government actions need to be visible, from a riverbank fence to global biofuel production.

Get into the detail of many government departments and you will see how little they know of outcomes, of where something is actually going, of performance, of whether and how a piece of legislation is having the desired effect, of the net energy saved as a result of its latest climate change policy, of how project funds were actually spent and with what benefit, of the deviation of a policy from its intended trajectory or of the actual performance of financial markets for savings and pension funds. The discipline imposed by dealing with reality is absent. For the politicians, a law is passed, victory declared and the new law forgotten as soon as the next one is debated.

Government accounting standards should be set through the Resulture, too. Loose standards have allowed governments to accumulate unsustainable debt, deferring current costs to future unrepresented and even unborn citizens. This is the same 'fiddling the books' through 'off-balance sheet' allowances usually found in the accounts of bankrupt companies.

10.1.4 Purpose of feedback

The purpose of feedback is to transform the performance of new governance systems, to ensure high-quality connectivity to the biophysical world, to reconnect governments with the people (civil society), and thus to contribute to the restoration of democracy as a lived experience and to a prevailing sense of empowerment. Cybernetic feedback would take priority attention away from passing laws and making other decisions to the results of actions, the changes needed, and what past results tell us about future changes. It would progress from issuing instructions to learning, and from the exercise of power for the benefit of those in power to the exercise of power for the benefit of the polity.

Feedback matters. It is a discipline on the end of the pipe furthest from the centre of power: if garbage is put in, governments will not be able to spin their way out of that decision. If delivery is poor, governments will not be able to duck and dive their way through years of underperformance before some accountability appears. If a government has bent to a preferential lobby, its detrimental results will show up. Feedback will cut many needless arguments in areas as diverse as air-conditioning and welfare, where the objectives are not either/or, but how much and how. Feedback cuts the pointless, the fruitless, the unintended and the perverse, and forces their abandonment. It means that we will not have to wait years for public pressure or a media campaign or a change of government to do what needed to be done all along. It focuses minds on priorities and on effectiveness and cuts out managerialism and proceduralism for their own sake, thereby saving money and taxes. It highlights issues – like unfit organisation – and compels change. It is the way to eliminate silo working and join up government in reality, as the feedback will be about overall purpose and not the sub-objectives of a government agency.

As the three-dimensional governance model will have brought the biosphere, technosphere and social purpose into the remit of the Resulture, so feedback on these subsystems will be institutionalised.

In STiP terms, we see in the fourth separation of powers and the feedback and challenge it produces, purpose coming to the fore in purposeful actions, removal of institutional 'weeds' through the abandonment program, multiple perspectives being applied, an end to systematic Weberian bureaucracy, a stimulus to deframing and reframing situations of concern, pathway dependencies being challenged and opportunities to relocate activities – like education – in that subsystem of the model where they will work efficaciously.

10.1.5 Results of feedback

Once feedback mechanisms are embedded and functioning, much would change simply because results, and trends in results, would be visible. No longer would a government or an initiating minister want to ignore non-performance and failure, or hide behind partial statistics or spun anecdotes, or want to defend the indefensible. The ambience in assemblies, parliaments and congresses would shift away from adversarial 'proving' right and wrong by whatever means, and towards collective inquiry and endeavour. With results doing the talking, in the early days much needless activity and procedure would be dropped, and zero-outcome acts of governing abandoned. Savings would be substantial. Government would become less complicated and more effective – essential when maintaining human–biosphere relations will take so much effort. Public sector bodies would look outward to the results as judged by others and become less internal and less ends to themselves.

This should prove to be a relief for politicians, themselves trapped in a system of endemic underachievement. Today's politicians have the misfortune to work in a world of make-believe. In the absence of hard results concentrating all of our minds on why they exist, governments become seduced by the political science fiction world of the 24-hour news agenda, announceables, initiativitis and the personal preferences of ministers. They are easy to criticise, but politicians and government officials are incarcerated in the past. The inadequacies of every system in the world have meant that governments observe and learn only randomly from the outcomes of their actions. Often they stop listening to and seeking to understand the public. The countervailing force to the comfort blanket of photo shoots is to face the actual outcomes of legislation, regulation, statutory duties, instruction to local governments, public education campaigns, changed benefits, altered taxes, contracts with the private sector and transfer of assets from civil society. But this is not institutionalised at any place in our constitutions – organisations are institutionalised, but not the fundamentals for making organisations work. If *we* were politicians, *we* would fail in this system too.

Politicians will hate this discipline – until they see its value. Feedback is a strong discipline on governments and parliaments, but for its politicians it procures significant immunity from vested interests, powerful lobbies and the news media – delayed gratification. The news media will lose influence and potentially become a 'fourth estate' once more – respected and valued. Big companies will lose power and become more competitive. We will get better government. Feedback delivers real political power in that much more is actually changed for good. For the public as citizens and consumers, and as a society, it procures performance and a lot less cost and tax. For the biosphere it gains focus, pace and real solutions: government by results.

Results are the equivalent of judgement day awaiting every government proposal – its results will be examined, monitored and evaluated, regularly and publicly. This is an overdue discipline on everyone in government, on corporate lobbies, and on us as citizens.

10.1.5.1 Feedback to us as citizens

Public feedback has another vital result. It educates electorates, questions our prejudices and infuses democracy with intelligence. Effective feedback is not a private matter between a governmental organisation and its political masters. Transparency is essential to good civil government.

10.1.6 What are 'results'?

The term results, here, is used as in its meaning of something that occurs or exists because of something else that has happened – what systems thinkers call measures of performance of a system. Thus, a government action may lead to a result, which is as clear-cut as in the situation that exists at the end of a contest. It may be a result in a positive direction, but no more than that is known. It may be ambiguous. It may have no effect, or it may have counter-intentional results. Results can include side effects, such as through the monopolisation of public goods leading to the erosion of their value.[6] In all cases, results include their costs, both governmental and non-governmental. Such estimates would follow Enrico Fermi's[7] maxim to 'never make something more accurate than absolutely necessary', just good enough to work out whether a law is worth keeping, for example. The dimension of time and trends in results is always a consideration and usually instructive. The term 'results' includes signals, responses, efficacy of response and response times. It includes the delay and attenuation of the feedback signal in relation to taking control action or revisiting purpose.

In aid-funded projects, Perrin distinguishes between two ways of understanding accountability: 'accountability up', that is, responsibility towards the donors in order to justify the money spent, and 'accountability down', that is, responsibility toward the beneficiaries of aid in order to assess whether the program met their needs and helped them improve their situation (empowerment).[8] Feedback of results should always be aimed first at the objects of its purpose – the biosphere and sections of the population – alongside other stakeholders.

10.1.7 Note on metrics

Metrics are a part of feedback. But 'effective performance management systems require priorities and measures, not numerical targets. All numerical targets are arbitrary. Numerical targets predictably induce gaming and other dysfunctional behaviour, and trigger unhealthy internalized competition'.[9] The mayor of New York, Rudy Giuliani, reached a similar conclusion in the 1990s, saying that they distort and are self-defeating. Many performance measures fail to provide a meaningful account of actual performance.

> For years in policing and beyond, we've used the wrong type of performance information in the wrong way. We've introduced perverse incentives that cause good people to do the wrong things. I believe this situation has persisted because 'it's what we've always done' and many people are uncertain about the alternatives. However, alternatives are simple and free and can be implemented now at all levels; abandon the use of binary comparisons, league tables and numerical targets, then use contextualized performance information instead. Be clear about purpose, so you can set meaningful priorities, then use the right measures in the right way to understand the system, inform decision making, learn and improve.[10]

Statistical process control from the quality theory and practice in companies such as Toyota is one effective mechanism.

10.1.8 Presentation of feedback

To make it understood, the way in which feedback is presented can matter as much as its content. In a piece of research[11] asking: 'Why do so many Americans hold misperceptions?', factors contributing to the prevalence of these beliefs were examined. Providing information in graphical form reduces misperceptions. This effect is greater than for equivalent textual information. But people may reject information because it threatens their worldview or self-concept.

The Roslings define 'factfulness' as 'the stress-reducing habit of only carrying opinions for which you have strong supporting facts'.[12] Their book addresses several specific misperceptions from poverty to population and crime, and seeks their correction, not least through 'Trendanalyzer', the bubble chart tool they invented. The 'instincts', as they term them, that lead to these misperceptions are identified, and tools for more accurate perceptions are provided. This is all music to the ears of those of us who do not want the world to be run on lies. These tools are to be found at work in the production of all sound metrics. The Roslings continue:

> Rejection of uncomfortable facts is a form of defensive processing that protects one's self-identity; when one's self-integrity is affirmed in some other domain, people may be less likely to respond defensively.[13]

Cognitive biases creep into all of our decision making. When investing in financial markets, people are well advised to avoid them. The seven psychological sins you must not commit[14] are loss aversion bias, hindsight bias, status quo bias, egocentric framing, vividness bias, curse of knowledge effect and certainty bias. This advice applies equally to investing in public policy and government action, and to their news media reporting.

Digital dashboards are now in use in various cities[15] to use data to record goals, track performance, and monitor results. Once their impact has been understood, the Resulture would set up its own. Stafford Beer[16] ran the first version of such a feedback dashboard in 1971–1973 for Chile under President Allende – 'Cybersyn'.

10.1.9 Note on existing government evaluations

A word here on evaluation, as practised in government. It might be seen as sufficient for reliable feedback. It is a practice that took hold in the US in the 1960s and was taken up subsequently by European and other governments, and by aid agencies. Its intentions are sound in assessing programs and policies in operation to see what effect they are having. The lessons thus discovered should be incorporated into future decision making in order to achieve desired purposes. The process has often become mandatory and routine. Some evaluations do have effect, and the methods used for them have developed and are applicable to feedback. So far so good.

But as Nicoletta Stame and Jan-Eric Furubo found in their evaluation of the evaluation enterprise,[17] its benefits have got lost and unintended consequences have mounted. The theory behind evaluation depends upon the dissemination of the learning, understanding and take up by decision makers, and its application, *all within a voluntary context.* The assumption is that if sound analysis is presented to politicians and policy makers, then they will accept and use it. This can happen, but in practice it most often becomes the classic consultant's report with a very short shelf life. There is nothing in the governing systems to ensure the learning is applied. Decision makers have all sorts of other pressures on them, including vested interests – both personal and organisational – ideology, competing priorities, media campaigns, and, of course, preferential lobbying. The thought that somehow rationality will take over in this ramshackle political world is naïve. Nevertheless, huge effort continues to go into evaluation, especially by the OECD and other global bodies, perhaps in the hope that at some point an outbreak of common sense will occur. As we know it has not, shows no sign of doing so and will not because it is not situated in a viable system.

Evaluations also suffer from the way in which they are undertaken:

> Old problems, like lack of attention from decision-makers, or scarce use, cannot be solved by issuing a general prescription of doing evaluation even where it is not needed, what Dahler-Larsen calls the 'panacea problem'. In fact, for fear of non-use, evaluability assessments tended to 'straighten out' the evaluand, so that it became evaluable. In so doing, evaluation has had constitutive effects upon the practices of the people evaluated, who change their behavior to meet the test: a serious hindrance to innovation, creativity and risk-taking.[18]

Evaluations are usually commissioned by those commissioning the original work, whose interests are not always well served by finding that their program has not worked, or has been operationalised poorly, or was misconceived in the first place. Funders hold the power, and the evaluators bend to their wishes. Financial audits of companies can suffer from a similar malfunction in operation, at root a governance flaw.

Thus, evaluations as currently practised are not cybernetic – circular, causal chains that move from action to sensing to comparison with the desired purpose, and again to action. They just do the sensing and sometimes the comparison if the purpose is clear, and then become space junk suspended above the earth, interesting to look at on a clear night if you happen to glance up but of no active relevance to life down below.

Forss notes:

> The overall picture is one of evaluation as a 'systems-preserving' activity, an intellectual effort which is inherently conservative and that assists in defending rather than challenging the powers that be, the established wisdoms, the current technologies and administrative practices.[19]

10.1.10 Forms of feedback

Feedback depends on data. The data needed depends, first, on the aims or purpose of the action. For governments, this means being clear as to why something is being done – a discipline. If actions are not clear, then why are they being done? What use are they? Second, the form of data depends on its operational context. In some contexts, the form takes data or signals, which then need interpretation and response, if preprogrammed. In others, conversation is required, as this is feedback when done well.

The forms of feedback will vary, for example:[20]

- Legislation, regulations, statutory duties: Governments have large legislative programs. They also need programs to ascertain whether the legislation has had the intended effect, and whether the means of enforcement are effective
- Government bodies: For government bodies, a broad assessment of performance by stakeholders would provide prima facie evidence of a well-run or poorly run body. The best example of this method we have seen is the PROGRESS[21] process developed by the charity Antidote to improve schools.[22] Regulators would also be part of this stakeholder assessment, along with all bodies substantially funded by government – charities and the government private sector (those companies contracted to undertake public sector operations).
- Policies and programs: Take a policy, any policy, and ask if it is achieving its purpose – from energy and agricultural subsidies, planning and money laundering, to watchdogs for trading standards. There are tens of thousands, some long forgotten and still going, incurring taxes and burdening or immobilising governments with complexity.

Let's have a think about what a Resulture might mean for the EU's Emissions Trading Scheme, for example. What would a ruthless examination of its results against its purpose generate? If all we did was to consider the policy-maker-assessing-itself report, then we would find all is on target.

> The EU emissions trading system (EU ETS) is a cornerstone of the EU's policy to combat climate change and its key tool for reducing greenhouse gas emissions cost-effectively. It is the world's first major carbon market and remains the biggest one.[23]

The YouTube commentary presented by a smooth talker accompanied by calming music heralds its success. The system works by setting a cap on the total emissions of certain greenhouse gases by big polluters such as coal-fired power stations and steel works. Companies receive or buy allowances they can trade with one another, depending on whether they are above or below their emissions targets. These are traded on various markets. The price fluctuates as demand and supply change. 'Trading brings flexibility that ensures emissions are cut where it costs least to do so. A robust carbon price also promotes investment in clean, low-carbon technologies'.[24]

The EU's report on its own performance goes on to claim: The EU ETS has proved that putting a price on carbon and trading in it can work. Emissions from installations in the system are falling as intended – by slightly over 8% compared to the beginning of phase 3.

The EU is making progress in reducing emissions, down by 23% between 1990 and 2016, while its economy has grown by 53%. But to what extent has the

ETS contributed to this fall? There are many questions that should be asked – how much has it cost, what have been its unintended consequences, will the scheme be strengthened to make it work faster, is this realistic and could its spending be put to better greenhouse gas (GHG) reduction uses?

Businesses in the scheme have been surveyed. They tend to report that the scheme has had little impact on the changes they have made that have reduced emissions. Companies are generally well aware of the business risks of climate change and, being run by people looking to their futures, have other pressures on them such as insurance and investors. Disentangling causes from effects takes much more than a 'glossy brochure'. According to UBS Investment Research, the EU ETS cost \$287 billion through to 2011 and had an 'almost zero impact' on the volume of overall emissions in the EU. The money could have resulted in more than a 40% reduction in emissions if it had been used in a targeted way (e.g. to upgrade power plants).

Beware, though, as many of these businesses are in industries employing considerable resources to lobby the EU for favourable decisions. Reports from this quarter may have no more value than those from the EU.

A report from academic sources brings together the many evaluations of the scheme.[25] It is a mixed picture. 'Don't know' features prominently. Overall,

> academic studies with both "top down", and sector-based "bottom up" evaluations point to attributable emission savings in the range 40 – 80 MtCO2/yr, annual average (and point estimates of particular years) to date. This is about 2-4% of the total capped emissions, which is much bigger than the impact of most other individual energy-environmental policy instruments.

Enormous windfall profits have been made. The impact on managerial decision making has been small. Renewables and the financial crash have had the biggest impact on greenhouse gas reductions. It is not apparent that the ETS has played any role in these reductions.

Our purpose here is not to design a new ETS but to emphasise:

- How important independent feedback is,
- Why initiating corrective action can never be left to the policy owner, and
- That decision makers get far too attached to their decisions.

How would the next \$287 billion of EU budget be best spent for biosphere–human relations and planetary preservation?

10.2 The Resulture

Making feedback work for governing cannot happen without the fourth separation of powers. For the fourth separation to work, it has to be institutionally separate from the other branches: the executive or government, the legislature or lawmakers, and the judiciary or judges. A place to locate it is in reformed second chambers, which have the vetting and 'check and balance' role already in many existing systems. These second chambers (the senate, the upper house) would – with their own democratic legitimacy – be separate in their origin and composition from the political parties contesting executive power. Alternatively, a permanently convened Citizens Assembly, based in the social purpose subsystem of the governance model, merits consideration for this role (see Chapter 7).

In the second chamber model, its role should not be political – feedback and vetting of government processes is not a matter of political judgement but of independent and wise minds. At its simplest, maths is not a matter of politics. The second chamber would establish the working arrangements for this new form of institutional power, the Resulture. This would cohere and take direct responsibility for existing 'independent scorekeepers' of statistics and outcomes. Typically these scorekeepers include national audit offices, statistical offices, reporting functions from government departments (for example, on clinical efficacy in health services), and reports commissioned from universities and consultancies. Assessments from international bodies such as the OECD and the WHO would form part of the Resulture's information base. Further capacity would be put in place to cover all the many existing gaps in feedback. The backlog is considerable, and this will take time.

None of these bodies would be staffed by existing government administrators and officials nor have any connection with them. Each would hire and develop its own fit-for-purpose staff. Independence of feedback is not possible with common staffing. A source of feedback that would be independent and comprehensive would then be in place. Governments would then run on feedback, including pattern and trend analyses. The time and energy wasted in concocting and contesting results would be put instead to the task of positive change, to understanding and dealing with a complex world. Noise, yapping, and anti-feedback would retreat to the margins. We would all focus on doing what needs to be done.

The second chamber would become a hive of activity and information, fulfilling this role for the people and for society, the 'ticker tapes' of results pouring through. Once you are monitoring and using feedback, you really are performing a vital role in 'running the country'. This role is as important as the executive and the legislature.

10.2.1 Abandonment and enforcement powers

Cybernetic feedback requires not just the collection of data but having the means to ensure corrective action occurs as a result of analyses of that data. The Resulture would propose abandonment of laws, regulations, policies, programs, and bodies that are not effective, and it would require governments to amend those that need improvement. Effective enforcement by the Resulture – as the regulator of government – would be essential. Having as a 'long stop' the power to withdraw a budget from the ineffective would represent effective enforcement, perhaps alongside the power to call an election.

Other means to ensure corrective action follows feedback would be through technical vetting of decisions, design authorities and failure inquiries (described in the section below), and the change in culture emerging from the enactment of principles for systemic governing (see Chapter 11).

The second chamber would also take on other responsibilities to be depoliticised. It would make all regulator and other *independent* public body appointments, set budgets for regulators jointly with the executive, provide the top-level governance of public service broadcasters, and decide on – with a citizens' assembly and referenda if needed – proposed transfers of assets like water out of the social purpose element.

10.2.3 Local governance feedback

Similar, although smaller-scale arrangements for feedback, response and decision vetting would operate for local governance, with connectivity between feedback at different levels and jurisdictions. The design principle here would be that of a viable system with effective variety and responsibility, at relevant levels.

10.3 Problem-analysis-policy-approval-implementation-solution – PAPAIS

What would STiP mean for the way decisions and policies are made in government? Let us start with where many decisions are taken, at the centre of power.

10.3.1 Decision making by the 'tiny top'

Governments make thousands of decisions. One veteran minister of 13 years' service estimated there were about 30–150 per week, depending on the ministry. Multiply that up and the decision rate is tens of thousands per year at the national government level. Then add those made by local, regional and international governments. Those decisions may affect the way we live, our opportunities, our restraints and freedoms, our income and wealth, the form of society and the protection or exhaustion of our planetary home. These decisions range from the size of holes in trawler nets, planning permission for a new supermarket and parole for an offender serving 'life', to changing the entire system for secondary schooling, responding to grave water shortages and adopting an economic system.

Typically, these decisions are drawn up to the top of a government as if by a super magnet. Such is their volume and the way in which the organisation works; most decisions conclude by being decided by a handful of people. The 'top' may be a minister and advisers, or a committee of government officials. This 'top' surveys the land (or that bit it can see from its window), does some analysis

– maybe a lot, maybe a little – and makes a decision. In retrospect, some of these decisions work. Many do not.

Why do it like that, when so much knowledge exists outside the tiny top? How do they/we know that a decision is right, or is the only workable answer? Where are the options? The tiny top has limited capacity for due consideration, especially when so many of its past decisions are queuing up for 'rework'.[26] Ashby's law of variety applies to excess. There is so much to handle, 'control freakery' emerges as a response. Centralisation exacerbates the decision jam.

10.3.2 Decisions cannot be separated from actions

Structuring government to separate decision from action has trapped many a polity in pseudo change. Arguments may rage, tempers flare, news outlets campaign and righteous indignation abounds. A new law is proposed, debate is extensive, backroom deals are done and undone and finally – to much acclaim – a new law comes into being. Heroes are lauded and victory is declared, with much self-congratulation at the sheer energy and political dexterity shown. Except that the really difficult part is about to begin.

A decision is only a decision. It is words on a piece of paper. Nothing has actually changed. The world and our lives have not altered. A decision has meaning only when it is turned into action. *Then* it takes form.

Decisions cannot be separated from actions. But this is, mostly, how governments and politics work. The problem might be, for example, the sustainability of fish stocks. About one-third of the oceans' stocks are fished at levels that allow fish to repopulate. From the 1970s, the mesh size of trawler nets has been regulated and catches or fishing quotas established. All should now be well. Except that monitoring trawler nets hundreds of miles out to sea with crews seeking the quickest, biggest catch, under pressure to pay off the loan for an expensive boat, and able to land their catch at a 'flexible' port, is at best a challenge. One such EU inspector, alone on a trawler surrounded by a hostile crew, took to counting fish in secret using tiny pellets of silver foil he rolled from cigarette packets. A halibut pellet went into his left trouser pocket, redfish into his right, American flounder in one back pocket and dogfish in the other. Once on his own, he could record the catch and note it in a secret book. He kept another, which coincided more or less with the trawler's 'official' book. He was offered luxury hotels and sex workers as inducements. If he had disappeared over the side in rough weather, few would have been surprised. In designing the regulations, 'policy makers' would not have envisaged the lengths one ethical inspector would have to go to apply them – in practice. He declined further 'inspection' roles.

The presumption that all governments usually work to is problem-analysis-policy-approval-implementation-solution. A problem is identified. The centre analyses it by collecting statistics and data, reports and research papers by academics, think tanks and other subject specialists, modelling, comments from those with the time and money to answer formal consultations, and preferential lobbies. A policy is formulated, and this is put to an authorising body for approval – sometimes the congress/parliament/assembly where it is subject to limited vetting – but usually to a small group of ministers. The policy is implemented through laws, regulations, budget allocation and government agencies, and the problem is solved. Press a button and the light goes on. This is linear and as systematic as the political process allows. We saw this most clearly in the German policy process of Figure 2.3. Sometimes it works, sometimes not. Sometimes it has dire and unexpected consequences, as Chapter 2 found on why governance systems are failing.

Housing projects and estates to replace slums and low-grade homes in the 1960s and 1970s were one of the most visible political and social experiments of the twentieth century. The effort had spectacular unexpected consequences. In some places, the experiment has been accepted as the extraordinary failure it became in creating a new outlaw underclass and centres for crime, ruined lives, social immobility, an intimidating and degrading ambience, and a public expenditure drain. Many such estates have been demolished. In other places, the experiment rolls on. If only providing mass new housing had been understood not as an 'end-state' policy, but as an experiment or set of experiments in governance and design. Small scale, diversity, feedback, adjustment, acceptance of failure, participation, scaling up the successful – that was the way to do it. The social and economic costs that we are all still paying would never have arisen.

Very slowly, this lesson for housing has been learnt. But the lesson about the lesson has not: Problem to analysis to policy to approval to implementation to solution (PAPAIS) does not work. Having come up with this acronym, out of curiosity we searched for definitions. In Spanish, Papáis has the meaning Daddy. In the Urban Dictionary:[27] 'the sexiest man in the universe, his large penis could destroy the sun, and his butt hole is really a black hole' – amusing and perhaps psychologically insightful.

Privatisation of the state assets of the former Soviet Union was a policy pursued by the World Bank. Its concern was to get these assets operating under market capitalism to secure the benefits this can bring. These have followed significantly, although far from completely. Such was the urgency given to privatising – in effect at any price and with no time for experimentation and variety – one of the more unexpected results has been the rise of the Russian oligarchy as a national and international power and wealthy elite, the kleptocracy.[28]

The EU's policy of promoting biofuels to replace fossil fuels so as to reduce CO_2 release looked right to help counter climate change. The unintended consequences have found forests and habitats, notably of rare orangutans, being destroyed for palm oil production with the loss of CO_2 capture. Presuming an end-state in this case has been counterproductive. Organisations and their decision makers are not inclined to own up to serious errors and tend to hope the new problem of their making will go away.

Feedback should be embedded in implementation. Rather than waiting for the end state to occur and then assessing whether the experiment has 'worked', the changes should be monitored and adjustments made as the experiment progresses. Those aspects of the biofuels policy found to be actually, rather than theoretically reducing CO_2, would continue. Those not doing so would be quickly stopped. This is Systems Thinking in Practice.

In practice, new housing, state asset privatisation and biofuel production were all mass political experiments, and it would be far better to acknowledge and treat them as such. You might think that they are the exception to the otherwise universal applicability of PAPAIS. But consider the multitude of regulations. No matter how well thought through, in practice some work and some are ineffective, costly and counterproductive. Each regulation needs feedback on its results, and adjustment or abandonment. Their intentions may be sound, but their means of enactment are experiments. Neoliberal economics and responses to planetary degradation are gigantic political experiments. Outsourcing and privatisation are political experiments. Tax rates and welfare regimes are continuous political experiments. Attempts to improve health systems are invariably political experiments.[29] A particular school system may be robust for decades, then external change occurs – the internet. It's time not to PAPAIS the whole system – but to experiment.

Experiments do happen, but systemic experimentation is not the norm.

10.3.3 The 'end-state' fallacy

Political experiments entail so many variables that the notion of being able to 'policise' an end-state (a solution) into existence is as fallacious as expecting Doctor Who's Tardis to materialise. With even the finest, most learned and objective minds on the case, such certainty is not possible. The context changes too, as new technologies, attitudes or 'unknown unknowns' pop out of the woodwork to thwart the best-laid plans. This is especially the case with the biosphere and planetary destruction, where our knowledge of unfolding events is so limited. A PowerPoint presentation is not going to save the world.

The mindset underlying the linear systematic approach is the 'end-state fallacy'. Government machines are then built to turn the mythology into reality. China has really good machinery, leading some to ponder whether a one-party state is the answer to semi-impotent democratic governments. China has a long history of being hugely effective at delivering its centrally determined plans – sometimes leaving millions dead, sometimes achieving extraordinary results. 'According to the World Bank, more than 500 million people were lifted out of extreme poverty as China's poverty rate fell from 88 percent in 1981 to 6.5 percent in 2012'[30] (although the 500 million have not themselves been asked for their opinions, many live in urban poverty, unregistered and therefore without health or education services). The Chinese system of government also allows active experimentation in government innovations, aided by investment in two major schools for training China's future rulers. Based in Shanghai and Beijing, it is claimed that one school fosters 'why thinking' and the other 'how thinking'.

According to Micklethwaite and Wooldridge, what is being sought is to build a cadre immersed in understanding 'how to best administer'.[31]

In democracies, the 'strong leader' is in vogue to provide the potency, to muscle aside the flabby administration, and deliver various promised end-states by sheer force of personality. Some positive change can occur – and invariably some horrors – but transformation never does, despite the leader driving PAPAIS hard.

Politicians and government officials (and us) are trapped in the myth of policy. Competitive policy offerings – usually alongside the words 'hope' or other feel-goods – are the bait of elections. Inevitably they disappoint on enactment. It is this end-state fallacy, perhaps more than anything else that is resulting in so much disaffection with so many governments.

Party politics are locked into being 'right' in order to be re-elected. But in a world of such complexity and high rate of change, and with such huge challenges, this linear presumption is the major obstacle to successful government. Policy as a distinct pursuit is dead. It is arguable that policy is a fallacious concept altogether and policy making a fool's errand. Decision is hard-wired to its result. Purpose is alive and awaiting our embrace. Weary of perpetual failure, notable administrators and policy makers have themselves concluded thus. Has there ever been a policy that has turned out as intended, first time around? Perhaps, but this was the exception, not the rule. Systems of governing must change to reflect this.

It is entirely legitimate for government to analyse and produce a theory for a solution, just as science does. However, science does not accept the theory as the answer until it is confirmed experimentally. Governments routinely omit this rather crucial step.

With some urgency we must extricate and unburden ourselves from this orientation to the end-state and reorient to outcomes. Placed then in the context of STiP, the government machine can transform its operation to putting in place the *means* or *process* for resolving situations of concern – rather than attempting DIY.[32]

Achieving lasting beneficial change then becomes circular, cybernetic, experimental and deliberative – all within the values of inquiry, not personal power. The case studies from Somerset health and Shaldon flood defence described earlier point to the means (Chapter 5). As enactments take place, so experience tells whether, in practice, the intentions are being fulfilled. It takes maturity on the part of those in power to let go and enable the *system* to make beneficial change.

This is not as big a leap as it might first appear. Consider the functions of institutions that depoliticise interest rate setting and transfer responsibility to a central bank. Central bank independence is usually guaranteed by legislation and the institutional framework governing the bank's relationship with elected officials, particularly the minister of finance.[33] The Monetary Policy Committee of the Bank of England has this role. Its model for decision making is instructive. Five members come from the top posts of the Bank and four are appointed by the Chancellor of the Exchequer (or Minister of Finance). It meets monthly. Its members discuss and vote. The minutes and votes of each member are published – disagreements, opposing views, changes of mind. It is transparent. Expert commentators join in this dialogue through the specialist media, and in explanations to parliamentary committees. Independent economic statistics and research papers add to the knowledge base. Each member's personal constituency participates in discussions back at their university, bank, partnership or other place of work. Transparency brings a lot of knowledge, experience, and brainpower to bear. Challenge and difference are encouraged. At the end of each meeting, members vote, and the majority set the rate for that month. Round we go again, in wide deliberation and learning, to the next month's decision. Adjustments are made depending on the strength of the economy and inflation rates. Despite having the word policy in its name, there is no end-state. This is a process of reasonably open deliberation.

10.4 Systemic experimentation

Vincent Ostrom asserts that all human artefacts, including governments, 'require knowledgeable experimenters who know what they are doing' and that for the observer to understand the experiment, he or she must have access to knowledge of the design principles employed by the artisan. Using an electric generating station as his example, Ostrom explains,

> An observer taking Wilson's advice and looking at the living reality of a power plant generating electricity would not be likely to survive if he escaped from theory and attached himself to facts ... The operation of an electric utility always occurs subject to the intelligent discharge of human artisanship ... Such a utility may, in turn, be linked to water systems, or other systems of relationships, capable of generating and using electricity ... Human societies, thus, are constituted by the simultaneous operation of diverse experiments variously linked to one another.[34]

10.4.1 Crafting experiments through eight tests

In launching an experiment, we need to consider where to start. The foundation is humility. As a matter of course, these experiments would be well crafted and adjusted or indeed dropped as they proceeded. Their means of enactment would build in cybernetic feedback, deliberation, and open decision making, and thus be systemic.

This may look time-consuming. But in terms of the total time taken to achieve beneficial results, it compares favourably with the 'end-state' method (five years rather than ten years in the case of Shaldon flood defences). Outright failure takes years or decades, either before its initiators have moved on and an alternative end-state is attempted, or its demise is grudgingly accepted. Moderate results may be left to linger on in perpetuity. Time invested up front in preparation is rarely wasted in the long run.

A lot is now known about *how* to take good decisions (more accurately termed here 'designs for action'). The applied research is extensive. We have developed these eight tests for systems of governing:

1. **Framing test**
   What is the situation of concern, where are the boundaries drawn? Are they sufficiently wide?

2. **Purpose test**
   What is the point or purpose of this experiment? What is it intended to achieve, what results are desired (against which the feedback would be sought)?

3. **Engagement and stakeholder test**
   Has the experiment been developed from, and with the cohort of citizens it is aimed at? What would improve their lot or change their behaviour in ways that would realise the experiment's purpose? Are the interests of all stakeholders at the table or does the stakeholding have to be built? Where successful implementation requires public engagement, use Engage–Deliberate–Decide.

4. **Insider test**
   Knowing how industries and organisations work *on the inside* is key to regulating them successfully. Is inside knowledge being used?

5. **Other countries test**
   How have other countries dealt with this situation? Have they been successful? Modern governments have been running long enough to learn from each other, for similar-country-based practice to be assessed and used to at least *inform* home policies. The OECD and others are prime sources.

6. **Systems thinking test**
   This is the test to determine if the experiment takes account of the inconvenient variables, if it is joined up, if it is holistic, if it has considered the knock-on effects and the potential unintended consequences. Systemic design should be in evidence (Chapter 8).

7. **Capability test**
   How will the experiment co-deliver the purpose? If so, how, and what evidence is there to show this? Who will do this? What capacities, skills, resources, organisation, and governance will this require?

8. **Value test**
   What would the experiment cost to execute, including costs to the public? What is its value?

Test, enjoy mistakes, learn from results.

The rigour and extent of application of the eight tests will vary. The intent is to 'train' governments to working in this way to get 'designs for action' right the first time, or as right as they can be before experimentation. The application of these tests would stop most preferential lobbying. Large companies, industries and other lobbyists would still be heard – as stakeholders, customers, and insiders – but on an equal footing with the less powerful. As the success rate of decisions improves, so will the 'rework' backlog reduce. In place of focusing on doing 'something', governments would focus on doing something well. This would mean doing less and achieving more.

10.4.2 Vetting decisions/designs for action

Asking or urging governments to change their behaviour does not work. The system has to be so constructed as to *require* that change, in this case to make the tests stick. There would therefore be two clauses in the constitution. One would be to allocate authority to the government administrators to ensure the tests are applied *as* decisions/designs for action are developed. As of now for the process for drafting, vetting and passing legislation, politicians would come into government with established processes in place for decision making, which they would then follow as the norm.

The second constitutional requirement would allocate authority to the second chamber to vet whether the tests had been properly applied and to refer back those that had not. This is not a challenge to a political judgment, but a check on the efficacy of the decision. Again, this is not as much of a leap as it might at first sight appear. Systems of government vary in the checks and balances decisions have to pass. The Singapore government requires probably the most stringent through the use of 'decision trees'.

Other governments do or have trialled what is, in effect, a technical vetting alongside a political vetting or scrutiny. But, as today's second chambers are bodies of politicians with party political allegiances, most jurisdictions simply apply a *political* vetting on a *political* decision. Both political and technical vetting are needed.

If the quantity of designs for action is high, the second chamber would be selective in their vetting. The constitutional court would be available for citizens to challenge decisions. As the new governance overall becomes established, less would be attempted, with more relational capital, the capability to reach accommodations amongst different interests and the eight test process would become the norm.

10.4.3 Design authorities

In the 1700s, the insurers, Lloyd's of London, faced the challenge of how to prevent ships sinking so often. Ship owners, designers, builders, distributors and government shared this interest. Their incentive was clear – to limit payouts, as was the objective – to make better ships. From these beginnings arose the now universal institutions described below.

Today, industry and insurance specialists and university researchers come together within formalised structures of technical committees, working groups, and certified verification agents to develop and apply design standards and to investigate operational failures. These standard-setters work under the aegis of, amongst others, the International Electrotechnical Commission (IEC) and the International Organization for Standardization (ISO). Founded in 1947, the ISO was one of the first organisations granted general consultative status with the United Nations Economic and Social Council. It is an independent, non-governmental organisation, the members of which are the standards organisations of the 163 member countries. In STiP terms, we see here multiple perspectives, second-order cybernetic feedback, knowing-in-action, and emergent standards. Each is, in effect, a Resulture.

The function of the design authorities in our new system of governing would be the same as those used throughout the world to improve safety, reliability, and performance in many fields of engineering and elsewhere – aircraft, ships, railways, wind turbines, oil and gas drilling, bushfires, flooding, and so on. The standards they set range from the prescriptive or 'shall' to recommended practice to technical specification to guideline (best advice). Standards evolve as definitive knowledge is acquired.

Such flexibility is key. Having standards does not mean standardisation. In some areas, ISO has attempted to produce systematic standards for situations that are inherently systemic. The result is bureaucracy and frustration. Much of the benefit from design authorities is in the sharing of knowledge and the learning this entails, not prescription. At Shaldon, local standards were in effect developed locally for its flood defence. But the process used of EDD could have had a design authority standard, adopting established engagement processes that work.

Unlike most current regulators that look only through their 'rear view mirror' at what has happened, design standards organisations seek to anticipate future challenges and risks. The process utilises 'working groups of open-minded experts speculating on possibilities, using physics, experience, and probability-based reliability theory in formulating their guidelines'.[35] Some are obvious – the consequence of hurricanes of increasing ferocity for offshore wind turbines – some far less so. The operating principles that have emerged are: rigour in decision making; failure being accepted and not ignored; reliability engineering as an essential tool; specifying the conditions to be taken into account in design; and the *consequences* of failure determining the significance or weight of a standard. This works. Use of standards:

- aids in the creation of products and services that are safe, reliable, and of good quality
- helps businesses increase productivity while minimising errors and waste
- safeguards consumers and the end users.

These are sound objectives for the 'products and services' of governmental organisations. What, for example, would a standard to 'safeguard consumers and the end users' of sanctions look like? Many of the challenges the world and governments face are amenable to the same 'engineering standard' process. But countries mostly still deal with these unilaterally and through political systems, with haphazard results. River basin management for sustainable water supply, vehicle pollution in cities, education for population limitation, intervention in civil war and post-war social and economic reconstruction are all examples of where knowledge is now sufficient for standards to be established. Once these are in place, the rate of learning will increase and the boundaries of ignorance will be reduced. Codification of different cultural, national, and tribal characteristics and matching the forms of education that work in these conditions (adaptation) will, again, be analogous to shipbuilding, where standards vary with the type of vessel.

Process infrastructure – for example, the digital dashboards and social innovation labs referenced above – would also be a subject for a design authority. This could cohere the learning from the many current experiments in these fields, understand their results, and set standards for their design. Over time, design authorities would move functions such as education, health, wellbeing, and environmental quality from an ideological, short-term cycle common to many ministries and locate them in the social purpose subsystem (see Chapter 7).

10.4.4 Failure inquiries

Failure inquiries in the new system would follow the well-established methods of air and train crash investigations. In practice, these are systemic inquiry processes. Their purpose is not to blame or to find the guilty, but to identify what happened, its causes and how to prevent these in the future. In this atmosphere, those involved are better able to speak straight rather than covering up. Everyone is committed to organisational learning and prevention.

For governments, such investigations would range from wildfires, flooding, the banking crash of 2008, poor tax collection, child protection failures, the fate of a specific failed project on, say, health improvement, to train service failures and deaths in custody. The potential for learning and improvement is vast.

With some urgency we must extricate and unburden ourselves from the orientation to the end-state and reorient to outcomes. Placed then in the context of STiP, the government machine can reform to putting in place the *means* or *process* for resolving situations of concern. Achieving lasting beneficial change then becomes circular, cybernetic, experimental and deliberative, all within the values of inquiry, not personal power.

The next chapter brings together the thinking in this book into a set of principles for systemic governing.

Notes

1 Lawton, G. 2017. Thoughtlessly thoughtless. *New Scientist* 236 (3156): 28.
2 *The Secret Life of Chaos*. BBC program presented by Professor Jim Al-Khalili.
3 Fazey, I. Schäpke, N., Caniglia, G., Patterson, J., Hultman, J., Van Mierlo, B., Säwe F., et al. 2018. Ten essentials for action-oriented and second order energy transitions, transformations and climate change research. *Energy Research & Social Science* 40: 54–70.
4 Straw, E. 2014. *Stand & Deliver: A Design for Successful Government*. London: Treaty for Government.
5 Ibid.
6 Fotos, M. 2013. *Vincent Ostrom's Revolutionary Science of Association*. Working paper for the Yale Center for the Study of Representative Institutions.
7 Schwartz, D. 2017. *The Last Man Who Knew Everything: The Life and Times of Enrico Fermi, Father of the Nuclear Age*. New York: Basic Books.
8 Furubo, Jan-Eric and Nicoletta Stame, eds. 2018. *The Evaluation Enterprise: A Critical View*. Aldershot: Routledge.
9 Guilfoyle, Simon. 2016. *Kittens Are Evil: Little Heresies in Public Policy*. Axminster: Triarchy Press.
10 Ibid.
11 Nyhan, B. and J. Reifler. 2018. The roles of information deficits and identity threat in the prevalence of misperceptions. *Journal of Elections, Public Opinion and Parties*: 1–23.
12 Rosling, Hans with O.Rosling and A. Rosling Ronnlund. 2018. *Factfulness: Ten Reasons We're Wrong about the World – And Why Things Are Better Than You Think*. New York: Flatiron Books
13 Ibid.
14 Agyemang, E. 25–31 May 2018. Seven psychological sins you must not commit. *Investors Chronicle*.
15 http://www.civicdashboards.com/city/new-orleans-la-16000US2255000/ (Accessed 15 April 2019).
16 https://en.wikipedia.org/wiki/Stafford_Beer (Accessed 15 April 2019).
17 Furubo op cit. See note 8 above.
18 Ibid.
19 Forss K, Marra, M., and Schwartz, R., eds. 2011. *Evaluating the Complex: Attribution, Contribution and Beyond*. Comparative Policy Evaluation, New Brunswick, NJ: Transaction Publishers.
20 Straw, E. 2014. op. cit.
21 PROGRESS is a radically different model of school accountability. It explores what might be learned from the history of Antidote – an organisation set up to foster more emotionally supportive school environments – to inform the development of such a model. It starts with pupil, staff, and parent surveys to describe their experience of the school, using the data that emerges to have conversations with each other to develop an explanation about what it means and a strategy for improvement. Every school should engage in this sort of process every year. League tables of public examination results are too blunt an instrument, and unlike the PROGRESS process do not stimulate solutions as well as highlight problems. Independent surveying and confidential reporting averts the syndrome of the untouchable but largely ineffective head teacher. All government agencies should find out how their stakeholders experience them and be held to account for responding to the findings. Board members would then have the judgment of the people and organisations they are there for and not airbrushed data from management in the annual review.
22 Park, James. 2018. Turning the tide on 'coercive autonomy': Learning from the antidote story. *Forum* 60(3): 387–396. http://doi.org/10.15730/forum.2018.60.3.387.
23 https://ec.europa.eu/clima/policies/ets_en (Accessed 20 September 2018).

24 Ibid.
25 Laing, T., Sato, M., Grubb, M., and Comberti, C. 2013. *Assessing the Effectiveness of the EU Emissions Trading System*. Centre for Climate Change Economics and Policy Working Paper 126. London: Grantham Research Institute on Climate Change and the Environment.
26 Rework was the term used in manufacturing for all the parts of an assembly not made to specification, which post quality control were then sent back for further machining to get right. The cost in time, money and organisational complexity was high. This was a bane of 'old world' engineering and led to the demise of much of the West's manufacturing industry. Starting with the automotive industry, Japanese companies revolutionised the process with 'zero defects', 'right first time' and similarly purposeful intentions. Today, either a company's manufacturing is world class or it's not in business. These attitudinal changes, translated into practice, are at the heart of this book.
27 Urban Dictionary is a crowdsourced online dictionary for slang words and phrases, with 14 million unique readers as of November 2014. https://en.wikipedia.org/wiki/Urban_Dictionary (Accessed 11 April 2019).
28 Kleptocracy is a government with corrupt leaders who use their power to exploit the people and natural resources of their own territory in order to extend their personal wealth and political power. Typically, this system involves embezzlement of funds at the expense of the wider population. https://en.wikipedia.org/wiki/Kleptocracy (Accessed 15 April 2019).
29 The US and the UK have been in the midst of political experiments with their health and school systems for 20+ years, without ever acknowledging it. Pitched as end-state policies, they still have not worked.
30 https://en.wikipedia.org/wiki/Poverty_in_China (Accessed 24 January 2019).
31 Micklethwaite, J. and Wooldridge, A. 2014. *The Fourth Revolution*. Harmondsworth: Penguin.
32 DIY, the acronym in English for 'Do It Yourself' – often applied to home maintenance.
33 https://en.wikipedia.org/wiki/Central_bank (Accessed 9 May 2019).
34 Allen, B., ed. 2012. *The Quest to Understand Human Affairs: Essays on Collective, Constitutional, and Epistemic Choice*, p. 265. Lanham, MD: Lexington Books.
35 Manwell, James. Professor of Mechanical Engineering, University of Massachusetts Amherst. Secretary of the International Electrotechnical Commission 61400-3-1 Working Group.

11

PRINCIPLES FOR SYSTEMIC GOVERNING

11.1 What sort of principles?

As you read this, the term 'principles' may evoke several 'takes' on what *sort* of principles. These might fall into the overarching or fundamental such as liberté, égalité, fraternité or to the relationship between people and the state, such as parliamentary sovereignty, or to the behaviour of governments, like open and accountable.

The difficulty lies in finding principles with widespread acceptance. Take fairness, which we think provides a unifying narrative, but is a word with different implications embedded in different people's minds. For us, the notion of fairness between citizens, between generations, between sexes, between ethnic groups, between employers and employees, between nations and between humans and the biosphere, forms the basis for just, peaceful and sustainable societies. But that same word may be challenged by those who observe empirically that 'life is not fair', or that 'personal responsibility' is a more effective foundation, or that fairness implies the state being a soft touch. A similar fate awaits harmony, equality, tolerance and so on.

We want to avoid the sort of values programs so beloved by large organisations – private and public – and management consultants. Through these means, top managements are in search of control and organisational alignment. In practice, they usually end up with a glossy brochure and mandatory e-learning course, 'rolled out' and espoused by dutiful spokespeople but which does not connect with the prevailing culture. Political ideologies are essentially corporate values programs, and as wasteful.

We want to avoid the temporary imposition of principles. In the absence of a strong constitution, winning political parties tend to impose their preferences, for these then to be replaced by another set from another party at the next election.

The difference we emphasise is between a standard manifesto of promises, on the one hand, and a governance model laid out in a constitution based on sound principles that would produce real improvement, on the other. The system should do the job. There would be no need, as now, to rely on the inherently unreliable process of competing parties proposing competing solutions well after the problem arises, one of which may or may not get implemented, relatively well or relatively badly.

It is instructive to recall the principles of the late founder of IKEA, Ingvar Kamprad, in his *Testament of a Furniture Dealer* of 1976:

- To create a better everyday life for the many people
- No method is more effective than the good example
- Low price with a meaning
- Development is not always the same thing as progress
- Expensive solutions to any kind of problem are usually the work of mediocrity
- Exaggerated planning is the most common cause of corporate death
- By always asking why we are doing this or that, we can find new paths
- Only while sleeping one makes no mistakes
- The fear of making mistakes is the root of bureaucracy and the enemy of development
- No decision can claim to be the only right one
- Time is your most important resource.

There is a lot of systems thinking here, which has made IKEA the global success it has been (although even this visionary leader omitted the biophysical world). We are seeking principles, similar in a way to Kamprad's, in that they choose themselves by being essential to our future, and around which societies and the world can cohere. Importantly, principles can be put into effect in different ways. If they were not we would all suffer, as maintaining our capacities to generate difference is the only reliable pathway to a viable future.

We have to formulate, articulate and rearticulate the enduring principles we need *collectively*. The principles we propose are emergent and cybernetic. In relation to the law, for example, this element of the diamond model requires major surgery. We could itemise what that surgery should be. Under current governing systems, little would change as a result. A systemic way through starts with what would make good change happen. For example, independent and public feedback on the *results* of the law in its many incarnations – from the legislative framework for water provision to inquests into deaths in custody – would act as a major pressure to change and as a counterweight to the vested interests of lawyers and their lobbying power, and to the inertia of government.

The good news is that we are not starting from scratch. Some constitutions do set out some meta-unifying principles which have the support of most people. Further, the Declaration of Human Rights, developed after World War II, is widely accepted and covers much ground. It can be abused by being ignored or overplayed, but as declared, it is sound and in no need of repetition here. The new proposed principles are set out below. We have grouped them into a set of five, according to the schema below. In all, 26 principles are listed; in your reading of the book you may well find more. In what follows, we address each group sequentially, but always keeping the whole set in mind.

Biosphere and people	Democracy and subsidiarity	Fourth separation of powers: The world can't run on lies	Governments	Companies

1 The biophysical world is incorporated as the central partner in our governing systems.

This, the very first principle, might be thought of as 'Inclusive Trusteeship'.

> Even though *Homo sapiens* has become a major agent in shaping the circumstances of its own existence, the future of our species depends on the survival of other living species and on our sustainable use and replenishment of finite planetary resources. Recognising this truth, a viable political economy for the future must be symbiotic with Planet Earth, enabling us as its custodian-stewards to hold it in trust for future generations.[1]

We cannot work to improve humanity's lot without cherishing the natural world we are part of. The production and distribution of goods and services has to be organised according to planetary sustainable patterns. The planet we share with all other living species shall be put before profit and growth for growth's sake. Principled pragmatism must become the watchword of social life, and its subsidiary, economic management.

2 People and constitutional sovereignty: All political power resides in the people, who delegate a defined measure of that power to a government and other institutions.

This avoids the practical impossibility of the people making and enforcing laws and running large public sectors. The principle goes hand in hand with that of *Constitutional Supremacy*, whereby the Constitution – setting out the governing system – becomes the supreme law of the land and cannot be altered save by wide popular consent. Constitutional Supremacy embodies the notion of a constitution, written and accessible, that in principle invalidates any laws that are inconsistent with it and of entrenchment whereby the constitution's provisions cannot, for example, be repealed by a Parliament. Under this principle of People Sovereignty minority interests shall be protected, through mandatory deliberation and engagement (EDD) and through key decisions requiring a supermajority – typically two-thirds of those voting.

This principle may seem to be of distant relevance until a long-standing prime minister or executive president seeks to become an elected dictator – as in Hungary, Poland, and Turkey. With Parliamentary Sovereignty (as opposed to People Sovereignty), a party with a majority can change the constitution to allow it to do what it wants. This is equivalent to a football match where, when one team takes the lead it is free to change the rules of the game to its advantage. In effect, the game is no longer externally governed. It becomes a lottery of power.

3 Rule of law: All members of a society (including those in government) are equally subject to publicly disclosed legal codes and processes.

The rule of law is the 'authority and influence of law in society, especially when viewed as a constraint on individual and institutional behaviour'.[2] For the principle to happen in practice, the judiciary must be constitutionally separate from government and politics. Their authority is delegated from the people. Governments, parliaments, and religious entities shall have no power to control, influence, or appoint the judiciary. In Russia, this is not the case, and the judicial system is used freely against the government's opponents. In South Africa, the very strength of independence of the judiciary has prevented it from going the way of Russia.

People Sovereignty is dependent on the rule of law. This is fundamental to the operation of any fully accountable and democratic governing system, to holding the egos of politicians and officials in check, and to preventing dictatorial tendencies (whether by an individual or a party).

4 A Constitutional Court adjudicates on interpretation of the constitution. Its decisions are binding.

A Constitutional Court is where disputes over the interpretation of the constitution, or acts thought to be outside it, are heard and judgments made. The court needs to have a sound grasp of government, democracy and politics. Judiciaries tend to fail when they assume all of life is amenable to the legal mind. Where the judiciary is drawn from a sufficiently wide experiential and educational base, then the constitutional court would be a branch of the existing Supreme Court. Where not, a new court would be established with a set of judges equipped with the necessary attributes.

Deliberation, not adversarial case-making, would be the usual process for decision-making by courts.

It is also possible to create new courts. A national or international biosphere court would shift thinking and power. The Land and Environment Court in New South Wales, Australia, was established in 1980 'to create a specialised "one stop shop" for environmental, planning and land matters … [that had previously been] … dealt with by a range of different tribunals and courts. There was no environmental law as it is now known'.[3] Arguably, this court's remit has been too narrow and instrumental, reflecting understandings and political imperatives that existed at the time of its creation. However, rulings in early 2019 point to the court itself actively reframing its concerns by banning a company bid to mine 21m tonnes of coal over 16 years. Greenhouse gas emissions contributing to climate change were listed amongst the reasons for preventing the application.

The role of the Resulture (see Section 11.3 below) in making such courts effective through providing comprehensive and transparent information is significant.

> Key to environmental governance in a 'democratic' mode are rights for the public freely to access information about environmental matters, to participate meaningfully in environmental decision-making and to seek enforcement of environmental laws through access to justice. These three 'pillars' of environmental democracy are articulated internationally in Principle 10 of the Rio Declaration and treaties such as the Aarhus Convention.[4]

5 Diversity of Lifestyles: All lifestyles are accepted – within the constraint of not harming others or the biosphere.

The role of diversity in responding successfully to biophysical breakdown extends to our lifestyles. Those at the social margins of developed societies may prove to be the more resilient. City dwellers typically have no experience in contending and working with the biosphere. Indigenous societies, nomads, travellers, off-grid pioneers, farmers, rejectors of consumerism, self-organising groups, local economic and social innovators, and all those experienced in adaptation represent an insurance policy for us all. These 'alternative' skills could prove vital. They need conserving. Every language in the world holds value in the culture it represents. The Kurds are likely to survive long after their oppressors: Presidents Erdogan and Assad in Turkey and Syria.

Modern politics and the media have a tendency to impose limitations on lifestyles, and to stigmatise 'alternatives'. These alternatives may be more robust than those now thought of as conventional and accepted. We do not know. But in an unknown future, it is dangerous to reject them.

Diversity of lifestyles – along with all other forms of diversity – is also a human right. Political parties and the media should stop privileging one lifestyle over another. The only constraint should be the one that applies to us all: not to harm others or the biosphere.

6 Explicit democratic decisions shall be made as to what is in and what is out of the Commons.

The Commons has been progressively taken over by the state and private ownership. This has had societal benefits in its more efficient use and exploitation through the market economy. But this has been to the detriment of the biophysical world, to local access and use, and to our sense of collective responsibility and control. For air quality and oceans, our governance systems are failing or effectively absent.

The basics of life – air, water, land – are, or should be, in the commons for the people to then decide the means of their management and use. The economistic takeover of utilities – whether as private businesses or as sources of revenue for the city or state – has meant that revenue is not linked to providing less of a valuable 'commodity' in need of sustaining. The rules for the operation of utilities should, amongst other aims, reward efficiency and reduced usage.

No one has yet sought to privatise the air, but it is regarded as free to pollute and with it, us and all species. This cannot continue. Much land has or is being privatised – legally or otherwise – from the forced seizures of the Enclosure Acts (in the nineteenth century about one-sixth of England was stolen by the state and typically its ownership 'transferred' to the MPs or their associates voting for the Acts) to today's similar acts in the Amazon rainforests. We need to think again how land should be treated – and therefore taxed – between the rights of the Commons and the benefits and obligations of private ownership.

The internet is now a major source of the commons, providing common knowledge: Wikipedia, common open source software like Linux, and a commons for free interchange: social media. Open source is a demonstration of how commons practice can create significant value and is a challenge to those who say only competition can do so. Blockchain technology may become a form of commons providing the collective space for money exchange. Public service providers – such as the BBC – are or shall be a form of commons.

Biosphere and people	**Democracy and subsidiarity**	Fourth separation of powers: The world can't run on lies	Governments	Companies

7 Elections shall be representative.

This means using a good system of proportional representation, limited and proportionate political party funding, voter registration at birth, and electoral boundaries set independently of government and parties by the second or vetting chamber, or an independent electoral commission.

8 A right to deliberative referenda shall exist; specific issues shall be resolved through Engage-Deliberate-Decide.

Voting is not the only means to enact a democracy. Representative democracy is essential, but has severe limitations. Participative and deliberative democracy are means to think, to develop social learning, to act responsibly, to learn from mistakes. They are, too, vital enablers of decentralisation. Citizens used to these forms of democracy – Switzerland and California, for example – know this and are well practised in their use. Chapter 9 on the Constitution reports on the recent exemplary example in Ireland for abortion.[5]

9 Central government only undertakes tasks or makes decisions which localities cannot or which require uniform regulation.

Switzerland as a nation was built from its Cantons upwards. Such was their diversity of language and culture that they only agreed to become one country on the basis that federal power was limited and local power protected. Its constitution states: 'The principle of subsidiarity must be observed in the allocation and performance of state tasks'.[6] The strength of local government and the active participation of citizens have served Switzerland well – democratically, in terms of citizen responsibility, and in the effectiveness of decisions and services. Ashby's Law that we referred to earlier, holds true in setting the limits to the authority of national governments. High levels of centralisation – as governments are wont to do – do not work. Much has to be done regionally and locally.

Subsidiarity is also about strengthening civic society. The more detached people are from any form of democratic power, the more detached they will be from civic society, and their responsibility for it. Subsidiarity engages people in solving problems from litter to traffic to unemployment. It restores a sense of agency.

Some argue against subsidiarity on the grounds that public services will vary between locales – termed a 'post code lottery'. In other words, one person may receive a different standard of public service from another, depending on where they live. In practice even in highly centralised countries, service standards vary considerably other than for simple functions. Most public services depend on local delivery. Eliminating variance is not possible. The upside to decentralisation is experimentation and subsequent transfer of the best outcome from one area to another. Thus, variation in delivery leads to improving standards and flexibility, and reducing the impractical load on the centre. Subsidiarity is also good for the personal commitment and motivation of public sector staff who have a sense of ownership and responsibility for the service rather than being mere deliverers of a top-down edict.

Subsidiarity depends on the existence of sound local governance connecting people and place, and on local tax raising and spending.

Biosphere and people	Democracy and subsidiarity	**Fourth separation of powers: The world can't run on lies**	Governments	Companies

10 A fourth separation of powers shall be incorporated in every system of government for the independent feedback of results through a Resulture.

The three established separations of powers – legislature, executive, and judiciary – have stood for a long time. They are essential. A fourth separation of powers is also essential to bring discipline and reality to the work of governments by providing the institutional means for the independent and timely collection and publication of the results of all that they set out to do (see Chapter 10 for an explanation of the term results). These institutionalised forms shall include design authorities, failure inquiries, and other means for corrective action. The term we have used for this fourth separation is the Resulture. This shall be as separate as the judiciary.

11 Statutory duties for the behaviour of politicians and officials at work, including the duty of straight speak, shall be set.

The fourth separation would also extend to the utterances of politicians and government officials through a set of statutory duties. Do we elect politicians to lie to us? That would be absurd. Yet that has become the norm. Do we employ officials to utter corporate speak and not learn from mistakes by pretending they have not happened? That too would be absurd. But that is the norm, too.

The governing system needs to be explicit as to what is expected of public office. Such a requirement would also act as a protection for ministers and managers who feel under pressure to toe the party or official line. All need boundaries in their work, to have it made clear what is expected and what is unacceptable, and to act as a counterbalance to the forces of perversion. A clear set of duties would help to create a different ethos.

These are the duties proposed:

- To speak straight, to say publicly what is really going on, and to avoid corporate speak, spin, obfuscation, evasion, gagging clauses, and lying.
- To approach each decision in a spirit of inquiry and learning.
- To make decisions transparently and openly at every stage and level of the political process, enabling people to see how decisions are made and their basis.
- To resist abuses of power and patronage and promote democracy at every level.
- To be non-discriminatory, ethical, and committed to diversity in all forms.
- To know that politicians exist to produce beneficial results (and not announcements, initiatives, or unworkable policies).

12 The first statutory duty of straight speak for politicians and officials shall apply also to the media.

The media is diversifying rapidly. This can only be a good thing. Having multiple perspectives is a systemic principle. Diversity is a principle of wide applicability to species, lifestyles, political parties and the media.

Nevertheless, the traditional media can still play a significant role in influencing government. Much of this influence has been a drag on effective responses to climate change and other degradations. We see no reason why the first statutory duty for politicians – *to speak straight* – should not apply also to the traditional media. This duty would not prevent stories being published, but would require their basis to be stated explicitly. We cannot escape acts of interpretation – and we will each be open to doing this differently because of our traditions of understanding – but we can expect responsibility to be taken for the interpretations that are made and exploration/deliberation around them. Is this piece of 'news' based on a straight report, the news outlet's interpretation, an official government leak, a reading of the tea leaves, or what? Do not dress up opinion as fact, one source as multiple sources, old news as new news and so on. The world cannot run on media lies either.

The internet and social media have made diversification possible. At the same time, local traditional newspapers have gone into decline and often extinction, leaving a hole where these organs had done a genuine job in investigating and reporting failure and abuse in local governments (noting that some have become as biddable as national newspapers in their local reporting).

In the small city of East Lansing, in the state of Michigan, USA, where the population is around 50,000, one group is filling the gap:

> Watching our city government came as something of a shock. While the policies were consistently liberal – in favor of the arts, the environment, and the unions – the behaviors were troubling. We saw cronyism, unmanaged conflicts of interest, and a general attitude that citizens are at best naive bores.
>
> We had no dedicated news organization to keep the people informed – to provide the transparency and accountability that the press ideally does. In a one-party town like East Lansing, a 'news desert' is especially dangerous. But in our town, as all over America, the Internet had gutted the local news economy, leaving us thirsting.
>
> So I did something I never thought I'd do. I used my skills as a professional historian and mainstream writer to become a local investigative reporter. Then, in 2014, I assembled a board and created a foundation to bring in donations from our community to provide news, hiring regular citizens and teaching them how to be local reporters. We've had 110 citizens report for us so far.[7]

This scheme is worthy of a new term – 'citizen scrutiny' – in part, a local Resulture. There is clearly much wrong with East Lansing's governing system, but even had it been all right, this civic society act has an important place: it harnesses the internet and social media for good and extends democracy. We can see such citizen scrutiny taking a formal role in local governance.

13 We each have a duty to think before we speak.

The new governance is designed to inform and educate us as much as governments. We, too, make assumptions, feed off our prejudices, hear what we want to hear, believe some fake news, or simply exist in ignorance. The more we understand, the better decisions we will make in democratic expression, in the news we choose to consume, in the discussions we hold with neighbours.

'Every nation gets the government it deserves', said Joseph de Maistre. This used to be the case – and still is in those countries where sufficient democracy exists for citizens to make a difference. Part of the purpose of the new governance is to restore the force of de Maistre's most famous quote.[8]

Personal responsibility will grow as systemic government develops. The onus is then on the citizens to use this wisdom in the decisions they are party to and to be active in running their societies. Two centuries ahead of social media, de Maistre also said: 'False opinions are like false money, struck first of all by guilty men and thereafter circulated by honest people who perpetuate the crime without knowing what they are doing'. We have to think, no matter how tempting the morsels of seductive confirmation bias laid before us. Open our eyes. Look and watch. Do not be duped.

14 Eliminate institutionalised bribery: No one shall benefit financially or electorally, directly or indirectly, now or later, from a decision in which they are involved or have influenced.

Corruption of all forms is detrimental. Whilst national laws typically outlaw straight financial bribery, several forms of bribery are legal and as detrimental. For the separation of powers to work in practice, a separation of people is required, too. Institutionalised bribery is endemic in places. It comes in several forms:

- The 'revolving door' for politicians, regulators, and civil servants to become employed in companies or industry associations. The employment bribe is in return for access to lobby, loose regulation, tax breaks, or company breaks. Where a civil servant is looking for such a post, then he/she will be spending more time on cultivating relationships with the potential employer and less energy on taking a firm regulatory line. A minister will see their long term income prospects arising from giving tax breaks to private equity firms today.
- Awards and honours in the control of the government, given in return for party funding or favourable news coverage.
- Unfunded and unusually high pensions for government officials, self-awarded, locking in administrators to their jobs, when they and we would be better served by change. These forms of pension produce organisational complacency and a strong focus on maintaining the status quo at the expense of institutional reform.
- Compensation committees setting pay for senior managements with a similar revolving door or mutual backscratching.
- Buying and selling of companies where managements receive large sums – nominally to tie them in – if the transaction proceeds regardless of the merits of the sale. These same institutional bribes have occurred in the demutualisation of pension funds, building societies, and roadside recovery services.

All of these forms of bribery have facilitated the expansion of neoliberalism and its wealth and power elites as well as its 'ethnic cleansing' of other forms of market capitalism.

Biosphere and people	Democracy and subsidiarity	Fourth separation of powers: The world can't run on lies	**Governments**	Companies

15 Governments shall serve democracy, and be effective, stable, adaptable, accountable, and open.

The 'enlightened constitution' model (see Chapter 9) proposes that constitutional governments should be stable, adaptable, accountable, open, and serve democracy. Effective might have been added. A few countries still manage the full house, but in many these principles are in retreat. Some governments are failing on all counts. Power and privilege have always hidden behind secrecy.

Evidently we must be more prescriptive in the modern world to fulfil the objectives of the enlightened constitution. What do we want from a system of governing? Essentially, a system is required that generates the most beneficial change, is balanced in its decisions and operations between the biophysical world and people, the rich and others, big organisations and individuals, in the application of laws, in the distribution of welfare, in the raising of taxes and between current and future generations. The many day-to-day governmental bodies (and their close relatives in the private sector contracted to government) would be run at high levels of service, as judged by the consumers/citizens and be satisfying to work in. It would not fund itself on unsustainable debt.

The system would provide routes for us as individuals to influence and understand its decisions – when we want to. It would not have to be fought to contribute to solving a public problem, and would take the noise out of the relationship between government and individuals. In other words, it would rebalance power between the citizen and the government.

Such a system would give agency to the biosphere and civic society, exclude ideology and prejudice for their own sake, proscribe preferential lobbying, eliminate patronage, and reduce the power and influence of companies, banks, and the news media. This new governing system would immunise politicians against business power, gut reactions, and media frenzy. It would stop as much as it starts, achieve more and attempt less and minimise waste. It would attract different kinds of politicians with contrasting formative experiences and the skills and the temperament to get things done.

Principles 16–20 also relate to governments. Their rationale and explanation can be found in Chapter 10 (Making Beneficial Change) so are not repeated here.

16 The purpose of government is to produce beneficial change.

17 Recognise that most 'decisions' by government are political experiments.

18 Designs for action shall be put into practice in the knowledge and positive acceptance that feedback may result in their amendment.

19 Beneficial change most often results from working with the affected population through the medium of STiP.

20 Technocratic democracy: Government designs for action shall be disciplined through their vetting.

21 Everyone pays their taxes.

The laws on taxation shall be written so as to prevent avoidance. If, in whatever form and in whatever jurisdiction, an individual earns £100,000 and the effective tax rate is 30%, then that is what is paid. The same applies to companies. This has been difficult to achieve. But an unlikely source – President Trump and the US Congress – may have produced part of the answer.[9] As part of his often criticised overhaul of the tax system, under a new rule any US firm with a global tax rate below 13.1% (to rise to 16.4% in a few years) must pay the difference up to that level to the US Treasury. Parking or hiding profits in low-tax countries or in tax havens would no longer be an incentive, as their effective tax rate will be below 13.1% and the long arm of the federal tax authorities will reach out. Nations considering cutting their corporate tax rates below this level to lure multinationals should find this to no longer be effective. Time will tell how well this will work and whether other countries/regions will follow suit, but experiments such as these are needed. One such trial would be a *global tax adjudicator* to determine where profit has arisen and therefore how much tax is due to each country. Countries should also require tax havens to operate with transparency in asset ownership, as a control.

Current experiments with basic income are innovations to be monitored and expanded systemically. In a similar vein, experiments with an annual ground rent/land value tax advocated by the Land Research Trust and others represent the opportunity to shift the burden from the 'deadweight taxes' of excise, VAT, payroll, and personal income to forms of taxation aimed at boosting economies and nurturing communities.[10] Further study is needed to assess the impact on the biosphere of different forms of taxation. Penalising our labour through its taxation and privileging company investment in resource consumption through capital expenditure tax allowances would be one place to start. A crucial hypothesis to test is whether taxing income – our labour – in place of taxing land value is a significant contributor to climate change and biodiversity loss.

Biosphere and people	Democracy and subsidiarity	Fourth separation of powers: The world can't run on lies	Governments	**Companies**

22 Companies shall act in the interests of people and the biosphere.

The cascade of principles listed above has set the terms for companies – the biosphere and people take precedence. Companies are here to be entrepreneurial without damaging the environment or us, and to develop technology without it controlling us.

Companies shall be brought into the situations in which we live. In terms of the governance model, companies cannot be disconnected from civil society or from the biophysical world. They shall no longer operate without reference to their impact on us as humans or on the biosphere.

23 End-to-end producer responsibility: Producers are responsible for all impacts of their activities and products, from raw material extraction to product recycling/disposal.

At present, company responsibility typically starts with its receipt of the materials it has purchased and ends with the use of their products by consumers. Companies are variously liable in law for the safety of their products in use by humans, for aspects of damage to the environment whilst manufacturing, and to very varying degrees, the quality of work life of their employees and recycling/disposal of their products.

Extended Producer Responsibility (EPR)[11] is the term given to making companies responsible for their receipt-to-end impact. Under EPR, producers are given a significant responsibility – financial and/or physical – for the treatment or disposal of post-consumer products. Assigning such responsibility should provide incentives to prevent waste, promote product design for the environment, and support the achievement of public recycling and materials management goals. Within the OECD, the trend is towards the extension of EPR to new products, product groups, and waste streams such as electrical appliances and electronics.

This new model of governance requires that this responsibility shall extend to pre-consumption, that is, to the sourcing of materials and components for their products and to their methods of production, including the treatment of employees and to all impacts of consumption and post-consumption.

This principle and the next are the means to establish the 'circular economy' —an economic system aimed at minimising waste and making the most of resources.[12] Beginning in 1966, far-sighted thinkers have proposed ideas on these lines. There is now a Platform for Accelerating the Circular Economy (PACE).[13]

24 Company duty to inform: For each product or service, consumers shall be informed of the biosphere and human impact of its sourcing, manufacture, distribution and post-use treatment.

Ignorance is a convenience for us all. Not knowing how the shirts on our backs are made, under what conditions, the chemicals used to process the cloth, and where the discharges go, relieves us of any nagging doubts as to the ethics of our consumption. But consumers do have considerable power for good when they are properly informed, as happened with some chemical additives in sweets – the 'e' number flavours and colours. Detailed research showed the effects of each additive, especially on children's behaviour. Enough consumers stopped buying products with potentially dangerous 'e' numbers that their use was reduced. Similar changes have been made where consumers have been given the opportunity to buy 'fair trade' products – like coffee beans and bananas – which are produced under reasonable working and financial conditions for their producers.

In all of these systemic improvements, labelling has been key – a cybernetic effect. The leaflets found with approved medicines set out what the medicine is for, when not to use it, what not to do whilst ingested, how to use it, possible side effects, their chances of occurring and how to store it. The user is thus fully informed and can consider its benefits against its side effects before use. Is my condition such as to risk a 1 in 1000 occurrence of conjunctivitis, for example? This honest discourse with consumers is our purpose *for all products*. It could be called *producer straight speak*. This might have a place in the fourth separation of powers. The world cannot run on company lies, either.

To provide easier-to-apply labelling, a scheme similar to that used for the energy efficiency of kitchen appliances could be established. The higher the rating the better (least energy use) and more consumer desirable. Competition has driven up standards of products' energy use. Under the proposed universal duty to inform, we would as consumers have the opportunity to decide whether to buy something made in a sweatshop using chemicals discharged into rivers, for example, or take notice of the energy consumed by a single Google search (20 searches are approximately equivalent to turning on a 60 watt light bulb for 6 minutes).

Greater awareness of the GHG discharge and other pollution caused by our purchases would inform future choices. Thus, for significant producers – air travel being the obvious one – its carbon production would appear alongside the price. Energy companies – public or private – would accompany their bills with an independent breakdown of its sources – renewable and non-renewable - and GHG produced.

The intent here is to emphasise that we are all responsible. The direct effect of labelling in reducing emissions may be limited, but in creating awareness, our decisions in other spheres of life – elections – would be better informed by that sense of biosphere responsibility.

Reducing choice through being aware of the consequences of a product may feel to some like another restriction on personal freedom, in an age when people have lost a lot through the impositions of governments and companies. In a way,

greenhouse gas = GHG

the freedom to pollute is one of the few left. The system of governing we are proposing would restore much of the freedom lost in the last 40 years through reallocating power between people and governments and companies. People would thus feel liberated and willing to cede the freedom to pollute in return for far greater, and ethical and aesthetic, freedoms.

25 Systemic inquiry shall accompany investment commitments in the technosphere; thereafter, end-to-end producer responsibility applies.

A tricky balance is to be struck between embracing the fruits of technology and exercising due caution with respect to their effects – both unintended and unexpected or emergent. On the one hand, imposing regulation and the time this takes can delay the benefits. On the other, before society has had the time to think much about it, the technology can take hold, whether for good or bad.

Producers should have the responsibility for anticipating the effects. Civil society must have a say. For some technologies the potential effects are obvious and can be considered systemically through deliberative democracy – gene modelling and GM foods, for example. For others, surprise may be in store – Uber and Airbnb, for example. In these latter cases, experimentation would be the way forward – small in scale and sufficient in number to identify their consequences and how they might be regulated to realise the benefits whilst limiting the disbenefits. Producers would be responsible for the social and other clean-up costs of those disbenefits.

As John Naughton, former professor of the public understanding of technology at the Open University, puts it:

> There are ethical issues in the development and deployment of any technology, but in the end it's law, not ethics, that should decide what happens, as Paul Nemitz, principal adviser to the European Commission ... points out ... Just as architects have to think about building codes when designing a house ... tech companies 'will have to think from the outset ... about how their future program could affect democracy, fundamental rights and the rule of law and to ensure that the program does not undermine or disregard ... these basic tenets of constitutional democracy'.[14]

26 In transitioning from polluting to non-polluting activities, communities and companies shall be supported fairly.

Industries have and will have to transition away from polluting activities. Some may take the view that oil or coal companies are simply bad and should be left to exit these industries and that their employee communities should find other work. But we have all benefited from them in many ways, and transition will occur quickest with state and international assistance. There is enough experience available now in handling closure and successful development of alternative economic activity for this to be applied generally. The Polish and Australian coal industries have to close soon. How can that best be organised, and with what assistance?

These 26 principles apply as much to one-party states, dictatorships and global governance bodies as they do to democracies. Enlightened leaderships will have to compensate for the absence of democratic pressures.

The collated principles can be seen in Box 11.1. In the final chapter – "What Next?" – a short overview of the means to put these principles into effect is outlined.

BOX 11.1 PRINCIPLES FOR SYSTEMIC GOVERNING

Biosphere and people

1. The biophysical world is incorporated as the central partner in our governing systems.
2. People and constitutional sovereignty: All political power resides in the people, who delegate a defined measure of that power to a government and other institutions.
3. Rule of Law: All members of a society (including those in government) are equally subject to publicly disclosed legal codes and processes: the rule of law.
4. A Constitutional Court adjudicates on interpretation of the constitution. Its decisions are binding.
5. Diversity of Lifestyles: All lifestyles are accepted – within the constraint of not harming others or the biosphere.
6. Explicit democratic decisions shall be made as to what is in and what is out of the Commons.

Democracy and subsidiarity

7. Elections shall be representative.
8. A right to deliberative referenda shall exist; specific issues shall be resolved through Engage–Deliberate–Decide.
9. Central government only undertakes tasks or makes decisions which localities cannot or which require uniform regulation.

Fourth separation of powers: The world can't run on lies

10. A fourth separation of powers shall be incorporated in every system of government for the independent feedback of results through a Resulture.
11. Statutory duties for the behaviour of politicians and officials at work, including the duty of straight speak, shall be set.
12. The first statutory duty of straight speak for shall apply also to the media.
13. We each have a duty to think before we speak.
14. Eliminate institutionalised bribery: No one shall benefit financially or electorally, directly or indirectly, now or later, from a decision in which they are involved or have influenced.

Governments

15. Governments shall serve democracy, and be effective, stable, adaptable, accountable, and open.
16. The purpose of government is to produce beneficial change.
17. Recognise that most 'decisions' by government are political experiments.
18. Designs for action shall be put into practice in the knowledge and positive acceptance that feedback may result in their amendment.
19. Beneficial change most often results from working with the affected population through the medium of STiP.
20. Technocratic democracy: Government designs for action shall be disciplined through their vetting.
21. Everyone pays their taxes.

Companies

22. Companies shall act in the interests of people and the biosphere.
23. End-to-end producer responsibility: Producers are responsible for all impacts of their activities and products, from raw material extraction to product recycling/disposal.
24. Company duty to inform: For each product or service, consumers shall be informed of the biosphere and human impact of its sourcing, manufacture, distribution, and post-use treatment.
25. Systemic inquiry shall accompany investment commitments in the technosphere; thereafter, end-to-end producer responsibility applies.
26. In transitioning from polluting to non-polluting activities, communities and companies shall be supported fairly.

Notes

1 Independent Constitutionalists UK. *Declaration.* http://icuk.life/declaration.html (Accessed 15 April 2019).
2 *Oxford English Dictionary.*
3 http://www.lec.justice.nsw.gov.au/Pages/about/history.aspx (Accessed 20 February 2019).
4 Worker, J. *What Does Environmental Democracy Look Like?* World Resources Institute. http://www.wri.org/blog/2014/07/what-does-environmental-democracy-look. (Accessed 15 February 2019).
5 O'Toole, F. 2018. If only Brexit had been run like Ireland's referendum. *The Guardian.* Wed., May 30. https://www.theguardian.com/commentisfree/2018/may/29/brexit -ireland-referendum-experiment-trusting-people (Accessed 18 January 2019).
6 *Federal Constitution of the Swiss Confederation* of 18 April 1999 (Status as of 23 September 2018).
7 https://www.theguardian.com/commentisfree/2018/may/28/news-journalism-politics-democrats-republicans (Accessed 10 November 2018).

8 Joseph-Marie, comte de Maistre, 1753–1821. Philosopher, lawyer, and diplomat who advocated social hierarchy and monarchy in the period immediately following the French Revolution.

9 https://www.thetimes.co.uk/article/trump-s-triumph-in-war-on-tax-avoidance-hhsp8f7m7 (Accessed 10 November 2019).

10 https://landresearchtrust.org/wp-content/uploads/2018/10/taxed.to_.death_.pdf (Accessed 10 March 2019).

11 OECD. 2001. *Extended Producer Responsibility: A Guidance Manual for Governments.* Paris: OECD Publishing.

12 https://en.wikipedia.org/wiki/Circular_economy (Accessed 10 May 2019).

13 How they are approaching this is described on their website: https://pacecircular. org/ (Accessed 6 January 2020).

14 Naughton, John. Don't believe the hype: The media are unwittingly selling us an AI fantasy. *The Observer* 13 January 2019.

The means to a far better end:

- Being aware of and changing our traditions of understanding
- Applying Systems Thinking in Practice, consistently

12.

WHAT NEXT?

12.1 The Will

In contemplating what we can do next, the core challenge for us all is the *Will*. We know what we need to do, but do we have the will to determine that we are going to clean up and preserve our magnificent planetary home and create balance in power, wealth and well-being? Do I as an individual have the will, which will then combine with the wills of others, to create the political will to complete the task? The answer, as Arthur Schopenhauer would have told us almost 200 years ago, is that the intellect calls the tune, but the will decides whether to dance.[1]

We can see this simile playing out all around us as our collective political wills have become the playthings of various elites. The depressing actuality of our collective political wills having become bewildered and listless is long-standing.

'The intellect calls the tune' – the argument has never been stronger for a return to the roots of our knowledge, based on rigorous processes of knowing; supported by clear and comprehensive method in our actions; informed by available discourse and expressed in conversation with our communities – or STiP.

How we construct this intellect – our own intellect, that mental wallpaper which we build by means of our experience and our media diet – radically determines if we will boil in our indifference and fecklessness like proverbial frogs, perhaps literally as the biosphere becomes too hot for human existence.

We are neither naïve, nor ignorant, nor innocent. We are capable of understanding each other, with and through all our games and agendas, our confusions, complications and distractions, and without judgement. We are also capable of asserting our unmediated experience of the world – of simply, pragmatically and effectively expressing our personal moral truth. And we should. To quote a well-known reader of Schopenhauer, Winston Churchill – 'We shape our buildings, and afterwards our buildings shape us'. We shape our political environment through our example, our speech, our confrontation and our engagement.[2]

We have no need to continue on the path of decline and permanent degradation. The alternative takes no more than the reinvention of institutions and organisations that were only human inventions in the first place. Schopenhauer's lesson is simple: political wills are easily bewildered; but they will dance if the intellect calls the right tune. Is this hard? Not with the Will.[3]

All manner of acts and innovations are happening throughout the world. Between starting this book and writing this final chapter, our sense is that the mood has shifted significantly, possibly dramatically. All of us have the capacity to consolidate and accelerate this shift. In many respects, what needs to be done is to face up to what has to be done and do it, with vigour and determination. Let no obstacle get in the way. We can challenge every excuse for inaction, dissect the framing, demand of those in power actions now, not distant targets, limp laws or words. If you have power, use it.

With the Will, the next question is where to apply it – where is my sphere of influence? Where can I have impact? Let's consider that in terms of acts that are collective, individual and at work. What follows are various ways for you to be active. Some are specific to people with certain responsibilities, some are open to us all. Your choice is possibly best made on the basis of your enthusiasm.[4]

12.2 Collective acts

Over only a few months in early 2019, the Climate Strikes[5] and the Extinction Rebellion[6] have struck quite a chord. As we write, this does not look like diminishing. Led mainly by the young, people are demanding serious, sufficient and urgent action. Frustration and dismay abound at the shuffling pace and commitment of dominant organisations in the state and private sector elements of the governance model. Children and young people – those who face most damage – are rebelling against the possible extinction of the human race. It is impressive to observe how much systems thinking is in use in the way these movements work.

Non-violent direct action has an extraordinary history – from Daniel O'Connell in Ireland in the first half of the nineteenth century to Mahatma Gandhi in India in the first half of the twentieth century – in opposing colonialism and achieving major constitutional and societal change. Modern colonialism comes in the form of neoliberalism. Protest comes in many forms, large and small, loud and soft. Well-aimed protest and campaigning has a vital role. Perhaps this is an act for you. Its time seems to be well and truly here.

Avaaz and other *online campaigning groups* have stepped into the gaping hole of government feedback and produced data and knowledge on some significant results of government policies and decisions. A cold draught of accountability has been felt by some politicians as well-aimed campaigns, built around petitions, have countered pockets of preferential lobbying and inertia. Even though they are limited in their reach by funding and lack of institutionalisation, these campaigns have expanded the means to experience and contribute to democracy.

Their focus is usually on single issues. Our concern is that this becomes a palliative, offering hope to active citizens through periodic success but able only to impact a handful of the multitude of injustices, as their cause – the governing systems – remains the same.

The reformation of governance requires second-order change. The online groups already run campaigns at this level and, if you are active in one of these, we encourage you further in this direction – and thus, in the process, extending your significant *public education role.*

Many other people and organisations in various roles from *fact checkers and feedbackers to open source software developers and citizen scientists,* all operating within civil society, represent fresh shoots to be initiated and encouraged as people act collectively to do what they have to do to replace governments of diminishing returns. In many respects, civil-society action replacing irrelevant government is the most effective protest you could make.[7]

Local activism with an effective local government, or without where it is not, is vital. This *art of association* has a long history. Writing in 1835

in the infancy of the United States, Alexis de Tocqueville was astonished that unlike other countries (which deferred to government and existing power structures to solve problems), Americans independently came up with their own organizations to solve the problems of the day. This ability to identify problems, form institutions, and address them, de Tocqueville observed, made Americans exceptional. Each new need immediately awakens the idea of association. The art of association then becomes the mother science; everyone studies it and applies it.[8]

Margaret Mead concluded similarly: 'Never doubt that a small group of thoughtful, committed citizens can change the world. Indeed, it is the only thing that ever has'.[9] Local groups are today developing community energy schemes, recreating local economies using public sector purchasing power, establishing local food growing and distribution, training in skills to connect unemployed people to employers needing staff and building community-based social care models, amongst many other examples of the art of association.

Perhaps above all for everyone as a citizen, an imperative is to avoid being sucked into *traditional party politics* through arguing over this or that policy – a first-order change. We know this is usually an ineffective process, is system-preserving, and will not save our relationship with the biosphere. Systems thinking raises the debate to a second-order change and to new systems, including constitutions. Where there are political parties campaigning at this level, get involved.

If you live where an established and accessible process to *change the constitution* exists, nationally or locally, you can use it. You can raise a specific issue – for example, eliminating coal, giving rivers legal status, rights over drinking water, sustainable fair food, end-to-end producer responsibility or the fourth separation of powers – and run with it. Presented with a well-reasoned case, campaigners have been surprised at the wider public's positive response.

Donate. If you have money to spend, rather than spending it on (polluting) stuff, consider using it to donate to campaigners and protesters, bio-litigators, fact-checkers, local development groups, second-order change political parties and other acts of association.

It may aid your motivation to see these *collective acts* in context. They are all examples of *civil society* springing purposefully into action, often in the face of institutional inaction and governmental opposition. Each represents a rejection of the decomposition of society into a series of transactions marshalled by the economic and governmental systems. People are acting in ways that are connected across the elements of the three-dimensional governance model (Chapter 4). In other words the new model is being practiced, if not yet knowingly institutionalised.

12.3 Individual acts

This book opened with an invitation to think differently, to think about your thinking, and to understand what it is you do, when you do what you do. Many ways of doing this have been covered. Our intention is that some of these will have stimulated you to *challenge your own mental models* and to review your worldview. Appendix 1 describes how your authors have come to think differently – our pathways to systemic sensibility. It may provide further stimulation.

As an aide-memoire and daily stimulus, Figure 12.1 provides a set of *systems practices* you can use every day.

Many of us have our immediate thinking framed by the media we read. This is as good a place as any to reframe from where you start. As we write this epilogue, a new book has appeared to explain why changing your media diet can change the world, titled *You Are What You Read*.[10] The author, Jodie Jackson, tells a story about her mother-in-law:

> Eva's belief that the world is more dangerous than it used to be lies in her perception of the world. This perception is created, not through experience – because the truth is that experientially things have improved – but through hearing stories about the world, stories told to her by the news. Hers is not an uninformed belief, it is an ill-informed one – and an incredibly common one at that. ... I came to realise it was not me, but the news industry that was damaged. I have grown tired of reading so many inflammatory headlines charged with opinion over fact and emotion over reason, designed to bolster conflict rather than aid resolution.

Fear paralyses. Balanced and positive news liberates.

Which practice will you apply today?

Engaging in systems practice is an ongoing activity – like a muscle, it continually needs to be exercised. Use these prompts to help you apply systems practices every day.

 Step back from the details to **see the bigger picture** and explore what else may be influencing a situation. *What else is going on here?*

 Be aware of your mental model and how it influences your perspective and actions. *What beliefs and values inform how I see, engage, and react to this situation?*

 See yourself in the system and how you engage, contribute and influence it. *What is my role in this situation? What can I influence?*

 Engage diverse perspectives to see a situation from different vantage points. *Who has a different perspective from my own on this situation and how might they see it? Whose voice is not being heard?*

 Be present in the moment and **listen deeply**, without trying to 'fix' a problem. *Am I listening or waiting to talk? Am I suspending judgement and criticism? Am I being open to new information?*

 Question assumptions to surface what has informed them and to question if they are true. *What assumptions am I making about this situation and how can I test them?*

 Uncover unintended consequences before committing to a decision or action. *What else might happen if we do this? What adaptations need to be made as a result?*

 Use visual modelling to make sense of, or explain a complex situation, which may reveal new insights. *Can I draw or illustrate this situation with diagrams, metaphors, relationships or symbols?*

 Look for connections and relationships between parts to gain new insights about the whole. *Which parts have a connection? What is their relationship? Is there an emerging or reoccurring pattern?*

 Reflect regularly on a situation, interpret and give it meaning to draw deeper learning. *What did I intend to happen and what actually happened? What does it tell me about the system? How can I work with this new insight?*

 For further information, visit preventioncentre.org.au/resources/learn-about-systems August, 2018

We would like to acknowledge and are grateful for the work of others to identify and develop systems practices. Our practices are drawn both from these existing resources and our own experience working in systems. There are many more practices, but we feel these are the most practical for everyday use.

FIGURE 12.1 Systems practices for day-to-day use. *Source*: Davidson, S. and Morgan, M. 2018. *Systems Practices*. The Australian Prevention Partnership Centre and The Tasmanian Department of Health. Used with permission.

One colleague has switched his media diet to avoid the mainstream as much as he can, and instead consumes media whose aim is to provide knowledge and knowing. These range from *The Conversation* – a daily collection of research-led journalism by academics on current issues; Sam O'Nella, CGP Grey, Mark Blyth and many others on YouTube; *The Mint* – a weekly summary promoting economic pluralism; *Resonance FM*, a radio station with no news breaks offering a very different slant on the world; *Investors Chronicle* – essential if you want to understand the world of the financial markets; *The Land* – similarly for the uses and control of land; *New Scientist* – the world's most popular weekly science and technology magazine; *The Week* – a digest of the news providing at least two sides to every story; and anything else likely to present a different framing and open his mind.

Beyond the UK, there will be other media possibilities that can be compiled into new ecologies for understanding. Sources that are refreshing and enjoyable. To think differently, consider avoiding daily news programs and traditional newspapers as much as possible. Tune in to something else. Take nothing at face value, probe, reflect.

Exiting or limiting traditional news media will help with a major obstacle to change, which is *being judgemental* – or critical, fault-finding, censorious, condemnatory, disapproving, disparaging, deprecating, negative, overcritical, scathing. Such (understandable) reactions can arise in all sorts of circumstances. Here are four ways to ward off these reactions.

First, where a company or government body is doing something objectionable, its visible head will often be deemed a 'bad' person, often without their critics having met them. Many 'good' people work in organisations that they wish were different. The situation of concern is the system that produces the objectionable results and often not the people in it. Try to avoid labelling people from afar.

Second, each of us may dislike one or other politician. But that is not the point. The point is what the person says and does. This is the place to engage. The work of Plato or Einstein is not judged on the basis of whether we like them, but on the quality of their thinking.

Third, is any form of moral superiority. It may have some justification, but no one was ever motivated by being told they are morally inferior. At an Extinction Rebellion meeting, one activist proposed rescinding membership of a conservation NGO as its mission stating that the most pressing global issue is conserving endangered species and not climate change. Besides the tactical naivety of creating division with people fundamentally on the same side, leading on emotive species extinction, like gorillas, is a potent entry point to its causes – biosphere destruction. Variety is good for persuasion too. There are many pathways to pursue.

Fourth is the notion that most of the 'masses' are stupid, unable to grasp the issues, easily duped, etc. This is music to the ears of elites – 'leave it to us'! The 'masses' are not stupid when engaged, as every deliberative process has demonstrated. Galileo Galilei's famous quote is always worth bearing in mind: 'I have never met a man so ignorant that I couldn't learn something from him'.[11]

As you meet people with whom you disagree, you can seek to *understand where they are coming from*, listen, discuss and invite them to think about their thinking. At a climate crisis protest, two teenage girls wandering by became interested and asked: 'What is climate change?' It would be easy to ridicule and dismiss. Instead, a discussion ensued. They understood. They joined. We are all in this together – one planet – and will get out of our predicament far faster if we act together.

Consider *your consumer power* in the widest sense. You can use it in the decisions you make on which media to read, which companies to buy from, and which products and services to buy. You can also be far more demanding in your relations with big organisations, to oppose and where possible reject lopsided terms of trade and to object to being farmed for profits.

In another recent book, *Stuffocation*[12], James Wallman

> introduces us to the innovators who are turning their backs on all-you-can-get consumption, and trading in materialism for "experientialism" – where they find more happiness, live more meaningful lives, and express status more successfully, through experiences rather than stuff. Experientialism does not mean giving up all our possessions, but it does mean getting over our obsession with them, and transforming what we value. We have to focus less on possessions and more on experiences. Rather than a new watch or another pair of shoes, we should invest in shared experiences like holidays and time with friends. With intriguing insights on psychology, economics and culture, *Stuffocation* is a vital manifesto for change. It has inspired those who have read it to be happier and healthier and to live more with less.

Everyone has a two-way relationship with the planet. Your biosphere needs you and we need it. But what can you best do in terms of *adapting your lifestyles*? This is complicated. Several books provide data to help in these choices.[13] Thinking systemically about the consequences of your actions and total personal carbon footprint should lead to some lifestyle shifts. Perhaps the biggest decision is whether to have children, and if so, how many? How significant is meat and dairy consumption? Where do all those chemicals from weed killers or household cleaning products go and what do they kill? How has this pair of slacks been made? Do you really need it? Are alternative forms of 'consumption' with less pollution – like walking or singing – just as satisfying when tried? Some changes are easy, some represent more of a lifestyle challenge – like less travel. Many will also require institutional change – so imagine you're creating a new game. Think up the new rules that will make the game work. Imagine who the other players are or could be.

12.4 Working acts

Change the conversation wherever you are. Places of work – in their broadest sense – are a good place to start. Think systemically about your organisation, discuss with other thinkers, and start to broaden the internal conversation. In practise, this happens continuously in the work-arounds employees and customers/citizens use to make misplaced processes and bureaucracy function. Make these workarounds explicit. Good organisations can promote this – to their advantage. Study *Systems Thinking in Practice* and encourage your organisation to make it core in its learning curriculum. Employ, if you can, professional Systems Thinking Practitioner Apprentices.[14] Look to the institutions that surround you and ask: Do these offer systemic or systematic affordances? Look in particular to the 'evaluation' industry and challenge the underlying thinking and practices.[15]

Many organisations overuse systematic management – especially in the corporate control function of HR, compliance, health and safety, procurement and finance – when *systemic management* is what's required. Organisations that use the systematic and the systemic in the right places are far more successful and sustainable.

Where might these changed conversations go in different places of work? If you have one of the roles below, there is much to consider.

Enlightened politicians of independent mind have a major role to play, by deserting the end-state fallacy and adopting STiP and experimentation as the norm in making beneficial change; utilising citizens' assemblies and wide deliberation for constitutional change most immediately for the fourth separation of powers; asserting or reasserting the powers of local and regional government within a systemic framework; and re-energising civil society through support and depoliticisation. Politicians of the future will have to embrace modes of practice based on 'power with', or 'delegating power to', rather than assuming 'power over'.

Public sectors and their officials also have a major role to play. You can follow suit and adopt STiP. This would have value in itself in making beneficial change, and it frees up resources of money, time and energy that are urgently needed for the clean-up.[16]

National audit and statistical offices have no need to wait to be asked or given permission to widen their scope. These institutions can take as much as they can of the Resulture's role in the independent collection of data and examination of results. The fundamental truth is that the world cannot run on lies. It has been and still is: governments lie, politicians lie, officials lie, companies lie, the media lies, elites lie and some citizens ignore their impact on the biosphere. The shameful consequences of this now surround us. The clean-up should have started in earnest 20 years ago. Any institution with, at least, some authority can put its weight behind the real world becoming a potent force in governance.

Researchers, wherever you may be, can expand the work pioneered by Arend Lijphart and others in analysing the relationships between systems of governing and lived experience, and the impact of a constitution on government performance. The more data there is, the greater the appreciation of the significance of a constitution, and specifically where and how change would benefit a particular country, its people and the biosphere.

In this world of captured or severely constrained *foundations and think tanks*, some do work independently of the prevailing order. The Global Challenge Foundation, the Open Society and others are fora to gather around as they focus on the systemic causes rather than single issues. Captured think tanks are to be avoided.

If you are in a *business*, then encourage the thinking in the direction of those companies that have stopped facing backwards, hoping the future will go away, and have got with the program. Sustainable business depends on a sustainable planet. If that's not sufficient motivation, then consider that past acts can become crimes. Certain forms of pollution have long been criminal acts. It cannot be so long before 'carbon criminal' and 'ecocide' become commonplace terms with the managers of greenhouse gas producers facing imprisonment.

Those working in the *insurance industry* know that it has been and is at the forefront of climate change. It sits within a cybernetic feedback loop: entities insure against risks, then one occurs – for example, a flood, insurers pay out, premiums go up, and the question then is how to reduce the risks (as with the origins of design authorities in Chapter 10). Insurers cannot wish climate change away.

'The insurance industry's role as society's risk manager is under threat', said Maurice Tulloch, chairman of global general insurance at Aviva and chair of ClimateWise. 'Our sector will struggle to reduce this protection gap if our response is limited to avoiding, rather than managing, society's exposure to climate risk'. The ClimateWise coalition of 29 insurers, including Allianz, Aon, Aviva, Lloyd's, Prudential, Swiss Re and Zurich, conclude that the industry must use more of its $30tn of investments to help fund increased resilience of society to floods, storms and heatwaves.[17]

But your role in insurance is more than this. The origin of the entire industry was in shipbuilding when prevention became the objective, not cleaning up after a shipwreck. Preventing ships sinking – or now our planetary home – is, or should be, the insurance industry's purpose today.

The *audit industry* uses the term 'going concern' in order to decide whether to sign off on a company's accounts. 'A going concern is a business that functions without the threat of liquidation for the foreseeable future, which is usually regarded as at least the next 12 months'.[18] With a stable planet, 12 months may be sufficient. With an unstable one, it is not. Fossil fuel and deforestation-dependent companies are not going concerns. The threat to company sustainability extends far beyond these industries.

Auditors and their national and international accounting standards bodies have to reconsider just how far into the future the term 'going concern' applies. In the current circumstances, it is not credible for this to be only one year. Auditors should require realistic company plans to exit their highest polluting activities as a condition for their approval of company accounts.

Judges and courts have an essential role to play. Where the law is clear, you can ensure it is applied effectively and with appropriate force. Where the law is open to interpretation or is unclear, then judges can follow the example of those jurisdictions that have erred on the side of the biosphere.

> The past year brought about several precedent setting court decisions and a growing number of lawsuits seeking to tackle climate change. In May, the Supreme Court of Colombia ruled in favour of a group of 25 children and youth, holding that their constitutional right to a healthy environment was being violated by deforestation in the Amazon. In October, the Hague Court of Appeal upheld an earlier decision concluding that the Netherlands is violating the right to life by failing to take adequate measures to reduce greenhouse gas emissions.[19]

Curative (not palliative) comedians, satirists, and dramatists have a great opportunity to rip to shreds the unfairly powerful. Their true selves are waiting to be revealed. Their revelation will reduce their influence and power. The BBC comedy classic of the 1960/1970s, *Monty Python*, did this for Great Britain's class-ridden society, which had pertained for centuries. Through mocking the behaviour of the aristocracy and upper classes, judges, civil servants, bankers, television presenters and others, it publicly acknowledged and contributed to the end of overbearing social snobbery. Today's list of the unfairly powerful has changed. It now includes CEOs who really think they are worth it; lobbyists and lobbying; cavalier financial market traders; the offshore elite who think they have earned it; thoughtless property developers; people traffickers; compensation committees; narcissistic political dictators; members of legislatures who feel important whilst ignoring the many holes in their ship of state; modern day, social fascists instructing the masses on what not to say; deadweight bureaucracies in the public and private sectors; and vice-chancellors who think a university is just a business. Insightful exposure will reduce their power. Lampooning will see them shrivel.

12.5 Creating new human dramas

Copenhagen, a play written by Michael Frayn and first presented in 1998, deals with the technological realisation of nuclear fission and atomic weapons.[20] Frayn's tightly written drama is about the most significant technological development made by humans – but it is not about the technology per se. It is actually a play about being and doing – being a scientist and doing science – as well as a play about human ethics and morality, particularly about offering and accepting explanations of what we do when we do what we do.

Frayn's concern is with the historical timing of particular explanations realised through the praxis of the physicists Niels Bohr and Werner Heisenberg, which intersect with the rise of totalitarianism and a world war. Together these created the context for the emergence of a technology containing, for the first time, the possibility of anthropogenic self-destruction – the atomic bomb. Thus far, humans have successfully navigated this threat, but the longer-term systemic implications remain unresolved (i.e. waste storage and the potential for uncontainable radiation to come about through human error and technological failure and, potentially, access to material for bomb making by 'terrorists'). Since Frayn wrote *Copenhagen*, we have become much more aware of anthropogenic climate change and the features of the Anthropocene. The overarching metaphor of his play, and the 'drama' of our lives, is living with human-induced uncertainty.

Governing nowadays is about production under conditions of uncertainty, where we as citizens and decision makers have to perform on a public stage to create common understandings.[21] This is what happened in Shaldon, where EDD was successful and DAD was not (Chapter 5). As we are all dramaturgists,[22] creators of the performance of our futures, there is liberation in knowing that we could make it possible to have agency to be co-creators of a life well lived.

Notes

1 https://en.m.wikipedia.org/wiki/The_World_as_Will_and_Representation (Accessed 9 April 2019).
2 https://www.parliament.uk/about/living-heritage/building/palace/architecture/palacestructure/churchill/
3 We are indebted to Philip Tottenham for his explication and interpretation of Schopenhauer's work.
4 See Russell, D.B. and Ison, R.L. 2000. Enthusiasm: Developing critical action for second-order R&D. In Ison, R.L. and Russell, D.B., eds. *Agricultural Extension and Rural Development: Breaking out of Traditions*, pp. 136–160). Cambridge: Cambridge University Press.
5 The School strike for climate (also known variously as Fridays for Future, Youth for Climate and Youth Strike 4 Climate) is an international movement of school students who are deciding not to attend classes and instead take part in demonstrations to demand action to prevent further global warming and climate change. https://en.wikipedia.org/wiki/School_strike_for_climate (Accessed 24 April 2019).
6 Extinction Rebellion is an international movement that uses non-violent civil disobedience to achieve radical change in order to minimise the risk of human extinction and ecological collapse. https://rebellion.earth/the-truth/about-us/ (Accessed 24 April 2019).
7 See Wagenaar, Henk. 2019. Making sense of civic enterprise. Social Innovation, Participatory Democracy and the Administrative State. *Partecipazione e conflitto* 12(2): 297–324, for some of the possibilities and constraints.
8 Katz, Bruce. 2018. https://www.linkedin.com/pulse/bigideas2019-welcome-new-community-institution-bruce-katz/ (Accessed 4 April 2019).
9 Doubts exist as to whether Mead actually said this. But its point remains. https://nevalalee.wordpress.com/2010/12/15/as-margaret-mead-never-said/.
10 Jackson, Jodie. 2019. *You Are What You Read*. London: Unbound.
11 Robert Johannsen in his book *The Alternative. A Green Manifesto* (2019) argues that change is undermined by those who personalise, polarise and escalate arguing instead of seeking systems approaches that depersonalise, depolarise and de-escalate.
12 Wallman, James. 2017. *Stuffocation: Living More with Less*. Harmondsworth: Penguin.
13 Berners-Lee, Mike. 2010. *How Bad Are Bananas? The Carbon Footprint of Everything*. London: Profile Books. Berners-Lee, Mike. 2019. *There Is no Planet B: A Handbook for the Make or Break Years*. Cambridge: Cambridge University Press.

14 For example, this Masters level apprenticeship is under development in the UK – https://www.instituteforapprenticeships.org/apprenticeship-standards/systems-thinking/ (Accessed 23 May 2019).

15 Follow the example of Andrew Mitchell. See Mitchell, A. 2019. *Second-Order Learning in Development Evaluation. New Methods for Complex Conditions.* Cham: Palgrave Macmillan.

16 Initiatives reported here are worthy of tracking: https://oecd-opsi.org/category/systems-thinking/ (Accessed 23 May 2019).

17 Cambridge Institute for Sustainability Leadership. 7 December 2016. *ClimateWise Launches Two Reports That Warn of Growing Protection Gap Due to Rising Impact of Climate Risks.*

18 https://en.wikipedia.org/wiki/Going_concern (Accessed 13 May 2019).

19 *The Status of Climate Change Litigation.* 2017. UNEP. http://wedocs.unep.org/bitstream/handle/20.500.11822/20767/climate-change-litigation.pdf?sequence=1&isAllowed=y (Accessed 8 April 2019).

20 Frayn, M. 1998. *Copenhagen.* London: Methuen Drama.

21 Hajer, M.A. 2009. *Authoritative Governance: Policy-Making in the Age of Mediatisation.* Oxford: Oxford University Press.

22 A dramaturgist is someone who writes, or creates, plays.

APPENDIX 1

Two lives invested in systemic sensibility

A.1 Do you ask: why?

The word 'why' comes from Old English. When used interrogatively, the usual effect is to initiate an inquiry that asks: what for or by what means? Asking 'why?' is the essence of systemic sensibility.

Between about the ages of four and seven, children become very curious and ask many questions. There is an emergence in the interest of reasoning and wanting to know why things are the way they are. Children realise they have a vast amount of knowledge but are unaware of how they acquired it.[1]

This ups the ante for adults. No longer are toddlers absorbed by exploring; they are becoming aware of their *being* separate from their parents. They are semi-autonomous, have volition. Knowledge starts to be constructed: how and why does this work, does this happen, does this make that?

As a patient person, keen to add to a child's limited understanding of the world he or she has joined, your dialogue may go like this:

Child: 'Why are you going upstairs, daddy?'
Daddy: 'I'm going to the bathroom to wee.'
Child: 'Why is that person fat?'
Mummy: 'He eats too much'

These questions can go on and on: Why does he eat too much? The initial question might be a real showstopper: Why time, mummy? Patience has its limits (why otherwise would there be a word for it). You may be busy, involved, had an intense day. Many times we have simply not known the answer.

To cover this eventuality, you may resort to: Because it is, or the calm-preserving diversionary tactic of: What's that over there – shall we play I Spy?

This is the child's first lesson in being limited and in the limitations of life.[2]

Schools take up the task of development and knowledge provision. Much is learnt. But the inquiring mind becomes the constrained mind as well. School curricula are, by definition, limited – as are understandings of knowledge and knowing. This has a social purpose: acceptance of the way things are is a more contented state than incipient dissatisfaction. The organs of society – both benign and exploitative – pursue the path of stability, the former motivated by harmony, the latter to maintain the status quo.

Bit by bit, children slot into their societal-determined roles, teenage rebellion blows itself out and adults become contained by relationships, work or, for some, just survival.

Except, some adults do not. We are two of those malcontents who have been unable to stop asking the question 'why?' You might ask us: Why? For Ed, patterns have been passed on by his contrary parents, and superbly but unwittingly reinforced and extended by a traditional British boarding school of its time. Radicalisation is not a new phenomenon. At the heart of our condition is a rejection of imposed authority. Authority should be earned, not taken.

As a child, Ray exhausted his grandparents as they drove to their remote farm, Journeys End. One complained to the other that his every second breath carried the words: 'But why?' Before he could read, Ray sat on his patient father's knees of an evening whilst he read the day's paper. What was he reading and why, demanded Ray.

The why question is forever in our heads. The train is jammed full. Why? Because it is half term, we are informed disembodiedly and disingenuously. But this is an entirely predictable event. Why were extra trains not put on for half term? Because the contracts under which the trains operate do not require this, and the train companies make more profit with overcrowding. Conversely, extra trains mean extra cost. These companies are driven by profit, and this translates into top management bonuses.

So why are these contracts so deficient for passengers? Because they were developed by civil servants who have no noticeable expertise in the complexities of contract management or of railway systems.

Why? Because the civil service continues to practise the 'generalist' model whereby 'clever' people are presumed to be able to do any of the hundreds of diverse tasks within government.

So why, in a democracy, do not the politicians intervene on behalf of the passengers? Because no accurate feedback of the results of these contracts for passengers exists. In their absence, politicians rhetorically massage statistics to 'prove' all is well. Some do not bother with this veneer – they go for the plain lie.

Why no feedback? Because the system of governing does not require it.

Why? Because these systems (turned into law by legislation and constitutions) were developed centuries ago, long before governments ran train services.

The answer that we would have been surprised and pleased to hear announced is: The train is over-crowded due to the inadequate contracts produced by inexpert civil servants and the absence of independent and public feedback, all the fault of the defective system of governing.

Rather than leaping on the obvious answer, posing successive 'whys' in the manner of a five-year-old is a good way of getting to the 'root cause' of a problem. We might be tempted to shout at the train manager. But it is not her/his fault. The true villain is the framework of institutions, laws, contracts, and rules, the 'governance system' for, in this case, running the trains. The quality of its governance determines the performance of any organisation. That something so far away and intangible as governance should be the real cause of squashed passengers is not how we usually see things.

Being both 'why' people, we were prone to thinking systemically without having named it. We also both worked in a world that did not. Our early careers were spent working in situations we experienced as messy, or complex, trying to improve them. This did happen, but mostly only at the margin. Either we were missing something or others were. We refused to let go of our systemic sensibilities.

A.2 Cultivating systemic sensibility

Through a series of experiences – related below – the scales gradually fell from Ed's eyes.

A.2.1 London's Central Line

In 2000, one of London's biggest and most intractable problems was the train system known as The Underground: much of it still is. This reached its nemesis in 2003 with the closure of the whole of the Central Line and its 49 stations. This line carries 500,000 people a day. A train had derailed in a tunnel after its engine fell off (no one knew why), injuring 32 passengers. Rather than a straightforward journey home, my new route involved a convoluted journey underground, overground, and a bus, lift, or taxi. One night, after a long day, I came out of the station at 11:00 p.m. to find no buses operating or taxis for hire, so I walked home for an hour through the cold, beautiful, snow-covered Epping Forest.

My frustrated mind turned to this: how on earth could one of the world's most advanced cities manage to disrupt its essential transport infrastructure, the lives of so many, and its economic activity so foolishly, and with such little interest from those in power? Surely, keeping the engine attached to the train is a key task for rail operators. Who was responsible, first for trains with detachable engines, and second for sorting them out when they went wrong? And where was the sense of urgency? It took three months for the Line to fully reopen. To whom did this matter?

The answers were fuzzy. Responsibility for London Underground lay with the Department for Transport in central government, which is run by civil servants. None had any operational experience of commuter railways, nor of running a large organisation like London Underground, or of attaching engines to trains. Neither had the ministers, who were unable to interrogate the rail management and challenge its decisions. In terms of public pressure, the chain of accountability was as strong as a cardboard bicycle lock. It wound its way from us, the users and voters, through to the national government and the election of a political party every four or five years, through its many priorities, on to a minister of the day with his or her agenda, onward to the civil servants and thence to London Underground. In other words, the next time the government might feel some heat over this issue was two years hence at the general election, by which time that issue would have been put to bed and forgotten politically. In effect, there was zero accountability of London Underground to the public.

In many modern countries, the metro is the responsibility of the city government, run by executive mayors. These are politicians who, rather than having to work through unelected officials (who can control most of what happens and are immune from public pressure), are elected to get things done – that is, to act in an executive capacity. The electors then know who to hold responsible. In local governments, non-functioning train lines become top priority very quickly. In national governments local issues come way down the pecking order.

When the Central Line was closed, London had recently elected its *first* executive mayor, Ken Livingstone. Here was another piece of the governance jigsaw. However, the government of Tony Blair prevented the transfer of control of London Underground to the GLA (Greater London Authority) until 2003, after itself signing controversial, flawed and ultimately failed private finance initiatives for track maintenance. Why they stopped the transfer was as much to do with political and personal jealousy as contracts – the new mayor had stood for office as an independent against the wishes of his party's hierarchy. Even worse, he was popular and competent. Once he got hold of the Underground it started to be managed more for its passengers than for the rail union's officials and drivers.

As an executive mayor, he brought in hardened and experienced metro managers from New York. The service improved considerably as he delivered what he had been elected to do. The same Ken Livingstone who was leader of the former chaotic and abolished Greater London Council (GLC), under new governance became a mayor of considerable achievement. It is the system not the person.

Totting this all up, the underlying reasons that led to the engine dropping off were as follows: an unaccountable London Underground; civil servants without the experience or any idea of how to run a large metro service, nor interest, nor organisational motivation; no feedback or monitoring of results by Parliament; prime ministers with too much power; and no executive mayor in control.

Two political parties, three prime ministers, five governments and a herd of transport ministers had between them created, or allowed the conditions for, something which should never have happened. And none of them meant to.

There was no single cause, no headline howler. It was the system – the system of government to, in this case, run the trains – that was at fault.[3] Contrary to what many in power would have us believe – that the system we have is essentially the only one possible, that foreigners may do things in other ways but those ways would not work here (why?), that you mess with our age-old democracy at your peril (how large is their vested interest?), or whatever other rationale for feet-dragging is trotted out – there are all manner of ways to run governments and public services. The UK happens to have one way. The government system for running the Underground was changed. It now looks more like those in every other modern city. Do not say it cannot be done – it can – but not by using the thought processes usually employed by those within these government systems. A different perspective and discipline are needed: systemic, non-ideological, organisational.

In the case of London Underground, it was transformed through major changes in its governance initiated by politicians. Fixing the top is surely their role? So vote for the political party that will most likely fix this, and many other problems? This does happen for anything outside the centre – sometimes well, sometimes badly. But not for the centre itself. Governments stand ready to reform everything – other than themselves.

A.2.2 Political Parties

Election night in 1997 came with a landslide win for New Labour and its charismatic leader, Tony Blair. After 18 years of Conservative Party rule, this was energising for those seeking change. The first half of the party's 13 years in office achieved quite a lot, the second half little.

Of those achievements, the majority proved to be temporary. As an influential advisor to ministers and their advisers, I started by introducing fresh proposals (particularly Relative Values: A Comprehensive and Sustained Programme to Improve People's Relationship and Parenting Skills)[4] to considerable effect, but finished by watching with resignation as some of those proposals put into sound practice were abandoned by the next minister or government.

The critical realisation for me was that party politics is an accumulator. Its lure is based on the prospect of 'our' beliefs/ideology/principles/lifestyle prevailing in government. When 'we' are in the ascendancy, all will be well. 'We' are better people, after all. Except that the *overall* quality of government people receive is not determined by the decisions and practices of the party in power *today*. The quality of education children are receiving today is the result of the accumulation of decades of government. The whole is the *sequential* sum of the parts. By the time the minuses have been added to the pluses, little may have changed for the better.

Thus, the nirvana on offer at election time is merely one set in a timeless tennis match. Our actual experiences are determined perhaps 10–20% by today's government and 80–90% by its predecessors. Think of it as an accumulator bet on the horses. To win your bet, every horse has to come first, not just one or two. We will only get a world-class health service if every bet (or government) comes home. In other words, I should want 'your' party to succeed as much as 'mine'.

I came, slowly and reluctantly, to realise that the competition of political parties, far from being the means to solve enduring problems, is but one part of a complex system. I perceived that there are other means to provide many answers, and that for really contentious or complex issues, some are far better being above party politics. At the election in Finland in 2015, all the parties agreed on a common policy for schools. This is not an argument for elite technocracy but for democratically accountable expertise from multiple sources.

Politics has a strange lure. It is as addictive as heroin. Even now, and against my better judgment, I am drawn into siding with a leader and a party, even though I know that their impact will disappoint, even though I don't want it to. But politics has the merit of immediacy. Something does have to be done. That party with that leader represents the best chance of at least something changing. The zigzag has to continue. If only politicians realised just how much better they could do if housed in a well-designed and fully refurbished system. There is the palliative of today and the curative of the future.

But there is no time to think ahead. The bustle of news, who is up and who is down, protecting your back (especially from those within your own party), the grind of the ministerial decisions in red boxes, announcements, policy initiatives plucked out of a brainstorm, feeling important, a voting division, a committee, constituents – so the world of Westminster goes on in a blur of underachievement.

The psychological flaws of many politicians are manifest. These do not help. Equally, however, I realised that if I were in that system, I would struggle to perform any better, even with the best of motives.

Sleaze became an issue for New Labour as 'cash for honours' hit the headlines. Such institutional corruption, far from being the behaviour of 'your' party with 'mine' above this sort of thing, is endemic to many systems of government. If as in the UK, controls on political party funding are lax, and governments have the gift of patronage available in the form of honours like knighthoods, then cash for honours will result. Change the rules.

Other systemic issues came to mind during this expedition in politics. Two-party states – the US and UK – have less good government than those with PR (proportional representation). The human and economic waste of zigzag policies, easier manipulation by media owners and business, under-representation and stifled views, over-representation and the dominance of tiny minorities in governments are all the product of this duopoly. But proportional representation by no means solves all of the problems of governing. Further, PR comes in several forms, some better than others.[5]

The US has a stronger institutional structure around government than the UK, providing better checks and balances and higher standards of implementation, but this is sabotaged by the huge power of business lobbying resulting from uncapped political party donations, in turn the result of a politically appointed Supreme Court.

Governments are struggling around the world. We may blame the leader – usually the first port of call. Then we blame the party or parties in power, politicians in general, the upper house, the regulators, civil servants and the bureaucracy, the electoral system, funding of political parties, representative democracy, business lobbying or the economic system. Having detached myself from the tendency to pick out only one of the above from the line-up, I no longer blame individuals or groups for the overall failings, nor hope for the one great leader who will descend and deliver us.

A.2.3 Government machinery

As a 'senior influential adviser' I saw the frustrations of ministers attempting to put their programmes into practice. Few people inside a system can see its flaws. This is true of all of the many organisations I've worked in. One recently retired MP commented that only a handful of people inside Westminster understand that the system they attempt to work in is holed below the waterline. The parallel with the Palace they occupy is striking: they have to move out for a full restoration over many years, as they cling on to the barely floating present.[6]

The most dominant group in this system of governing is the senior civil service. Having worked with and alongside this cadre both as an adviser and consultant for 30 years, the civil servants demonstrated a continuing inability to translate policy into effective practice. The 'why' questions started to roll, the upshot of which was a report proposing the specialisation and professionalisation of the civil service. The 'generalist' civil service model of 1855 introduced to stop 'cronyism' did not work in the complex world of implementing societal change. The prime minister and his chief of staff took it on, and the head of the civil service introduced a package of reforms. Nothing changed. The Whitehall civil service saw it off, as it has done with every other attempt at reform before and since.

When one of the civil service's defending allies in the House of Lords during the most recent (Conservative) reform attempt was asked why he remained committed to the 1855 model, he replied that removing power from the civil service would put more into the hands of the executive or government, which already had too much. This is true because of the very limited checks and balances in the notional constitution of the UK. My mistake was to pick out only one component from the whole system.

As an antidote, established in 2003, the Prime Minister's Delivery Unit (PMDU) took some key government objectives, especially in health and education, and drove them forward systematically, with weekly reviews by the PM. This had some effect until their sponsor – the prime minister or their head – left or moved onto other priorities. Later, the original head of the PMDU became a consultant and was successful in selling this mechanism to governments around the world – with the same result. A conversation with a former staffer of such a unit in Indonesia reinforced this realisation – it was closed with a change of President. For consistent delivery to work, then, mechanisms have to be set in stone in the system and not rely on the occasional appearance of a knowledgeable leader.

By the late 2000s, I had spent many, many hours in discussions with ministers, lords, advisers, senior civil servants and heads of public bodies, and also came to realise just how little of what we discussed in these supposedly powerful chambers would actually translate into beneficial action on the ground. I arrived at the point where sitting around government tables inventing policies was an exercise in futility. Little changed and even less for the better.

Nothing is as straightforward as it might seem in those rambling corridors, buildings, extensions, and lean-tos of UK government. A plus here may look like a solution to be grasped, only for an associated minus to cancel it out. A functioning system cannot be created by cherry picking.

A.2.4 Working in a large partnership

Working for over a quarter of a century in a global partnership developed an emerging awareness that whilst I might have some talent, I was but part of an organisation, along with everyone else with a job. To illustrate, consider my colleagues advising on that modern plague of tax avoidance. PricewaterhouseCoopers (PwC) is home to some very intelligent minds whose task it is to develop schemes for clients to minimise taxes legally. They have been hugely successful – to the detriment, of course, of people who, as a result, pay more than their fair share.

You might regard these tax advisers as 'bad' people who, if only they got some ethics, would cause avoidance to cease. But success for clients is what gets rewarded and the income pays the partners very well. For avoidance to end, the rules have to change. These same advisers will then work happily to a different set of rules. All organisations – including governments – are the same. Their outcome behaviour is as good or bad as the rules by which they operate.

Partnership is a very powerful form of organisation, providing the partners exercise proper governance of the management. The latter, like most managements and governments, want to break free of control. This invariably ends in tears and diminishing profits. All governance has to be strong. It should lead, and managements (and governments) should follow. Never let them off the leash.

Most (all?) compensation committees setting the pay of top managements are a sham. A combination of wanting to encourage the CEO and of 'you scratch my back and I'll scratch yours' is the norm with notionally independent members of these committees. This same scam is now common in the setting of vice chancellors' pay in British universities. These business practices tend to infect all organisations eventually. An American member of the global board on which I sat commented that, in contrast to another increase proposed by our committee, the CEO be paid very little, as he wanted the power so much.

Another source of systemic sensibility is travel – it broadens the mind. My work has brought exposure to the ways of others and an appreciation of the influence of national cultures and different systems of governing in Hungary behind the Iron Curtain, Thailand, Singapore, Nigeria, several Western European countries and the US, along with working with the EU, World Bank and USAID.

The huge strides forward of Japanese consumer goods companies were ever present in much of the consulting work at PwC.

The Dutch are direct, the Thais are humble and full of humour and Hungarians under communism were not up for a discussion on economics. Each country has significant differences in its characteristics. Work with them and respect them. They are not wrong, just different, and if you look carefully, just possibly better.

The 'special relationship' between the US and the UK is a narcissistic fetish. I made an early mistake in New York when I assumed that because I had a good relationship with an American that he would use some of his valuable time to do something for me. No – it's business, Ed, not personal. Americans will do something for you if you have something to offer that they want. Otherwise they will not. Why would they? The special relationship is a construct to reassure the Conservative Party and senior civil servants that they still matter in the world. They do not. Clinging to a once glorious past is no substitute for getting to grips with now and the future.

One of the other lessons of too much time spent in airports was that because we are an island, learning in British governmental and political institutions and amongst its people is restricted. On mainland Europe, it takes only a car journey to be in a different jurisdiction, to experience different ways of running schools, rehabilitation of offenders, tax collection, funding local government, lighting the streets, and so on. Inevitably, one or more of these methods may work better than others. This is an opportunity to examine and trial. National pride has no value in operating public services to high standards. Alas, British government is usually too proud to learn.

A.2.5 Acquiring systems literacy

Alongside day-to-day practical experience, education provides the means to grasp the theories that advance systemic sensibility. For me, this started with Manchester Business School (MBS), where at that time, 1971–1973, research and thinking in organisational behaviour was taking off. Two years there opened my eyes to what education could be. Largely project- and seminar-based, my time there introduced me to consulting, computer programming, statistics, and microeconomics, alongside some of the complexities of the human condition. MBS fielded some of the finest thinkers (which I appreciated only years later), including Professor Stafford Beer,[7] still revered as one of the heroes of systems thinking.

Learning is lifelong and does not stop with university. PwC is one of the finest vocational education bodies in the world. It has to be. Advisers must always be ahead of their clients; if they're not, they have no value. Alongside many books, conferences, psychometric tests, and videos of oneself in action – always telling – some of the highlights were:

- Leadership of Professional Services firms at Harvard Business School, which taught me how 'alignment' of any organisation is the means to high performance. The concept is to get all the motivators of behaviour pointing in the same direction. Conversely, if the speeches say do X and the appraisal and pay systems say do Y, then Y is what will happen, no matter how impassioned the speeches.

- Strategic Leadership at Templeton College, Oxford University,[8] which taught me that its constitution and the ethos of the leading group determine the success or failure of an organisation, even one as large as a government.

For my first book,[9] interviewing hundreds of people, from MPs, Lords and civil servants to sound engineers, doctors, and gardeners, taught me just how much intelligence is out there – the wisdom of crowds – and why Labour lost the 2010 election.

More recently, the internet as a portal to the many, often unsung, thinkers and writers producing fine work, which is different and usually more perceptive than the mainstream, has taught me that lifestyle diversity is as important for human survival as biodiversity is for species. Working with academics at the Open University and elsewhere has kept the brain spinning and introduced me to the many layers of systems thinking. Almost as significant is having a 17-year-old son, who regularly extends my mind with YouTube channels from Vox, Vsauce and others.

That, then, is how I got to systems thinking, and to that point of understanding that little will change until we grasp that the present system as a whole is itself what stands in the way of successful government. This has become critical with the threat to the planet we inhabit. We can no longer muddle on.

Meanwhile, beginning on the other side of the world, Ray's systemic sensibility journey was unfolding.

A.3 Living a systemic sensibility

It is hard *not* to live a systemic sensibility growing up in a farming community. Financial destitution would have been the result of ignoring the wider world and the biosphere. The narrative of our family was one of Depression-era struggle, surviving on trapping rabbits (in plague proportions) and selling their pelts – the job of my mother from an early age. Boom followed bust with a change in wool prices during World War II and the Korean War – the vagaries of commodity cycles were ever present. There were also the multiple sources of adversity to be overcome – distance and poor roads, drought, sometimes flood; rabbits, foxes, eagles (I am ashamed to admit – they took lambs), snakes and feral weeds. Working on my parents' farm from age 11, I acquired a range of skills that have had little application since. Practices and context co-create each other.

Across the creek from our house, my great aunts offered limitless love and attention. Their yard was a treasure trove of distraction, experimentation, and interest; there I created my own garden and cubby house in the old chicken shed before starting school. My natural inquisitiveness and the frequent family visitors to their house exposed me to stories, different perspectives, and the politics of family.

My childhood was never decoupled from the broader world. I grew up with stories of World War I, in which my grandfather had fought on the Western Front, and World War II, in which my father served briefly. Bathurst (NSW) had a large Army camp, so there were photos of my mother picnicking and dancing with soldiers. My maternal grandfather was very active in local government in the days when councillors were non-party political. As a grazier (not farmer) he leaned politically to the right and was firmly anti-Catholic. Sectarianism was rife. In contrast, my paternal grandfather had been a fireman on the state railways, where he had worked with Ben Chifley, local hero and Labor Prime Minister of Australia. I grew up experiencing politics from multiple perspectives. My paternal grandmother, descended from a long line of teachers, but thwarted through family tragedy in her own education, imbued the value of continued learning; as did their collective experience of the Great Depression.

Reflecting on Bathurst (NSW) in the 1950s compels me to describe this as one of the most benign periods in human history. The shooting of JFK, the moon landings and then Vietnam impinged. Was it all downhill from there in terms of a lived experience of safety, humour, community, and gossip and grudges, or is it just the natural process of aging? I gradually became aware of life beyond Bathurst such that by age 18 I could not wait to escape its confines, to experience the world I had discovered in books and through the stories of excellent teachers within the state education system. I left in 1971.

Looking back, my formative years imbued me with a systemic sensibility. How you started out created a path from which it was difficult to shift. Relationships were key – and they could be good or bad – other perspectives deserved an airing, even if you did not agree. One should strive to have the courage of one's convictions – if something is not working, then fix it. War is not an answer to anything, and a group of committed people can do much to change their circumstances, but this requires constant vigilance. Voting – and thus participating in a democracy – is a responsibility as much as a right. Much later I realised it took good luck and some good management to become aware of the limitations built into our manners of living, our cultures, and ways of thinking and doing. I felt a bit like a fish suddenly becoming aware of the water. And then getting fish to cooperate to sustain their existence.

A.3.1 Agriculture

My family and schooling convinced me that history matters. Studying agriculture, it was hard to see that what was being taught was within a particular narrative framing, largely associated with European settlement and making good. We had no idea what it meant that aboriginal people had been in Australia for 65,000 years. Both the secondary and university curricula had almost nothing to say on the matter.

Influenced by my maternal grandfather, who in the 1960s had begun work-ing with a young agronomist who was successfully pioneering the aerial sowing of improved pastures on very hilly, rough, sheep-grazing country (a 'technol-ogy' that improved farmer productivity by a factor of five), I decided to study agricultural science at university. I was seduced by the greening a brown land[10] narrative, as many well-meaning people were.

I majored in 'General Agriculture', the closest I could get to a systems approach (though I was not really aware that this was what I was doing at the time). I wanted to combine my concerns for plants, animals, people and social purpose within whole farms in my study. This was not the best career enhancing option – those academics who favoured this approach were highly valued in rural areas but not usually promoted in the university.

Agricultural Economics was a major part of the curriculum. Much later I realised why I did not like it – it never dealt with people as people, and many of the underlying assumptions did not gel with my experience.

I studied agriculture feeling totally confident that science could resolve prob-lems of food supply as well as deal with externalities – it was the period of sig-nificant investment in the chain of international agricultural research centres (CGIAR) devoted to major commodities and regional agricultural issues. The virtues of the 'Green Revolution' were being touted. The spectre of Thomas Malthus informed thinking. I became aware of what was happening and left undergrad studies with an added conviction – that agricultural research and development, especially in the tropics and developing countries, could make major improvements in people's lives. I sought ways to gain experience in these parts of the world.

Relationships formed during this period were and remain significant. One of my lecturers became a friend, and later we wrote together two editions of the *Agronomy of Grassland Systems*. When we began, we both conceptualised grass-lands and biological/ecological systems as nested in human activity systems. By the second edition, I felt we had to change the overall framing to understand grasslands as if they were socially constructed systems.

After leaving university, my first job was with the 'Soil Con', the Soil Conservation Service of the New South Wales state government. My job title was Extension soil conservationist: regional, located in a small office in Braidwood (population about 2,000) on the southern tablelands.

I learned how effective local action could be enhanced by learning from oth-ers in the community – to not see oneself as the holder of all the expertise. I also saw how autonomy and creativity declined the closer one was to a regional or head office. Later, I could have said that public service bodies are corrupted, Janus-faced organisations – pretending to look both ways but always answerable up the chain of command to the Minister. Many private sector service provid-ers are much the same. On my first day, a deputy commissioner, forced to make small talk with a group of graduate recruits, asked how we had fared in our exams. When told I had done OK, graduating with honours, he said that in the

Soil Con that wouldn't help much. Little did I realise he was right – the organisation prided itself on its anti-intellectualism. When I resigned after 14 months to travel through Asia and Europe – the classic overland trip of young Australians – I vowed never to return to the public service, a vow I have upheld.

Travelling through 11 Asian and Middle-Eastern countries and 13 European countries over 21 months, working in three of them, experiencing the German hospital system for nine weeks and constantly encountering other people, whether in restaurants, buses, trains, relationships, etc., was a most profound, life-altering experience. Memories of restaurant conversations include arguments as to why the Shah of Iran should be overthrown, draft dodging, land clearing, dam building, the role of the military in governance (Indonesia, Thailand, and Burma), and experiencing ethnic tensions first-hand – Islamisation then becoming evident in Malaysia. Later, Naipaul's *Among the Believers* was insightful reading. I refused to use a camera so as to be open to my surroundings, unmediated by a lens: I purposefully chose to work in a non-English-speaking country, despite having no foreign language skills. I managed for emergence by writing to researchers in Australian agricultural aid-projects in Southeast Asia asking to visit. PhD study and a life partner were just two of the emergent outcomes.

Field research for my PhD followed in Bali, Indonesia, an island where the 'culture' that contributes to the word agriculture stands out, that is to say, the rise of agriculture came from the move from nomadic to sedentary lifestyles, and this allowed humans to develop culture. Studying how climate affects flowering behaviour of plants in the field in Bali and labs in Brisbane sensitised me to the fine-tuning that exists between climate and biological and ecological processes.

A.3.2 Tanzania early 1980s: development

My first arrival in Africa was in Dar-es-Salam in 1980, again a profound experience. My growing awareness that so much done in the name of development has failed led me from 1986–1996 to be concerned with the process of problem/opportunity formulation for research and development (R&D). I discovered and followed the work of Robert Chambers, who used the term 'development tourism' to describe what I had experienced. As an explanation for the failure of development, I became fond of Russell Ackoff's notion that the only form of development possible is self-development.[11] Let me attempt to explain what I mean by this.

I need to ask you to think of how the Tanzanian project came about. Who might have been involved in naming the problem as low or unreliable beef supply for Dar es Salaam? How might FAO (the Food and Agriculture Organisation of the United Nations, headquartered in Rome) have become involved? Who might have represented them? Possibly a technical expert who saw the problem and may have proposed potential solutions based only on their own experience. Also, what organisations comprising what institutions were likely to have been involved as stakeholders in the project, how might their histories have circumscribed the modes of action of those involved? Further, how might the particular trajectories of action of the individuals and social groups involved have been constrained or enhanced by their traditions of understanding? Questions like these were asked by many development workers during the 1980s. This led to the emergence of a plethora of different research approaches, such as rapid rural appraisal (RRA) and participatory learning and action (see below), which attempt to involve multiple perspectives in the process of 'problem formulation', and which refocus on participation and local or contextualised knowledge.

The Tanzanian experience allowed me to see, eventually, that 'problems' do not exist 'out there' in 'nature'. My realisation that problems and opportunities come into being through the involvement of people in the braiding of language and emotion and by social processes through which agreement is reached about what constitutes a problem was confronting but revealing. It led me to raise questions such as:

- What do we mean when we speak of knowledge?
- What do we mean by research and development?
- What is meant when we speak of learning?
- (As a theme which weaves each of these together): What do we mean when we speak of human communication?[12]

I soon became aware that 'development tourism' was not confined to the practice of development; it exists in most organisations where silos exist and one part knows little of, or has poor relations with, others. Every centralised administrator who designs policy with limited engagement with other perspectives, or only with the 'usual suspects', imposes development tourism on the citizenry. Much development still does not work well because it has not committed to long-term self-organising 'self-development'. Instead, it remains an ideological and political 'toy' of the so-called developed countries. At the University of Sydney, I pursued the 'problem metaphor'. This seemed to be the neglected critical first step in the project cycle – how were problems formulated and who was involved in this process?

A.3.3 Distinguishing 'enthusiasm': breaking out of the trap of 'information transfer'

Perhaps the most profound insight I gained as an educator and a would-be development practitioner was that I could not take responsibility for someone else's learning. My role in this milieu was of facilitating others in ways that enabled them to take responsibility for their own learning. Unfortunately, many academics (and others with expertise) find this difficult, or impossible, to do – to give up their identity as someone with knowledge which has to be dispensed to others.

In late 1986, a tutor and I began exploring the potential of RRA, a qualitative survey methodology, in Australia.[13] RRA was then increasingly being used in third world countries to better formulate problems for research. We were particularly concerned to develop good group function as a means of breaking down strict disciplinary boundaries, and a participant observer was invited to join us so as to evaluate our group process. Thus began a 30-year collaboration, the first of many cross- or interdisciplinary collaborations in my professional life.

The impetus for the RRA had come from concerns about how and why particular research questions were asked and our strong feeling that the supposed clients of research – in this case, farmers – were rarely active participants in formulating the research questions. We spent a week in the field.

Dusk was approaching on a dust-choked road somewhere in central Western New South Wales as we returned from the end of our intense but absorbing week, a week involving visits to many farms and families to hear about their histories and the issues they now confronted.[14] We were reflecting on what we had heard and our dissatisfaction with our team meeting over lunch earlier in the day, in which several members had begun to develop a typology of farmers in terms of 'information rich' and 'information poor'. These descriptions – very much in vogue at the time – simply did not fit with our experience. There was a stereotyping of what constituted 'information' in the literature which was heavily biased towards whatever was technically 'the go-to' at any point in time. Our experience was that farmers were information rich about those farming practices which they judged to be important to them. Some of these practices were proving to be financially advantageous, whilst others seemed to be breaking even or, occasionally, operating at a loss.

Our experience was that farming families wanted to engage with us around those practices that best tapped into their energy, captured their imagination, or represented what they most wanted to do. The generic term that best expressed this complex phenomenon was 'enthusiasm'.

We asked: how much of the current R&D leads to 'change that makes a difference'? The R&D literature is replete with examples of first-order change – change within the existing system, or more of the same. There appeared to us to be few cases of second-order change, change so fundamental that the system itself is changed.[15] Second-order change entails stepping outside the usual frame of reference and taking a meta-perspective.

We proposed that it might be possible to trigger enthusiasm in people by valuing and appreciating them for who they were, for what they were doing, and how they thought, as we'd done in very open-ended interviews. Our proposition assumed all people were information rich and thus capable of making the best sense of their realities.

The concept of 'triggering' is critical here, as we concluded that enthusiasm was already present and was not something that could be instilled by others. The assumption was that everyone is enthusiastic about certain key features of what they consider needs to be done. They are not enthusiastic about everything, even though they might perform effectively across a wide range of practices. What became obvious to us was that each individual possessed a reservoir of unexpended energy or excitement which was a resource for collective action if it could be organised effectively, elicited, and brought together in some manner. We saw the opportunity of developing a process to provide a mechanism for the expression of enthusiasm as a research question.

A.3.3.1 Enthusiasm as theory, driving force and methodology

We wanted to incorporate the idea that enthusiasm is several things. It is an intellectual notion or a theory, it is an emotional driving force (not necessarily connected to any reality-testing process) and it is a methodology (an observable strategy to go from A to B). We wished to do all three things as best we could.[16] The word enthusiasm comes from the Greek, meaning 'the god within'. Our work showed how 'enthusiasm' could be built into a functional R&D system. Later I came to realise that enthusiasm was central to my own life and that of others I encountered in groups, projects, teams and organisations.

What we did would now be called co-research, co-inquiry or co-design with pastoralists in semi-arid Western NSW, who were seen by the research funders as 'being slow to adopt the latest technology' as developed from research they had funded. In many ways, the R&D corporations projected worries about their own roles onto pastoralists who were generally capable of significant innovation in their own right – especially with good facilitation. The R&D system was failing, and perhaps continues to fail. It is not that R&D is not needed, but it fails in the traditions of understanding on which it is built.

A.3.4 Higher Education

I have operated in three distinct models of higher education (HE). They have left me with strong views on the social purpose of a university and the extent to which current HE policy and governance, in the main, fails citizens. This is largely a product of neoliberalism and government policies.

A.3.4.1 Traditional, didactic universities

The first university I experienced, and later returned to, was the traditional didactic, expert-led model, characterised in the 1970s by tiered lecture theatres, some terrible *avant garde* TV lectures in vast arenas (which did nothing for learning), and a centre-to-periphery way of thinking. Research was what mattered. If you were interested in enhancing student learning, you ran the risk of undermining your career. But like-minded people with progressive concerns about learning banded together and could be very supportive. And I was also interested in research.

My undergraduate educational model was essentially about passing exams and writing good assignments. Living in a university residential college was like becoming a member of a 'getting-good-marks community of practice'. Good for us, but not so good if you were not one of the lucky ones able to reside in a campus college (or as today, forced to work long hours to make enough money to keep you at university). As one of the first in my family to attend university, I was there thanks to Commonwealth Scholarships – a significant investment by the state in me. The election of the Whitlam Labor government also meant I did not have to go to fight in Vietnam – or make a choice about conscientious objection.

A.3.4.2 Experiential Learning at Hawkesbury

In early 1982, fresh from my PhD, I joined the academic staff of what was then Hawkesbury Agricultural College in Richmond, NSW – a very different HE model from the one I was used to. Hawkesbury is notorious in some circles as one of the more fascinating attempts to radically reorient HE. Several authors have charted the transformation from a traditional – some would say, pedestrian – agricultural curriculum into an innovative, systemic and experiential student-centred curriculum.[17] The experiences there were amongst the more powerful of my professional life. Some of the relationships I developed there have also been the most enduring.

I was actively involved with others in devising the new process for assessment and graduation. Our system gave power and responsibility to students for applying for progression based on a competency matrix that had been constructed collaboratively (this was well before competency based-assessment became highly instrumental and was of a 'tick the box' type now only too common). Our matrix included autonomy in learning, systems agriculture, and effective communication across thinking, knowing, and doing.

Kolb's[18] experiential learning model featured strongly in the new learning system design. Some students were able to do great things because they already were, or became, 'conceptualisers'. But many students interpreted the requirement as being able to relate what they had done to the Kolb model in a way that merely regurgitated it (i.e. they were not able to conceptualise their self-directed work). They went experience → reflect → act, leaving out conceptualise after reflect. Often the reflection was weak, as well. This is, unfortunately, a widespread phenomenon. Praxis fails when a concept, or set of concepts, have not been embodied.[19]

On some occasions students experienced the model as illuminating. They appreciated that individuals had different learning styles and that the failure of education to recognise this was a failure of 'the system', not of them as learners. At other times, students found it difficult not to feel labelled as a particular 'type' of learner, which they experienced as confronting and sometimes disabling. The realisation that remains was that experience is prime when considering the design of learning (and researching) systems. The ongoing failure of education is, in the main, not transforming learners into active conceptualisers capable of critical reflection, nor fostering lifelong learning in students who are capable of taking responsibility for their own learning.

The Hawkesbury experiment in radical, student-centered learning, which began in 1979, lasted in various forms for 15–20 years before it was no more. Why? In short, if you want to pursue another paradigm that puts you on a different trajectory to the mainstream, then constant co-adaptation is needed to maintain viability. It is demanding on all involved. Perhaps Mao knew this when pursuing constant revolution. To succeed, some powerful rules of the game have to be changed. Put another way, a niche that enables viable co-evolution needs to emerge.

A.3.4.3 The Open University (UK)

The UK Open University (OU) is my third model of HE. I went there (moving continents and family) to be in a Systems group, as I'd been impressed with their teaching materials in earlier posts. I was, too, enamoured with the OU's espoused social purpose, or mission, and interested in the nature, and thus future, of 'the university'. This interest was manifest in my concerns for the design and enactment of 'learning systems', which is what I saw the OU doing. I thought technology would become increasingly important, but being aware that TV learning and computer-aided instruction had all failed, I was keen to understand the interplay between what Toffler called 'high tech with high touch'. This interest persists – hence my scepticism regarding MOOCs (Massive Open Online Courses).

My time at the OU has included:

- A lot of successful program design.
- Cultivation of Systems alumni relations in a climate where the organisation has never taken these seriously.
- A strong research performance.
- Conducting a successful internal action research process that did away with a dysfunctional department and created a new organisation and structure (Centre of Complexity & Change) that flourished for a period – until factors in the environment were so inimical that I became involved in trying to change the University.
- Putting into practice what we taught. At first this was framed as supporting the then VC to build a stronger senior team. It failed, as it succeeded in challenging the VC who really wanted to continue to divide and rule. The second attempt was PersSyst (a partnership of Systems and Personnel) with another VC. It lasted for five years, now largely dissipated. Why? Attempts to mainstream were its undoing, because its rationale was never built into the central governance function of the University.

The OU may be characterised by its extraordinary world-leading distance learning – still in high demand and highly valued and applying little of this vast reservoir of innovation and practice to its own organisation.

A.3.5 Governance

In 1994, I was fortunate to be in South Africa just after the historic elections. The euphoria and sense of possibility remains with me. My purpose was a 'learning-based consultancy', involving a team of 13 South Africans and non-South Africans. Our focus was land reform, agricultural extension, and rural development. Derick Hanekom, still an ANC minister in 2019, was involved.[20] This process brought to the surface the prevailing view then existing in the Ministry of Agriculture that the trajectory for 'development of black farmers' was to provide the conditions for them to become like white farmers. This embodied particular views of what it was to be a farmer, a focus on productivity often through commercial cropping, and a range of other unquestioned assumptions. Senior officials found it impossible to conceptualise agriculture as only a part of possible rural livelihood systems, despite the local realities of widespread artisanal activity, extended kinship networks, complex livestock owning patterns, and the importance of remittance wages from distant miners, who often invested in cattle as a form of saving.

The South Africans were keen to create a Ministry that dealt with Rural Development. We argued against it, saying that it would fail unless '"rural development" became everyone's business in the new governance arrangements'. It did fail.

Since that time, my ongoing relationship with SA has brought to the surface lessons for governance reform and misdirected innovation, notably massive state capture and systemic failure of the praxis of governance. Positive discrimination went too far too quickly – understandable at one level – but could have been designed differently. The whole of the SA state is occupied by people who are there because of their connection to the ANC, not because of their capability to do the job. But its constitution, the rule of law, and democratic voting have thus far proved robust.

The trajectory of the new SA state was evident from our process consultancy. Over drinks in the LAPC (Land and Agriculture Policy Centre), I asked the South Africans, all former activists: 'What are you doing so that what happened under apartheid never happens again?' The most convincing answer was to institutionalise a dialectic between civil society and the state. How? I asked. By diverting state resources to maintain a vibrant civil society that would help, challenge, and provoke that state. Did this happen? Well, the locals in our group began to move from being activists one day to members of the new government the next. The writing was already on the wall – when in government their earlier commitments were soon forgotten. What might have happened if SA had institutionalised this dialectic? In my current work in SA on the systemic governance of the Olifants River catchment, I am working with the NGO AWARD to create a set of dialectical governance institutions.[21] Governance as feedback and the creative fostering of difference have been part of my life.

A.3.6 Systemic Musings

Living with a systemic sensibility creates a trajectory for living – one that can be highly rewarding and deeply frustrating at the same time. When I started blogging in 2006, I called it 'systemic musings'. My motivation came from a feeling of repression – a need to get things off my chest. The blog has been a form of personal catharsis, but over the years has become less so as I have become inured to events in a world lacking systemic sensibility and practice. I sometimes experience this widespread failing as overwhelming. I understand why some well-meaning academics become activists. But there are not enough. My blogging has fallen away. This book means I am still having a go. I am also sustained by the success of our postgraduate program in Systems Thinking in Practice[22] at the OU. The feedback from students whose lives are transformed, through their changed understandings and practices, is evidence of what can be done.

A.4 Enabling systemic sensibilities to flourish

These vignettes from lives lived in the pursuit of 'why?' offer glimpses of what might be possible if the systemic sensibilities we humans have are allowed to flourish from birth or, where lost, to be recovered. We know this from careers in and outside PwC and from designing and delivering Systems education programs at the OU for nearly 50 years.

Notes

1 Piaget called it the '*intuitive substage*'
2 This is also a good example of what Humberto Maturana says is so special about humans – that we seek explanations. He posits that to be accepted, an explanation must satisfy two criteria – it must propose a mechanism, and it must have a relational/interpersonal element (i.e. who the explainer is in relationship to the explainee).
3 There was no purposeful system of governance in place till the Greater London Authority took over.
4 Straw, Ed. 1996. *Relative Values*. London: Demos.
5 Australian style PR (proportional representation) still delivers zigzag policies. Germany and New Zealand less so, but in Germany the emergent property is loss of difference, except on the far right.
6 The Palace of Westminster, home of the UK parliament
7 Author of *The Brain of the Firm*, and developer of Cybersyn, used to run Chile's industries during President Allende's term – see https://en.wikipedia.org/wiki/Project_Cybersyn (Accessed May 20 2019).
8 Chalmers Hague, Sir D. and Young, M., eds. 2007. *The Oxford Strategic Leadership Programme 1982-2007*. Oxford: Oxford Said Business School.
9 Straw, Ed. 2014. *Stand & Deliver: A Design for Successful Government*. London: Treaty for Government.
10 Barr, N. and Cary, J. 1992. *Greening a Brown Land: Australian Search for Sustainable Land Use*. Basingstoke: Palgrave MacMillan.
11 Ackoff, Russell. 1991. *Ackoff's Fables: Irreverent Reflections on Business and Bureaucracy*. New York: John Wiley & Sons.

12 These are all themes taken up in Ison, R.L. & Russell, D.B. 2000. Exploring some distinctions for the design of learning systems. *Cybernetics and Human Knowing* 7(4): 43–56. Also later by Ison, R.L. 2017. *Systems Practice. How to Act.* London: Springer and the Open University and in new supported open-learning courses developed at the UK Open University in the period 1998–2018.

13 See Ison, R.L. and Ampt, P.R. 1992. Rapid rural appraisal: A participatory problem formulation method relevant to Australian agriculture. *Agricultural Systems* 38: 363–386.

14 The 'we' in this story includes David Russell (e.g. see Russell, D.B. and Ison, R.L. 2017. Fruits of Gregory Bateson's epistemological crisis: Embodied mind-making and interactive experience in research and professional praxis. *Canadian Journal of Communication* 42 (3): 485–514).

15 Watzlawick, P. 1976. *How Real Is Real?* New York: Random House; Russell; D.B. and. Ison, R.L. 1993. *The research-development relationship in rangelands: An opportunity for contextual science.* Invited Plenary Paper, *Proceedings of the IVth International Rangeland Congress*, Montpellier, France. 1991. 3: 1047–1054.

16 In work later published in the book *Agricultural Extension and Rural Development. Breaking Out of Knowledge Transfer Traditions*, we explicate how an R&D system could be designed and conducted based on triggering enthusiasm and facilitating joint action among those with shared enthusiasms.

17 See Bawden, R.J. 1985. Problem-based learning: An Australian perspective. In D. Boud, ed. *Problem Based Learning in Education for the Professions*, pp. 43–57. Sydney: HERDSA (Higher Education Research and Development Society of Australia); Bawden, R.J., Macadam, R.D., Packham, R.G., and Valentine, I. 1984. Systems thinking and practices in the education of agriculturalists. *Agricultural Systems* 13: 205–225; Bawden, R.J. Ison, R.L., Macadam, R.D., Packham, R.G., and Valentine, I. 1985. A research paradigm for systems agriculture. In J.V. Remenyi, ed. *Agricultural Systems Research for Developing Countries*. ACIAR (Australian Centre for International Agricultural Research) Proceedings No 11, pp. 31–42. Canberra: ACIAR; Bawden, R.J. and Packham, R.G. 1991. Systemic praxis in the education of the agricultural practitioner. *Systems Practice* 6: 7–9; Bawden, R., Packham, R. Macadam, R., and McKenzie, B. 2000. Back to the Future. Reflections from Hawkesbury. In Learn Group, eds. *Cow Up a Tree. Knowing and Learning for Change in Agriculture. Case Studies from Industrial Countries*. Paris: INRA.

18 One of the main theoretical ideas that underpinned the 'autonomy in learning' strand was the work of David Kolb (1976) and his model of experiential learning – see Kolb, D. 1984. *Experiential Learning: Experience as the Source of Learning and Development.* Upper Saddle River, NJ: Prentice Hall Inc.

19 Reyes, A., and Zarama, R. 1998. The process of embodying distinctions – A reconstruction of the process of learning. *Cybernetics and Human Knowing* 5: 19–33.

20 https://en.wikipedia.org/wiki/Derek_Hanekom (Accessed 20 November 2018).

21 See http://award.org.za/project/resilience-in-the-limpopo-basin (Accessed 20 November 2018).

22 http://www.open.ac.uk/postgraduate/qualifications/f47 (Accessed 14 January 2020).

APPENDIX 2: GLOSSARY[1]

Active listening Listening in such a manner (giving verbal and non-verbal cues) that it gives rise to the experience of being heard unconditionally. It is often a cathartic experience for the person being listened to and is emotionally demanding on the listener.

Affordance Explains the relationship between, for example, an iPhone4 and a hand – there is a comfortable and practical fit. The quality or property of an object or system in effect defines its possible uses or makes clear how it can or should be used. The environment offers an animal or human the affordances of being a resource and support. The animal or human must in turn possess the capabilities to perceive the environment and to live in it. An affordance happens in the relationship between two elements – it is not a property of one alone.

Biosphere The worldwide sum of all ecosystems. It can also be understood as the zone of *life* on Earth, a closed system (apart from solar and cosmic radiation and heat from the interior of the Earth), and largely self-regulating (see Box 4.1).

Boundary A form of distinction made by someone or some group: the act of making a boundary judgment produces a distinction – a system and the environment of a system. The relationship between the inner and outer is mediated by a boundary (think of taking a pen and drawing a circle on paper). In the social world, making boundary judgments is a political act replete with power. A shift in boundary is a conceptual act which may, or may not, have some physical characteristics as well. A system can't come into existence conceptually without a boundary.

Circular causality A sequence of coupled cause and effect relationships that lead back to the starting point. In a living organism, however, it is only ever possible to move towards a future, so the return point is never 'the same'. The same is true of a social system. Feedback loops are a form of circular causality. Multiple causality can hold relationships that are linear and/or circular. Circular causality needs to be distinguished from linear, or systematic causality where a first event, factor, or action is supposed to be the single cause of a second, or at least its principal and overwhelming, cause. In this form, feedback is missing.

Co-evolution   A process of mutually accommodating changes between at least two entities over time, for example, a gut and a selection of microorganisms, whose co-evolutionary *trajectory* has been significantly perturbed by the introduction of antibiotics and the cult of cleanliness taken to extremes. Governance can be understood in co-evolutionary terms, for example, a company and the market for its products, or the biosphere and humans.

Communication   (i) Communication is understood by some to be a simple feedback process (as in a heater with a thermostat) involving information, but is not to be confused with human communication, which has a biological basis. (ii) A theory of cognition which encompasses language, emotion, perception, and behaviour communication amongst human beings which gives rise to new properties in the communicating partners, who each have different experiential histories. *Conversation*, a turning together, as in a dance routine, is the basis of human communication.

Connectivity   Elements may be connected to each other in many different ways (i.e. what constitutes a relational dynamic can be manifested in many different forms). If there is no connectivity between a set of elements, then there is no system. In the human microbiome, if the connections were between good and bad bugs, or the relationships had been destroyed by antibiotics, then what we could call a healthy microbiome system would not exist.

Conversation   The experience of understanding that is generated by the flow of emotions. Because the flow of our language and our emotions are so delicately interwoven, it follows that emotional matching is the precursor of semantic congruence. The meanings in the conversation will only match when the emotion matches. Whole cultures arise through communication networks of conversation leading to widespread agreement about concepts and values and a comfortable ability to live together with a certain amount of mutual understanding – all achieved through conversation.

Dialectical relationship   A relationship that continuously exposes and holds together both sides of any distinction and keeps them connected in a recursive way (e.g. the parliament creating the parliamentarian and the parliamentarian creating the parliament). The parliamentarian and the parliament are now seen as a complementary pair: they are distinct but related. The dialectical and recursive process allows us to look at the quality of the relationship as a variable in policy and research.

Difficulty   A neologism invented by Russ Ackoff for a situation considered as a bounded and well-defined problem where it is assumed that it is clear who is involved and what would constitute a solution within a given time frame.[2]

Dualism   Describes antagonistic or negating opposites: mind/matter, objective/subjective, Brexit/Remain. Two concepts form a dualism when they belong to the same logical level and at that level are perceived as opposites: either/or. The logic behind this dialectic is negation. Negation takes a proposition p to another proposition, not-p. Not-p is interpreted intuitively as being true when p is false, and false when p is true. This fuels pugilistic media interviews and adversarial politics.

Duality The wave/particle paradox in quantum physics was resolved by appreciating that the behaviours of each element in the pair are complementary and constitute a duality rather than a dualism. Taken together, they do not negate each other but create a unity or a coherent whole. Reframing conceptual pairs as dualities rather than dualisms stimulates relational thinking and practice. Following this logic, the following pairs need not be understood as self-negating but as expressions of a relational dynamic in which the whole is different to the parts: control – autonomy; constraint – freedom; environment – system; social world – biophysical world; yin–yang. When recognised as pairs participating in a relational dynamic, more operational possibilities open up that may be more rewarding than a *dualism*.[3]

Emergence Generally understood with the phrase 'the whole is more than the sum of the parts' or the variant 'the whole is different to the sum of the parts'. An emergent property of flooding is often a shortage of safe drinking water. The wetness of water cannot be understood from the properties of the hydrogen and oxygen molecules from which it is formed. In the book, we talk about managing for emergence and make the point that emergence does not result from deterministic, engineered interventions.

Environment That which surrounds, that is to say, all that is outside the system boundary and which is coupled with, or affects and is affected by, the behaviour of the system. Alternatively, it is the 'context' for a system-of-interest. A system and its environment can be said to co-evolve, or not.

Feedback This may be understood in two basic forms. These are either positive (or reinforcing) or negative (or dampening – as in flattening an oscillation) feedback. The former can be understood as increasing the input into a system, the latter decreasing it, and thus, if left unattended, both can destroy a system. For example, more bad bugs in the microbiome increase bowel inflammation which in turn creates better conditions for bad bugs which together create what is known as a vicious circle. Research is trying to find ways to break the vicious circle by adding good bugs at the right time. Feedback is relevant in all domains. The idea that we give feedback to each other in groups or the workplace means the same in process terms. Giving feedback is designed to avoid growing divergence, alienation, lack of communicative efficacy (i.e. products of positive feedback) and to move towards convergence of purpose, enthusiasm, or mutual respect by listening, talking, debriefing, etc., (i.e. initiating negative feedback processes).

Fractal structure Fractal comes from the Latin *fractus* meaning broken or uneven. It is 'a structure that is characterised with self-similarity (i.e. it is composed of such fragments whose structural motif is repeated if the scale changes)'.[4]

Framing When you point a camera, you are framing a subject. Different photographers will use different framings to convey different moods and meanings. The same occurs in life in framing a situation through our education, work experience, family values, mass media, and so on. We build in filters. An economist will see government in a different frame from a sociologist. Reframing facilitates a fresh perspective and new answers. When an Italian sociologist was asked about his country's approach to road safety, he reframed the issue by replying, 'Build better hospitals'. Framing involves the social construction of a social phenomenon – by mass media sources, political or social movements, political leaders, or other actors and organisations.

Framing choice   'Framing can manifest in thought or interpersonal communication. Frames in thought consist of the mental representations, interpretations, and simplifications of reality. Frames in communication consist of the communication of frames between different actors'.[5] The effects of framing can be seen in many journalism applications. With the same information being used as a base, the 'frame' surrounding the issue can change the reader's perception without having to alter the actual facts. In the context of politics or mass-media communication, a frame defines the packaging of an element of rhetoric in such a way as to encourage certain interpretations and to discourage others. For political purposes, framing often presents facts in such a way that implies a problem that is in need of a solution. 'Members of political parties attempt to frame issues in a way that makes a solution which favours their own political leaning appear as the most appropriate course of action for the situation at hand'.[6]

Governance   'Governance comprises all of the processes of governing – whether undertaken by the government of a state, by a market or by a network – over a social system (family, tribe, formal or informal organisation, a territory or across territories) and whether through the laws, norms, power or language of an organized society'.[7] It relates to 'the processes of interaction and decision-making among the actors involved in a collective problem that lead to the creation, reinforcement, or reproduction of social norms and institutions'.[8] In lay terms, it could be described as the political processes that exist in and between formal institutions. In this book, we favour a metaphor for governance, or governing (the practise) based on the Greek 'to steer', as in a sailing ship, and from which the word cybernetics is derived.

Hierarchy   Layered structure; the location, or embedding, of a particular system within a continuum of levels of organisation. This means that any system is at the same time a subsystem of some wider system and is itself a wider system to its subsystems.

Initial starting conditions   When, how and with whom you start out determines where you end up. The referendum design that led to Brexit in the UK or the rapid passage in the UK Parliament of the Article 50 legislation that specified the original leave timetable each comprised a set of initial starting conditions that were incapable of dealing with the complexity that had to be managed. This concept applies in particular to non-linear phenomena, or in situations best framed as messes, wicked, or complex.

Institution   The rules of the human game 'in which individual strategies compete … [they] include any form of constraint that human beings devise to shape interaction' (e.g. formal arrangements such as law or constitution, or informal arrangements such as customary land tenure or meal times).[9]

Institutionalisation   Is the process when an understanding or practice is made into an institution which then assumes a place or life of its own in activities of a group, project, organisation or nation. Citizen assemblies, for instance, are a concept and a form of practice that have gained some informal institutionalisation, or, as in Ireland are fully institutionalised in formal governance systems.

Interdependence   The condition where the interactions of elements (relationships) are necessary to maintain each of those elements. Interdependencies operating in a system give rise to emergence (see above), or, put another way, a whole and its parts can be said to be interdependent. A health-giving microbiome will be the product of a set of interacting, interdependent microbes that depend on each other yet together produce something that is more than the sum of these parts (emergence).

Knowing-in-action Premised on the understanding that all knowing is doing, then knowing is emergent from action, rather than knowledge (reified knowing) as an input to, or precursor for, action. This understanding offers a creative duality (knowing/knowledge) as well as an alternative framing to the mainstream view for practice.[10]

Layered structure hierarchy A key notion in developing systems literacy is thinking in terms of a layered structure which is evident in the use of concepts such as a *system* within a *supra-system* (or meta-system) and being made up of *subsystems* which in turn can be made up of *sub-subsystems*. It is possible to speak of nested levels, moving up and down levels of conceptual abstraction, and of a *fractal structure*, in that it is possible for infinite *recursion* or the unfolding of a *pattern* which repeats itself. For example, if one thinks of the human as a system, then we can also think in terms of various subsystems – a circulatory system, an immune system, an endocrine system, a nervous system, and so on. Please note this is not an attempt to classify parts of the human, but a means to appreciate or understand how the human functions *as if* it were a system.

Measure of performance The criteria against which a system-of-interest formulated by an observer is judged to have achieved its purpose. Data collected according to measures of performance are used to modify the interactions within the system.

Mess This is another neologism coined by Russ Ackoff. It refers to a set of conditions that produces dissatisfaction. It can be conceptualised as a system of apparently conflicting or contradictory problems or opportunities. A problem or an opportunity is an ultimate element abstracted from a mess.[11]

Microbiome The human microbiome is the combined genetic material of all the microorganisms in the gut (nearly 50% of our DNA). Understanding the microbiome is as important as understanding the human genome. As a field of study it has been marginalised in science until relatively recently.

Monitoring and control Monitoring consists of observations related to a system's performance in the form of prescribed measures or data. When these observations are outside a specified range, action is taken through some avenue of management to remedy or 'control' the situation.

Multiple perspectives A term that encompasses multiple and possibly heterogeneous viewpoints, representations and roles. The more perspectives that are brought to bear, the more understanding of a situation of concern will be available for its improvement. The frame is expanded. A *perspective* is a way of experiencing that is shaped by our current state and circumstances, as these are influenced by our unique personal and social histories, where experiencing is a cognitive act.

Neologism A word that is invented (or coined) and introduced into the language at a moment in time that refers to a new phenomenon or conceptual distinction.

Networks An elaboration of the concept of hierarchy which avoids the human projection of 'above' and 'below' and recognises an assemblage of entities in relationship (e.g. organisms in an ecosystem). Networked entities may be totally parallel, embedded, or partially embedded (structurally intersected).

For purposeful action in networks, some form of boundary choice (and thus system formulation) is always needed.

Organisation A commonly used but poorly understood term, which is often confused with the term 'institution'. In this book, both terms are used in very specific ways. The organisation of 'a system' is the particular set of relationships, whether static or dynamic, between components which constitute a recognisable whole – a unity. Organisational relationships have to be maintained to maintain the system – if these change the system either 'dies' (this may be physical or conceptual 'death') or it becomes something else.[12] As an organisation, the Roman Catholic Church has existed for a long time. At the moment it is grappling with the issue of celibacy of its priests and its response to child abuse. The question it faces is whether by abandoning celibacy it will continue to be the same organisation. In using this concept it is important to appreciate the difference between organisation and *structure*.

Pathway lock-in/dependency Pathway dependence explains how, for any given circumstance, the set of decisions faced is limited by the decisions made in the past or by the events experienced. In economics and the social sciences, path dependence can refer either to outcomes at a single moment in time, or to long-run equilibria of a process. In common usage, the phrase implies either (i) that history matters, or (ii) that the predictable amplifications of small differences are a disproportionate cause of later circumstances, and, in the strong form, that this historical hangover is economically and managerially inefficient.[13]

Pattern The repetition, in form, of relations. A common practice of Geoffrey Bateson was to present patterns of relationships in the form of stories as he sought to create patterns of explanatory connection across multiple fields in the social and natural sciences.[14]

Perspective A way of experiencing shaped by a person's current state and circumstances as these are influenced by their unique personal and social histories, where experiencing is a cognitive act.

Praxis Purposeful, theory-informed practical action.

Problematique The complex of issues associated with a topic, considered collectively. Specifically, the totality of environmental and other problems affecting the world. The term was used by Hasan Özbekhan in the first report to the Club of Rome in 1969 entitled *The Predicament of Mankind – The Problematique*.[15]

Purpose What a system does or exists for from the perspective of a person or persons; the raison d'être of a system-of-interest formulated by someone and achieved through the particular transformation that has been ascribed. Two forms of behaviour in relation to purpose have also been distinguished. One is *purposeful behaviour*, which can be described as behaviour that is willed – there is thus some sense of voluntary action. The other is *purposive behaviour* – behaviour to which an observer can attribute purpose.

Recursion The description of a circular relationship such as the one that connects action and experience – all knowing is doing and all doing is knowing – every act of knowing brings forth a world of experience.

Reification The transformation of an abstract concept into material (thingness) form (e.g. justice into a marble statue, or ecosystems into entities that can be mapped in the world).

Resources Elements (e.g. matter, energy or information) which are available either within the system boundary or present outside the system in a manner that the system can access, and which enable a desired transformation to occur.

Second-order change Change that is so fundamental that the system itself is changed. In order to achieve second-order change, it is necessary to step outside the usual frame of reference and take a meta-perspective.[16] *First-order change* is change within the system, or more of the same.

Situation-of-concern This might also be termed the area of interest. In everyday language we might refer to the 'problem' or the 'issue'. Situation-of-concern avoids immediate labelling, allows for reframing, and is neutral as to any causal connection between the situation and its 'solution'.

Social purpose The pursuit of purpose – articulation and rearticulation – to achieve social ends. To pursue social purpose requires an understanding of what it means to be social. That is, it requires understanding that the social arises in the reciprocal experience of others – humans, other species, the biosphere – arising as legitimate others in our living (i.e. the operation of the biology of love or mutual acceptance).[17]

Steady-state Applies within the context of an open-system (i.e. to the flow of materials and elements that constitutes a system-of-interest), such as the changing ecology of bugs in the microbiome in which one species or configuration comes to dominate over a period of time (e.g. a period of stability). Humanity, in relation to the biosphere, has passed from a long relatively steady-state period into one of exponential change which may lead to *tipping points*.

Structure The structure of a system is the set of current concrete components and relationships through which the organisation of a system is manifest in a particular setting. Thus the organisation 'human X' may comprise over time a different set of structural elements such as microbes, skin cells, liver cells – they may even lose an arm or a leg or an organ such as a kidney, yet conserve their organisation and thus their living.

Structural coupling Structural coupling happens when two or more systems in recursive interactions defined by the properties of their components undergo congruent structural changes or mutual adaptation.[18] A shoe becomes comfortable through the recurrent interaction between the foot and shoe where each 'shapes' the other. Break the cycle of interaction and the phenomenon disappears, as when a comfortable shoe is not worn for a year or so and then put back on. We ask whether the ongoing structural coupling of social and biophysical systems is a useful framing for what requires governing in the future.[19]

Structure-determined system When we seek a mechanic to fix a car, we treat the car as a structure-determined system (i.e. systems operate according to how they are made through the operations of their components).[20] Examples of structural determinants of governance systems include the three-year election cycle in Australia and the UK's first-past-the-post voting system. Each helps determine what is, and is not, possible.[21] We ask what might be revealed or concealed by considering governance situations *as if* they were structure-determined systems.

System An integrated whole, as distinguished by an observer, whose essential properties arise from the relationships between its parts; from the Greek 'synhistanai', meaning 'to place together'.

System change (whole system change)   An evolving framing for transformative change discourse and practice primarily, but not exclusively, in the fields of sustainable development, social entrepreneurship and social innovation.[22]

System, closed   A system closed to its environment in terms of deterministic inputs. For example, humans are closed systems with respect to information. It is our history and the configuration of our nervous system (structure) that determines what does or does not perturb our cognitive processes.

System, open   A system open to its environment for the transfer of resources (materials, money etc.) needed to effect the transformation of the system.

System-of-interest   The product of distinguishing a system in a situation in relation to an articulated purpose, in which an individual or a group has an interest (a stake). A constructed or formulated system-of-interest to one or more people may be used in a process of inquiry. It is also a term suggested to avoid confusion with the everyday use of the word system.

Systematic thinking or practice   Methodical, regular and orderly thinking about the relationships between the parts of a whole or the stages of a process. Systematic thinking usually takes place in a linear, step-by-step manner.[23]

Systemic reformation   This is what is needed in the Anthropocene to challenge ways of thinking about the world and the place of humans in it. Systemic reformation is also a period of great institutional reform. In comparison to religious reformations of the past, we face a greater challenge and have less time to effect the transformations needed.

Systemic sensibility   An aesthetic held by all humans based on awareness and openness to relational thinking and dynamics. Humans are born imbued with systemic sensibility that arises from our evolutionary past, our biology, and, for the fortunate, their manners of living experienced as children. Some retain this sensibility. Others lose it over time when subjected to the prevailing paradigms, practices, and institutions of Western civilisation. Asking 'why?' is an essence of systemic sensibility.

Systemic thinking or practice   The type of thinking that arises from the evolutionary trajectory of cognition. In humans, this form of thinking takes place through the systemic action of our own cognitive system in a manner that is not limited to language and logic (background systemic thinking). Within language (i.e. in the foreground), it refers to the understanding of a phenomenon within the context of a larger whole. To understand things systemically, literally means to put them into a context and to establish the nature of their relationships.

Systems literacy   The extent to which systems concepts, traditions, methods, and approaches are appreciated and understood by a practitioner (e.g. the concepts listed in this glossary).

Systems thinking in practice capability   Combines systemic sensibility with systems literacy to engage in both systemic and systematic thinking and practice which is effective in changing, or improving action, in a given situation or set of circumstances.

Tame problem   A neologism coined by Rittel and Webber for situations where what a problem was, and thus what a solution could be, were easily known and agreed.[24] Tame and *wicked* (see below) problems are framing choices for situations.[25]

Technosphere 'All of the structures that humans have constructed to keep them alive ... on the planet: houses, factories, farms, mines, roads, airports and shipping ports, computer systems, together with its discarded waste'. It 'is the novel ecosystem created by technologies interacting with the natural ecosystem, or biosphere' (see Box 4.2).[26]

Tipping point 'The time at which a change or an effect cannot be stopped'.[27] For example, the earth has already passed the tipping point in terms of global warming. Beyond a tipping point, what the system is changes because of irreversible changes in the relational dynamics of the components.

Tradition A network of pre-understandings or prejudices from which individuals, culturally embedded, think and act. This is how we make sense of our world.

Trajectory A trajectory is a path of travel in a relational dynamic. It is only really knowable after the event. The myriad of human languages and how language brings forth different understandings of, and relationships with, the biosphere exemplify different trajectory possibilities. Purposeful interventions are possible in an attempt to change a co-evolutionary trajectory through changes to the relational dynamics between structurally coupled systems that realise changes in qualities, emergent properties and viability (including liveability).[28]

Transformation What a system does. Transformations are changes, modelled as an interconnected set of activities or processes which convert an input to an output which may leave the system (a 'product') or become an input to another transformation. Transformations are sometimes referred to as processes.

Trap A term derived through analogy with a lobster pot by Geoffrey Vickers. This is a way of thinking and acting which is difficult to escape from, and no longer relevant to the changed circumstances.[29]

Wicked problem Part of the neologism wicked/tame coined by Rittel and Webber to refer to situations where there is contestation over what a problem might be and thus what might constitute an improvement. It is a framing choice for situations that warrant systemic responses.[30]

World view That conception or understanding of the world which enables each observer to attribute meaning to what is observed. Sometimes the German word *Weltanschauung*, which refers to both attitude as well as concept, is used synonymously.

Notes

1 Material in this glossary draws on a range of sources, including Open University Systems courses. It relies heavily on material from Francois, C., ed. 1997. *International Encyclopaedia of Systems and Cybernetics*. Munchen: K. Sauer. Also Ison, R.L. 2017. Systems practice: How to act. In *Situations of Uncertainty and Complexity in a Climate-Change World*. 2nd Edition. London: Springer; The Open University. The website Principia Cybernetica. 2009. http://pespmc1.vub.ac.be/DEFAULT.html is also an important source (Accessed 7 April 2019).

2 Ackoff, R.L. 1974. *Redesigning the Future*. Wiley: New York.

3 Ison, R.L. and Straw, E. 2018. Duality, dualism, duelling and Brexit. *OpenDemocracy* https://www.opendemocracy.net/en/can-europe-make-it/duality-dualism-duelling-and-brexit/ (Accessed 9 April 2018).

4 https://www.google.com/search?client=firefox-b-d&q=fractal+structure (Accessed 13 April 2019).

5 Druckman, J.N. 2001 The implications of framing effects for citizen competence. *Political Behavior* 23 (3): 225–256.

6 van der Pas, D. 2014. Making hay while the sun shines: Do parties only respond to media attention when the framing is right? *Journal of Press/Politics* 19 (1): 42–65.

7 https://en.wikipedia.org/wiki/Governance (Accessed 2 April 2019).

8 Hufty, Marc. 2011. Investigating policy processes: The governance analytical framework (GAF). In Wiesmann, U., Hurni, H. et al., eds. *Research for Sustainable Development: Foundations, Experiences, and Perspectives*, pp. 403–424. Bern: Geographica Bernensia.

9 See North, D. 1990. *Institutions, Institutional Change and Economic Performance.* Cambridge University Press: Cambridge.

10 Cook, S.D. Noam and Brown, John Seely. 1999. Bridging epistemologies: The generative dance between organisational knowledge and organisational knowing. *Organisational Science* 10 (4), July–August.

11 Ackoff, R.L. 1974. op. cit.

12 Ceruti, M. 1994. *Constraints and Possibilities. The Knowledge of Evolution and the Evolution of Knowledge.* Lausanne: Gordon and Breach.

13 https://en.wikipedia.org/wiki/Path_dependence (Accessed April 4 2019).

14 Bateson, G. 1978. The pattern which connects. *The CoEvolution Quarterly* (Summer): 5–15.

15 http://blogora.wikifoundry.com/page/Remembering+Hasan+%C3%96zbekhan (Accessed 13th April 2019).

16 Watzlawick, P. 1976. *How Real Is Real?* New York: Random House.

17 Ison, R.L. 2019. Towards cyber-systemic thinking in practice. *World Futures (Special Edition)* 75 (1) & (2) DOI: 10.1080/02604027.2019.1568797.

18 Maturana, H. R., Verden-Zöller, G., and Bunnell, P. (eds.) 2008. *The Origin of Humanness in the Biology of Love*, p. 169. Exeter: Imprint Academic.

19 Maturana, Humberto and Varela, Francisco. 1987. *The Tree of Knowledge - The Biological Roots of Human Understanding.* Boston: New Science Library, Shambala Publications.

20 Ibid., p. 158.

21 Ison, R.L., Alexandra, J., and Wallis, P.J. 2018. Governing in the Anthropocene: Are there cyber-systemic antidotes to the malaise of modern governance? *Sustainability Science* 13 (5): 1209–1223.

22 See http://systemschangeeducation.com/portfolio-item/what-is-your-definition-of -systems-change/ (Accessed April 7 2019); and Systems-Change-Education-Report. FINAL.pdf.

23 Systematic and systemic thinking and practice can be understood as a reframing of the hard and soft systems traditions, respectively, as formulated by Peter Checkland. This reformulation arises from experience as systems educators, where the terms hard and soft hindered effective learning.

24 Rittel, H.W.J. and Webber, M.M. 1973. Dilemmas in a general theory of planning. *Policy Science* 4: 155–169.

25 Ison, R.L., Collins, K.B., and Wallis, P. 2014. Institutionalising social learning: Towards systemic and adaptive governance. *Environmental Science & Policy* 53 (B): 105–117.

26 https://www.eurekalert.org/pub_releases/2016-11/uol-en113016.php (Accessed 13 April 2019).

27 https://dictionary.cambridge.org/dictionary/english/tipping-point (Accessed 12 October 2018).

28 Ison, R.L., Alexandra, J., and Wallis, P.J. 2018. Op. cit.

29 https://www.triarchypress.net/growing-wings---mental-traps.html (Accessed 13 April 2019).

30 Rittel, H.W.J. and Webber, M.M. 1973. op. cit.

INDEX

intersection of system change + racial equity
is in civil society reforms
p.102 CDE   ck ice for local conditions
           then try experiments.
Think systemically + make govts do it too.
p.110 The world needs to sustain this shift in thinking.

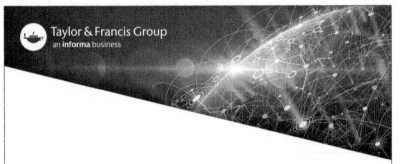

A p.130 Systemic / systematic practice is a duality
(bricolage). Use the "design turn" to take
useful action.